TO URANIA

Selected Poems 1965–1985

JOSEPH BRODSKY

VIKING

The author wishes to express his gratitude to Miss Ann Kjellberg for her invaluable help in editing this collection

VIKING

Published by the Penguin Group
27 Wrights Lane, London w8 5tz, England
Viking Penguin Inc., 40 West 23rd Street, New York, New York 10010, USA
Penguin Books Australia Ltd, Ringwood, Victoria, Australia
Penguin Books Canada Ltd, 2801 John Street, Markham, Ontario, Canada l3r 1b4
Penguin Books (NZ) Ltd, 182–190 Wairau Road, Auckland 10, New Zealand

Penguin Books Ltd, Registered Offices: Harmondsworth, Middlesex, England

Many of these poems were originally published in Russian by Ardis Publishers in *Uraniia*, 1987, and *Chast'rechi*, 1977
This selection of poems in translation first published in the USA by Farrar, Straus & Giroux, New York, 1988
Published simultaneously in Canada by Collins Publishers, Toronto
First published in Great Britain in hardback by Viking 1988
Published simultaneously in paperback by Penguin Books
1 3 5 7 9 10 8 6 4 2

Acknowledgments are made to *Cross Currents*, *The New York Review of Books*, *The Paris Review*, *Partisan Review*, *Ploughshares*, *The Times Literary Supplement*, and *Vanity Fair*, where some of these poems originally appeared in somewhat different form. The following poems first appeared in *The New Yorker*: "Eclogue IV: Winter," "Sextet," "To a Friend: In Memoriam," "Galatea Encore," "Kellomäki," "Belfast Tune," "Eclogue V: Summer," "Polonaise: A Variation," "October Tune," "In Memoriam," and "The Fly"—all in slightly different form.

Printed in Great Britain by
Richard Clay Ltd, Bungay, Suffolk

A CIP catalogue record for this book is available from the British Library

ISBN 0-670-81439-3

Contents

To Urania

May 24, 1980

I have braved, for want of wild beasts, steel cages,
carved my term and nickname on bunks and rafters,
lived by the sea, flashed aces in an oasis,
dined with the-devil-knows-whom, in tails, on truffles.
From the height of a glacier I beheld half a world, the earthly
width. Twice have drowned, thrice let knives rake my nitty-gritty.
Quit the country that bore and nursed me.
Those who forgot me would make a city.
I have waded the steppes that saw yelling Huns in saddles,
worn the clothes nowadays back in fashion in every quarter,
planted rye, tarred the roofs of pigsties and stables,
guzzled everything save dry water.
I've admitted the sentries' third eye into my wet and foul
dreams. Munched the bread of exile: it's stale and warty.
Granted my lungs all sounds except the howl;
switched to a whisper. Now I am forty.
What should I say about life? That it's long and abhors transparence.
Broken eggs make me grieve; the omelette, though, makes me vomit.
Yet until brown clay has been crammed down my larynx,
only gratitude will be gushing from it.

[*1980 / Translated by the author*]

3

To a Friend: In Memoriam

It's for you whose name's better omitted—since for them it's no
                                                    arduous task
to produce you from under the slab—from one more *inconnu*: me,
                                                    well, partly
for the same earthly reasons, since they'll scrub you as well off the
                                                    cask,
and because I'm up here and, frankly, apart from this paltry
talk of slabs, am too distant for you to distinguish a voice,
an Aesopian chant, in that homeland of bottle-struck livers,
where you fingered your course to the pole in the moist universe
of mean, blabbering squinchers and whispering, innocent beavers;
it's for you, name omitted, the offspring of a widowed conductress,
                                                    begot
by the Holy Ghost or by brick courtyard's soot circling all over,
an abductor of books, the sharp pen of the most smashing ode
on the fall of the bard at the feet of the laced Goncharova,
a word-plyer, a liar, a gulper of bright, measly tears,
an adorer of Ingres, of clangoring streetcars, of asphodels' slumbers,
a white-fanged little snake in the tarpaulin-boot colonnade of
                                                    gendarmes in full gear,
a monogamous heart and a torso of countless bedchambers—
may you lie, as though wrapped in an Orenburg shawl, in our dry,
                                                    brownish mud,
you, a tramper through hell and high water and the meaningless
                                                    sentence,
who took life like a bumblebee touching a sun-heated bud
but instead froze to death in the Third Rome's cold-piss-reeking
                                                    entrance.
Maybe Nothing has no better gateway indeed than this smelly
                                                    shortcut.
Man of sidewalks, you'd say, "This will do," adding, "for the
                                                    duration,"
as you drifted along the dark river in your ancient gray, drab
                                                    overcoat
whose few buttons alone were what kept you from disintegration.
Gloomy Charon in vain seeks the coin in your tightly shut shell,

4

someone's pipe blows in vain its small tune far above heavy, cumulous
                                                                curtains.
With a bow, I bid you this anonymous, muted farewell
from the shores—who knows which? Though for you now it has no
                                                             importance.

[*1973* / *Translated by the author*]

October Tune

A stuffed quail
on the mantelpiece minds its tail.
The regular chirr of the old clock's healing
in the twilight the rumpled helix.
Through the window, birch candles fail.

For the fourth day the sea hits the dike with its hard horizon.
Put aside the book, take your sewing kit;
patch my clothes without turning the light on:
golden hair
keeps the corner lit.

[*1968 / Translated by the author*]

A Polar Explorer

All the huskies are eaten. There is no space
left in the diary. And the beads of quick
words scatter over his spouse's sepia-shaded face
adding the date in question like a mole to her lovely cheek.
Next, the snapshot of his sister. He doesn't spare his kin:
what's been reached is the highest possible latitude!
And, like the silk stocking of a burlesque half-nude
queen, it climbs up his thigh: gangrene.

[*1977* / *Translated by the author*]

7

Lithuanian Nocturne

To Thomas Venclova

I

Having roughed up the waters,
wind explodes like loud curses from fist-ravaged lips
in the cold superpower's
innards, squeezing trite wobbles
of the do-re-mi from sooted trumpets that lisp.
Nonprincesses and porous
nonfrogs hug the terrain,
and a star shines its mite clouds don't bother to tamper
with. A semblance of face
blots the dark windowpane
like the slap of a downpour.

II

Greetings, Thomas. That's my
specter—having abandoned its frame in a fleabag somewhere
overseas, rowing through
whipped-up thick northern cumulus, thereby
tearing from the New World—which wings homeward,
and this thoroughfare
duly brings him to you.

III

Late Lithuanian dusk.
Folk are scuffling from churches protecting the commas
of their candle flames in trembling brackets of hands;
in the freezing courtyards
chickens peck in the sodden sawdust,
over stubbled Zhemaitija's contours
snow's aswirl like the ashes from burnt-out celestial wards.
From the doors flung askew,
fish soup's odor is oozing. A youngster, half naked,
and a kerchiefed old hag chase a pig to the sty.
And a cart-riding Jew,

8

late for home, drums the village's cobblestone, trying to make it,
yanks the reins hard
and bellows "Gerai!"

IV
Sorry for the invasion.
Take this apparition for, let's
say, an early return of the quote back to its Manifesto's
text: a notch more, say, slurred, and a pitch more alluring
for being away.
Thus don't cross yourself, etc.,
and don't torture gauze curtains: I'll vanish as fast as
roosters herald the day.
Sorry for the intrusion.
Don't reel into a bedroom in fright:
it's just frailty that widens its reach at the cost of state borders.
Like a stone that avenges a well
with its multiple rings,
I buzz over the Baltic, like that ill-fated flight
of Girenas and Darius, the immortals!—
but on less brittle wings.

V
Evening in the Empire,
in a destitute province. A conifer force
wades the Neman and, bristling with darkening lances,
takes old three-storied Kaunas; a blush of remorse
sweeps the stucco as darkness advances,
and the cobblestones glisten like bream in a net.
At the opera, up soars a patterned
curtain, while in an archway the object of passion
gets divided by three, with, I bet,
no leftovers. The dark thrills the calm
tulle. A star, shining in a backwater,
does so all the more brightly: like a card played in suit.
And your delta-like palm
drums the pane, flowing into the outer
dark—a cheerless pursuit.

9

VI

Every speech after midnight
develops a blind man's technique.
Even "homeland," by touch, feels like Lady Godiva.
Cobweb-shaded, the mikes
of the secret police in a bard's quarters pick
up the mattress's sighs, and the dripping saliva
of the national anthem: the tune that dislikes
using words. Here reticence reigns. Trembling leaves
torn between their reverse and their surface
irritate a lamppost. Spurning loudspeakers, a man
here declares to the world that he lives
by unwittingly crushing an ant,
by faint Morse's
dots of pulse, by the screech of his pen.

VII

That's whence that mealy grain
of your cheeks, your quite addressless, senseless
stare, your lisping, your hair
with its shade of weak colorless tea down the drain;
that's whence, too, one's whole life's honest, hesitant sentence:
a comma-bound affair.
It is thence also its
upward spinoffs: my washed-out appearance
in your windows; uprisings—with threats to invade—
of sharp willow twigs, etc.;
ocean's pages, one's leafings through them in the quest for a period,
a horizon, a fate.

VIII

Our cuneiform, Thomas! With my margin-prone
predicates! with your subjects, hearthbound and luckless!
Our inkpot alliance! Its splurge!
Doodling lace, herringbone,
Roman writ *cum* Cyrillic, harking to Magnavox's
ends-*cum*-means demiurge!
Our imprints! In damp twisted sheets
—in that flabby brainlike common cotton—
in our loved ones' soft clay, in our children without us, or

as a bruise that still sits
on the firmament, brought on-
to its cheek by a youngster whose sore
eye was trying to fathom the distance from that
famed Lithuanian inn,
to the multieyed face gazing sideways
like some old squinting Mongol beyond our spiked earthly fence,
poised to put fingers in-
to his mouth—that old wound of your namesake!—to find its
tongue and alter, like seraphs and silence
do, his verbs or their tense.

IX

Thomas, we are alike;
we are, frankly, a double:
your breath
dims the same windowpane that my features befuddle.
We're each other's remote
amalgam underneath,
in a lackluster puddle,
a simultaneous nod.
Twist your lips—I'll reply with the similar grimace of dread.
I'll respond to your yawn with my mouth's gaping mollusc.
I'll cry rivers to your
hundred-watt swollen tear overhead.
We're a mutual threat,
Castor looming through Pollux,
we're a stalemate, no-score,
draw, long shadows' distress
brought to walls by a match that will die in a minute,
echoes tracing in vain the original cry
as small change does its note.
The more life has been ruined, the less
is the chance to distinguish us in it
with an indolent eye.

X

What do specters live by?
By the refuse of dreams,
borders' dross, the chaff of mute odd numbers or even,

for addresses are what makes reality hark
back. A lane gnashes, gumlike, its porches agleam;
like a simpleton's cheese, alleys' yellow is eaten
by the fox of the dark
hours. Avenging its permanence, a
place stuffs time with a tenant, a lodger—
with a life-form, and throws up the latch.
And an epoch away
I still find you in this dog-eared kingdom of cudgel
forests, plains, well-preserving one's features, one's thinking and such,
but above all, the pose:
in her many-miled, damp
hemp nightgown, in her high-voltage curlers,
dormant Mother Lithuania's taking her rest
by the shore, as you're gluing your plump
lips to her bare and colorless
glassy half-liter breast.

XI
There are places in which
things don't change. These are a substitute
for one's memory. These are the acid
triumphs of fixative. There each mile
puts striped bars into focus; one's suit
gravitates to a silhouette, added
to one's thinking. Meanwhile,
soldiers keep growing younger. The past
peers ahead with a wary
eye, well matching the khaki attire of youth,
and one's fate, like a border trespasser, reels fast
into brittle old age with its spittle, its aching, its weary
shuffling down the infinity-reeking night pavements. In truth,
night's the border where reality, like
Tartars, threatens the kingdom
of what has been lived through with a raid, or perhaps vice versa;
where logs
join their trees and split back into logs, where daylight
grabs what night's left unhidden
under tight eyelids' locks.

XII

Midnight. Cries of a jay
sound human and charge Mother Nature
with the crime of thermometers: with zerocide.
His bleak shield thrown away
and sword ditched, Prince Vytautas is ready to venture
our flatulent Baltic, with the Swedes out of sight
but in mind. However, the land
overtakes him, assuming the shape of a lengthy
pier, to catch up with freedom long fled
climbing over flat ladderlike waves. In the end,
the best-built beaver dam in the woods cries a-plenty:
tears gleam silver and lead.

XIII

Midnight in a deciduous region,
in a province the shade
of topcoats. Belfries' wedges. A swatch of a cloud
to enshroud a contiguous nation. Below,
haystacks, pastures, a glade
of roof tiles, colonnades, brick, cast-iron; and—proud
in his boots—a by-blow
of the state. Midnight's oxygen gets
flooded with interference, with weather reports, news, and prayers,
with the Vizier of Woes
and his rounded numbers, with anthems, sextets,
jigs, decrees, with anathema-sayers,
banning things no one knows.

XIV

A specter wanders in Kaunas. It enters, by chance,
a cathedral. Runs out. Drifts along Laisvis Boulevard. Enters
empty "Tulpe," slumps down on a chair.
Yet the waiter who'd glance
in this corner will spot just white napkins, or embers
of the cabs outside, snowflakes circling—and stare
at the street. You would envy, I think,
me: for invisibility comes into fashion
with the passage of years—as the body's concession to its

soul, as a well-taken hint
of the future, as Paradise's fathom-
like attire, as a drawn-out minus that fits
everyone. For all profit from absence, from stark
nonextension: a mountain, a valley,
a brass pendulum plate with two glimmers to serve,
the Almighty that gazes from stars
downward, mirrors, a squealer,
corridors, you yourself.

XV

A specter loiters about in Kaunas. It is
but your thoughts of me added
to the air, but a vacuum rampant, and not
that tempestuous sermon of social bliss.
So don't envy me at it,
simply note
in this faint apparition a kin
or an aspect of air—like these words, with their fear of the morning,
scattered thinly at midnight by some slurring voice—
a sound more like houseflies
bravely clicking a tin,
and which won't satiate
the new Clio adorning
checkpoint gowns, but in which
ever-naked Urania is to rejoice!
Only she, our Muse
of the point lost in space, our Muse of forgotten
outlines can assess, and in full,
like a miser, the use
of small change, immobility's token
paid for flights of the soul.

XVI

That's whence, Thomas, the pen's
troth to letters. That's what must explain gravitation,
don't you think?
With the roosters' "Time's up,"
that light-entity rends
its light self from its verbs and their tense,

from its hair-shirted nation,
from—let's loosen the trap—
you: from letters, from pages, from sound's
love for sense, from incorporeality's passion
toward mass, and from freedom's, alas,
love for slavery's haunts—
for the bone, for the flesh, and
for the heart—having thus
liberated itself, that light-entity soars up to ink-
like dark heavenly reaches,
past blind cherubs in niches,
past the bats that won't wink.

XVII

Muse of dots lost in space! Muse of things one makes out
through a telescope only! Muse of subtraction
but without remainders! Of zeroes, in short.
You who order the throat
to avoid lamentation,
not to go overboard,
that is, higher than "la"!
Muse, accept this effect's
little aria sung to the gentle
cause's sensitive ear,
and regard it and its do-re-me-ing tercets
in your rarefied rental
from the viewpoint
of air,
of pure air! Air indeed is the epilogue
for one's retina: nobody stands to inhabit
air! It is our "homeward"! That town
which all syllables long
to return to. No matter how often you grab it,
light or darkness soon darn with their rapid
needles air's eiderdown.

XVIII

Every thing has a limit: the horizon that splits
a round eye; for despair, it is memory; often
it's the hand's fabled reach.

Only sound, Thomas, slips,
specter-like, from the body. An orphan
sound, Thomas, is speech.
Push the lampshade aside, and by staring
straight ahead
you'll see air *en face*:
swarms of those
who have stained it
with their lips before us.

XIX
In the kingdom of air!
In its equality of
gulps of oxygen to our syllables! In the transparent
lumped-like-clouds exhalations of ours! In that
world where, like our dreams haunt the ceiling,
our O's
shape the vault of the palate,
where a star gets its shine from the vat
of the throat! That's how the universe
breathes. And that's what a rooster's sharp yokel
meant by sparing the larynx the draught's dry assaults.
Air, the tongue's running course!
And the firmament's a chorus of highly pitched vocal
atoms, alias souls.

XX
That is why it is pure!
In this world, there is nothing that bleaches
pages better (except
for one's dying) than air.
And the whiter, the emptier, which is
homelike. Muse, may I set
out homeward? To that out-loud
realm where witless Boreas
tramples over the trophies of lips in his flight,
to your grammar without
punctuation, to your Paradise of our alphabets
and tracheas,
to your blackboard in white.

XXI

In the sky
far above the Lithuanian hills
something sounding like a prayer
for the whole of mankind, droning cheerlessly, drifts
toward Kurshskaya Point. This is St. Casimir's
and St. Nicholas's mumbling in their unattainable lair
where, minding the passage of darkness, they sift
hours. Muse! from the heights where you
dwell, beyond any creed's stratosphere, from your rarefied ether,
look, I pray you, together
with those two,
after these pacified sunken plains' sullen bard.
Do not let handmade darkness envelop his rafter.
Post your sentinels in his back yard.
Look, Urania, after
both his home and his heart.

[*1974 / Translated by the author*]

Twenty Sonnets to Mary Queen of Scots

I

Mary, I call them pigs, not Picts, those Scots.
What generation of what clan in tartan
could have foreseen you'd step down from the screen
a statue, and bring life to city gardens—
the Luxembourg, to be precise? I came
here to digest a Paris lunch and stare,
with the dull eyes of a decrepit ram,
at the new gates and into ponds. And here
I met Your Highness. And to mark that meeting
and since "all the dead past now lives anew
in my cold heart," by way of greeting,
I'll stuff the old gun full of classic grape-
shot, squandering what remains of Russian speech
on your pale shoulders and your paler nape.

II

The war to end all wars produced ground zero.
The frying pan missed fat that missed pork chops.
Mary, I was a boy then, and saw Zarah
Leander approach the scaffold, clippety-clop.
Whatever you may say, the axman's blade
equates the ditches to the lofty reaches
(cf., our luminary rising late).
We all came to the surface from the pictures,
but something calls us, at the hour of gloom,
back to the Spartacus, whose plushy womb
is cozier than a European evening.
There the stars hang, the grandest a brunette;
there are two features, everybody queuing,
and not an empty seat, I bet.

III

I, who have traveled half my earthly road,
make my appearance in the Luxembourg
and contemplate the petrified gray curls
of thinkers and of scribblers. Gents and broads

1 8

are strolling to and fro; a whiskered
blue copper glistens from the thicket;
the fountain purrs, the children laugh,
and not a soul to greet with "Bugger off."
And you, untiring, Mary, stand and stand,
in the stone garland of your girl friends—stunned
French queens of once-upon-has-been,
in silence, with a sparrow in your hair.
You'd think the garden was a cross between
the Pantheon and *Déjeuner sur l'herbe*.

IV

The beauty whom I later loved—quite likely
more tenderly than you loved Bothwell—had
some features similar to yours ("My God,"
I automatically whisper, lately
recalling them). Moreover, we,
like you, did not make a happy pair.
Wearing a mackintosh, she went off somewhere.
To sidestep the straight line of destiny,

I cut across another line—whose edge
is sharper than a knife blade: the horizon,
Mary. With neck above that thing outstretched—
not for the oxygen but the breathtaking poison
that bursts my Adam's apple with a squeal—
the larynx's sort of grateful for the deal.

V

The number of your lovers, Mary, went
beyond the figure three, four, twenty, twent-
y-five. A crown, alas, gets dented, bent,
or lost between the sheets with some odd gent.
That's why a monarchy comes to an end
while a republic may be permanent
(see ancient pillars or a monument).
And your Scots barons neither couldn't, nor can't
think otherwise. They wouldn't relent
in pressing their quite sordid argument—
that is, that they, your Scottish lords, can't see

what makes a throne so different from a cot.
O *rara avis* of your century!
To your compatriots you were a slut.

VI

I loved you. And my love of you (it seems,
it's only pain) still stabs me through the brain.
The whole thing's shattered into smithereens.
I tried to shoot myself—using a gun
is not so simple. And the temples: which one,
the right or left? Reflection, not the twitching,
kept me from acting. Jesus, what a mess!
I loved you with such strength, such hopelessness!
May God send you in others—not a chance!
He, capable of many things at once,
won't—citing Parmenides—reinspire
the bloodstream fire, the bone-crushing creeps,
which melt the lead in fillings with desire
to touch—"your hips," I must delete—your lips.

VII

Paris is still the same. The Place des Vosges
is still, as once it was (don't worry), square.
The Seine has not run backward to its source.
The Boulevard Raspail is still as fair.
As for the new, there's music now for free,
a tower to make you feel you're just a fly,
no lack of people whom it's nice to see,
provided you're the first to blurt "How's life?"

Paris by night, a restaurant . . . What chic
in words like these—a treat for vocal cords.
And in comes *eine kleine nachtmuzhik*,
an ugly cretin in a Russian shirt.
Café. Boulevard. The girlfriend in a swoon.
The General-Secretary's-coma moon.

VIII

In my decline, in a land beyond the seas
(discovered in Your Highness's time, methinks),

2 0

splitting my animated frame between
a stove and a divan with busted springs,
I muse how just a few words would have been
enough for us, if fate had crossed our paths:
you would have simply called me "dear Ivan,"
and I'd have answered with one word, "Alas."

Scotland would have been our mattress then.
I'd have displayed you to the haughty Slavs.
Port Glasgow would have seen a caravan
of satins, Russian cakes, and shoes of bast
come sailing in. And we'd have met our fate
together. Severed by a wooden blade.

IX

A plain. Alarum. Enter two. The clash
of battle. "Who are you?" "And you yourself?"
"Us? we are Protestants, we don't observe . . ."
"And we are Catholics." "Ah, bloody Papists!" Crash!
And then the corpses lie about like trash,
the endless din of crows' first-come-first-served.
And later—winter, sleigh rides through the slush.
A shawl from Persia. "Persia! Ah! what nerve!"
"A land where peacocks make their peahens blush."
"Yet even there a queen at night can shush
her shah." "Or mate him, playing chess up north
in a cute Hollywood-style modest castle." Slash:
a plain again. Time: midnight. Enter two.
And drown you with their wolfish who-is-who.

X

An autumn evening. All but with the Muse.
Alas, not heeding the relentless lyre.
That's nothing new. On evenings such as these
you'd play for kicks even the army choir.
Becoming yesterday, today won't use
new sheets of paper, pen, or oatmeal's mire
and let the crippled Hamburg cooper cruise
night skies at length. About the secondhand,
soiled, scratched, or badly dented items:

2 1

time seems a teeny bit more confident
than fresh tomatoes, and at least won't bite them.
The door may creak: death, having failed to knock,
will stand before you in her moth-holed frock.

XI

A clang of shears, a momentary chill.
Fate, envying the sheepfolk for their wool,
knocks off our crowns and bridal wreaths at will—
quite indiscriminately. And the heads as well.
Farewell, young dudes, their proud dads, their ill-
kept promises, divorces, all to hell.
The brain's like a skyscraper in whose still
tight shell each cell ignores another cell.
That's how the twins in distant Siam swill
their booze: one does it, but they both feel swell.
No one has shouted to you, "Watch out!"
Nor did you, Mary, know enough to shout,
"I am alone"—while boring God and pew
with Latin pleas—"There are a lot of you!"

XII

What is it that makes History? Well, bodies.
And Art?—a body that has lost its head.
Take Schiller, say. Young Friedrich served his notice
to History. You never dreamt, I bet,
a Jerry'd get, out of the blue, so hot as
to resurrect the ancient case, long dead.
It's not his business to discuss your quotas:
who had you or who didn't in a bed.

But then, perhaps, like every other Hans,
our Fritz was simply frightened of the ax.
And secondly, dear Mary, let me stress:
there's nothing, barring Art, sublunar creatures
can use to comprehend your gorgeous features.
Leave History to Good Queen Bess.

2 2

A ram shakes out his ringlets, alias fleece,
inhaling lazily the scent of hay.
All round are standing Glencorns, Douglases,
et al. These were the words they spoke that day:
"They have cut off her head." "They have, alas."
"Just think what those in gay Paree will say."
"The French? About the head of some poor lass?
Now, were it aimed above the knee, they may . . ."
"She's not a man, though. Came out in her shift."
"That's not enough to rest one's case upon . . ."
"You could see through it. Shameless!" "What of it?
Could be she's got no gown for putting on."
"Yeah, she's no Russian. 'Ivanov,' I mean,
suggests a wench whichever case it's in."

Love is more powerful than separation, but
the latter is more lasting. Plus, the greater
the statue, the more palpably it ain't her.
Her voice, her wits, smell, finally, are cut
off. While one blames it on the granite that
you won't kick up your legs to starry heights, for
so many fingers' failure to decipher
your petticoats, one has to punish but

one's awkward self. It's not 'cause so much blood
and so much water—equally blue—
have flowed under the bridge, but since the brass
bed screams at night under a lonely lad,
I'd have erected, too, a stone for you,
but I would cut it in transparent glass.

Your ruin, Mary, wasn't the grooms who'd got
no carpenters to raise the roofbeams higher
in that small chamber where they bravely fought;
nor was it that smart ink, which only fire
makes visible (and you were never caught);

nor that Elizabeth loved England's plot
indeed more than you did your Scottish shire
(which is the truth, though some will cry it's not);
nor those good tunes the Spaniard would admire,
especially coming from a royal throat;
no, what they killed you for—let's clear the mire—
was something to which they, in those old days,
could see no end: the beauty of your face.

XVI

As corners vanish, softened by the dark,
a square, too, gradually becomes a sphere.
The crimson wood, like a doused fire,
peers into night with all its pores of bark,
in silence, listening to cranes up there.
Triggered by swishing leaves, a setter's bark
flies to the seven stars that mutely stare
on withered winter crops, forlorn and stark.

How few among those things that once could cause
a tear of pleasure have survived the passage
into the humus shade, how little stays.
The fountain pen now has to stick to those
that failed to heed another season's message,
to squeak and echo "Melancholy Days."

XVII

The thing that dragged from English mouths a shout
of wonderment, that still impels
my own two lips—keen for a lipsticked pout—
to use foul epithets, that rang the bells
for Philip, sending his great painter out
and ordering the great Armada sail;
it was—it seems I can't complete the big
buildup of phrases—well, your wig,
red, lying fallen from your fallen (wow,
that's rich!) head, was your one and only bow
to any audience (with no free seat),
and though it didn't cause a major fight

2 4

among spectators, it was such a sight
it brought your enemies to their cold feet.

XVIII

To one whose mouth has said farewell to you,
not just to anyone, isn't it all the same,
whatever tasteless crusts he has to chew
in years to come? I'll wager you became
accustomed to the lack of do-re-mi.
And if you didn't, don't be cross with me:
ratlike the tongue goes scurrying through a mound
of rubbish, seeking treasure left behind.

Forgive me then, fair idol on the lawn.
Yes, separation is no fool, to own
them measly peanuts. For between us lie
eternity and ocean. Literally.
Plus Russian censorship, in case you ask.
They could have done the job without an ax.

XIX

The Scots have wool now, Mary (and it all
looks spick-and-span like from the cleaners, great).
At six o'clock life judders to a stall,
leaving no mark upon the sunset's plate.
The lakes—unnumbered as in days gone by—
have spawned strange monsters (serpentine and frisky),
and soon they'll have their private oil supply,
Scotch oil, to go in bottles meant for whiskey.
It looks like Scotland got along just fine
without you, and England too, one hears.
And you in this *jardin* of French design
don't look the madcap of those yesteryears.
And there are dames through whose silk folds I'd rummage—
but the comparison would do you damage.

XX

With simple pen (rebellious, not true!)
I've sung this meeting under foreign eaves

2 5

with her who taught me from the screen a few
facts of the heart on '48's cold eves.

Now judge, ye of all races and beliefs:
(a) if he learned his lessons (one or two),
(b) the new setting where a Russian lives,
(c) moments of grammatical voodoo.

Nepal's far capital is Katmandu.

Being absolute, the arbitrary gives
a helping hand to everything we do.

Leading the life I lead, I am grateful to
the sheaf of previously snow-white leaves
of paper, rolled for simply blowing through.

[*1974 / Translated by Peter France and the author*]

North Baltic

To C.H.

When a blizzard powders the harbor, when the creaking pine
leaves in the air an imprint deeper than a sled's steel runner,
what degree of blueness can be gained by an eye? What sign
language can sprout from a chary manner?
Falling out of sight, the outside world
makes a face its hostage: pale, plain, snowbound.
Thus a mollusc stays phosphorescent at the ocean's floor
and thus silence absorbs all speeds of sound.
Thus a match is enough to set a stove aglow;
thus a grandfather clock, a heartbeat's brother,
having stopped this side of the sea, still tick-tocks to show
time at the other.

[*1975 / Translated by the author*]

The Berlin Wall Tune

To Peter Viereck

This is the house destroyed by Jack.
   This is the spot where the rumpled buck
stops, and where Hans gets killed.
   This is the wall that Ivan built.

This is the wall that Ivan built.
   Yet trying to quell his sense of guilt,
he built it with modest gray concrete,
   and the booby traps look discreet.

Under this wall that (a) bores, (b) scares,
   barbed-wire meshes lie flat like skeins
of your granny's darnings (her chair still rocks!).
   But the voltage's too high for socks.

Beyond this wall throbs a local flag
   against whose yellow, red, and black
Compass and Hammer proclaim the true
   Masonic dream's breakthrough.

The border guards patiently in their nest
   through binoculars scan the West
and the East; and they like both views
   devoid, as it were, of Jews.

Those who are seen here, thought of, felt,
   are kept on a leash by the sense of Geld
or by a stronger Marxist urge.
   The wall won't let them merge.

Come to this wall if you hate your place
   and face a sample of cosmic space
where no life forms can exist at all
   and objects may only fall.

28

Come to this scornful of peace and war,
    petrified version of either/or
meandering through these bleak parts which act
    like your mirror, cracked.

Dull is the day here. In the night
    searchlights illuminate the blight
making sure that if someone screams,
    it's not due to bad dreams.

For dreams here aren't bad: just wet with blood
    of one of your like who's left his pad
to ramble at will; and in his head
    dreams are replaced with lead.

Given that, it's only time
    who has guts enough to commit the crime
of passing this place back and forth on foot:
    at pendulums they don't shoot.

That's why this site will see many moons
    while couples lie in their beds like spoons,
while the rich are wondering what they wish
    and single girls eat quiche.

Come to this wall that beats other walls:
    Roman, Chinese, whose worn-down, false
molars envy steel fangs that flash,
    scrubbed of thy neighbor's flesh.

A bird may twitter a better song.
    But should you consider abortion wrong
or that the quacks ask too high a fee,
    come to this wall, and see.

[*1980*]

Dutch Mistress

A hotel in whose ledgers departures are more prominent than arrivals.
With wet Koh-i-noors the October rain
strokes what's left of the naked brain.
In this country laid flat for the sake of rivers,
beer smells of Germany and seagulls are
in the air like a page's soiled corners.
Morning enters the premises with a coroner's
punctuality, puts its ear
to the ribs of a cold radiator, detects sub-zero:
the afterlife has to start somewhere.
Correspondingly, the angelic curls
grow more blond, the skin gains its distant, lordly
white, while the bedding already coils
desperately in the basement laundry.

[*1981*]

Allenby Road

At sunset, when the paralyzed street gives up
hope of hearing an ambulance, finally settling for
strolling Chinamen, while the elms imitate a map
of a khaki-clad country that lulls its foe,
life is gradually getting myopic, spliced,
aquiline, geometrical, free of gloss
or detail—be it cornices, doorknobs, Christ—
stressing silhouettes: chimneys, rooftops, a cross.
And your closing the shutters unleashes the domino
theory; for no matter what size a lump
melts in your throat, the future snowballs each "no"
to coin a profile by the burning lamp.
Neither because there is a lot of guilt
nor because local prices are somewhat steep,
nobody picks this brick pocket filled
with change that barely buys some sleep.

[*1981*]

The Fifth Anniversary

June 4, 1977

A falling star, or worse, a planet (true or bogus)
might thrill your idle eye with its quick hocus-pocus.
Look, look then at that locus that's better out of focus.

.   .   .

There frowning forests stand decked out in rags and tatters.
Departing from point A, a train there bravely scatters
its wheels toward point B. Which station hardly matters.

There causes and effects are drowned in murky waters.
One's corpse there lies unseen; so does, of course, one's foetus.
It's different with birds; but eggs don't beg for photos.

At dusk a Steinway grand twangs out a thin B-minor.
There musty jackets hang, the moth their redesigner.
On rocks, enchanted oaks nod to a passing liner.

.   .   .

There a puddle in the yard is neither round nor square.
There single mothers pot their daughters in day care.
A boisterous mountain stream strives for the third shore there.

A kid stares down his dad there all the way to breeches.
There rockets carry up crafts filled with barking bitches
plus officers whose pay suggests the upper reaches.

There weeds submit to green: a sort of common harness.
A principle of sound owes to a bee that's harmless.
A copy, sparing its original, stays armless.

.   .   .

In winter, Arctic winds shake parks to herald foul days,
and radiators which absorb the dust in hallways
possess more ribs than girls. A freezing man, though, always

3 2

prefers the former, which, in turn, appear more eager.
At tea, a candy hurts a tooth that's scarcely bigger.
A sleeping guard enjoys wet dreams and pulls the trigger.

There on a rainy day a sulphur match looks shocking.
They say, "It's only us," with rotten smirks while knocking.
There fish scales shine with tin, in lakes where fish are soaking.

. . .

There having voted yes, they sob in toilet corners.
There icons in the church turn black from incense burners.
The army shows who's who to folks across the borders.

There orchards burst in view, thus aping epic horsemen.
The liquor store's long queue needs only you to worsen.
Behind you and in front, you find the same stiff person.

There snatches of old tunes hang in the air they brighten.
Wheat left the zeal of state: it's a collector's item.
There martens quit the woods, whose branches fail to hide them.

. . .

There even when you lie flat on a sheet of cotton,
your shadow dwarfs a palm in Palestine, begotten
most likely in a dream. There deserts lie well-trodden

by sugar bowls' houseflies, which trek on foot, old-style.
There under rakish roofs small windows squint hostile.
The world map is replaced there by a large Holstein

a-mooing on a hill, awash in sunset's slobber.
There steel mills far away belch heavy smoke and clobber,
though no one needs all that; no matter drunk or sober.

. . .

There owls hoot late at night on matters vain and ashen.
No leader seems quite fit to stop green leaves' ovation.
There brain folds spurn straight thought for being out of fashion.

3 3

The hammer-hugging sickle there adorns the banner.
But nails are not struck home and weeds submerge the planner:
into the Great Machine someone has lobbed a spanner.

Apart from these, there are no enigmas, signs in heavens.
The landscape's dull, and its horizon's notched with cave-ins.
There gray is all the rage—the tint of time and cabins.

.   .   .

I grew up in those parts. I used to share a cigarette
with their most gifted bard. Was kept, a guilty secret,
in cells. Admired lead skies, as well as windswept liquid.

There I thought I would die. From boredom or from terror.
If not in friendly arms, then at their hands. But there or
somewhere nearby. Today I see my error.

I see that I was wrong. For on a stage the actor
means less than backdrops do. Space is a greater factor
than horsemen. Space won't tell the front legs from the back two.

.   .   .

Well, I'm no longer there. The sense of loss, as much as
this was indeed a loss, is best displayed by statues
in galleries, or by their vases' mute "Don't touch us."

The place sustained this loss. Some moss combined with lichen,
encountering the hole I've made, will quickly stitch it.
A connoisseur of hues won't tell you later which one

is missing. This feels odd but constitutes a variant.
It would be odder still to lie there low and ironed
or play a warrior valiant and nudge an aging tyrant.

.   .   .

So I'm no longer there. All things have rules to reckon.
I never liked fat cats, and never kissed an icon.
And on a certain bridge, a black cast-iron Gorgon

3 4

seemed in those parts to me the truth's most honest version.
So later having met her in gigantic person,
I haven't turned to stone and let my lumpy portion

of savage screams go stale. I hear the Muse's prattle.
I sense the thread within strained by the Parcae's shuttle:
the spheres still tolerate my CO_2 life rattle,

.   .   .

as my free-flapping tongue, a glutton for clear lyric
sends its Cyrillic thanks into the blue acrylic
to fate—since fate can grasp the meaning in Cyrillic

as well. I face pure space, which tolerates no columns
nor torsos of Apollos, nor pyramids, nor chorus.
There, it appears, I need no guide; at least, it follows.

Scratch on, my clawlike pen, my pilgrim staff, my salvage!
Don't rush our shuffling words: the age wheel-deep in garbage
won't overtake us and won't grab you, barefoot savage.

.   .   .

This won't be heard up North, nor where hot sands hug cactus.
I don't know anymore what earth will nurse my carcass.
Scratch on, my pen: let's mark the white the way it marks us.

[*1977 / Translated by the author*]

Polonaise: A Variation

To Z.K.

I

Autumn in your hemisphere whoops cranes and owls.
A lean nation's frontier slips off like a loosened harness.
And though windows aren't sealed yet, your camisole's
cleavage adds to the shadows the parlor harvests.
As the lamps flare up, one may well denounce
one's own curves as jarring the jigsaw puzzle
of the rooms whose air savors every ounce
pecked by Frederyk's keyboard-bedeviled nozzle.
In the full moon, the stubble gets lavished with
nobody's silver by sloughy waters.
Roll on your side, and the dreams will blitz
out of the wall like those fabled warriors
heading east, through your yard, to dislodge the siege
of tall hemp. Still, their hauberks won't hide their tatters.
Yet, since they look alike, you, by getting hitched
only once, let an army across your mattress.

II

Reddish tiles of the homestead, and the yellow shade
of its stuccoed dwellings, beset with shingles.
Either cartwheels are craving an oval shape
or the mare's hoof, hitting the cow-moon, shimmies,
and slumped haystacks flash by. Alders, nothing-clad,
in their basket carry away the river.
And the leaden plow in the furrowed clouds
bodes no good to gray winter crops racked with fever.
To your woolen stockings and linen hem
burdocks cling like nobody's child that loses
in the end its grip. And space is stitched firm
with the threadbare rain, and Copernicus turns out useless.
Still, the iris gleams, and the milky tint,
with those scattered birthmarks, your dress effaces.
Long a silhouette to yourself, you won't
fall into anyone's fond embraces.

III

I admit that one's love should be greater, more
pure. That one could, like the son of Cronus,
size up the darkness, perfect its lore,
and drop, unnoticed, within your contours.
That one could reconstruct, pore by pore, your true
looks, with idle atoms and mental power;
or just peer at the mirror and state that you
are me: for whom do we love but ourselves? Yet chalk one up for Fate: your watch
may be running behind, for in our future
already that bomb has exploded which
leaves intact only the furniture.
Does it really matter who's run away from whom?
Neither time nor space is matchmaking for us
who took full advantage of sampling some
of those ages to come, and whatever follows.

[*1981 / Translated by the author*]

The New Jules Verne

To Lev and Nina Loseff

I

A perfect line of horizon. Without a blot. A swanky
clipper, whose Franz Liszt profile keeps stabbing
the waves. Tight cables are creaking. A naked monkey
with a scream leaps out of the naturalist's hot cabin.

Dolphins bounce along. As someone remarked somewhere,
only bottles in bars experience no seasickness.
A squall tears off the punch line of a joke, and the captain's bare
fists in a flurry challenge the mizzen's stiffness.

At times, the piano tinklings waft from the lounge: pure, guileless.
The navigator ponders the course, scratching behind his ear.
And the blueness of space straight ahead blends inside the spyglass
with the blueness of space withering at the rear.

II

You can tell a passenger from a sailor
by the swishing silk of his underwear,
by the quality of what he eats and where,
by the repetition of some meaningless question and a general air
                                                      of failure.

You can tell a sailor from a lieutenant
by the absence of an epaulette,
by the age that he's at,
by the nerves wrung tight like cables, or, say, a pennant.

You can tell a lieutenant from a captain
by the stripes, his hazel eyes' razzmatazz,
by the snapshot of Blanche or of Françoise,
by his reading of Kant, Maupassant, Karl Marx, and his buying
                                                    smokes by the carton.

You can tell a captain from the Admiralty
by the lonely thinking, by the profound disgust

toward anything that is blue and vast,
by the memory of his in-laws, which loses, he thinks, its accuracy.

And only a ship acts always as though she could
be another ship. Combing the waves that hold her,
a ship resembles at once an albatross and an alder
from under whose feet the ground has slipped for good.

III
Exchanges in the Lounge
"Of course the Archduke is a monster! And of course it matters!
But he's trying his best, whereas his subjects, they . . ."
"Masters resent their slaves, slaves resent their masters.
Feels like a vicious circle!" "Like a sort of ring buoy, I'd say."

"What a splendid sherry!" "Gosh, you know, I couldn't sleep a wink.
It's this frightful sun: it burns your skin through the bodice."
". . . but what if we've sprung a leak!? I've read leaks are hard
to notice.
Imagine, we've sprung a leak! And we are—to sink!

Has this ever happened to you, Lieutenant?" "No, but I have had
a sour
experience with a shark." "Yeah? But I mean, a leak. What if . . ."
"Well, then you'll finally meet the passenger from 8–F."
"Who is that?" "She's the governor's daughter, sailing to Curaçao."

IV
Exchanges on the Deck
"I, Professor, too, as a kid, wanted, and badly so,
to discover some insect, or, better still, a virus . . ."
"Right. And what happened?" "Well, science involves new values . . .
Plus, the usual tsuris . . ." "Sorry?" "You know: the dough."

"What is man, anyway? I tell you: he is a gnat!"
"But back there, in Russia, monsieur, do you also have rubber,
as in . . ."
"Valdemar! I said stop it! You bit my lip, you rat.
Don't forget, Valdemar, that I am . . ." "I am sorry, cousin."

"Listen, buddy." "Well, what?" "What is that thing far off?"
"Where?" "On the right." "I see nothing." "At two o'clock,
                                            out there."
"Oh, that . . . maybe a whale. Got any smokes?" "Nope. Zero . . .
but—it's rising! It's rising so fast! And it is, by Jove . . ."

V

The sea is more various than the terra
firma. It's harder for you to grapple
with, not to mention stare at.
A fish is more intricate than an apple.

The land means four solid walls, a ceiling.
We are scared of wolves or of bears. Although some are ready
to detect in the latter a human feeling
and address one as "Teddy."

The sea has no room for these sorts of worries.
A whale, in its primordial splendor,
won't respond to a name like Boris;
Dick is a better tender.

The sea is filled with surprises; some are unpleasant.
Many a maritime upheaval
can't be ascribed to the evil crescent
of the moon or the human eye's lesser evil.

Ah, sea dwellers' blood is colder than ours. Their goggle
mesmerizes even fishmongers. The late Charles Darwin
would have quit legislating his gentle jungle
had he tried some limited scuba diving.

VI

Exchange on the Bridge

"Captain! We're passing the fathoms where *The Black Prince*
went down. For reasons unknown." "Navigator Benz!
Return to your cabin and sober up!"
". . . the fathoms where the Russian *Tsarina*, too, took the rap
and was lost . . ." "Navigator Benz! I'll banish you to the can!
Do you hear me?!" ". . . for reasons un . . ."

The clipper's unswerving on its blue track.
Africa, Asia, the New and the Old World lag
behind. Taut sails look like question marks in profile.
Space's answer is in the back.

VII

Exchange in a Cabin

"Irina!" "Ah, what?" "Take a look at that thing, Irina."
"But I am asleep." "All the same. Look!" "Where?" "In the porthole.
What is that?" "Looks like somebo . . . like samba . . .

like submarine . . .
Huh?

What did you say?" "But it coils!" "So what. In the water, all
things coil " "Irina!" "What? Where are you dragging me? I am
completely naked."
"Yes, but just look!" "Oh, stop pushing me!" "You see?" "Well, I
look. Yes, it coils. But I think—I take it—
But it's a gigantic octopus! And it's climbing in! Nikolai!!!"

VIII

The sea is ostensibly lifeless, yet
it's full of monstrous life-forms which your mind-set
won't grasp until you hit the king-size sea-bed.

At times, this gets proven by what's been angled
or by shimmering waves whose rather languid
mirror reflects things happening under the blanket.

While on the surface, a man wants to sail fast and be there first.
Submerged, he gets this wish reversed;
suddenly he feels a thirst.

There, underneath, man feels dry within.
Life appears to him short and green.
Submerged, man can be only a submarine.

From the mouth, bubbles are bursting free.
In the eyes, an equivalent of sunrise replaces glee.
In the ears, a colorless baritone keeps uttering: "One. Two. Three."

4 1

"Dear Blanche, I write this to you sitting inside a gigantic octopus.
A miracle, but the stationery and your picture survived. This jelly
is hard to inhale. Yet in a sense it's populous:
there are a couple of savages, both playing the ukulele.
Main thing: it's dark. I strain my eyes and listen.
Sometimes I make out some arches and vaults. When I write, it also
                                        becomes less black.
I resolve to examine the metabolic system.
That's the only railroad to freedom. Kisses. Your faithful Jacques."

"It's like being back in the womb . . . Still, one should be grateful
for the octopus. Sharks are worse. So is water as such—for
                                        yours truly.
Am still searching. The savages brought a grapefruit.
But when I ask for directions, all I hear is 'Hoolie-hoolie.'
All I see are infinite, slippery, coiling tunnels.
Some peculiar, tangled system that's hard to memo-
rize. And unless I'm delirious, yesterday in these trammels
I bumped into somebody who calls himself Captain Nemo."

"Nemo again. Invited me to his rooms. I went.
He says he has reared this octopus as a protest
against society. Well, earlier, I understand,
he was married, with kids. But his wife—the hottest
pants in town . . . and so forth. And he had no choice. He says
the world drowns in Evil. The octopus ('opus' for some) avenges
hubris and heartlessness, alias earthly ways.
Promised me immortality if I don't leave the trenches."

"Tuesday. Supper at Nemo's. Caviar, cognac, *fromage*—from, I
guess, both *Prince* and *Tsarina*. The savages served: good manners.
We discussed the matter raised yesterday, that is, my
immortality; Pascal's *Pensées*; recent La Scala tenors.
Just think: evening, candles. The octopus all around.
Nemo with his goatee and baby-blue, nay, prenatal
eyes. If I think of his loneliness, my heart starts to pound . . ."

That's the last Mlle Blanche Delarue heard from Jacques Benz,
                                        navigator.

x

When the ship doesn't arrive at the port of call
on time, or later on, the Business
Manager says in his office, "Hell!"
The Admiralty says, "Jesus."

Both are quite wrong. But how could they know what had
transpired? You can't interrogate a seagull
or a shark with its streamlined head.
Nor is sending an eager

doggie down the track of much help. And anyway, what sort
of tracks are there at sea? All this is valiant
bunk. One more triumph—via the absurd—
for waves contesting dry land.

Oceanic events are, as a rule, abrupt.
Still, long afterward, the waves toss the remnants of their brief sally:
life vests, splinters of masts, a rat—
none with fingerprints, sadly.

And then comes autumn. And later on, winter cuts
in. The sirocco tatters awnings that summer fancied.
Silent waves can drive the best attorney nuts
with their show of a sunset.

And what gets crystal-clear is that it's dumb to grill
(turning your vocal cords into a shortwave's risen
pitch) the blue ripples perfecting their sharp-as-steel
line of the horizon.

Something bobs up in the papers, burying under their slants
the facts, driblets really. Who can crack it . . .
A woman wearing brown clutches the drapes and slumps
slowly onto the carpet.

The horizon's improving. The air's filled with iodine and salt.
Far away, breakers pummel with great abandon
some inanimate object. And the bell of old
keeps tolling grimly at Lloyd's of London.

[*1977 / Translated by the author*]

43

Lines on the Winter Campaign, 1980

The scorching noon,
the vale in Dagestan . . .
MIKHAIL LERMONTOV

I

A bullet's velocity in low temperatures
greatly depends on its target's virtues,
on its urge to warm up in the plaited muscles
of the torso, in the neck's webbed sinews.
Stones lie flat like a second army.
The shade hugs the loam to itself willy-nilly.
The sky resembles peeling stucco.
An aircraft dissolves in it like a clothes moth,
and like a spring from a ripped-up mattress
an explosion sprouts up. Outside the crater,
the blood, like boiled milk, powerless to seep into
the ground, is seized by a film's hard ripples.

II

Shepherd and sower, the North is driving
herds to the sea, spreading cold to the South.
A bright, frosty noon in a Wogistan valley.
A mechanical elephant, trunk wildly waving
at the horrid sight of the small black rodent
of a snow-covered mine, spews out throat-clogging
lumps, possessed of that old desire
of Mahomet's, to move a mountain.
Summits loom white; the celestial warehouse
lends them at noontime its flaking surplus.
The mountains lack any motion, passing
their immobility to the scattered bodies.

III

The doleful, echoing Slavic singing
at evening in Asia. Dank and freezing,
sprawling piles of human pig meat
cover the caravansary's mud bottom.
The fuel dung smolders, legs stiffen in numbness.

4 4

It smells of old socks, of forgotten bath days.
The dreams are identical, as are the greatcoats.
Plenty of cartridges, few recollections,
and the tang in the mouth of too many "hurrahs."
Glory to those who, their glances lowered,
marched in the sixties to abortion tables,
sparing the homeland its present stigma.

IV

What is contained in the drone's dull buzzing?
And what in the sound of the aero-engine?
Living is getting as complicated
as building a house with grapes' green marbles
or little lean-tos with spades and diamonds.
Nothing is stable (one puff and it's over):
families, private thoughts, clay shanties.
Night over ruins of a mountain village.
Armor, wetting its metal sheets with oil slick,
freezes in thorn scrub. Afraid of drowning
in a discarded jackboot, the moon
hides in a cloud as in Allah's turban.

V

Idle, inhaled now by no one, air.
Imported, carelessly piled-up silence.
Rising like dough that's leavened,
emptiness. If the stars had life-forms,
space would erupt with a brisk ovation;
a gunner, blinking, runs to the footlights.
Murder's a blatant way of dying,
a tautology, the art form of parrots,
a manual matter, the knack for catching
life's fly in the hairs of the gunsight
by youngsters acquainted with blood through either
hearsay or violating virgins.

VI

Pull up the blanket, dig a hole in the palliasse.
Flop down and give ear to the *oo* of the siren.
The Ice Age is coming—slavery's ice age is coming,

oozing over the atlas. Its moraines force under
nations, fond memories, muslin blouses.
Muttering, rolling our eyeballs upward,
we are becoming a new kind of bivalve,
our voice goes unheard, as though we were trilobites.
There's a draft from the corridor, draft from the square windows.
Turn off the light, wrap up in a bundle.
The vertebra craves eternity. Unlike a ringlet.
In the morning the limbs are past all uncoiling.

VII

Up in the stratosphere, thought of by no one,
the little bitch barks as she peers through the porthole:
"Beach Ball! Beach Ball! Over. It's Rover."
The beach ball's below. With the equator on it
like a dog collar. Slopes, fields, and gullies
repeat in their whiteness cheekbones
(the color of shame has all gone to the banners).
And the hens in their snowed-in hen coops,
also a-shake from the shock of reveille,
lay their eggs of immaculate color.
If anything blackens, it's just the letters,
like the tracks of some rabbit, preserved by a wonder.

[1980 / Translated by Alan Myers]

46

Café Trieste: San Francisco

To L.G.

To this corner of Grant and Vallejo
I've returned like an echo
to the lips that preferred
then a kiss to a word.

Nothing has changed here. Neither
the furniture nor the weather.
Things, in one's absence, gain
permanence, stain by stain.

Cold, through the large steamed windows
I watch the gesturing weirdos,
the bloated breams that warm
up their aquarium.

Evolving backward, a river
becomes a tear, the real
becomes memory which
can, like fingertips, pinch

just the tail of a lizard
vanishing in the desert
which was eager to fix
a traveler with a sphinx.

Your golden mane! Your riddle!
The lilac skirt, the brittle
ankles! The perfect ear
rendering "read" as "dear."

Under what cloud's pallor
now throbs the tricolor
of your future, your past
and present, swaying the mast?

47

Upon what linen waters
do you drift bravely toward
new shores, clutching your beads
to meet the savage needs?

Still, if sins are forgiven,
that is, if souls break even
with flesh elsewhere, this joint,
too, must be enjoyed

as afterlife's sweet parlor
where, in the clouded squalor,
saints and the ain'ts take five,
where I was first to arrive.

[*1980*]

The Hawk's Cry in Autumn

Wind from the northwestern quarter is lifting him high above
the dove-gray, crimson, umber, brown
Connecticut Valley. Far beneath,
chickens daintily pause and move
unseen in the yard of the tumbledown
farmstead, chipmunks blend with the heath.

Now adrift on the airflow, unfurled, alone,
all that he glimpses—the hills' lofty, ragged
ridges, the silver stream that threads
quivering like a living bone
of steel, badly notched with rapids,
the townships like strings of beads

strewn across New England. Having slid down to nil
thermometers—those household gods in niches—
freeze, inhibiting thus the fire
of leaves and churches' spires. Still,
no churches for him. In the windy reaches,
undreamt of by the most righteous choir,

he soars in a cobalt-blue ocean, his beak clamped shut,
his talons clutched tight into his belly
—claws balled up like a sunken fist—
sensing in each wisp of down the thrust
from below, glinting back the berry
of his eyeball, heading south-southeast

to the Rio Grande, the Delta, the beech groves and farther still:
to a nest hidden in the mighty groundswell
of grass whose edges no fingers trust,
sunk amid forest's odors, filled
with splinters of red-speckled eggshell,
with a brother or a sister's ghost.

The heart overgrown with flesh, down, feather, wing,
pulsing at feverish rate, nonstopping,

4 9

propelled by internal heat and sense,
the bird goes slashing and scissoring
the autumnal blue, yet by the same swift token,
enlarging it at the expense

of its brownish speck, barely registering on the eye,
a dot, sliding far above the lofty
pine tree; at the expense of the empty look
of that child, arching up at the sky,
that couple that left the car and lifted
their heads, that woman on the stoop.

But the uprush of air is still lifting him
higher and higher. His belly feathers
feel the nibbling cold. Casting a downward gaze,
he sees the horizon growing dim,
he sees, as it were, the features
of the first thirteen colonies whose

chimneys all puff out smoke. Yet it's their total within his sight
that tells the bird of his elevation,
of what altitude he's reached this trip.
What am I doing at such a height?
He senses a mixture of trepidation
and pride. Heeling over a tip

of wing, he plummets down. But the resilient air
bounces him back, winging up to glory,
to the colorless icy plane.
His yellow pupil darts a sudden glare
of rage, that is, a mix of fury
and terror. So once again

he turns and plunges down. But as walls return
rubber balls, as sins send a sinner to faith, or near,
he's driven upward this time as well!
He! whose innards are still so warm!
Still higher! Into some blasted ionosphere!
That astronomically objective hell

of birds that lacks oxygen, and where the milling stars
play millet served from a plate or a crescent.
What, for the bipeds, has always meant
height, for the feathered is the reverse.
Not with his puny brain but with shriveled air sacs
he guesses the truth of it: it's the end.

And at this point he screams. From the hooklike beak
there tears free of him and flies *ad luminem*
the sound Erinyes make to rend
souls: a mechanical, intolerable shriek,
the shriek of steel that devours aluminum;
"mechanical," for it's meant

for nobody, for no living ears:
not man's, not yelping foxes',
not squirrels' hurrying to the ground
from branches; not for tiny field mice whose tears
can't be avenged this way, which forces
them into their burrows. And only hounds

lift up their muzzles. A piercing, high-pitched squeal,
more nightmarish than the D-sharp grinding
of the diamond cutting glass,
slashes the whole sky across. And the world seems to reel
for an instant, shuddering from this rending.
For the warmth burns space in the highest as

badly as some iron fence down here
brands incautious gloveless fingers.
We, standing where we are, exclaim
"There!" and see far above the tear
that is a hawk, and hear the sound that lingers
in wavelets, a spider skein

swelling notes in ripples across the blue vault of space
whose lack of echo spells, especially in October,
an apotheosis of pure sound.
And caught in this heavenly patterned lace,

starlike, spangled with hoarfrost powder,
silver-clad, crystal-bound,

the bird sails to the zenith, to the dark-blue high
of azure. Through binoculars we foretoken
him, a glittering dot, a pearl.
We hear something ring out in the sky,
like some family crockery being broken,
slowly falling aswirl,

yet its shards, as they reach our palms, don't hurt
but melt when handled. And in a twinkling
once more one makes out curls, eyelets, strings,
rainbowlike, multicolored, blurred
commas, ellipses, spirals, linking
heads of barley, concentric rings—

the bright doodling pattern the feather once possessed,
a map, now a mere heap of flying
pale flakes that make a green slope appear
white. And the children, laughing and brightly dressed,
swarm out of doors to catch them, crying
with a loud shout in English, "Winter's here!"

[1975 / Translated by Alan Myers and the author]

Sextet

To Mark Strand

I

An eyelid is twitching. From the open mouth
gushes silence. The cities of Europe mount
each other at railroad stations. A pleasant odor
of soap tells the jungle dweller of the approaching foe.
Wherever you set your sole or toe,
the world map develops blank spots, grows balder.

A palate goes dry. The traveler's seized by thirst.
Children, to whom the worst
should be done, fill the air with their shrieks. An eyelid twitches
all the time. As for columns, from
the thick of them someone always emerges. Even in your sweet dream,
even with your eyes shut, you see human features.

And it wells up in your throat like barf:
"Give me ink and paper and, as for yourself,
scram!" And an eyelid is twitching. Odd, funereal
whinings—as though someone's praying upstairs—poison the
daily grind.
The monstrosity of what's happening in your mind
makes unfamiliar premises look familiar.

II

Sometimes in the desert you hear a voice. You fetch
a camera in order to catch the face.
But—too dark. Sit down, then, release your hearing
to the Southern lilt of a small monkey who
left her palm tree but, having no leisure to
become a human, went straight to whoring.

Better sail by steamer, horizon's ant,
taking part in geography, in blueness, and
not in history, this dry land's scabies.
Better trek across Greenland on skis and camp

5 3

among the icebergs, among the plump
walruses as they bathe their babies.

The alphabet won't allow your trip's goal to be
ever forgotten, that famed point B.
There a crow caws hard, trying to play the raven;
there a black sheep bleats, rye is choked with weeds;
there the top brass, like furriers, shear out bits
of the map's faded pelt, so that they look even.

III

For thirty-six years I've stared at fire.
An eyelid is twitching. Both palms perspire:
the cop leaves the room with your papers. Angst. Built to calm it,
an obelisk, against its will, recedes
in a cloud, amidst bright seeds,
like an immobile comet.

Night. With your hair quite gone, you still dine alone,
being your own grand master, your own black pawn.
The kipper's soiling a headline about striking rickshaws
or a berserk volcano's burps—
God knows where, in other words—
flitting its tail over "The New Restrictions."

I comprehend only the buzz of flies
in the Eastern bazaars! On the sidewalk, flat
on his back, the traveler strains his sinews,
catching the air with his busted gills.
In the afterlife, the pain that kills
here no doubt continues.

IV

"Where's that?" asks the nephew, toying with his stray locks.
And, fingering brown mountain folds, "Here," pokes
the niece. In the depths of the garden, yellow
swings creak softly. The table dwarfs a bouquet
of violets. The sun's splattering the parquet
floor. From the drawing room float twangs of a cello.

At night, a plateau absorbs moonshine.
A boulder shepherds its elephantine
shadow. A brook's silver change is spending
itself in a gully. Clutched sheets in a room elude
their milky/swarthy/abandoned nude—
an anonymous painful painting.

In spring, labor ants build their muddy coops;
rooks show up; so do creatures with other groups
of blood; a fresh leaf shelters
the verging shame of two branches. In autumn, a sky hawk keeps
counting villages' chicklets; and the sahib's
white jacket is dangling from the servant's shoulders.

v

Was the word ever uttered? And then—if yes—
in what language? And where? And how much ice
should be thrown into a glass to halt a *Titanic*
of thought? Does the whole recall the neat shapes of parts?
Would a botanist, suddenly facing birds
in an aquarium, panic?

Now let us imagine an absolute emptiness.
A place without time. The air *per se*. In this,
in that, and in the third direction—pure, simple, pallid
air. A Mecca of it: oxygen, nitrogen. In which
there's really nothing except for the rapid twitching of a lonely eyelid.

These are the notes of a naturalist. The naughts
on nature's own list. Stained with flowerpots.
A tear falls in a vacuum without acceleration.
The last of hotbed neu-roses, hearing the
faint buzzing of time's tsetse,
I smell increasingly of isolation.

VI

And I dread my petals' joining the crowned knot
of fire! Most resolutely not!

5 5

Oh, but to know the place for the first, the second,
and the umpteenth time! When everything comes to light,
when you hear or utter the jewels like
"When I was in the army" or "Change the record!"

Petulant is the soul begging mercy from
an invisible or dilated frame.
Still, if it comes to the point where the blue acrylic
dappled with cirrus suggests the Lord,
say, "Give me strength to sustain the hurt,"
and learn it by heart like a decent lyric.

When you are no more, unlike the rest,
the latter may think of themselves as blessed
with the place so much safer thanks to the big withdrawal
of what your conscience indeed amassed.
And a fish that prophetically shines with rust
will splash in a pond and repeat your oval.

[*1976 / Translated by the author*]

Minefield Revisited

You, guitar-shaped affair with tousled squalor
of chords, who keep looming brown in an empty parlor,
or snow-white against laundered expanses, or
dark—at dusk especially—in the corridor,
strum me a tune of how drapery makes its cloudy
rustle, how a flipped-up switch ravages half a body
with shadow, how a fly prowls the atlas, how in the garden
outside, the sunset echoes a steaming squadron
of which there survived only a middy blouse
in the nursery, how hidden in the satin trousers
the comb of a Turkish dog trainer, when played, elevates his poodle
beyond Kovalevska, beyond its idol
to a happy occasion: that is, to yelping forty
times at some birthday, while wet and frothy
firework stars fizz and fade in the foggy trembling
glass, and carafes on a tablecloth feign the Kremlin.

[*1978 / Translated by the author*]

Near Alexandria

To Carl Proffer

The concrete needle is shooting its
heroin into cumulous wintry muscle.
From a trash can, a spy plucks the crumpled morsel—
a blueprint of ruins—and glances east.

Ubiquitous figures on horseback: all
four hooves glued to their marble bracket.
The warriors apparently kicked the bucket,
crushing bedbugs on the linen sprawl.

In the twilight, chandeliers gleam, akin
to bonfires; sylphides weave their sweet pattern:
a finger, eight hours poised by the button
relaxes fondling its hooded twin.

Windowpanes quiver with tulle's soft ply;
the besom of naked shrubs is bothered
by the evergreen rustle of money, by the
seemingly nonstop July.

A cross between a blade and a raw
throat uttering no sound whatever,
the sharp bend of a level river
glistens, covered with icy straw.

Victim of lungs though friend to words,
the air is transparent, severely punctured
by beaks that treat it as pens treat parchment,
by visible-only-in-profile birds.

This is a flattened colossus veiled
by the gauze thickening on the horizon,
edged with the lacework of wheels gone frozen
after six by the curb's gray welt.

Like the mouse creeping out of the scarlet crack,
the sunset gnaws hungrily the electric
cheese of the outskirts, erected
by those who clearly trust their knack

for surviving everything: by termites.
Warehouses, surgeries. Having measured
there the proximity of the desert,
the cinnamon-tinted earth waylays its

horizontality in the fake
pyramids, porticoes, rooftops' ripple,

as the train creeps knowingly, like a snake,
to the capital's only nipple.

[*1982 / Translated by the author*]

Tsushima Screen

The perilous yellow sun follows with its slant eyes
masts of the shuddered grove steaming up to capsize
in the frozen straits of Epiphany. February has fewer
days than the other months; therefore, it's more cruel
than the rest. Dearest, it's more sound
to wrap up our sailing round
the globe with habitual naval grace,
moving your cot to the fireplace
where our dreadnought is going under
in great smoke. Only fire can grasp a winter!
Golden unharnessed stallions in the chimney
dye their manes to more corvine shades as they near the finish,
and the dark room fills with the plaintive, incessant chirring
of a naked, lounging grasshopper one cannot cup in fingers.

[*1978 / Translated by the author*]

A Martial Law Carol

To Wiktor Woroszylski and Andrzej Drawicz

One more Christmas ends
soaking stripes and stars.
All my Polish friends
are behind steel bars,
locked like zeroes in
some graph sheet of wrath:
as a discipline
slavery beats math.

Nations learn the rules
like a naughty boy
as the tyrant drools
manacles in joy.
One pen stroke apiece,
minus edits plus
helping the police
to subtract a class.

From a stubborn brow
something scarlet drops
on the Christmas snow.
As it turns, the globe's
face gets uglier,
pores becoming cells,
while the planets glare
coldly, like ourselves.

Hungry faces. Grime.
Squalor. Unabashed
courts distribute time
to the people crushed
not so much by tanks
or by submachine
guns as by the banks
we deposit in.

Deeper than the depth
of your thoughts or mine
is the sleep of death
in the Vujek mine;
higher than your rent
is that hand whose craft
keeps the others bent—
as though photographed.

Powerless is speech.
Still, it bests a tear
in attempts to reach,
crossing the frontier,
for the heavy hearts
of my Polish friends.
One more trial starts.
One more Christmas ends.

[*1980*]

Folk Tune

It's not that the Muse feels like clamming up,
it's more like high time for the lad's last nap.
And the scarf-waving lass who wished him the best
drives a steamroller across his chest.

And the words won't rise either like that rod
or like logs to rejoin their old grove's sweet rot,
and, like eggs in the frying pan, the face
spills its eyes all over the pillowcase.

Are you warm tonight under those six veils
in that basin of yours whose strung bottom wails;
where like fish that gasp at the foreign blue
my raw lip was catching what then meant you?

I would have hare's ears sewn to my bald head,
in thick woods for your sake I'd gulp drops of lead,
and from black gnarled snags in the oil-smooth pond
I'd bob up to your face as some *Tirpitz* won't.

But it's not on the cards or the waiter's tray,
and it pains to say where one's hair turns gray.
There are more blue veins than the blood to swell
their dried web, let alone some remote brain cell.

We are parting for good, little friend, that's that.
Draw an empty circle on your yellow pad.
This will be me: no insides in thrall.
Stare at it a while, then erase the scrawl.

[1980 / Translated by the author]

6 3

Roman Elegies

To Benedetta Craveri

I

The captive mahogany of a private Roman
flat. In the ceiling, a dust-covered crystal island.
At sunset, the windowpanes pan a common
ground for the nebulous and the ironed.
Setting a naked foot on the rosy marble,
the body steps toward its future: to its attire.
If somebody shouted "Freeze!" I'd perform that marvel
as this city happily did in its childhood hour.
The world's made of nakedness and of foldings.
Still, the latter's richer with love than a face, that's certain.
Thus an opera tenor's so sweet to follow
since he yields invariably to a curtain.
By nightfall, a blue eye employs a tear,
cleansing, to a needless shine, the iris;
and the moon overhead apes an emptied square
with no fountain in it. But of rock as porous.

II

The month of stalled pendulums. Only a fly in August
in a dry carafe's throat is droning its busy hymn.
The numerals on the clock face crisscross like earnest
anti-aircraft searchlights probing for seraphim.
The month of drawn blinds, of furniture wrapped in cotton
shrouds, of the sweating double in the mirror above the cupboard,
of bees that forget the topography of their hives and, coated
with suntan honey, keep staggering seaward.
Get busy then, faucet, over the snow-white, sagging
muscle, tousle the tufts of thin gray singes!
To a homeless torso and its idle, grabby
mitts, there's nothing as dear as the sight of ruins.
And they, in their turn, see themselves in the broken Jewish
r no less gladly: for the pieces fallen
so apart, saliva's the only solution they wish
for, as time's barbarous corneas scan the Forum.

The tiled, iron-hot, glowing hills: midsummer.
Clouds feel like angels, thanks to their cooling shadows.
Thus the bold cobblestone eyes, like a happy sinner,
the blue underthings of your leggy blond friend. A bard of
trash, extra thoughts, broken lines, unmanly,
I hide in the bowels of the Eternal City
from the luminary that rolled back so many
marble pupils with rays bright enough for setting
up yet another universe. A yellow square. Noontime's
stupor. A Vespa's owner tortures the screaming gears.
Clutching my chest with my hand, at a distance
I reckon the change from the well-spent years.
And, like a book at once opened to all its pages,
the laurels scratch the scorched white of a balustrade.
And the Colosseum looms, the skull of Argus,
through whose sockets clouds drift like a thought of the vanished herd.

IV

Two young brunettes in the library of the husband
of the more stunning one. Two youthful, tender
ovals hunch over pages: a Muse telling Fate the substance
of several things she tried to render.
The swish of old paper, of red crepe de Chine. A humming
fan mixes violets, lavender, and carnations.
Braiding of hair: an elbow thrusts up its summit
accustomed to cumulus-thick formations.
Oh, a dark eye is obviously more fluent
in brown furniture, pomegranates, oak shutters.
It's more keen, it's more cordial than a blue one;
to the blue one, though, nothing matters!
The blue one can always tell the owner
from the goods, especially before closing—
that is, time from living—and turn the latter over,
as tails strain to look at heads in tossing.

V

Jig, little candle tongue, over the empty paper,
bow to the rotten breath as though you were courted,

follow—but don't get too close!—the pauper
letters standing in line to obtain the content.
You animate the walls, wardrobe, the sill's sweetbriar:
more than handwriting is ever after;
even your soot, it appears, soars higher
than the holiest wish of these musings' author.
Still, in their midst you earn yourself a decent
name, as my fountain pen, in memory of your tender
commas, in Rome, at the millennium's end, produces
a lantern, a cresset, a torch, a taper,
never a period—and the premises look their ancient
selves, from the severed head down to a yellow toenail.
For an ink pot glows bright whenever someone mentions
light, especially in a tunnel.

VI

Clicking of a piano at the siesta hour.
Stillness of sleepy mews acquires
C-flats, as scales coat a fish which narrows
round the corner. Exhaling quarrels,
inhaling a fusty noon's air, the stucco
flaps its brown gills, and a sultry, porous
cavity of a mouth scatters
around cold pearls of Horace.
I've never built that cloud-thrusting stony
object that could explain clouds' pallor.
I've learned about my own, and any
fate, from a letter, from its black color.
Thus some fall asleep while hugging
a Leica, in order to take a picture
of the dream, to make themselves out, having
awakened in a developed future.

VII

Eggshells of cupolas, vertebrae of bell towers.
Colonnades' limbs sprawled wide in their blissful, heathen
leisure. The square root of a skylark scours
the bottomless, as though prior to prayers, heaven.
Light reaps much more than it has sown: an awkward

body hides in a crack while its shadow shutters
walls. In these parts, all windows are looking northward,
where the more one boozes the less one matters.
North! A white iceberg's frozen-in piano;
smallpoxed with quartz, vases' granite figures;
a plain unable to stop field-glass scanning;
sweet Ashkenazy's ten running fingers.
Never again are the legions to thread those contours:
to a creaking pen, even its words won't hearken.
And the golden eyebrow—as, at sunset, a cornice—
rises up, and the eyes of the darling darken.

VIII

In these squinting alleyways, where even a thought about
one's self is too cumbersome, in this furrowed clutter
of the brain which has long since refused to cloud
the universe, where now keyed up, now scattered,
you trundle your boots on the cobbled, checkered
squares, from a fountain and back to a Caesar—
thus a needle shuffles across the record
skipping its grooves—it is altogether
proper to settle now for a measly fraction
of remaining life, for the past life craving
completeness, for its attempts to fashion
an integer. The sound the heels are scraping
from the ground is the aria of their union,
a serenade that what-has-been-longer
hums to what's-to-be-shorter. This is a genuine
Caruso for a gramophone-dodging mongrel.

IX

Lesbia, Julia, Cynthia, Livia, Michelina.
Bosoms, ringlets of fleece: for effects, and for causes also.
Heaven-baked clay, fingertips' brave arena.
Flesh that renders eternity an anonymous torso.
You breed immortals: those who have seen you bare,
they too turned Catulluses, statues, heavy
Neros, et cetera. Short-term goddesses! you are
much more a joy to believe in than a permanent bevy.

Hail the smooth abdomen, thighs as their hamstrings tighten.
White upon white, as Kazimir's dream image
one summer evening, I, the most mortal item
in the midst of this wreckage resembling the whole world's rib cage,
sip with feverish lips wine from a tender collar-
bone; the sky is as pale as a cheek with a mole that trembles;
and the cupolas bulge like the tits of the she-wolf, fallen
asleep after having fed her Romulus and her Remus.

X

Mimicking local pines, embrace the ether!
The fingertips won't cull much more than the pane's tulle quiver.
Still, a little black bird won't return from the sky blue, either.
And we, too, aren't gods in miniature, that's clear.
That's precisely why we are happy: because we are nothings; speckled
pores are spurned by summits or sharp horizons;
the body is space's reversal, no matter how hard you pedal.
And when we are unhappy, it's perhaps for the same small reasons.
Better lean on a portico, loose the white shirt that billows,
stone cools the spinal column, gray pigeons mutter,
and watch how the sun is sinking into gardens and distant villas,
how the water—the tutor
of eloquence—pours from the rusted lips, repeating
not a thing, save a nymph with her marble truants,
save that it's cold and fresh, save that it's splitting
the face into rippling ruins.

XI

Private life. Fears, shredded thoughts, the jagged
blanket renders the contours of Europe meager.
By means of a blue shirt and a rumpled jacket
something still gets reflected in the wardrobe mirror.
Let's have some tea, face, so that the teeth may winnow
lips. Yoked by a ceiling, the air grows flatter.
Cast inadvertently through the window,
a glance makes a bunch of blue jays flutter
from their pine tops. A room in Rome, white paper,
the tail of a freshly drawn letter: a darting rodent.

6 8

Thus, thanks to the perfect perspective, some objects peter
out; thus, still others shuffle across the frozen
Tanaïs, dropping from the picture, limping,
occiputs covered with wilted laurels and blizzards' powder—
toward Time, lying beyond the limits
of every spraddling superpower.

XII

Lean over. I'll whisper something to you: I am
grateful for everything: for the chicken cartilage
and for the chirr of scissors already cutting
out the void for me—for it is your hem.
Doesn't matter if it's pitch-black, doesn't matter if
it holds nothing: no ovals, no limbs to count.
The more invisible something is,
the more certain it's been around,
and the more obviously it's everywhere. You
were the first to whom all this happened, were you?
For a nail holding something one would divide by two—
were it not for remainders—there is no gentler quarry.
I was in Rome. I was flooded by light. The way
a splinter can only dream about.
Golden coins on the retina are to stay—
enough to last one through the whole blackout.

[1981 / Translated by the author]

To Urania

To I.K.

Everything has its limit, including sorrow.
A windowpane stalls a stare. Nor does a grill abandon
a leaf. One may rattle the keys, gurgle down a swallow.
Loneliness cubes a man at random.
A camel sniffs at the rail with a resentful nostril;
a perspective cuts emptiness deep and even.
And what is space anyway if not the
body's absence at every given
point? That's why Urania's older than sister Clio!
In daylight or with the soot-rich lantern,
you see the globe's pate free of any bio,
you see she hides nothing, unlike the latter.
There they are, blueberry-laden forests,
rivers where the folk with bare hands catch sturgeon
or the towns in whose soggy phone books
you are starring no longer; farther eastward surge on
brown mountain ranges; wild mares carousing
in tall sedge; the cheekbones get yellower
as they turn numerous. And still farther east, steam dreadnoughts
or cruisers,
and the expanse grows blue like lace underwear.

[1981 / Translated by the author]

7 0

The Bust of Tiberius

All hail to you, two thousand years too late.
I, too, once took a whore in marriage.
We have some things in common. Plus,
all round, your city. Bustle, shrieking traffic.
Damp alleyways with hypodermic youths.
Also, the ruins. I, a standard stranger,
salute your grimy bust in some
dank chamber storing echoes. Ah, Tiberius!
Here you're not thirty yet. The face displays
a greater confidence in trusted sinews
than in the future of their sum. A head
the sculptor severs in one's lifetime surely
sounds like a prophecy of power. All
that lies below the massive jawbone—Rome:
the provinces, the latifundists, the cohorts,
plus swarms of infants bubbling at your ripe
stiff sausage. A delight in tune
with nourishment by the she-wolf of tiny
Remus and Romulus—the mouths of babes indeed!
that sweetly incoherent mumbling
inside the toga! So we have a bust
that stands for the essential independence
of brain from body: (a) one's own, (b) one
that is Imperial. Should you be carving your
own likeness, you'd produce gray twisted matter.

You haven't reached thirty yet, thus far. Not one
arresting feature to detain observers.
Nor, in its turn, does your observant eye
appear to rest on anything before it:
neither on someone's face nor on
some classic landscape. Ah, Tiberius!
What does it matter what Suetonius
cum Tacitus still mutter, seeking causes
for your great cruelty? There are no causes in
this world—effects alone. And people
are victims of their own effects,

the more so in those steamy dungeons
where everyone confesses. Though confessions
dragged out by torture, like the ones in childhood,
are of a muchness. Far the best of fates
is really to have no part of truth.
It never elevates us. None,
Caesars especially. And at any rate
you seem a man more capable of drowning
in your piscina than in some deep thought.
Plus, shouldn't cruelty be termed a form
of speeding matters up, accelerating
the common fate of things? of a simple body's
free fall in vacuum?—in which, alas,
one always finds oneself when one is falling.

New year. A January pile of clouds
above the wintry town, like extra marble.
The brown, reality-escaping Tiber
and fountains spouting up to where no one
peers down—through lowered eyelids or
through fingers splayed. Another era!
And no one's up to holding by the ears
the wolves consumed with frenzy. Ah, Tiberius!
And such as we presume to judge you? You
were surely a monster, though perhaps more monstrous
was your indifference. But isn't it monsters
—not victims, no—that nature generates
in her own likeness? Ah, how much more soothing
(that is to say, if one should get the choice)
to be wiped off the earth by hell-bound fiends
than by neurotics. Still in your twenties,
with stony looks hewn out of stone, you look
a durable organic engine
of pure annihilation: not some dope,
a slave of passion, channel of ideas,
et cetera. And to defend you from
harsh tongues is like defending oak trees
from leaves, wrapped in their meaningless but clearly
insistent clamor of majority.

7 2

An empty gallery. A murky noontime
soiling tall windows with the distant drone
of life. A piece of marble in no fashion
responding to the quality of space . . .
It cannot be that you don't hear me speaking!
I, too, have often made that headlong dash
from rank reality. I, too, became an island
replete with ruins, ostriches. I, too,
struck off a profile with the aid of lamplight.
As for the things I've either coined or said,
it must be said that what I've said is useless,
and not eventually, but already: now.
Can't that be also that acceleration
of history? A bold attempt, alas,
by consequence to overtake causation?
And also in a total vacuum, which
gives no assurance of impressive splashdown.
Should one recant, then? rearrange the dice?
cut yet another deck of cards or atlas?
Who gives a damn: the radioactive rain
will scour us much the same as your historian.
Who'll come around to curse us, then? a star?
the moon? some wandering termite, driven
mad with its multiple mutations, fat
and yolklike? Probably. But having hit
something that's hard in us, it too, I reckon,
will shudder and give up its digging.

"Bust," it will utter in the tongue of ruins
and of contracting muscles. "Bust. Bust. Bust."

[*1981 / Translated by Alan Myers and the author*]

Seven Strophes

I was but what you'd brush
with your palm, what your leaning
brow would hunch to in evening's
raven-black hush.

I was but what your gaze
in that dark could distinguish:
a dim shape to begin with,
later—features, a face.

It was you, on my right,
on my left, with your heated
sighs, who molded my helix,
whispering at my side.

It was you by that black
window's trembling tulle pattern
who laid in my raw cavern
a voice calling you back.

I was practically blind.
You, appearing, then hiding,
gave me my sight and heightened
it. Thus some leave behind

a trace. Thus they make worlds.
Thus, having done so, at random
wastefully they abandon
their work to its whirls.

Thus, prey to speeds
of light, heat, cold, or darkness,
a sphere in space without markers
spins and spins.

[*1981* / *Translated by Paul Graves*]

The Residence

An attractive mansion on the avenue of Sardanapalus.
A pair of cast-iron lions with their hind legs complex.
In the hall, like a grinning footman, the black Steinway lets
the owner's fat-fingered, myopic, porous
grandniece poke its molars in broad daylight.
Lavender smells. Everywhere, including the kitchen,
outnumbering dishes, hang oils and etchings
depicting the Teacher, whose kinfolk might
still be living somewhere in Europe. Hence, sets of Goethe, plus
some Balzacs, chandeliers, capitals, gay putti,
and the very columns whose supple body
houses a battery of the "ground-to-ground" class.

But it feels the coziest in the eastern, i.e., his wing.
Bedroom windows hug poplars, or else it's alders.
And the cricket's chirr's softer than all those idle
bird feeders with their sensitive relay wink.
Here in the evening you may snap the lock, undress
to the lilac sweat shirt, to the matching long johns, whatever.
A far-off crow's nest in the branches suggests the beaver
of a Jewess he knew in his salad days,
but thank heaven they've split. And what really makes you crawl
to the bed are those eight-digit budget figures routinely hoarded
by the staff, or the last mortal screams of his confessed-it-all
son, apparently tape-recorded.

[1983 / Translated by the author]

Eclogue IV: Winter

To Derek Walcott

Ultima Cumaei venit iam carminis aetas;
magnus ab integro saeclorum nascitu ordo.
—VERGIL, *Eclogue IV*

I

In winter it darkens the moment lunch is over.
It's hard then to tell starving men from sated.
A yawn keeps a phrase from leaving its cozy lair.
The dry, instant version of light, the opal
snow, dooms tall alders—by having freighted
them—to insomnia, to your glare,

well after midnight. Forget-me-nots and roses
crop up less frequently in dialogues. Dogs with languid
fervor pick up the trail, for they, too, leave traces.
Night, having entered the city, pauses
as in a nursery, finds a baby under the blanket.
And the pen creaks like steps that are someone else's.

II

My life has dragged on. In the recitative of a blizzard
a keen ear picks up the tune of the Ice Age.
Every "Down in the Valley" is, for sure,
a chilled boogie-woogie. A bitter, brittle
cold represents, as it were, a message
to the body of its final temperature

or—the earth itself, sighing out of habit
for its galactic past, its sub-zero horrors.
Cheeks burn crimson like radishes even here.
Cosmic space is always shot through with matte agate,
and the beeping Morse, returning homeward,
finds no ham operator's ear.

III

In February, lilac retreats to osiers.
Imperative to a snowman's profile,

7 6

carrots get more expensive. Limited by a brow,
a glance at cold, metallic objects
is fiercer than the metal itself. This, while
you peel eyes from objects, still may allow

no shedding of blood. The Lord, some reckon,
was reviewing His world in this very fashion
on the eighth day and after. In winter, we're
not berry pickers: we stuff the cracks with oakum,
praise the common good with a greater passion,
and things grow older by, say, a year.

IV

In great cold, pavements glaze like a sugar candy,
steam from the mouth suggests a dragon,
if you dream of a door, you tend to slam it.
My life has dragged on. The signs are plenty.
They'd make yet another life, just as dragging.
From these signs alone one would compose a climate

or a landscape. Preferably with no people,
with virgin white through a lacework shroud,
—a world where nobody heard of Parises, Londons; where
weekdays are spun by diffusive, feeble
light; where, too, in the end you shudder
spotting the ski tracks . . . Well, just a pair.

V

Time equals cold. Each body, sooner
or later, falls prey to a telescope. With the years,
it moves away from the luminary, grows colder.
Hoarfrost jungles the windowpane with sumac,
ferns, or horsetail, with what appears
to be nursed on this glass and deprived of color

by loneliness. But, as with a marble hero,
one's eye rolls up rather than runs in winter.
Where sight fails, yielding to dreams' swarmed forces,
time, fallen sharply beneath the zero,
burns your brain like the index finger
of a scamp from popular Russian verses.

My life has dragged on. One cold resembles another
cold. Time looks like time. What sets them apart is only
a warm body. Mule-like, stubborn creature,
it stands firmly between them, rather
like a border guard: stiffened, sternly
preventing the wandering of the future

into the past. In winter, to put it bleakly,
Tuesday is Saturday. The daytime is a deceiver:
Are the lights out already? Or not yet on? It's chilly.
Dailies might as well be printed weekly.
Time stares at a looking glass like a diva
who's forgotten what's on tonight: *Tosca*? Oh no, *Lucia*?

Dreams in the frozen season are longer, keener.
The patchwork quilt and the parquet deal,
on their mutual squares, in chessboard warriors.
The hoarser the blizzard rules the chimney,
the hotter the quest for a pure ideal
of naked flesh in a cotton vortex,

and you dream nasturtiums' stubborn odor,
a tuft of cobwebs shading a corner nightly,
in a narrow ravine torrid Terek's splashes,
a feast of fingertips caught in shoulder
straps. And then all goes quiet. Idly
an ember smolders in dawn's gray ashes.

Cold values space. Baring no rattling sabers,
it takes hill and dale, townships and hamlets·
(the populace cedes without trying
tricks), mostly cities, whose great ensembles,
whose arches and colonnades, in hundreds,
stand like prophets of cold's white triumph,

looming wanly. Cold is gliding
from the sky on a parachute. Each and every column

looks like a fifth, desires an overthrow.
Only the crow doesn't take snow gladly.
And you often hear the angry, solemn,
patriotic gutturals speaking crow.

IX

In February, the later it is, the lower
the mercury. More time means more cold. Stars, scattered
like a smashed thermometer, turn remotest
regions of night into a strep marvel.
In daytime, when sky is akin to stucco,
Malevich himself wouldn't have noticed

them, white on white. That's why angels
are invisible. To their legions
cold is of benefit. We would make them
out, the winged ones, had our eyes' angle
been indeed on high, where they are linking
in white camouflage like Finnish marksmen.

X

For me, other latitudes have no usage.
I am skewered by cold like a grilled-goose portion.
Glory to naked birches, to the fir-tree needle,
to the yellow bulb in an empty passage—
glory to everything set by the wind in motion:
at a ripe age, it can replace the cradle.

The North is the honest thing. For it keeps repeating
all your life the same stuff—whispering, in full volume,
in the life dragged on, in all kinds of voices;
and toes freeze numb in your deerskin creepers,
reminding you, as you complete your polar
conquest, of love, of shivering under clock faces.

XI

In great cold, distance won't sing like sirens.
In space, the deepest inhaling hardly
ensures exhaling, nor does departure
a return. Time is the flesh of the silent

cosmos. Where nothing ticks. Even being hurtled
out of the spacecraft, one wouldn't capture

any sounds on the radio—neither fox-trots nor maidens
wailing from a hometown station.
What kills you out there, in orbit, isn't
the lack of oxygen but the abundance
of time in its purest (with no addition
of your life) form. It's hard to breathe it.

XII

Winter! I cherish your bitter flavor
of cranberries, tangerine crescents on faience saucers,
the tea, sugar-frosted almonds (at best, two ounces).
You were opening our small beaks in favor
of names like Marina or Olga—morsels
of tenderness at that age that fancies

cousins. I sing a snowpile's blue contours
at dusk, rustling foil, clicking B-flat somewhere,
as though "Chopsticks" were tried by the Lord's own finger.
And the logs, which rattled in stony courtyards
of the gray, dank city that freezes bare
by the sea, are still warming my every fiber.

XIII

At a certain age, the time of year, the season
coincides with fate. Theirs is a brief affair.
But on days like this you sense you are right. Your worries
about things that haven't come your way are ceasing,
and a simple botanist may take care
of commenting upon daily life and mores.

In this period, eyes lose their green of nettles,
the triangle drops its geometric ardor:
all the angles drawn with cobwebs are fuzzy.
In exchanges on death, place matters
more and more than time. The cold gets harder.
And saliva suddenly burns its cozy

8 0

tongue, like that coin. Still, all the rivers
are ice-locked. You can put on long johns and trousers,
strap steel runners to boots with ropes and a piece of timber.
Teeth, worn out by the tap dance of shivers,
won't rattle because of fear. And the Muse's
voice gains a reticent, private timbre.

That's the birth of an eclogue. Instead of the shepherd's signal,
a lamp's flaring up. Cyrillic, while running witless
on the pad as though to escape the captor,
knows more of the future than the famous sibyl:
of how to darken against the whiteness,
as long as the whiteness lasts. And after.

[*1977 / Translated by the author*]

Eclogue V: Summer

To Margo Picken

I

I hear you again, mosquito hymn of summer!
In the dogwood tepee, ants sweat in slumber.
A botfly slides off the burdock's crumpled
epaulet, showing us that it always
ranked just a private. And caterpillars show us
the meaning of "lower than grass." The rosebays'

overgrown derricks—knee-deep or ankle-
deep in the couch-grass and bindweed jungle—
shine blue from their proximity and their angle
to the zenith. The praying mantis's little
rakes shutter the hemlock's brittle,
colorless fireworks. The scruffy, whittled

thistle's heart looks like a land-mine which is
only half exploding its ruddy riches.
The cowbane resembles a hand that reaches
for a carafe. And, like a fisherman's wife, a spider
patches its trawl, strung out between the bitter
wormwood and the hedge mustard's golden miter.

Life is the sum of trifling motions. The silver
twilight of sedge's sheathed blades, the quiver
of many a shepherd's purse, the ever-
shifting tableau of horse sorrel, gentle
alfalfa's ditherings—these engender
our grasp of the rules of a stage whose center

cannot be found. At noonday both wheat and shabby
darnel cast northward their common shadow
because they are sown and shuffled
by the same windy sower about whose humors
the place is still rife with all sorts of rumors.
Give ear to the swishing murmurs

8 2

of cock-and-hen brushes! To what a daisy's
odd-or-even whispers! To how a drowsy
coltsfoot dubs these findings crazy.
To how a soft, wild-mint Leda, flattened
by a powerful swanweed, goes raving mad and
mumbles. Small grassplots of summer, flooded

with sunlight! Their homeless moths! Their nettle
pyramids! Their heat! Their total
stupor! Their fern pagoda's gentle
sway, or their ruined column
of anise, or a bent minaret of wild sage's solemn
bow—that's a copy, in grass and pollen,

of Babylon! Terzaromeville's verdant recent
version! The realm where, turning left, one's risking
ending up on the right side: everything's close, yet distant!
And a grasshopper in his pursuit of beauty—
of the cabbage butterfly in her pale tutu—
stalls, a knight at the crossroads, caught in dry blades' tutti.

II

Air, that's colorless in its core, seems, given
a landscape, blue—very often even
dark blue. The green perhaps gets enlivened
in a similar fashion. A passive grimace,
an eye's remoteness from the weed's the greenness
of the weed. In July, the seamless

flora's clear penchant to sunder
its ties with a botanist while darkening sanguine
leaves results in pale faces' suntan.
The sum of beautiful ones and ugly,
coming close or retreating, oddly
enough, can waste one's eye as badly

as these green/blue expanses. The color's humble
mask hides infinity's constant hunger
for details. Mass, after all, is hardly

the result of energy split by the square
of the speed of light (nay, sight!) somewhere
but the feeling of friction, of wear and tear

against one's own likes. Examine
space closely! Its selfsame garment
nearby and far away! Its ardent
obstinacy, with which green or bluish hollows—
their distance notwithstanding—always
sustain the pigment. Ah, this is almost

faith! A fanatic belief! The buzzing
of a fly stuck on flypaper doesn't
spell an agony but a dazzled
self-portrait in the Cyrillic *zh*. A semblance
of alphabet, warmth takes species across the sentence
of the horizon. A landscape shows just the settlers

left behind when their betters escaped to graceful
Asian palm trees. A July morning, faithful
to bedrooms, to shutters, flutters fistfuls
of jasmine banknotes, skipping
the acacia change of its seed pods splitting;
and the air's more diaphanous than a sleeping

beauty's lingerie. Sultry July! The surplus
of the green and the blue—of that threadbare surface
of existence. And a kind of solstice
of the luminary, stopped and splattering, like Attila before the battered
shield, fills one's orbs. The aforementioned outer

blue flaxlike stuff after all can't spin it
indefinitely. Light simply learns its limit
by means of a body because, within it,
light gets refracted, as at the finish
of too long a road whose beginning few wish
to consider. The finish, though, tends to furnish

butterflies, mallow, hay-scented fever,
a Seym or Oredesz type of river,
its banks strewn with luxuriating figures
of city-folk families; rosy naiads,
their risqué outfits which ignite us;
splutters, splashes; shrill jeremiads

of blue jays thrill pussy willows' bashful
branches obscuring the white parts of bathers
mooning as they wring swimsuits in bushes
upstream; ocher precipices, the pine-needle-
thick aroma, the heat, the nimble
sudden clouds tinting waves with a nickel,

fishlike sheen. All summer reservoirs! Most often
glimmering through foliage, molten
ponds or lakes—those orphan
parts of water surrounded by land; the rustle
of sedge and bulrush, moss-shammied muscles
of snarled snags, tender duckweed, and nascent

yellow nymphaeas, passionless water lilies,
algae or Paradise with no limits
for lines; and a water bug darts the liquid
blue, rather Christlike. And at times a perch is
splashing in order to catch a nervous
glimpse of the world, the way one peers out

a window and reels back afraid of falling.
Summer! The time for the shirt gone flapping,
for the old, animated polemic fumbling
about nightshades, toadstools, or garish,
wart-dotted, poisonous fly agarics;
for the quiet of forest clearings carried

by the peacefulness of their noontime slumber,
when your eyelids get lowered down by languor,
when a bumblebee, if it stung you,

did so because it was too myopic
and simply mistook you for blooming poppies
or a desirable cow dropping

and soared upward, distressed, in an awkward spiral.
The woods look like combs with their teeth in peril.
And a boy's revelation that he is "taller
than the bush though shorter than trees" will scramble
his brain for the rest of it! And a humble
nay! invisible skylark appears to tumble

his trills from on high. Summer! The season of exam cramming,
of formulae, of tossed coins, of a manic
pimpled look in boys, delays caused by panic
in girls; and the colonnade of a college
or bricks of some other seat of knowledge
haunt your dreams. Only fishing rods can abolish

with a swish those worries, the fears and burdens.
And we notice a singlet or else a bodice,
sandals, a bicycle in the grass; we notice
specifically its stainless pedals,
resembling a sergeant's bars or medals.
Indeed, their rubber pads, their metal

spell the future, the century, the whole deal,
Europe, a railroad whose branch, for real,
as though wind-shattered, produces rural
platforms—waterspouts, painted fences,
chickens, hedges, broad peasant faces
of women. In the meantime, each maggot forces

itself out of your tin can, soggy, sluggy,
homesick for its cowshed wall, for its muggy
shade. And then, later, a creaking buggy
lumped with burlap bushels, the clanging harness,
and the track that winds through the fields past harvest
time, and, at a distance, some church's harmless

bottle silhouette, haystacks, barns, stables—mainly
huts with their tarred sloping roofs and lonely
windows for whose sakes only
sunsets exist. And the spokes' shadow upon the shoulder
stretching all the way to the Polish border
runs along like some Fido, or a still bolder

Rover, catching foul mutterings of the driver;
and you stare at your toes or chomp on clover,
your thoughts drifting over to some freckled oval
in the town. And high up, in the very corner
of your eye, it's a crane, and not some infernal
thunderbird. Three cheers for normal

temperature: ten notches below the body's
standard. Three cheers for all things you notice.
For both the closest and the remotest
things. For everything that still matters,
for your shirt's drying tatters, for sunflowers' bent lanterns,
for the faint, distant waltz tune—"Manchurian Mountains."

IV

Summer twilight's fluttering window laces!
Cold cellars packed with milk jugs and lettuce,
a Stalin or a Khrushchev on the latest
news, jammed by cicadas' incessant rattle;
homemade bilberry jelly jars bat the rafters;
lime socks round apple orchards' ankles

look the whiter the darker it gets, like joggers
running beyond what the distance offers;
and farther still loom the real ogres
of full-size elms in the evening's bluing.
Kitchens, vast bottoms and head rugs brewing
something; the hellish fires phewing

in cookstoves' mica peepholes. Suppers on the verandas!
Potato in all its genres and genders,
onions and radishes in their grandest

fashion; tomatoes, dill, cucumbers—
all straight from the garden patch in great numbers;
and, finally, tired of their hide-and-seek, decanters

coated with dust! A soot-rich lantern,
a ballet of shadows dwarfing the wallpaper pattern,
geniuses of this high art, their ardent
admirers; samovar's armor; sugar
that you tell from salt by a fly, and shoo her
off. A nightjar's lonely pitch or super-

cilious frogs voicing every grievance
from their ditch. A silver pitcher glimmers
with your pink oval's distorted grimace,
rustling tabloids, burp-triggered tremors;
from the parlor wafts "Chopsticks," or else some tenor's
record. And Simonides' view on tendons

spares for a moment a keenly placid
stare at the wallpaper or hawthorn's flaccid
ramifications and twists: a glance at
a knee is never enough. The flesh is
dear indeed, since the fabric (bless its
patterns), by hiding the body, lessens

the resistance of skin—free of any pattern—
to one's upward gliding. Meantime, a patina
fogs half-empty tea glasses; prattling
dies; the flame in the lamp, too, suffers
shivers. And later, beneath the covers,
your brand-new pocket compass's needle quivers,

gleaming dully yet pointing north not any
less categorically than many
a prosecutor. Dogs barking, a dropping penny,
creaking joints of old chairs, or is that some invader?—
a sudden cackle in the hen coop, a whistling freight or
cattle train. Yet even these sounds later

8 8

cease. And naggingly, softly—even
softer perhaps than your ears are given
to discern—leaves, as countless as souls of all those who lived on
the earth before ourselves, blab something
in their burgeoning dialect; it's sounding
like dark tongues, though their tattered samplings—

smudges, cuneiforms, moon-spun vowels—
are unclear both to you and your wall for hours
as you toss and turn twixt the mounds and hollows
of the mattress, trying in vain to fathom
a sprouting hieroglyph, a phantom
comma, while outdoors the invisible rustling quantum

airs its China-like, powerful yellow anthem.

[*1981 / Translated by George L. Kline and the author*]

Venetian Stanzas I

To Susan Sontag

I

The wet hitching post of the quay: a sulky hackney
fights off sleep in the twilight, twitching the iron bay
of her mane; napeless gondolas, fiddling numbly
the out-of-sync silence, sway.
As the Moor grows more trusting, words turn the paper darker,
and a hand, short of snapping a neck, though keen on the gothic lace
of a stone kerchief crushed in the palm of Iago,
presses it to its face.

II

The piazza's deserted, the quays abandoned.
The café walls are more crowded than the café inside:
a lute's being strummed by a frescoed, bejeweled maiden
to her similarly decked Said.
Oh, nineteenth century! oh, lure of the East! and oh, clifftop poses
of exiles! and, like leucocytes in the blood,
full moons in the works of bards burning with tuberculosis,
claiming it is with love.

III

At night, there's nothing to do here. No sweet Duses, no arias.
A solo heel's tapping out a basalt street.
Under lamps, your shadowy shuddered alias
like carbonari postpones its hit
and exhales a cloud. At night here we hold soliloquies
to an audience of echoes, whose breath won't warm up, alas,
this resonant marbled fish tank, nor fill it with
anything save steamed glass.

IV

Golden scales of tall windows bring to the rippled surface
wedges of grand piano, bric-a-brac, oils in frames.
That's what's hidden inside, blinds drawn, by perches
or, gills flapping, by breams.
The retina's sudden encounter with a white ceiling's goddess

shedding it all but her cobweb bra
makes one dizzy. A doorway's inflamed raw throat is
gaping to utter "Ahhhh."

V

How they flitted their tails here! How they flapped here, breamlike!
How spurning and spawning they streamed to score
the mirror! And how that cleaving, cream-white
bodice's plunge could stir—
like a sirocco that roils the waters. How, in the middle
of the promenade, squalls were turning their pantaloons and skirts
into cabbage soup! Where are they all now—masks, stockings, middies,
harlequins, clowns, flirts?

VI

That's how chandeliers dim at the opera; that's how cupolas
shrink, like medusas, in volume, the tighter night hugs the place;
that's how streets coil and dwindle, like eels; that's how
                                        just-as-populous
squares mimic plaice.
That's how, treating his daughters, Nereus nears us,
pinching the combs from ladies' wind-ravaged curls,
leaving untouched the quays' yellow, nervous,
cheap electrical pearls.

VII

That's how orchestras fade. The city, while words are at it,
is akin to attempts to salvage notes from the silent beat,
and the palazzi, like music stands, stand scattered,
hoarded and poorly lit.
Only up where Perm's citizen sleeps his lasting sleep, a falsetto
star is vibrating through telegraph wires, reaches a minor key.
But the water applauds, and the quay is a hoarfrost settled
down on a do-re-mi.

VIII

And the loaded pupil of Claude, his limbs like half past eleven,
jettisoning his lines to the page's edge
in the struggle to keep all his gray mass level
despite the brandy's siege,

9 1

longs to undress, to cast off his woolen armor,
flop to the bed, press himself to the living, soft
bone's hot mirror from whose amalgam
no finger will scratch him off.

[*1982 / Translated by Jane Ann Miller and the author*]

Venetian Stanzas II

To Gennady Smakov

I

A sleep-crumpled cloud unfurls mealy mizzens.
Slapped by the baker, matte cheeks acquire
a glow. And in pawnbrokers' windows
jewelry catches fire.
Flat garbage barges sail. Like lengthy, supple
sticks run by hot-footed schoolboys along iron grates,
the morning rays strum colonnades, red-brick chimneys, sample
curled seaweed, invade arcades.

II

Dawn takes its time. Cold, naked, pallid marble
thighs of the new Susannah wade waves, being watched with glee
by new elders whose lenses squint, whirr, and gargle
at this bathing. Two-three
doves, launched from some pilaster, are turning
into gulls at the palaces opposite; that's the tax
here for flights over water—or else that's bed linen spurning
the ceiling for what it lacks.

III

Dampness creeps into the bedroom where a sleeping beauty,
dodging the world, draws her shoulder blades in.
That's how quail shrink sometimes at twig-snapping bootsteps,
how angels react to sin.
The window's sentient gauze gets fluttered by both exhaling
and inhaling. A pale, silky foam lashes stiff armchairs and
the mirror—an exit for objects, ailing
locally from their brown dead end.

IV

Light pries your eye—like a shell. Your helix,
in its turn like a shell, gets completely drowned
by the clamor of bells: that's the thirsty cupolas herding,
waterhole- and reflection-bound.
Parting shutters assault your nostrils with coffee, rags and

cinnamon, semen; with something transparent, pink.
And the golden St. George tips his lance at the writhing dragon's
maw, as though drawing ink.

V

Leaving all of the world, all its blue, in the rearguard,
the azure—squared to a weightless mass—
breasts the windowpane's gunport, falling headlong forward,
surrendering to the glass.
A curly-maned cloud pack rushes to catch and strangle
the radiant thief with his blazing hair—
a nor'easter is coming. The town is a crystal jumble
replete with smashed chinaware.

VI

Motorboats, rowboats, gondolas, dinghies, barges—
like odd scattered shoes, unmatched, God-size—
zealously trample pilasters, sharp spires, bridges'
arcs, the look in one's eyes.
Everything's doubled, save destiny, save the very
H_2O. Yet the idle turquoise on high
renders—like any "pro" vote—this world a merry
minority in one's eye.

VII

That's how some rise from the waters, their smooth skin stunning
the knobbly shore—while a flower may sway
in the hand—leaving the slipped dress scanning
the dry land from far away.
That's how they wash you in spray, for the immortals' ardent
perfume of kelp is what marks them from us and scares
pigeons off playing their crazy gambits
on the chessboards of squares.

VIII

I am writing these lines sitting outdoors, in winter,
on a white iron chair, in my shirtsleeves, a little drunk;
the lips move slowly enough to hinder
the vowels of the mother tongue,
and the coffee grows cold. And the blinding lagoon is lapping

9 4

at the shore as the dim human pupil's bright penalty
for its wish to arrest a landscape quite happy
here without me.

[*1982 / Translated by Jane Ann Miller and the author*]

Seaward

Darling, you think it's love, it's just a midnight journey.
Best are the dales and rivers removed by force,
as from the next compartment throttles "Oh, stop it, Bernie,"
yet the rhythm of those paroxysms is exactly yours.
Hook to the meat! Brush to the red-brick dentures,
alias cigars, smokeless like a driven nail!
Here the works are fewer than monkey wrenches,
and the phones are whining, dwarfed by to-no-avail.
Bark, then, with joy at Clancy, Fitzgibbon, Miller.
Dogs and block letters care how misfortune spells.
Still, you can tell yourself in the john by the spat-at mirror,
slamming the flush and emerging with clean lapels.
Only the liquid furniture cradles the dwindling figure.
Man shouldn't grow in size once he's been portrayed.
Look: what's been left behind is about as meager
as what remains ahead. Hence the horizon's blade.

[*1983*]

Galatea Encore

As though the mercury's under its tongue, it won't
talk. As though with the mercury in its sphincter,
immobile, by a leaf-coated pond
a statue stands white like a blight of winter.
After such snow, there is nothing indeed: the ins
and outs of centuries, pestered heather.
That's what coming full circle means—
when your countenance starts to resemble weather,
when Pygmalion's vanished. And you are free
to cloud your folds, to bare the navel.
Future at last! That is, bleached debris
of a glacier amid the five-lettered "never."
Hence the routine of a goddess, née
alabaster, that lets roving pupils gorge on
the heart of the color and temperature of the knee.
That's what it looks like inside a virgin.

[*1983*]

Variation in V

"Birds flying high above the retreating army!
Why do you suddenly turn and head toward our enemy,
contrary to the clouds? We are not yet defeated, are we?
True, we are scattered, but we still have some energy."

"Because your numbers diminish. You are less fit to listen
to our songs. You are no more an audience.
Vultures swoop in to replace us, and Valkyries. And the eastern
wind slams the fir horizons like jagged accordions."

"Cuneiform of the beaks! Explosions that sprout a palm tree!
Your tunes will be blown out of the sky, too, by the screaming
                                                    westerly.
We commit them to memory, which is a larger country.
Nobody knows the future, but there is always yesterday."

"Ye-ah! but our life span's shorter. There is no tomb or pyre
for our kind, but chamomile, clover, chicory,
thyme. Your valedictory runs 'Fire! fire! fire!'
We are less comprehensible. That's why we need a victory."

[*1983*]

Letter to an Archaeologist

Citizen, enemy, mama's boy, sucker, utter
garbage, panhandler, swine, *refujew, verrucht;*
a scalp so often scalded with boiling water
that the puny brain feels completely cooked.
Yes, we have dwelt here: in this concrete, brick, wooden
rubble which you now arrive to sift.
All our wires were crossed, barbed, tangled, or interwoven.
Also: we didn't love our women, but they conceived.
Sharp is the sound of the pickax that hurts dead iron;
still, it's gentler than what we've been told or have said ourselves.
Stranger! move carefully through our carrion:
what seems carrion to you is freedom to our cells.
Leave our names alone. Don't reconstruct those vowels,
consonants, and so forth: they won't resemble larks
but a demented bloodhound whose maw devours
its own traces, feces, and barks, and barks.

[*1983*]

9 9

Kellomäki

I

Dumped in the dunes snatched from the witless Finns,
a small veneered burg whose walls let one's sneezing fits
be echoed at once by a "Bless you" cabled from Sweden, yet
sporting no ax to split enough wood to heat
up a dwelling. What's more, certain houses aimed
at warming winter itself, using their black walls, and
bred lush flowers at eventide on blue
glass verandah rhomboids or squares; and you,
as though plotting a trip to the polar zone,
were falling asleep there with your thick socks on.

II

Flat, lapping swells of the sea starting with B, in curves,
resembling bleak thoughts about oneself, ran course
onto the empty beach and froze
into wrinkles there. The twitching gauze
of the hawthorn twigs at times would compel one's stark-
naked eye to develop a rippling bark.
Or else a few gulls would issue from the snowy haze
like the curls of the soiled-by-nobody's-fingers page
of a pallid, quietly rustling day,
and no lamp would light up till they flapped away.

III

In small towns one recognizes folk
not by face but by their queuing backs that flock
to the store. And on Saturdays the populace strung out, bound
caravanlike for the sandlike ground
flour, or string bags of smelts rending one's balance sheets.
In a little town usually one eats
the same thing as others. And to distinguish oneself from the rest, one could only try doodling on
a ruble with its sharp-*cum*-dull hardware
or seeing your things scattered everywhere.

IV

Notwithstanding all that, they were sturdy, those
abandoned matchboxes, stacked in white bundled rows
with two or three rattling, damp heads inside,
which, when feeding a sparrow, huddled to watch the sight,
family-strong, by the window whose trees as well
strove to merge into some baobab whose spill
of branches would overtake the sky's pink hem—
which indeed would happen round 6 p.m.,
when a book was slammed shut; and where once you sat
just two lips were remaining, like that vanished cat.

V

This outermost generosity, this—to denote true worth—
gift to exude, while freezing inside, the warmth
outside was binding tenants and habitats,
and winter considered the drying sheets its own linen. That's
what would stall conversations. A normal laugh
creaked like snow underfoot, leaving prints above
where it powdered the edges of sighs or shy
pronouns with hoarfrost, or turned some "I"
into a crystal, shot with hard turquoise,
that would melt like your tear to reduce the choice.

VI

Did it really happen, all that? And if yes, then why
now disturb the peace of these has-beens by
recalling details, testing shadowy pines by grip
—aping the afterlife (often accurately) when asleep?
Only those who believe (in angels, in roots) will rise
again. And what honestly could Kellomäki prize
as such, save its rail and its schedule of tin-plate links,
whistling from nonexistence, by which these things
would be gobbled up five minutes later, along with blurred
thoughts of love, plus those who have jumped aboard?

VII

Nothing. Winter expanses' slaked lime that would duly grab
from empty suburban platforms its daily grub
was leaving by conifer awnings, with their white load,

1 0 1

the present in its black overcoat, whose broad-
cloth, more sturdy than cheviot and *drap d'or*,
shielded one much better against the future or
the past than the station buffet's dim shack.
There is nothing more permanent than black.
That's what unleashes letters, or Carmen's breast;
that's why opponents of change hit their mattresses fully dressed.

VIII

Never again is that door to endure that key
with its curly goatee, nor is the switch to be
shoved up by one's heaving shoulder, to blind the stale loaf of bread.
This birdhouse has outlived its bird
and its cirrus or cumulous flocks. From time's point of view,
there is no "then," only "there." And "there," through
empty rooms, memory roams like a thief at dusk,
frisking the wardrobe, rummaging through the desk,
knocking over a novel by an unknown
—picking the pocket which is its own.

IX

In mid-life's thick forest, in that dark wood,
man, like a runaway or, better still, a hood,
tends to glance backward: now branches creaking, now water's sound.
But the past is neither that panther nor some greyhound
that leaps onto one's stooped shoulders and, having thrown
the prey to the ground, strangles it in its brown
furry embrace—for its shanks ain't so sweet anymore, alas;
and the liquid, Narcissus-resistant glass
of the river gets icy (the fish, having pondered its
tin-can, flickering silver bits,

X

swims away beforehand). Probably you could state
that you simply were trying to dodge the great
metamorphosis, much as those smelts did. That
every point in space is indeed B-flat,
and a true express, skipping points A, B, and
C, slows down as a rule at the farthest end
of the alphabet, letting the steam out from

1 0 2

its comma-like nostrils. That water, too, runs home
from the basin much faster than it pours in
through a couple of pipes, making the bottom win.

XI

One may nod and admit that the Lobachevsky sleds'
lesson was lost on this terrain. Or let's
say that Finland's asleep, nurturing deep disdains
for ski poles, aluminum-made these days—
that is, better for hands, as they say, for turns;
still, they won't teach a youngster how bamboo burns,
won't evoke palm trees, tsetse flies, fox trot,
monologues of a parrot—i.e., the sort
of parallels where, since the world there ends,
a naked scientist makes naked friends.

XII

In little towns' basements, storing all sorts of scraps,
like snapshots of strangers or playing cards, no maps
are ever kept, as though to block the threshold for fate's bold attempts upon defenseless flesh.
The wallpaper suffices; a populated site
is relieved by its pattern from outer ties
so completely the smoke would in kind decide
to coil back in the chimney, whitewashing its pale façade,
so that the blending of two into one would yield
but a cloudy spot on the laundered field.

XIII

It's irrelevant now to remember your name, or mine.
For your blouse or my waistband will do just fine
to confirm in a trifoliate mirror's splits
that anonymity truly becomes us, fits,
as it does in the end all that's alive, that dwells
on this earth, till the aimless salvo of all one's cells.
Things have their limits—that is, their length
or immobility. And our claim on that piece of landscape extended no farther than, should I say,
the woodshed's sharp shadow, which, on a sunny day,

1 0 3

wedged a snowpile. Scanning an alien scene,
let's agree that that wedge can be simply seen
as our common elbow, thrust into the outside;
the elbow that neither of us can bite
or, moreover, kiss. In that sense, I bet,
we really blended—though our standard bed
barely squeaked. For it chose, in its turn, to swell
and become the wide world. In which, on the left as well
there is a door. Which, for all its domestic clout,
may only be good for one's getting out.

[*1985 / Translated by the author*]

Ex Voto

To Jonathan Aaron

Something like a field in Hungary, but without
its innocence. Something like a long river, short
of its bridges. Above, an unutterable umlaut
of eyes staining the view with hurt.
A posthumous vista where words belong
to their echo much more than to what one says.
An angel resembles in the clouds a blond
gone in an Auschwitz of sidewalk sales.
And a stone marks the ground where a sparrow sat.
In shop windows, the palms of the quay foretell
to a mosquito challenging the façade
of a villa—or, better yet, hotel—
his flat future. The farther one goes, the less
one is interested in the terrain.
An aimless iceberg resents bad press:
it suffers a meltdown, and forms a brain.

[*1983*]

Elegy

About a year has passed. I've returned to the place of battle,
to its birds that have learned their unfolding of wings from a subtle
lift of a surprised eyebrow, or perhaps from a razor blade
—wings, now the shade of early twilight, now of stale bad blood.

Now the place is abuzz with trading in your ankles' remnants, bronzes
of sunburnt breastplates, dying laughter, bruises,
rumors of fresh reserves, memories of high treason,
laundered banners with imprints of the many who since have risen.

All's overgrown with people. A ruin's a rather stubborn
architectural style. And the heart's distinction
                                        from a pitch-black cavern
isn't that great; not great enough to fear
that we may collide again like blind eggs somewhere.

At sunrise, when nobody stares at one's face, I often
set out on foot to a monument cast in molten
lengthy bad dreams. And it says on the plinth "Commander
in chief." But it reads "in grief," or "in brief," or "in going under."

[*1985 / Translated by the author*]

106

The Fly

To Irene and Alfred Brendel

I

While you were singing, fall arrived.
A splinter set the stove alight.
While you were singing, while you flew,
the cold wind blew.

And now you crawl the flat expanse of
my greasy stove top, never glancing
back to whence you arrived last April,
slow, barely able

to put one foot before the other.
So crushing you would be no bother.
Yet death's more boring to a scholar's eye
than torment, fly.

II

While you were singing, while you flew, the leafage
fell off. And water found it easier
to run down to the ground and stare,
disinterested, back into air.

But your eyesight has gone a bit asunder.
The thought of your brain dimming under
your latticed retina—downtrodden,
matte, tattered, rotten—

unsettles one. Yet you seem quite aware of
and like, in fact, this mildewed air of
well-lived-in quarters, green shades drawn.
Life does drag on.

III

Ah, buggie, you've lost all your perkiness;
you look like some old shot-down Junkers,
like one of those scratched flicks that score
the days of yore.

Weren't you the one who in those times so fatal
droned loud above my midnight cradle,
pursued by crossing searchlights into
my black-framed window?

Yet these days, as my yellowed finger-
nail mindlessly attempts to fiddle
with your soft belly, you won't buzz with fear
or hatred, dear.

IV

While you sang on, the gray outside grew grayer.
Damp door-frame joints swell past repair;
drafts numb the soles. This place of mine
is in decline.

You can't be tempted, though, by the sink's outrageous
slumped pyramids, unwashed for ages,
nor by sweet, shiftless honeymoons
in sugar dunes.

You're in no mood for that. You're in no mood to
take all that sterling-silver crap. Too good to
let yourself in for all that mess.
Me too, I guess.

V

Those feet and wings of yours! they're so old-fashioned,
so quaint. One look at them, and one imagines
a cross between Great-grandma's veil
et la Tour Eiffel

—the nineteenth century, in short. However,
by likening you to this and that, my clever

pen ekes out of your sorry end
a profit and

prods you to turn into some fleshless substance,
thought-like, unpalpable—into an absence
ahead of schedule. Your pursuer
admits: it's cruel.

VI

What is it that you muse of there?
Of your worn-out though uncomputed derring-
do orbits? Of six-legged letters,
your printed betters,

your splayed Cyrillic echoes, often
spotted by you in days gone by on open
book pages, and—misprints abhorring—
fast you'd be soaring

off. Now, though, since your eyesight lessens,
you spurn those black-on-white curls, tresses,
releasing them to real brunettes, their ruffles,
chignons, thick afros.

VII

While you were singing, while you flew, the birds went
away. Brooks, too, meander free, unburdened
of stickleback. Groves flaunt see-throughs—no takers.
The cabbage acres

crackle with cold, though tightly wrapped for winter,
and an alarm clock, like a time bomb, whimpers
tick-tock somewhere; its dial's dim and hollow:
the blast won't follow.

Apart from that, there are no other sounds.
Rooftop by rooftop, light rebounds
back into cloud. The stubble shrivels.
It gives one shivers.

VIII

And here's just two of us, contagion's carriers.
Microbes and sentences respect no barriers,
afflicting all that can inhale or hear.
Just us two here—

your tiny countenance pent up with fear
of dying, my sixteen, or near,
stones playing at some country squire—
plus autumn's mire.

Completely gone, it seems, your precious buzzer.
To time, though, this appears small bother—
to waste itself on us. Be grateful
that it's not hateful,

IX

that it's not squeamish. Or that it won't care
what sort of shoddy deal, what kind of fare
it's getting stuck with in the guise of
some large nose-divers

or petty ones. Your flying days are over.
To time, though, ages, sizes never
appear distinguishable. And it poses
alike for causes

as for effects, by definition. Even—
nay! notably—if those are given
in miniature: like to cold fingers,
small change's figures.

X

So while you were off there, busy flirting
around the half-lit light bulb's flicker,
or, dodging me, amidst the rafters,
it—time—stayed rather

the same as now, when you acquire the stature
—due to your impotence and to your posture

toward myself—of pallid dust. Don't ponder,
decrepit, somber,

that time is my ally, my partner.
Look, we are victims of a common pattern.
I am your cellmate, not your warden.
There is no pardon.

XI
Outside, it's fall. A rotten time for bare
carnelian twigs. Like in the Mongol era,
the gray, short-legged species messes
with yellow masses,

or just makes passes. And yet no one cares
for either one of us. It seems what pairs us
is some paralysis—that is, your virus.
You'd be desirous

to learn how fast one catches this, though lucid,
indifference and sleep-inducing
desire to pay for stuff so global
with its own obol.

XII
Don't die! Resist! Crawl! though you don't feel youthful.
Existence is a bore when useful,
for oneself specially—when it spells a bonus.
A lot more honest

is to hound calendars' dates with a presence
devoid of any sense or reasons,
making a casual observer gather:
life's just another

word for nonbeing and for breaking rules. Were
you younger, my eyes'd scan the sphere
where all that is abundant. You are,
though, old and near.

1 1 1

XIII

So here's two of us. Outside, rain's flimsy
beak tests the windowpanes, and in a whimsy
crosshatches the landscape: its model.
You are immobile.

Still, there's us two. At least, when you expire,
I mentally will note the dire
event, thus mimicking the loops so boldly
spun by your body

in olden times, when they appeared so witless.
Death too, you know, once it detects a witness,
less firmly puts full-stops, I bet,
than tête-à-tête.

XIV

I hope you're not in pain, just lonely.
Pain takes up space; it therefore could only
creep toward you from outside, sneak near
you from the rear

and cup you fully—which implies, I reckon,
my palm that's rather busy making
these sentences. Don't die as long as
the worst, the lowest

still can be felt, still makes you twitch. Ah, sister!
to hell with the small brain's disaster!
A thing that quits obeying, dammit,
like that stayed moment,

XV

is beautiful in its own right. In other
words, it's entitled to applause (well, rather,
to the reversed burst), to extend its labor.
Fear's but a table

of those dependencies that dryly beckon
one's atrophy to last an extra second.

And I for one, my buzzy buddy,
I am quite ready

to sacrifice one of my own. However,
now such a gesture is an empty favor:
quite shot, my Shiva, is your motor;
your torpor's mortal.

XVI

In memory's deep faults, great vaults, among her
vast treasures—spent, dissolved, disowned or
forgotten (on the whole, no miser
could size them, either

in ancient days or, moreover, later)—
amidst existence's loose change and glitter,
your near-namesake, called the Muse, now makes a
soft bed, dear *Musca*

domestica, for your protracted
rest. Hence these syllables, hence all this prattling,
this alphabet's cortege: ink trailers,
upsurges, failures.

XVII

Outside, it's overcast. Designed for friction
against the furniture, my means of vision
gets firmly trained on the wallpaper.
You're in no shape to

take to the highest its well-traveled pattern,
to stun up there, where prayers pummel
clouds, feeble seraphs with the notion
of repetition

and rhythm—seen senseless in their upper
realms, being rooted in the utter
despair for which these cloudborne insects
possess no instincts.

XVIII

What will it end like? In some housefly heaven?
an apiary or, say, hidden
barn, where above spread cherry jam a heavy
and sleepy bevy

of your ex-sisters slowly twirls, producing
a swish the pavement makes when autumn's using
provincial towns? Yet push the doors:
a pale swarm bursts

right past us back into the world—out! out!—
enveloping it in their white shroud
whose winter-like shreds, snatches, forms
—whose swarm confirms

XIX

(thanks to this flicker, bustling, frantic)
that souls indeed possess a fabric
and matter, and a role in landscape,
where even blackest

things in the end, for all their throttle,
too, change their hue. That the sum total
of souls surpasses any tribe.
That color's time

or else the urge to chase it—quoting
the great Halicarnassian—coating
rooftops *en face*, hills in profile
with its white pile.

XX

Retreating from their pallid whirlwind,
shall I discern you in their winged
(a priori, not just Elysian)
a-swirling legion,

and you swoop down in your familiar fashion
onto my nape, as though you missed your ration

of mush that thinks itself so clever?
Fat chance. However,

having kicked off the very last—by eons—
you'll be the last among those swarming millions.
Yet if you're let in on a scene so private,
then, local climate

XXI
considered—so capricious, flippant—
next spring perhaps I'll spot you flitting
through skies into this region, rushing
back home. I, sloshing

through mud, might sigh, "A star is shooting,"
and vaguely wave to it, assuming
some zodiac mishap—whereas
there, quitting spheres,

that will be your winged soul, a-flurry
to join some dormant larva buried
here in manure, to show its nation
a transformation.

[*1986 / Translated by Jane Ann Miller and the author*]

Belfast Tune

Here's a girl from a dangerous town.
　　She crops her dark hair short
so that less of her has to frown
　　when someone gets hurt.

She folds her memories like a parachute.
　　Dropped, she collects the peat
and cooks her veggies at home: they shoot
　　here where they eat.

Ah, there's more sky in these parts than, say,
　　ground. Hence her voice's pitch,
and her stare stains your retina like a gray
　　bulb when you switch

hemispheres, and her knee-length quilt
　　skirt's cut to catch the squall.
I dream of her either loved or killed
　　because the town's too small.

[*1986*]

Afterword

I

The years are passing. On the palace's pumice façade appears
a crack. The eyeless seamstress's thread finally spears the midget
eye of the needle. And the Holy Family, the features drawn, severe,
comes half a millimeter more close to Egypt.

The bulk of the visible world consists of living types.
The streets are lit with a bright, extraneous
light. And at night an astronomer reckons, straining his
eyes, the total of sparkling tips.

II

I am no longer able to recall where or when events
occurred. This one, or any other.
Yesterday? A few years ago? On a garden bench?
In the air? In the water? Was I the matter?

And the event itself—an explosion or, say, a flood,
the lights of the Kuzbas derricks or some betrayal—
can't recall anything either, burying thus the trail
of myself or of those who either were saved or fled.

III

This, presumably, means that we are now in league
with life. That I, too, have become a segment
of that rustling matter whose fabric's bleach
infects one's skin with its neutral pigment.

In profile I, too, now can hardly be set
apart from some wrinkle, domino, patchwork, fig leaf,
fractions or wholes, causes or their effects—
from all that can be ignored, coveted, stood in fear of.

IV

Touch me—and you'll touch dry burdock stems,
the dampness intrinsic to evenings in late Marchember,

the stone quarry of cities, the width of steppes,
those who are not alive but whom I remember.

Touch me—and you'll disturb a little that which does
exist regardless of me, obviously in the process
not trusting me, my overcoat, my face—
that in whose book we are always losses.

v

I am speaking to you, and it's not my fault
if you don't hear. The sum of days, by slugging
on, blisters eyeballs; the same goes for vocal cords.
My voice may be muffled but, I should hope, not nagging.

All the better to hear the crowing of a cockerel, the tick-tocks
in the heart of a record, its needle's patter;
all the better for you not to notice when my talk stops,
as Red Riding Hood didn't mutter to her gray partner.

[1986 / Translated by Jamey Gambrell and the author]

At Karel Weilink's Exhibition

To Ada Stroeve

I

Nearly a landscape. The full figure count,
appearing in it, gradually flees
the influx of bare statues. Like a coal
turned inside out, the marble's blondish, bleached,
and the locale seems northern. A plateau;
the cabbage tousled by a polar blast.
It's all so very horizontal that
no one will clasp you to an anxious breast.

II

Perhaps—this is the future. Backdrop of
repentance. An old colleague's vengeance. One
distinct yet muffled expletive, "Get out!"
A martial artist's unexpected veer.
And this—the future's town. Your lidless eyes
stay glued to rampant garden growth, alert,
like lizards scanning tropical hotel
façades. And skyscrapers even more.

III

It's possibly the past. Despair's last swoon,
its limit. Common summit. Verbs that wait
in line to view the preterit entombed.
A storm of crumpled velvet settled, passed.
And here's the past's dominion. Paths grown dense
while straying in reality. Lagoons
preserving lapsed reflections. Eggshells glimpsed
externally by yolk's unscrambled pools.

IV

Clearly—perspective. Calendar of sorts.
Or rather, from inflamed and swollen throats,
a tunnel sunk to psychological
beyonds, unfettered by our features. For
the voice, acquainted better with the thick

and thin of failure's landscape than is sight,
the greater evil's handier to pick—
it reckons on the echo's kind response.

V

Perhaps it's—still life. Far away it seems
that everything within the stretchers is
part dead and certainly immobile. Clouds.
A river, over which in circles flies
a bird. A plain, unable quite to stage
a transmutation, dons another shape,
becomes the prey of canvas, postcard, page,
the vindication Ptolemy awaits.

VI

Perhaps it's—tidal zebras or a half
a tiger hide. A hybrid barricade
and rumpled dress that licks the supple calves
of balusters immune to sunburn; and
the time approaches evening. Stifling heat;
a lone mosquito's stubborn solo, whose
pitch hoists the sweaty hammer from its soft and sweet
forge, dies amidst the bedroom's loud applause.

VII

Perhaps—the decoration for a set.
A staging of the classic "Cause's Rude
Indifference to Parting from Effect."
In greeting creature comforts singers prove
less gentle than myopic; "fa" resounds
a short-lived "far." And, trembling, brilliant, slight,
above the wire of notes like faucet drops,
the moonspun trill of the soprano glides.

VIII

Clearly—a portrait, but without a lick
of varnish. Dark, a subtly surfaced pall
whose earthy tints quite naturally arrest
the eye—of one who's up against the wall.
A ways away, a compromise with white,

Olympians amass in storm clouds, sense
the stare aimed at their backs, the inside-out-
ward gaze, the painter's—i.e., the suicide's.

IX

Which is the essence of self-portraiture.
A step aside from one's own flesh and frame,
the profile of a footstool kicked toward
you, a long view on life when dues are paid.
This, then, is "mastery": ability
to not take fright at the procedure of
nonbeing—as another form of one's
own absence, having drawn it straight from life.

[*1984 / Translated by Jamey Gambrell*]

121

"Slave, Come to My Service!"

I

"Slave, come to my service!" "Yes, my master. Yes?"
"Quick, fetch my chariot, hitch up the horses: I'll drive to the palace!"
"Drive to the palace, my master. Drive to the palace.
The King will be pleased to see you, he will be benevolent to you."
"No, slave. I won't go to the palace!"
"Don't, my master. Don't go to the palace.
The King will send you on a faraway expedition,
down the unknown road, through hostile mountains;
day and night he will make you experience pain and hardship."

II

"Slave, come to my service!" "Yes, my master. Yes?"
"Fetch water, pour it over my hands: I am to eat my supper."
"Eat your supper, my master. Eat your supper.
Frequent meals gladden one's heart. Man's supper
is the supper of his god, and clean hands catch the eye of Shamash."
"No, slave. I won't eat my supper!"
"Don't eat your supper, master. Don't eat your supper.
Drink and thirst, food and hunger
never leave man alone, let alone each other."

III

"Slave, come to my service!" "Yes, my master. Yes?"
"Quick, fetch my chariot, hitch up the horses: I'll go for a ride in
the country."
"Do that, my master. Do that. A carefree wanderer
always fills his belly, a stray dog always
finds a bone, a migrating swallow is especially skilled in nesting,
a wild donkey finds the grass in the driest desert."

This text dates back to the eleventh or tenth century B.C. *and is known among Sumerian scholars as "The Dialogue of Pessimism." In antiquity it was regarded as a philosophical text; now some argue that it is, rather, a skit. For my translation, I used two interlinear renditions: one was taken from* Babylonian Wisdom Literature *by W. G. Lambert (Oxford, 1960); the other, from* Ancient Near Eastern Texts Relating to the Old Testament, *by James B. Pritchard (Princeton, 1955). —J.B.*

"No, slave. I won't go for a ride in the country."
"Don't go, my master. Don't bother.
The lot of a wanderer is always dicey.
A stray dog loses its teeth. The nest
of a migrating swallow gets buried in plaster.
Naked earth is a wild donkey's bedding."

IV

"Slave, come to my service!" "Yes, my master. Yes?"
"I feel like starting a family, like begetting children."
"Good thinking, my master. Start a family, start a family.
Who has children secures his name, repeated in posthumous prayers."
"No, slave. I won't start a family, I won't have children!"
"Don't start it, my master. Don't have them.
A family is like a broken door, its hinge is creaking.
Only a third of one's children are healthy; two-thirds always sickly."
"So, should I start a family?" "Don't start a family.
Who starts a family wastes his ancestral house."

V

"Slave, come to my service!" "Yes, my master. Yes?"
"I shall yield to my enemy;
in the court, I'll stay silent before my detractors."
"Right, my master, right. Yield to your enemy;
keep silence, my master, before your detractors."
"No, slave! I won't be silent, and I won't yield!"
"Don't yield, my master, and don't be silent.
Even if you don't open your mouth at all
your enemies will be merciless and cruel to you, as well as numerous."

VI

"Slave, come to my service!" "Yes, my master. Yes?"
"I feel like doing some evil, eh?"
"Do that, my master. By all means, do some evil.
For how otherwise can you stuff your belly?
How, without doing evil, can you dress yourself warmly?"
"No, slave. I shall do no evil!"
"Evildoers are either killed, or flayed alive and blinded,
or blinded and flayed alive and thrown into a dungeon."

1 2 3

"Slave, come to my service!" "Yes, my master. Yes?"
"I'll fall in love with a woman." "Fall in love, my master. Fall in love!
Who falls in love with a woman forgets his griefs and sorrows."
"No, slave. I won't fall in love with a woman!"
"Don't love, my master. Don't love.
Woman is a snare, a trap, a dark pit.
Woman is a sharp steel blade slitting man's throat in darkness."

"Slave, come to my service!" "Yes, my master. Yes?"
"Quick, fetch water to wash my hands: I am to make an offering
                                                    to my god."
"Make an offering, make an offering.
Who makes offerings to his god fills his heart with riches;
he feels generous, and his purse is open."
"No, slave. I won't make an offering!"
"Rightly so, my master. Rightly so!
Can you really train your god to follow you like a doggy?
All the time he demands obedience, rituals, sacrifices!"

"Slave, come to my service!" "Yes, my master. Yes?"
"I'll invest with the interest, I will loan for the interest."
"Yes, invest with the interest, make loans for the interest.
Who does so preserves his own; his profit, though, is enormous."
"No, slave, I won't lend and I won't invest!"
"Don't invest, my master. Don't lend.
To lend is like loving a woman; to receive, like siring bad children:
people always curse those whose grain they eat.
They'll resent you or try to reduce your profit."

"Slave, come to my service!" "Yes, my master. Yes?"
"I shall do a good deed for my nation!"
"Very good, my master, very good. You do that!
Who does good deeds for his nation has his name in Marduk's
                                                    gold signet."
"No, slave. I won't do a good deed for my nation."
"Don't do that, my master. Don't bother.

Get up and stroll across ancient ruins,
scan the skulls of simple folk and nobles:
which one of them was a villain, which one a benefactor?"

XI

"Slave, come to my service!" "Yes, my master. Yes?"
"If all this is so, then what is good?"
"To have your neck broken and my neck broken,
to be thrown into a river —that's what is good!
Who is so tall as to reach the heavens?
Who so broad as to embrace plains and mountains?"
"If that's so, I should kill you, slave: I'd rather you go before me."
"And does my master believe that he can survive for three days
                                                    without me?"

[*1987*]

In Italy

To Roberto and Fleur Calasso

I, too, once lived in a city whose cornices used to court
clouds with statues, and where a local *penseur*, with his

shrill "Pervért!
Pervért!" and the trembling goatee, was mopping
avenues; and an infinite quay was rendering life myopic.

These days evening sun still blinds the tenements' domino.
But those who have loved me more than themselves are no
longer alive. The bloodhounds, having lost their quarry,
with vengeance devour the leftovers—herein their very

strong resemblance to memory, to the fate of all things. The sun
sets. Faraway voices, exclamations like "Scum!
Leave me alone!"—in a foreign tongue, but it stands to reason.
And the world's best lagoon with its golden pigeon

coop gleams sharply enough to make the pupil run.
At the point where one can't be loved any longer, one,
resentful of swimming against the current and too perceptive
of its strength, hides himself in perspective.

[*1985 / Translated by the author*]

In Memoriam

The thought of you is receding like a chambermaid given notice.
No! like a railway platform, with block-lettered DVINSK or TATRAS.
But odd faces loom in, shivering and enormous,
also terrains, only yesterday entered into the atlas,
thus filling up the vacuum. None of us was well suited
for the status of statues. Probably our blood vessels
lacked in hardening lime. "Our family," you'd have put it,
"gave the world no generals, or—count our blessings—
great philosophers." Just as well, though: the Neva's surface
can't afford yet another reflection, brimming with "mediogres."
What can remain of a mother with all her saucepans
in the perspective daily extended by her son's progress?
That's why the snow, this poor man's marble, devoid of muscle power,
melts, blaming empty brain cells for their not so clever
locks, for their failure to keep the fashion in which you,
                                        by putting powder
on your cheek, had meant to look forever.
What is left is to shield the skull, with raised arms, against
                                                idle glances,
and the throat, with the lips' nonstop "She has died, she has died,"
                                                while endless
cities rip the retinal sacs with lances
clanging loud like returning empties.

[*1985 / Translated by the author*]

127

Gorbunov and Gorchakov

CANTO 1
Gorbunov and Gorchakov

"So, what'd you dream of this time, Gorbunov?"
"Oh, mushrooms mostly." "Mushrooms? Curious.
Again?" "Again." "You really make me laugh."
"And why is that? It's pretty serious.
Regularity in sleep's the stuff
the doctors seem to think is curing us."
"No offense—but you've not had enough
of all this fungus?" "Well, up here I guess
it's all I've got." "In Leningrad we have
so many dreams, but 'mushroom' clearly is

the one you're wedded to." "And what
are all you Leningraders dreaming, then?"
"Well, it depends. Of concerts forested
with bows. Of avenues and alleys. Men—
just faces. (All in all, they're fragmented.)
The Neva, bridges. Or a page I can
discern—although the nurse collects, come bed-
time, all our specs—without my glasses on!"
"That dream's too much for these dull eyes to read!"
"And then I dream myself back here again."

"Who needs real life? Just take a look around.
Now there's a dream. The day's gratuitous.
The dawn dims dreams like that. And how you groan
with rage when you're awakened. —Mickiewicz!
Try and keep it down, okay? —For one
of those I'd gladly slumber through to dusk,
miss supper, too . . ." "Sometimes my dreams are prone
to birds, to bullfinches, a kid who is
leaping puddles—and it's me . . ." "What's wrong?
Go on!" "I think I've got the flu. Do these

things interest you at all? What for?" "Beats me.
Just do." "I dream of childhood: sneaking through
an attic with my pals, just two or three
of us. And of old age—nowhere to go
to shake off *that* unholy mess, I see.
Old man, young brat . . ." "Bleak apposition, no?"
"Oh, Gorbunov, that's pure stupidity.
These dreams are only manufactured so
as to give our nights variety,
to give day's heritage a jolt or two."

"Now there's a conundrum, this 'heritage.'
A question, though, you can't ignore:
what *of* old age? You hardly act your age,
or even have gray hairs." "Or ever snore
quite like Babanov on the window ledge?
Or ever, like Mickiewicz does, resort
to bustling and garbled badinage?
What'd we get imagination for
if not to use it pump-like to discharge
old age into our dreams." "Forgive me, Gor-

chakov, but in that case it can't be true
it's you you're dreaming of." "The Crosses was
constructed for stone-headed fools like you.
And there they'll keep you living under glass!
So tell me who I'm dreaming of . . . yoo hoo!"
"Gor-kiewicz . . . or Gor-banov, no?" "You ass!
You're crazy, Gorbunov." "The face I knew—
as yours—with their gray hair. My friend, for us
there's daily self-deceit aplenty to
disgust." "Next they'll sew your pocket closed."

"I sport pajamas with no underwear
on as it is." "At times I see a ring
of burning logs, and stoves . . ." "A real one there!
Streets, conversations. Simply things. The string
and woodwind sections playing as a pair.

And women. And, perhaps, a spicy fling."
"Just yesterday I dreamt of silverware
for six." "Do they amount to anything—
your dreams—or whirl like chaos everywhere?"
"Some seem coherent, some just menacing."

"Herr Freud says we're imprisoned by our dreams."
"I've always heard that we are slaves to habit.
Apparently you're stumped by what this means."
"No, I can see the page on which I read it."
"Freud was a liar." "Liars come in reams . . .
Now let's suppose you're in the mood to have it—"
"You mean the thing in pants?" "Or out, it seems
—but dream your face with titmice gnawing at it.
No gossip's more explicit than your dreams."
"And so this brings us to your mushrooms, *ibid*."

"They're just like islands. (Mushrooms even sprout
like little islands.) And the same can stand
for streets and alleys, dead ends, words. Throughout
our lives we speak in spurts, or tend to. And
between the spurts, like silence, all about
is grass. But you can touch them with your hand!
And so they have unbounded rights, and what
sustains the solid ground on which I stand
seems as unsteady as a rocking float
the Neva's currents bear away from land."

"Then you're just like those fishermen who face
the water, watching where their bobbins go,
for hour after hour lodged in place?
I've got it right?" "So far, exactly so."
"And, during supper, fashioning new shapes
of lures, light-hearted, in the evening's glow?"
"And hiding mealworms in my tackle case!"
"You'll be locked in here forever." "No!
Why are you aggravating me?" "Because
my name is Gorchakov, as well you know."

1 3 3

CANTO 2
Gorbunov and Gorchakov

"Had supper?" "Yeah, some vegetables, a dish
of Jell-O." "Things keep looking up, I see.
And what's outside?" "The starry fields." "What's this?
Another Galileo, doubtlessly!"
"With the departure of Aquarius
around the twentieth of February, we
see Pisces in ascendancy, the fish-
sign pledging rivers will again run free."
"And what about the earth?" "The earth?" "Well, yes.
What's down below?" "That alley edged with trees."

"You know what, Gorbunov? Your case is sad:
a neo-Newton-*cum*-analysand.
There's this guy Khomutov, who says amid
the lockups' retching, histrionics, and
the noise, 'Name's Hamilton, and I'm not mad.'
And yet he snores just like a Khariton."
"Erecting all our seaports, Peter had
to bring the Teutons in to get it done.
The names were harder than the work they did.
Our Khomutov may be a Hamilton."

"The heater's on, and yet I feel a chill."
"Don't lean against the window, then." "Why not?
You think your shiny pets above us will . . . ?"
"Are you convinced?" "Oh no, I'm full of doubt:
I see the snowdrifts and the lane. That's all."
"Look over there: Aquarius is out,
he's bending with the Dipper." "We'd do well
to have a telescope. You wouldn't shout
so much." "A telescope! In here? Like hell!"
"What *are* you getting so worked up about?"

"You've put your filthy feet up on my cot.
At least you could have taken off those mold-
y slippers first." "I'm cold. You know, the thought
devoted to your chanterelles has told

on me. I'm chilled down to my bones without
my slippers on. And so you shouldn't scold."
"Did Freud dream up such progress? That I doubt.
And progress is a thing we should uphold:
the activist, he dreams a rainy wood;
the passivist contracts a nasty cold."

"Your chanterelles are hazards to the sane.
Beware, they're far from harmless, Gorbunov.
How much importance do you give to them?"
"As much as I give love." "And what is love?"
"The end to loneliness." "The very end?"
"It's being able, once, to stand above
the bed and, by just bending over in
the silence, with your hands, brow, breath, touch life."
"What are you staring at? The stars? The lane?"
"The opposite of empty narrative."

"Toss me an apple." "Catch." "Just tell me this:
what are your mushrooms, if you know at all?"
"Whenever I see toadstools in the grass
or forest floor, I find that I recall,
well, love. It's in the mind, or blood perhaps,
for always like an echo, dim but real,
I feel it." "That's just habit and, alas,
the mind's penchant for going general."
"The hands do that. Upstairs what's striking is
a total dearth of the habitual."

"So in the darkness of your sleep you dream
of chanterelles?" "Yes, constantly." "And so
you dream of love?" "It's all the same . . . You seem
to think that's strange." "Not strange. It's sinful, though.
Yes, sinful, and, to tell the truth, I deem
the whole thing utterly disgraceful." "No!"
"What's got you smirking now?" "You're such a scream."
"Toss me an apple, won't you?" "Sure, although
you'll never catch all that the mushrooms mean."
" 'Mushrooms'? That's polygamy, you know.

There now! I planted that one on your chin!
The bitterness I feel is manifest
in my reproach." "You tell me it's a sin,
but sin is something punished in the flesh,
and how can Gorbunov be punished when
life's agonies lie focused in his breast
as in a prism? Is the future clear
of obstacles?" "Apparently we're guests
at someone's wake." "Apparently my grin
makes me, today at least, an optimist."

"And the Last Judgment?" "That's just memory
in flashback, like a film. Why magnify
Apocalypse? Come on, what's it to me?
Five months spent in a wasteland. Merely five.
Well, I've blown half my life and I would be
content to sleep with mushrooms till I die.
I know, however, when and where I'll flee
before the Fiery Angel of the Sky . . ."
"Pain crushes pride." "No, not a bit. The tree
of pride sucks up our suffering to thrive."

"You're saying you don't fear the dark?" "It has
its landmarks, and with some of them I am
acquainted rather well." "You swear it does?"
"Plenty. Just give a whistle and they'll come."
"Vanity's mother is inventiveness."
"I doubt the wisdom of that apothegm.
A man's soul never feels the loss of space."
"And of dead creatures would you say the same?"
"I think the soul, while living in this place,
assumes the features of its mortal frame."

CANTO 3
Gorbunov in the Night

It's night. The hospital. The hostile ground . . .
This hardly qualifies for tragedy . . .
Besides, the tougher life a mortal's found,

the smoother things will seem on Judgment Day
for this soul, when the sentences resound.
I feel, when life is really wretched, I
could tolerate with ease a second round.
That's why inside the man—a child, and why
the mushrooms got me here, though all they meant
to me is out there somewhere, far away.

I dream of chanterelles, but never dream
now of my wife . . . It seems that's as it ought
to be. As fabric tears where thinnest. Some
truth in—got her pregnant, guess I thought
I'd make her stay. The reasoning of a bum.
Apparently I finally bottomed out.
Don't know about my soul, although I am
about my eardrums' health in little doubt:
I hear Babanov now—he's humming, comb
in mouth; a sheet is rustling on a cot.

I hear a voice amid these nighttime sounds—
not auricular hallucination, for
the ear's outfitted even with defense
against the pressure at the ocean's floor.
Besides, I'm contradicted by its sense,
that voice—consistent, hollow, sure.
Whose voice is it? Can't be my wife's. And since
persistently the supernatural world
stays silent as my wife, it can't be saints.
Oh, how I wish I had my muffler here!

It's night. The hospital. The lane, the drifts
of snow. An alder hums, contesting heaven.
Kike-wise the night nurse in the hallway lifts
his Jewish telescope and peers in, laughing.
My pupil's shrinking, shrinking—it resists
the bed contracting on me like a coffin.
And my blood bubbles like bicarbonates.
My ankle freezes as it comes uncovered.
My mind divides the way a microbe splits
and in the silence multiplies forever.

1 3 7

Yes, two of us, before the altar. Inasmuch . . .
She left, and somewhat irritated, maimed,
I crave an interlocutor to match.
Yes, there were two. Indeed, so two remained.
Relieving February, enter March:
that's how the altar, in its turn reminding one of guardsmen, like the still night-watch,
because of how the calendar's designed,
obstructs the silence, my assault on which
creates another force field here inside.

She left. I am possessed by, I possess
myself. Myself? Well, maybe I should call
for Gorchakov? . . . Hey, Gorchakov! . . . I guess
the bed-bell's rung. But is it, after all,
so senseless for one pair of vying lips,
especially without a music hall,
to sing as two? I watch them as they press
together, syllable by syllable.
I am—a circle cleaved. Thus, more or less,
we're magnets, horseshoe-shaped, identical.

Night. Night. My lips performing a duet.
You think that it's too good for you? I say
that there's a special coziness in it.
It is a contradiction, yes, but they
are close. Almost a family when bit.
And all the more so in a brief display.
The upper lip is like a groom, to wit:
The lower lip is like his fiancée.
But that which splits in two will surely split
into two hundred just as easily.

And everything that's been twofold is then
accountable, is then no longer moot.
The solitude dilemma's answered when
it's split. Despair divides my soul like wood—
in two—and yet it's not that I remain
beside it *tête-à-tête*. Two-souledness would

seem atheistic, but it's not the flame
that logs require: the inverse makes it hot.

O God in heaven, if you're so designed
that you can listen to two voices blast
at once from but one set of lips and find
in them not noise but strife between the past
and future, raise to you my coughing mind
and plant its microbes where your light is cast.
Divide among them with your mighty hand
the sum of these convulsive thoughts and days.
And leave the fraction of me left behind
to triumph over silence then, at least.

But if I really need a listener, send,
O Lord, without delay, a denizen
of heaven down to me. I won't pretend
to be superior to him in sin
or sarcasm. He wouldn't comprehend
them anyway. But if that's out, well then,
let cherubs and not Gorchakov ascend
above the filthy hole they keep me in,
and, like your blessing, circle to the end
above the sobbing and surveillant men.

CANTO 4
Gorchakov and the Doctors

"Well, Gorchakov, make your report." "You mean
on Gorbunov?" "Of course, on Gorbunov."
"His mental operation is, when seen
in toto, dialectical, but half
of all his statements clearly contravene
the Party's views, and several, as to both
events and things, are new to us." "A sign
his blood is not nitrogenous enough,
and thus we see disintegration in
the patient's self-controlling operative."

"His chin is puffy, asymmetrical.
His brows close-knit and thick. His nose is mapped
with intersecting veins that twist and swell."
"Bad kidneys, I should say." "His forehead, wrapped
in compresses and asymmetrical as well,
is like a knot of arteries that snapped.
His weakness and his god's the chanterelle.
With women, you might say he's handicapped.
'The inner world is made majestical;
the outer, correspondingly, is scrapped'—

now there's your standard Gorbunov-ish line.
In regular pronouncements more or less
like this one, one can easily divine
all his wrongheaded—his non-Partyness."
"A leftward shift. He's out to undermine
our trusted Marxist principles." "There is
too little evidence." "Well, does he whine
at atmospheric changes?" "Does he miss
the fairer sex a lot?" "No, there he's fine,
his manner, really, the antithesis,

in fact, of a . . . oh, what's it called? I say . . ."
"Composure, Gorchakov." "A paramour."
And how's he down below? . . . *Déshabillé*,
his privates . . ." "Strictly business. Out the door,
the can, and back again three times a day.
If you'll forgive my crudeness." "Say no more.
And have a glass of water." "Water?" "Hey!
You were expecting cognac?" "No! I'm sure
I never touch the stuff!" "Then tell us why
you licked your lips when I began to pour."

"I'm not sure why . . . Some memory of water."
"Water? What?" "I can't remember what.
I'm sorry . . ." "Supper, did you drink a lot, or—"
"No . . . you've tied my mind up in a knot . . .
But wait! I see . . . a man . . . and sands like Tartar
hordes a-whirling round . . . He hasn't got
a drop to drink; he's thin; it's hotter, hotter . . .

1 4 0

Sun is at . . . what do you call it . . . at
the zenith. Hostile ground. It's getting harder
now to see. Then, boom, a well . . ." "Proceed!"

"Then everything again is empty, dead!
The well, well, disappeared with all the rest . . ."
"Gorchakov? What's wrong?" "I've lost my head.
I'm sorry. I admit I was impressed
when with such majesty today he made
his full idealism manifest."
"Who? Gorbunov?" "Of course! Who else? He said . . .
I . . . er . . . oh, please forgive me, I digress."
"No, no. Don't worry. Please, do go ahead."
"I'm too involved with Gorbunov, I guess.

Non-Party! *That's* what's wrong with him!
Indeed! And when the temperature approaches
zero, he moves to that end of the room . . .
well . . . toward the heater . . . to the left." "Prodigious!"
"Is he at all religious?" "Is a hymn?
He is exceedingly relig-religious!
Sometimes I am afraid the day will come
he'll kneel and summon God from heaven's reaches
down to bless the sanitorium."
"Well, being so non-Party, sure he's anxious."

"So: 'deviations to the left.' " "Ha-ha!"
"Dear colleague, what's so funny?" "Just the plain
stupidity of what you said just now.
Observe: the heater, as we ascertain,
is left of Gorchakov, it surely . . ." "Ah,
is right of Gorbunov! Like king and queen
in chess. Well, to be safe we won't withdraw
the other option but instead maintain
the presence of the two phenomena."
"What good's a song without a good refrain?"

"Well, Doctors, do we have our diagnosis?
Staple this; now, Gorchakov, please sign
here, at the bottom." "Haven't got my glasses."

"Won't mine do?" "They might. Let's see: 'We find
some deviations to the left at places' . . .
That's for sure! . . . 'and to the right' . . . That's fine!
They're both correct. We'll fix these lordly asses.
Either we'll exterminate their kind,
or—" "Thank you, Comrade Gorchakov. It pleases
us to let you off at Eastertime."

"I thank you, friends. Mere thanks don't say enough
to thank in full . . . What now? Should I salaam?
Where's Gorbunov? I've got to open up
his eyes! My God, not one true word . . . I am—
but who am I so self-reproaching of?
To hell with woodsy paranoiacs! Damn!
The warp's gone crazy under which the woof
has lost its thread while sliding home.
It's so peculiar now that Gorchakov
speaks Gorbunov's maniac idiom."

CANTO 5

A Song in the Third Person

"He said to him." "And then he said to him."
"And then he said." "He answered." "And he said."
"Then he." "And he then said into the wind."
"He gazed into the dark and said." "He said
again to him." "But, so to speak, to say
he said is not the same as saying what
he said." "And then he said, 'Don't lose your way
in details; all is clear. That's that.' "
"The one he-said flows on into the next."
"Until he-saids of sin and penance flow
together." "Silent on the table rests
he-said." "And in the end they form a row,
like Tartar yokes." "And then he said to him."
"And he connected his he-said, in line
with that he-said, whose echo echoed thin."
"And then he said to him, and filled the time."

"And then he said." "It is as when a stone
is thrown into a pond. The rings—one, two,
six . . ." "And he said." "The rings are really one,
although the radius is stretched, it's true."
"He-said—a ring." "He-said—another ring."
"And his he-said collided with the ground."
"His own he-said came like a boomerang
back to slap him." "No more new worlds around."
"He said." "He said." "He said." "He said." "He said."
"A train!" "And on a line without an end."
"And starting at the station of He-said."
"And who would want to make the tracks his bed?"
"And then he said." "But in response he said."
"He said, then vanished." "On the platform see
he-said." "He said." "But if he-said's a dead
object, should not the same be true of he?"

"And he to him." "And he." "And he to him."
"All right, let's say the evening has begun."
"And he to him." "And it's no idle whim
to think the two together are but one."
"A question—'he.' " "Whose answer is—'to him.' "
"And vice versa." "Yes, they are the same."
"Though there's a strip of light dividing them."
"Only so that each can have a different name."
"Is he related, then, to him?" "Does not
the world of senseless objects boast of some
relations closed to analytic thought?"
"If not a relative, a sort of chum?"
"What won't the judge's chamber analyze!
The judge sits down; his glasses have no glass."
"Then what is he to him?" "A thin disguise
for the he-said." "That beats in-laws, I guess."

"A massive building. Featureless façade.
Two faces pallid from the stench they breathe."
"They are not here." "And where could they have gone?"
"To the he-said-to-him or to the he."
"A massive building. Through the window peer
two silhouettes." "And pandemonium,

1 4 3

as in a station." "Never silence here?"
"Just in the gaps between he-said-to-him."
"A 'said,' you know, requires she."
"But we've been talking of the said of he."
"But, all in all, the silence pleases me."
"Anathema resounds less threateningly."
"So in this place they're scared of silence?" "No,
they are united by he-said, the way
they are by time and place. It is as though
some grand instinct to incest were at play."

"And that's a form of action, isn't it?"
"Oh yes, for they are full of interplay."
"And will they never quit?" "They'll never quit."
"No doubt it's like a proper noun that way."
"That's right. A proper noun is concentrate.
Substitutions, alterations, slight
omissions—such things cannot enter it."
"And that's the vehicle of questions, right?"
"That's it precisely! Indirect discourse
is in reality the most direct."
"And this is something anyone ignores
at peril of his happiness." "Detect-
ing all pronouncements that he-said recites,
like children by the church doors waiting, one
appears almost to enter in the heights
achieved *before* the dialogue's begun."

"Well, what'd you dream about, He-said-to-him?"
"The doctors are too near." "So what? Go on."
"I dreamed of waves. I dreamed that I could swim
far out to sea." "Unrealistic! Un—"
"Already he's forgotten all about
his mushrooms." "That's impossible!" "Could be."
"He's simply speaking for them both, no doubt."
"That sort of thing absorbs infinity."
"I saw a host of waves pass in review
as clearly as could be. And as they passed
I saw the sky, and just as clearly, too . . ."
"That's something like a double-barreled blast."

1 4 4

". . . the crests, like manes of horses when
they drag a sinking cart, their only thought
is breaking loose." "And weren't there drowning men
or shipwrecks?" "Aivasovsky I am not!
I saw the spuming breakers. And the shore,
a giant horseshoe . . . And, a distance off,
the he-said bustling through the clouds. It wore
the smile of Gorbunov, of Gorchakov."

CANTO 6

Gorbunov and Gorchakov

"Well, what'd you dream of this time, Gorbunov?"
"But I've already told you all about
my meeting with the doctors." "Knock it off.
I overheard it all myself just out
there in the hall." "I'm saying, Gorchakov—"
"That you dream only of the sea, no doubt."
"That's right, the sea." "You are beyond belief."
"I don't insist on your belief. It's not
important." "What a tangled web you weave
with all your lies. It's easy to pick out

a bad egg by its putrid odor! Phew!"
"Just shut your mouth!" "Why should I shut my mouth?"
"Oh, Gorchakov, I know you through and through . . ."
"X-ray technician now?" "Your 'funny' stuff
is out of place, you know. You might live to
regret it." "Oh, imagine that!" "Don't laugh . . .
Why is it the commission always knew
what we'd discussed as soon as you'd gone off?
You played the stoolie for them, didn't you?
So quit your bride-like blushing, Gorchakov."

"You're angry." "I'm not angry." "Don't torment
me, Gorbunov." "I you? That's funny!" "See,
you're angry." "No, I'm not. And if you want,
I'll even swear to God." "But that would be

1 4 5

unpleasant for you." "I'm not hesitant."
"You seemed to say that with sincerity."
"Now you're starting that again? I can't
believe you think it's worth it watching me."
"So then you'll swear to it. I bet you won't
believe me if I do." "Well, probably."

"And *I* don't follow what you mean by that."
"I'm mixing up the chaff and wheat." "You are
unable to believe in anything! No, not
in words, or even holy signs." "There's war
in the Crimea—smoke is all about.
That's something, isn't it? I quote from our
grandfather Krylov . . . Prison's what you've got
ahead, you know." "You ought to go before
they send you." "Hey, what are you gaping at?
"Orlova and Ulanova, two stars."

"I think I'll wander down the hall." "Why?" "Oh,
no reason, just a headache. It's a crime
the way you're always asking questions." "Go
to hell." "What are you after, pal, sublime
illumination?" "Maybe. How 'bout you?"
"You shit! I'm sure you play the stoolie, slime."
"I'm just extending my horizons." "Though
without beliefs." "A skeptic in my prime!
Denunciations, conversations—so
it goes. All helps to brighten up the time."

"And somehow time helps brighten up the days."
"I think my head is better." "So you won't
reveal your dream? Come on, no more delays."
"Oh, all that's sad and ugly. I just want
to watch the lights reflecting on the glass."
"Well, shadows from the boardwalk, friend . . ."
"Ulanova! Orlova, too, who stays
in darkened background!" "Coffee's cold." "They meant
a lot, you know. We were at war, and they
were symbols, of a kind, for our home front."

1 4 6

"The second half of February. Look
at what the hands are pointing to." "It's just
zero's radius." "The numbers?" "Like
the border of a plate . . . I somewhere crossed
this service, *à la* Meissen—" "I relate
to counterfeits." "—*King's Workshop* was embossed
on it, and under that a sun like light
that's beaming from a gasolier." "A glass
of gin right now . . ." "A water bottle I'd
not turn away tonight, if it were passed.

Look there! The shadows stream across the lane!"
"Excuse me, I would rather like to see
us turn the conversation back again . . .
to clocks." "What for?" "You judge more cruelly
than I deserve." "Your own lips are to blame."
"So, is it really zero?" "Yes." "But why?"
"Because outside is emptiness." "But then
inside it's warmer than outside can be."
"But one can simply call a heated room
a product of the freezing earth and sky."

"And what about the woodpiles?" "Well, I guess
they're links between outdoors and in—" "Oh, Lord,
the wind is whistling through the crevices!
I'm freezing cold, and hungry as a bear."
"Physicians aren't as big as sicknesses."
"An inner sanctum's greater than a door."
"It is, you know, a shelter nonetheless."
"Don't be a hypocrite. And furthermore,
remember, Gorchakov: the utterness
of uttered words surpasses disbelief by far."

"Yes, as cold is larger than the heat."
"So, too, the clock hands are inferior
to time." "The hollow in the tree can't beat
the tree." "Though hollows are superior
to squirrels." "Who are certainly more sweet
than eagles." "And the fish . . . that thing . . . so pure . . ."
"I want my body naked, head to feet!"

1 4 7

"Where there's a radius, there's, as it were,
a fork and plate." "And burnt wood—" "Can't compete
with my hot-water bottle, that's for sure."

CANTO 7
Gorbunov and Gorchakov

"Had supper?" "Yeah, a plate of day-old greens.
It's always greens." "We've got the right to eat
bird food here. Still, it's no use making scenes."
"But why do they refuse to give us meat?"
"Look, there's new firewood stacked up between—"
"I have a perfect right to be upset!"
"No, the administration's right. I mean,
it's right within the radius it's set."
"But neither gut nor cranium's too keen
to squeeze inside it." "Let us not repeat

a conversation we've already had . . .
Besides, my kidney's acting up." "But I—
I am outside the radius." "You're mad!
Then who's this standing here?" "A shell, you see."
"When I was young, the soul's infinitude
was something on which one had much to say."
"But me, I'm *married*. Don't you understand?
My wife—and daughter—both outside the ra-
dius." "You need a bracing shower, friend."
"You know one in the neighborhood?" "Well, try

Opochka Station." "Some place you dreamed?" "Like hell!
More likely you dreamed me." "But it's a day
by train out in the provinces!" "You really get around." "I should escape this." "Why
waste the time and effort? I can tell
you've really put down roots here, anyway."
"You've put down roots here, too." "In general,
I've gotten lazy, though I am, they say,
swift as the wind. It's really not my style
to walk around in hiking boots." "Okay,

calm down." "I'm calm." "How much'd you make?" "A few
hundred, old currency." "Where at?" "A place in . . ."
"Are you thinking I'll report on you?"
"Who would deny himself the fine sensation?"
"*My* silence ain't enough to save you." "True.
Yes, well, you know, on reconsideration . . ."
"You'd rather think me traitor through and through
than try to speculate on a location."
"Alas, my genealogy is too
ignoble to perform such speculation."

"So why attack the menu?" "It's the rut
of eating . . . Well, I'm not a veteran
in here, and this unvaried menu—" "But
you're using restaurants as comparison."
"I'm stretching out the radius somewhat
to get my family in." "They slaughter one
fat lamb a night at home, no doubt." "Well, what
I'm getting at is that it's still too soon
for me to sacrifice the past." "Oh, cut
the crap." "Why call it crap?" "It's overdone."

"I've stretched the radius's distance way
out to my home." "So much the worse, my friend."
"I'm only one leg of the compass. They,
the stationary leg, support me." "And
somehow this helps to brighten up the day,
this wider radius that you command?"
"The narrower. Down here that's just the way
things are: some move as strangers, others stand
still." "Though a stationary lamppost, say,
reflected in a puddle, will expand."

"I'm moving! Look!" "I don't know where the start
is, but I know the end's in Leningrad
snowdrifts." "I move, therefore I am. Descartes
would envy me." "Of course! It makes me glad
to see enthusiasm from the heart."
"As for me, this slumming in your head
is simply boring." "What about your chart:

1 4 9

the Dipper and the skyline, and all that?"
"Aries: it ascends, curating March."
"A telescope's the thing I wish we had."

"Precisely! Then the both of us could see
those fixèd stellar feet." "Progenitors
of motion." "Making the stability
of both Opochka and Kamchatka ours."
"Born late in March, it is my destiny
to wander. I've been fingerprinted . . . stars
are such unstable points of gravity
they set us all to trembling . . ." "Of course,
as one born under Aries, you should be
beneath a cap of Karakulan furs."

"You think I'm trembling from cold?" "That's why
your toes are turning blue." "And you? What is
your sign?" "Well, I belong to Gemini.
Born under Gemini, in May." "I guess
that makes you warm." "I guess." "Come on. Don't try
to play the genius with non-geniuses!"
"Compared to you it's clear enough that I
am scarcely cold at all." "Oh, stop with this!"
"But, Gorchakov, what's wrong?" "It's all a lie!"
"Oh no, it's true—the months and all." "Alas,

we can't afford a telescope. And thus
we'll never see our distant sponsors." "You're
forgetting that, although the radius
is scorned in life, the compass will endure
forever, Gorchakov." "It's hideous—
the possibility of dying here,
believing it's the end." "Ridiculous!
You won't die." "No? You think not?" "Yes." "You're sure?"
"Of course. We cannot carry on into the next
the burden we, in this life, have to bear."

CANTO 8
Gorchakov in the Night

Your line assures me immortality!
My brain, like convolutions in the bed-
clothes—flooded by the glimmer (towering
above my tiny flame) your words have shed.
Colitis is a curse! . . . thoughts clamoring
inside my head like demons in a brood.
Your torch can't seem to set aglow my wick!
Oh, Gorbunov, your words have set my blood
to seething through my cranium, the way
a spark ignites the chips of bone-dry wood.

He's gone . . . He's left me only monologue.
And the night dial's radius . . . He's stored
some apples as security and lobbed
off like Pilate! In the corner curled,
I will inspect the folding of my robe.
I have a salad bowl—I can discard
its dried remains and doff it like a rogue
in a veritable bowler. Where's this starred
empyrean? The ceiling and the rug.
The window—the reflection of the ward.

Night. Windows swirl the ward and double it.
The bulwarks of infinity. They're all
encased in shutters, though, and don't permit
their own reflections farther than the wall.
In that space—rear end forward—one's a bit
uncertain just whose bed is whose. I'd fall
asleep now if I could, though I admit
I'd like to kill myself in general.
And thus—since here a thing's its opposite—
risk delving deeper still into my soul.

I'd like to fall asleep . . . The orderlies
are still on duty . . . Is the room's reflection
helping them? It merely multiplies
the mess . . . Infinity's multiplication.

I watch myself expand before my eyes;
the panes, encouraging imagination,
press a mile into the space that lies
between the bunks. The fiery sensation
gazing at that distant star implies
that gravity is just degeneration.

Regularity in sleep's the core—
indeed, what helps us to recuperate.
So what do I need Gorbunov, then, for?
Whatever for? . . . Shall we abbreviate
our speech by Gorbunov? No gossip's more
explicit than a dream. No eye as great
as dreams. Herr Freud of course has written we're
imprisoned by them . . . Strange to meditate
on this again . . . When there's no other cure,
the grave, of course, will make a hunchback straight . . .

But these disordered musings are the state
that follows from the silence of the nearby beds. I feel my very self's at stake
when I don't have an interlocutor.
It is in words alone that I partake
of life. They need a witness and an heir!
And, Gorbunov, you are, make no mistake,
my judge. While I am but an agent here,
connecting sleep and sleeplessness, to make
appraisals of front teeth beyond repair.

It's night. The window vent. Oh, if the guard
would only open it! But it's no use.
My face and shoulders are securely barred
in its reflected surface. If the nurse
would open it, a leak would surely start
in the reflection, and, in turn, induce
a wayward patient who was so inspired—
especially since it isn't far—to loose
his face at least en route to Leningrad.

1 5 2

Oh, Gorbunov! Like any simpleton,
I feel I'm nothing but the radius
a clock hand makes! To wait for me—beyond
the bordered plate or here—I'd have to guess
pitifully, there isn't anyone.
For these dimensions are, for you, alas
too circumscribed. Ahead your martyrdom
is waiting: it's been fitted to your size.
The horror there's a variation on
a ladder's rung, a little door, the pass

where you're expected for too long. My sin
is only that my call won't get to you.
You, Gorbunov! As long as I am in
this world, I know I must surrender to
your power! To you I raise my prayers. I can
go nowhere that your words do not pursue
me. Come to me, I beg you, speak again!
I have to hear your words resounding through
the air. If I've denounced them, it has only been
because I cannot part with them, I know.

Forgive me when you leave me here at last.
It isn't that I fear our parting when,
with walking papers crumpled in my fist,
I finally stretch to you my parting hand.
Like all one has to bear—the catalyst
of boredom and indifference—my friend,
do not resent me, crave revenge. At best
I'm like an echo which continues sound
to save it, in the end, from being lost:
I love you and betray you, too, to pain."

CANTO 9
Gorbunov and the Doctors

"Well, Gorbunov, we've brought you here to tell
us everything." "About?" "Your dreams." "About
the compass." "And your daughter." "And the shell."

"And give us names, details." "Let's see. I doubt
my daughter figures in my dreams at all.
In fact, I'm sure of it." "Oh, cut it out!"
"Come on!" "I dreamed about the sea." "Oh hell!"
"Let's do without the wet stuff." "And without
'anchors aweigh' and 'o'er the seas' as well."
"About Opochka . . ." "Can't imagine what

you're after that one for." "For your own good."
"A line that smacks—" "It's necessary. We—"
"—that smacks of questions that Red Riding Hood
asked Granny. You'll recall, I'm sure, that she
inquired about the ears . . . 'Don't be afraid . . .'
She answers, 'Oh, I am afraid . . .' 'Tee-hee—
the better, pet, to hear you with.' " "Who would
have figured that he would turn out to be
a coward." "Anyway, the girl is saved."
"There is a plus in everything, you see."

"Say something, Gorbunov." "You realize
that we'll get angry if you make us wait
too long." "What are you waiting for?" "For lies
unmet by protests to evaporate."
"And then?" "Well, then I think it would be nice
to speak on equal terms, don't you?" "I hate
his whimpering, his stupid shrugs and sighs.
Nurse, an injection will facilitate . . ."
"He's trembling." "Naturally. The needle's size
has caused his thinking to accelerate."

"Well, Gorbunov, recalled your dream?" "It was
the sea. Just that." "No chanterelles?" "In short,
alas, there are no more of them." "Alas?"
"A habit. I got used to their support."
"It often happens, when their women pass
away or go away, that men resort
to words of grief like that." " 'Alas'—a man's
word, when it's said in quotes." "But it's the sort
of word one's likely to hear widows use."
"We'll put that down as well in the report."

"Dreams bare the secret canvas of a man,
of what takes place inside." "And what the eyes
observe is of less interest to us than
what's hidden, for the reason that—" "What lies
outside is Gorchakov. I know." "Well then,
the point is not the mischievous disguise
he has assumed; it's what your dreams make plain:
you gravitate to darker depths." "I guess
I'm dreaming like the Neva flows, you mean.
But mouths of rivers speak not of demise,

but just the opposite: of procreation."
"It's scarcely bearable that any freak
or bum should dump descendants on the nation."
"A pity. For the river, as the Greek
philosopher remarked, though flowing, stays in
one place." "Which is the problem all men seek
to solve." "And Newton's moral." "There! He's raising
Newton!" "And Lomonosov." "Outside?" "A week
in February. Time of hibernation,
denunciations, snowstorms." "It's unique

among the months, in terms of days." "A kind
of cripple." "Don't you think it easier
to live through?" "Shamefully. In fact, I find
it easier than easy to endure."
"And rivers?" "What about them?" "Don't they bind
themselves in ice?" "But it was man we were—"
"Know what awaits you?" "I suspect a signed
certificate committing me." "Yes, sir.
Considering the things you have in mind,
We'll have to keep you on forever here."

"What for? . . . However, well, it's obvious
one must control oneself to be let go."
"And call for Gorchakov." "One can discuss
the stars with him." "Of course." "Which goes to show
that there's a plus in most things." "Yes, a plus!"
"And he, like God, is omnipresent, though
he's in the habit of denouncing us."

1 5 5

"It's nails that hold a horseshoe up, you know."
"How strange that Gorbunov, nailed to the cross,
must look for help from Gorchakov below."

"But why exaggerate like this? Why mumble
these Golgothan thoughts?" "But can't you see
that this is a catastrophe." "You bundle
eternity up with catastrophe."
"Eternity's the bung that plugs the bunghole.
That's why he doesn't want eternity."
"Yes, this is all too hard for him to follow."
"Hey, Gorbunov, you want a cup of tea?"
"Oh, why have you forsaken me?" "Dear fellow,
whom are you calling now?" "He seems to be

lamenting Gorchakov again." "Why not
his daughter or his wife? Why Gorchakov?"
"The whole thing's egotism." "You sure we've got
it right? It's really Gor—" "Hey, Gorbunov!
Look here, your fate has been decided." "What
of Gorchakov's?" "Well, live with the rebuff:
we're freeing him. You're on your own. I'd not
waste sighs on such a creep." "From this day forth,
as usual, my friend, when life is shot,
eternity begins." "Speech signing off."

CANTO 10
A Conversation on the Porch

"A massive city in its twilight shroud."
"The streets, like lines in ledgers, parallel."
"A massive madhouse stands." "Looks like a void
existing at the center of the well-
planned universe." "The gate obscures from view
an icy courtyard filled with snow and cords
of wood." "Which is a conversation, too,
since all these things have been described in words."
"Out here are men, and there, the lunatics
who know internal and eternal pain."

1 5 6

"Not 'men' themselves?" "But can one ever fix
the title to one's neighbor?" "They're not men?
The expressions in the eyes, the stance, the frame:
head, sturdy shoulders, legs, and arms that reach . . ."
"The moment that we give a thing a name,
that thing's transformed into a part of speech."
"But what about the body?" "It obeys
the rule." "And what about this place?" "It's called
a madhouse." "And the days?" "Their names are days."
"Oh, everything's transformed again to old

Gomorrah, built of greedy words. But how
do they come by the right?" "—A word that rings
a nasty bell." "My head's already so
besotted with these words devouring things."
"No question that it causes heads to spin."
"As seas make Gorbunov's; it's for the birds."
"And so it's not the sea that surges into shore, but words are overlapping words."
"And words are sort of holy relics." "Yes,
though once things hung . . . Names are defense
against the very things that they express."
"Against the sense of life?" "Well, in a sense."
"Do they defend against the Passion, too?"
"Against all passions." "God forbid!" "For He
designed His lips for words . . . But then He drew
forth words in His defense." "Well, basically,
that's why His life is so prophetic. It's
insurance that we won't go down, but swim."
"And thus His life's the one thing that admits
two meanings." "It's, therefore, a synonym."

"But what about eternity? Does it
resemble He-said in a Cossack coat?"
"It is the only word that hasn't yet
devoured its earthly object in its throat."
"A hardy word-shield!" "Hardly." "Yet the man
protected by the cross is saved, at least."
"Not fully so." "You mean the synonym
can give no greater guarantee than this?"

1 5 7

"That's true." "But what of love? Can love not stem
the tide of aimless chatter?" "Either you've
descended from the sphere of seraphim
or you're confusing potency with love."
"No word is so devoid of telltale signs."
"And there's no cover that has so devoured
its object, obfuscating its designs.
And nothing is so rending as a word."
"But try regarding this objectively;
to wit: the general observation seems
to be that words are also things, so we
are saved at last!" "It's then the silence comes.

Silence is the future of the days
that roll toward speech, with all we emphasize
in it, as, in our greetings, silence pays
respect to unavoidable goodbyes.
Silence is the future of the words
whose vowels have gobbled up internally
the stuff of things, things with a terror towards
their corners; a wave that cloaks eternity.
Silence is the future of our love;
a space, not an impediment, a space
depriving love's blood-throbbed falsetto of
its echo, of its natural response.
Silence is the present for the men
who lived before us. And, procuress-like,
silence gathers all together in
itself, admitted by the speech-filled present. Life
is but a conversation in the face
of silence." "Gestures, quarrels, men incensed."
"A twilight talking to a murky close."
"With walls that stand like arguments against."

"A massive city in its twilight shroud."
"A speech by chaos, rendered plain as hell."
"Here stands the massive madhouse, like a void
existing at the center of the well-
planned universe." "Goddamn this draft!" "Your curse
won't hurt my ears. My friend, it isn't life

1 5 8

before me but a victory of words."
"And verily the nouns are verbalized!"
"A bird flies upward from its nest when food
is what the little bird is looking for."
"Indeed, a star that climbs above the field
seeks out a brighter interlocutor."
"And all night long, as far as one can view,
with postal slowness, in its turn, the plain
keeps up the conversation." "How can it, too?"
"By means of jaggedness in the terrain."
"But can one, at such distance, hear enough
to know which blabbermouth he bothers with?"
"The higher pitch belongs to Gorbunov,
to Gorchakov, the low." "For what it's worth."

CANTO 11
Gorbunov and Gorchakov

"So, what'd you dream of this time?" "Nothing new."
"Then I won't ask." "What's this? You feeling racked
by shame or something suddenly?" "No, view
it simply as a sense of measure, tact."
"How very generous." "What can I do?
This place has gotten to me. And the fact—"
"What fact?" "That I have landed here." "Oh, you
are capable of causing cardiac
arrest. Just take your facts and go to . . . to . . ."
"Come off it now. We've got to interact."

"And who am I to you?" "I wouldn't know."
"No matter . . . So I guess you're leaving. When?"
"Right after Easter." "And from here you'll go . . . ?"
"Home." "They won't hesitate to take you in?"
"They won't." "Where do you live?" "The address? Oh,
I never give that out to anyone."
"That strikes me as a lie." "If you say so."
"Don't tell me fairy tales." "But then again
you won't be coming by to visit." "No?
And why is that?" "Because the outcome's been

159

decided." "Then you're right." "I think I am."
"You *think* so?" "Oh, I'm sorry! That popped out
by accident. I've no right to dream
of doubt." "So tell me, when you're home, about
the house, how d'you think you'll pass the time?"
"That's my concern." "You're the one who thought
that we should 'interact.' And yet your tone
is hardly conversational. It's odd."
"It's just my nature." "Well, an apple, then,
to change your mood?" "Okay, a nibble, but
I promise I won't take the goods and run . . .

'Lift 'n' heave'—that's my kind of work. Believe
me, pal, all others are superfluous."
"My eyes are being shrouded! Lift 'n' heave,
take 'er away—oh, that's synonymous
with all that happens to me now." "Be brave.
We promise not to drop you." " '*We?*' What does
'we' mean?" "Don't be afraid. Before I leave
I'll teach you palmistry." "If that's the case
I turn my back on you." "You mean that we've
no friendship left? There's no more to discuss?

You could be kinder." "Evidently this
is what my genes designed." "Existence, though,
determines—" "Tea?" "Okay . . . deter—" "I guess
it's cold. You want it warmed a bit?" "Uh, no . . .
cold's fine . . . determines consciousness."
"I'd take that sentence left to right." "Ah, so
you think I am a Jew?" "This apple was
plucked from the tree of knowledge by a Jew."
"No, it was Eve who did the plucking, ass."
"Eve may have, but it seems he did it, too."

"But still, he was a genius in his way.
He founded science, and he's got a name
that's sonorous, in any case." "Let's try
to skip the names. That palindrome
would set them chopping off my hands today."
"You know, he, too, consigned himself to pain.

And now he has whole peoples in his sway."
"Panmongolism! There's a loaded term."
"He was condemned as well." "You mean to say
he was condemned to parting?" "Just condemned."

"But what is parting?" "Must we linger on
this word?" "It's for my files. Elucidate
the ways of parting." "They depend upon
from whom one parts. That's what's at stake.
Where you remain. Can you remain as one,
named So-and-so, in such a place and state?
And if from someone close, to whom he's gone
and for how long." "And if forever?" "Wait . . .
You stand and gape into the dark, alone—
the sort of dark that lowered lids create

for sleeping in. And so you shudder now
and then from grief. The darkness, being real,
is clearly visible. Though now, you know,
there isn't any sea or chanterelle."
"And even in the spring you think it's so?
The springtime makes it easier, I feel."
"I doubt it." "—doubt it gazing at the snow."
"You're like a thing extracted from a field."
"Unlike a gum, the earth's not bleeding, though."
"This evidently is as God has willed.

And what does parting mean to you?" "Decay . . .
Doors closed behind you as you disappear.
And, if it's day, the brilliance of the day."
"And if it's night?" "At night the atmosphere
comes into play—perhaps a single stray
light or a bench in some deserted square."
"And does the memory of a loved one stay
with you for long?" "You'd better be more clear."
"Well, after losing me what will you say?"
"In general, loss isn't hard to bear."

"If that's the way you feel about it, why
go on about our 'friendship'?" "In this instance

we're the better for the fact that we
live here together at this little distance:
the reason being that to really be—"
" 'Really to be'! Or, better yet, 'existence' . . ."
"—to really cease to be . . . Nonentity
will make my absence give, for one who listens
to the plain, it's plain monotony."
"You mean, therefore, that you will be my silence."

CANTO 12
Gorbunov and Gorchakov

"Have you had supper?" "Have indeed. And you?"
"Uh-huh." "How'd you like the cabbage mush?"
"In texture, cabbage mush gives little to
the palate; and it didn't fill me much."
"It's watery and empty as a rule—
so quoth the proverb." "Sad." "Could use a dash
of vinegar, for pungency, it's true."
"Well, all is empty." "But one emptiness
tastes different from another one." "I do
yearn for a thing to sink my teeth in, yes."

"In this hell-hole into which we're cast,
there's nothing left to do but to begin
a month before the start of Lent to fast."
"I guess you're speaking of the madhouse, then."
"Our geography is small, at best."
"And afterwards?" "You're always asking! When
is afterwards?" "When crucifixion's past."
"And what's that mean?" "It's just an idiom."
"You'd think they'd use some basil leaves at least."
"As usual they'd mix the bromide in."

"Yeah, none of this will turn out well, I fear.
This bromide is unhealthy, nasty stuff."
"It's dispossessing all of us of hair.
Just look at any pillow: daily fluff
is sacrificed by our Babanov there,

1 6 2

Mickiewicz sheds his eyebrows, and I have
now lost the battle on my crown. I swear
the dope makes you anemic." "Cools you off
between the devil and the rib—that's where
it sits, so we don't wreck our brains with love."

"I took it in the army." "You alone?"
"No, everyone. We called it 'Unmanalov' or
'Antihardon,' 'cause with just a dram
we all forgot Ulanova-Orlova."
"Mine was dark, but now it's gone so blond!
The warp is gone on which this rug was woven.
It won't make the gray it would have gone . . ."
"But don't forget the basic circumstances given."
"And what, dear sir, is that supposed to mean?"
"That you won't need it at the rate you're going."

"You're right." "Don't shake." "I'm cold." "Here, put your hands
beneath the blanket." "Thank you. Tell me, what
is love?" "I told you . . ." "But I know that sounds
each bear their various boundaries; they've got
many different levels." "Love still stands
for parting's preface." "No!" "I'm willing that
I be a monument to lies, who sends
his children and their progeny to fart
upon his head!" "Come on, don't be a dunce.
I said that 'cause, as usual, I'm bored."

"Damn the draft in here! It chills the blood!"
"They've puttied shut the cracks." "Now there's a joke.
The radiator's cold as well." "It's cold
and dirty in this place around the clock."
"There's a star above that tree I could
discern without a telescope." "You look
at one; no star ascends without a brood."
"It's just occurred to me, just as a lark:
what if they chopped the cross for firewood—
would its image rise again in smoke?"

1 6 3

"You're nuts." "I'm only showing some concern
for your affairs." "Praiseworthy charity!
What are you really after, though?" "The churn
of warmth back in a cold extremity."
"You said it. Mine are all about to turn
to ice." "I'm right." "There's inhumanity
in that." "Let's lay the logs star-shaped to burn."
"You're right. Stars bring to mind eternity—
unlike the cross, I am ashamed to own."
"I'd rather say a bad infinity."

"What time is it?" "Apparently it's night."
"Oh, please, don't start in on the zodiac."
"I know my wife and daughter are outside."
"Well, what I said of love is as exact
for marriage." "For myself, I wouldn't mind
it someday. But for you it's a mistake."
"My marriage irritates you, I've divined."
"You should have wed the darkness." "I can't hack
monotony. Indeed, I take delight
in each domestic jam and cul-de-sac."

"What time is it? It's almost zero." "Oh.
That late." "Since I have no mathematic prowess,
I'll tell you I consider every 0
a forerunner of plus." "My lips, empowered
by yawning and by biting, quickly go
to circle." "What's achieved, then, when you throw it
all into a single heap?" "The snow-
capped pinnacles where unscaled Elbrus towered."
"Did earth create concavity that's so
immense?" "It showed itself to be a coward."

"If mountains are to be your leitmotif,
then think about Golgotha; March 15,
the Ides of March, is almost here, and I've
made up my mind to jump in some ravine."
"Or wrap yourself up in a cloud, as if
in some black Persian veil. And in that scene
you'll play the spirit." "Well, you measure with

1 6 4

a yardstick of your own. However, mine
won't measure that two-headed summit. It
just presses all the courtyard snowdrifts down."

CANTO 13
Conversations about the Sea

"One is immortal, goes your argument.
But to the sorrow of your prophecy,
I am already half an invalid.
Your light cannot drive off the dark from me—
not any more than night-lights by the bed
drive off my dreams. I don't reproach you. We
must stop reproach. Isn't that the point?
Before my open or my shutting eye
something mighty always seethes ahead
as if it were the sea. I think it is the sea.

It's night. The hospital. On hostile ground.
I cannot bear to listen to you lest
I tremble from the cold and shame about
that torch. Because the sea will never best
its own concavity. I won't go down
into it, though. Though truth is dearer . . . Trust
I won't allow you into any harm!
Enough of that! It seems you hardly rest
in certainty that it's the sea around
us and not simply . . . woe. Oh, *why* this test?"

"Perhaps it is indeed the sea . . . the cries
of gulls above a woman tossing crumbs
of bread from off a pier. And like the waves
her flounce flaps in the wind; her ragged hem
is slapping at her shoes. So, in a blaze
of screeching battle, there she stands alone:
she tosses bread and stares into the haze . . .
As if, become farsighted for a time,
she holds a bee in Turkey in her gaze."

"Yeah, that's the sea. Precisely that. The deep
of life from which, like knights in chain-mail coats,
so very long ago we all sprang up
that if you hadn't struck this distant note
again just now, I would have let it sleep,
forgetting that, in fact, the world has got
a bottom and horizon and a type
of space besides this one where it's our fate
to stare at painted walls, a lilac stripe.
But 'he that hath ears to hear, let him be mute.' "

"There's something bigger in the world than us,
a thing that warms us, though it doesn't warm
itself; that, with the help of Boreas,
stuffs hollows up with hills, collecting them
around to be of one another's use.
I feel as though I'm striding through a dream:
upstairs to light, downstairs to the abyss,
up to the threshold of Elysium,
all by myself, amid the blooming crests
where Nereus' escalators hum."

"But ocean's a too-foreign element
to buy the story of some 'Tally ho'
across it. Ice of course is different.
No, Gorbunov, the end of all your woe
is not in sight. It seems that you are meant
to measure out your grief in years—you know,
just like they did in Exodus. I can't
say where each year your wanderings will go,
where water's woven into sky . . . this tent
of sky's so broad, for whom can one man howl?"

"My soul's too weak for calling. From now on,
wherever fate sees fit for me to be,
from Paradise to squatting in the john,
not painted walls but waves are what I'll see.
And that's not bragging, Gorchakov. A man
like me, in such celestial disarray,
well, what would he be pleading for? For one

who hath the ears to hear, artillery
repeat of waves is far more pleasant than
a tearful prayer that this cup pass from me."

"But that's a sin! . . . What's wrong with me? Today
I, cursing you, forgot that woodpile scene's
details: you asked about (as I replay
it in my head) my dreams. And in response
I tried to speak my mind, that dreams employ
the heritage of day. And then it seems
you called my mushrooms islands. I reply:
How hard it is beneath our craniums!
And now you see the sea—to that I say,
Absurd! Though yours has greater rights, the dreams

are both the same." "And sleep?" "The doctors' cure:
the core of cores." "And like in streams, we sink
in it." "We sink into the darkness. Your
imagination sucks. What cripple-think!"
"Sleep's an exit from the blackness." "Gorbunov forgets the age we're trapped within.
I tell you that your dream's not new!" "But nor
is man." "Why speak of man?" " 'Cause man's a thing
that dreams alone can take the credit for."
"And what about a man is most distinct?"

"The eyelids. Close them, you see darkness, right?"
"But in the light?" "In light, too, as a rule . . .
And suddenly you see, your eyes shut tight,
a feature. One, a second . . . third . . . You feel
your ears hum; your mouth's cold. The height
of sky. And children running down the quay. A gull
is catching bread crumbs midway through its flight."
"Am I not there? On that embankment?" "All
I see, that moment, everything in sight
is real—more real than you there on your stool."

Conversation in a Conversation

"But that's delirium! You hear? So look,
we need a witness . . . Here, Babanov, you.
Now, in a robe without a belt or hook,
I'll perch upon this stool in public view.
Well, Gorbunov, you see me, right?" "I took
no notice." "Even of my long johns' hue?"
"No." "I'll obliterate your portrait! Look
here, Gorbunov! The sea becomes a stew
now that the wind is kicking up! You snake,
you hear?" "I have already answered no."

"So that's the way it is! Well then, let's use
our fists! Taught! Blockheads must be taught a lesson!
Take that! Well now, can you conjecture whose
hand hit you—mine? Babanov's?" "In that session?
um, well, was it . . . Gor-banov's?" "You refuse
to blame me! You'd forgive my sins! Your ocean
will burst the faucets soon, and you'll know whose!"
"He-he." "What are you laughing at, you crashing
idiot! You fool!" "Hey, what's the noise?"
"Get out of here, Mickiewicz!" "I'm the boss in

here, and if a pal has closed his eyes,
the more so as it's night already, those
around him should, I think, shut up." "You flies!
I slugged him, well, because . . . he didn't close
his eyes from pain." "I really do advise
you to shut up." "Mickiewicz, your brain loose
or what? What's wrong with you? It isn't wise,
you know, opposing me." "I'll bust your nose!"
"Ouch, ouch, my corns!" "What's going on, you guys?"
"Damned if I know." "Someone got his toes

stepped on." "Watch it, I hear the doctors!" "Jeez-
us Christ! Get in the sack, quick!" "I'm in bed."
"And, Gorbunov, don't you so much as sneeze.
Just cover up and . . ." "But he's really dead

asleep already." "What?" "I hear the keys!"
"Asleep? Impossible! You're cracked!" "I said
shut up, you fool!" "Babanov, don't you tease."
"Leave him alone." "I only want a bit . . ."
"Just you try squealing, Gorbunov." "But he's
asleep." "Oh no. We're really in for it."

"How should you greet your doctors?" "Showing some
respect . . . Get up, you crippled lunatics!"
"You got a gripe about the grub, you scum?"
"There was a fight in here. I heard it." "Nix,
my friend, there wasn't." "Don't be quarrelsome.
The night clerk said he heard a fight." "I'll fix
that liar!" "Save your tricks. We're not so dumb."
"Whose stream is that?" "Some dick's." "Who mentioned dicks?
I asked you whose it is, not where it's from."
"Yes, whose? An eagle's?" "Yours, you Cossack pricks."

"Mickiewicz!" "Yeah?" "Well, wipe it up, you creep!"
"We keep the peace here. Better learn your place."
"What's wrong with Gorbunov?" "Uh . . . he's asleep."
"So get to sleep and don't disturb the peace."
"We're on our way." "That's right. Bad little sheep."
"We're going." "We'll hear houseflies buzz
you'll be so quiet. Got it? Not a peep!"
"Excuse me, fellows, but I've got to piss."
"Tomorrow." "Gorchakov, they're in your keep."
"Here's news for you: a sputnik is in space."

"They've gone." "Hey, Gorchakov! What's that? Your piss?"
"Go f——." "All right, let's close our little eyes."
"I'd love to have a cake for Easter." "Yes,
to break the fast. Some butter, some good-size
salami . . ." "You should have asked the doctor." "Guess
you could've—he was asking, doctor-wise."
"In the confusion I forgot." "I wish
you'd shut . . ." "Hey, look at Gorchakov, you guys!
He's whispering to Gorbunov, his lips
pressed close." "He's trying to apologize."

1 6 9

"You're really sleeping? Far as I can tell,
you're really sleeping . . . how the strands are wound
in knots! I cannot understand myself . . .
For God's sake, please forgive, forgive me, friend.
Here, let me fluff this battered pillow full.
How's that? . . . my self and self are out of tune.
Forgive me . . . This is more than I can well
perform. Now, sleep . . . to speak of glances, one
could not find much to pause on here, where all
is obstacle. On obstacles alone.

Sleep, Gorbunov. Until they sound
retreat. I only want to guard your rest.
To hell with it! with the alarum's round!
Though obstacles are new to you, I'm used
to them. Forgive me for my bragging, friend.
Forgive me my disharmony, at best.
Sleep, sleep, and I will wait beside your bed.
Not over you, not under, but here next
to you . . . Don't care how many years they send
you up! I'll wait to meet your opened eyes.

What do you see? The sea? Two seas or more?
You wander wave-filled hallways . . . Fishes stare
with dumb expressions out of every door.
I'm right behind you . . . But from God knows where
ten thousand bubbles bubble up before
my eyes . . . And I can't follow, I can't bear
the pressure . . . What? What's that? My mind's gone . . . or
hallucinating conversation . . . Look there!
Down from the north the wind's begun to roar!
The pillow's squashed, the part has left your hair."

[*1968 / Translated by Harry Thomas*]

170

Notes

To a Friend: In Memoriam / *Natalia Goncharova (1812–63):* Pushkin's wife.

Lithuanian Nocturne / III. *Zhemaitija:* Lithuanian name for Samogitia, a historical region of western Lithuania. / IV. *Stasis Girenas (1893–1933)* and *Steponas Darius (1896–1933):* American aviators of Lithuanian origin, who crashed near Soldin, Lithuania, after successfully flying across the Atlantic. They were widely believed to have been shot down by the Nazis. / XII. *Prince Vytautus (c. 1350–1430):* Grand prince and most famous monarch of early Lithuania. / XXI. *St. Casimir (d. 1484):* Patron saint of Lithuania. *St. Nicholas (d. 324):* Patron saint of Russia.

Twenty Sonnets to Mary Queen of Scots / I. *"all the dead past now lives anew in my cold heart."* From a popular nineteenth-century Russian love song. / II. *Zarah Leander:* Swedish actress and singer popular in the 1940s. She played Mary, Queen of Scots, in the German film *Das Herz einer Königin.* / VI. *Parmenides:* Greek philosopher of the Eleatic School, c. 515 B.C. / X. *crippled Hamburg cooper:* From Gogol's *Diary of a Madman.*

Minefield Revisited / *Sophia Kovalevska (1850–91):* A celebrated mathematician.

Eclogue IV: Winter / VII. *Terek:* A river in the Caucasus. / IX. *Kazimir Malevich (1878–1935):* Russian suprematist painter.

Eclogue V: Summer / I. *"cock and hen":* A children's guessing game played with meadow grass. *Terzaromaville:* Moscow is traditionally identified as the "Third Rome." / IV. *Simonides (556–468 B.C.?):* Greek lyric poet.

Kellomäki / XI. *Nikolai Lobachevsky (1793–1856):* Mathematician who proposed the theory that parallel lines converge in infinity.

The Fly / VI. *"six-legged letters":* The Cyrillic letter Ж indicates the *zh* sound.

Afterword / *Kuzbas:* Acronym for an industrial region in Siberia.

Gorbunov and Gorchakov / Gorbunov (from the Russian *gorbun,* "hunched") and Gorchakov (from *gor'kii,* "bitter") are patients in a "psychiatric hospital" on the outskirts of Leningrad. / I. *dreams:* The Russian *son* means both "sleep" and "dream." *The Crosses:* A prison in Leningrad. / V. *Ivan Aivazovsky (1817–1900):* Seascape painter. / VI. *Ivan Krylov (1768–1844):* Satirist and poet, famous for his fables. *Lyubov Orlova (1902–75):* Film star. *Galina Ulanova (b. 1910):* Dancer with the Bolshoi Ballet. / IX. *Mikhail Lomonosov*

(1711–65): Russian scientist, scholar, poet. / xi. *Panmongolism, say. How much there is to that:* Parody of Soloviev's epigraph to Blok's poem "The Scythians." / xii. *Elbrus:* Highest peak in the Caucasus. / xiii. *like knights in chain-mail coats:* From Pushkin's *Tale of Tsar Saltan.*

The View Was
Exhausting

Mikaella Clements
& Onjuli Datta

REVIEW

First published in the USA in 2021 by Grand Central Publishing

First published in Great Britain in 2021 by
Headline Review
An imprint of HEADLINE PUBLISHING GROUP

1

Cataloguing in Publication Data is available from the British Library

Hardback ISBN 978 1 4722 7171 6
Trade paperback ISBN 978 1 4722 7172 3

Typeset in Bembo Std

Printed and bound in Great Britain by Clays Ltd, Elcograf S.p.A.

Headline's policy is to use papers that are natural, renewable and recyclable
products and made from wood grown in well-managed forests and other
controlled sources. The logging and manufacturing processes are expected
to conform to the environmental regulations of the country of origin.

HEADLINE PUBLISHING GROUP
An Hachette UK Company
Carmelite House
50 Victoria Embankment
London EC4Y 0DZ

www.headline.co.uk
www.hachette.co.uk

For our family

SAINT-TROPEZ

CHAPTER ONE

Win went down to meet Leo herself, in the lobby of La Réserve on the first day. He was sitting on his suitcase, one hand in his pocket. White T-shirt and jeans, brown leather shoes. He looked patient.

"Hello," Win said.

Leo smiled and raised his eyebrows in that old, familiar way. He had buzzed his hair short since she'd last seen him. He stood up, reaching for her, and she said, "Oh, there's no cameras here, it's okay."

He held his hands up in surrender, then leaned back and grinned. "You look good."

It was quiet in the lobby. The green and gold light drifted around them, salt in the air and wildflowers poised in the still afternoon while light-footed staff flitted about pretending not to have noticed them. Win had forgotten what it was like to stand under Leo's fixed gaze. She was used to attention, but in a chaotic, excitable way; flashes and screams and outpourings of emotion. Leo's attention had focus and purpose, like a calm hand on her shoulder.

She still felt shaken, fragile from jet lag and the flight itself. There had been turbulence over the Atlantic, and although it was a red-eye, no one had slept. Win spent most of it trying to focus on scripts and avoiding conversation with her publicist. People's phones kept lighting up in the gloom around her. She had pretended not to know that all of the messages were about her.

When they finally landed and made it to Saint-Tropez in the early morning, she still felt too unsettled to sleep. She'd spent the better half of the day on her laptop in bed, reading emails and doing her best not to go online. She looked out the window at the view only once; some fans had strung up a huge banner angled toward her suite, ON T'ADORE WHITMAN in pink glitter paint on a bedsheet. Several fresh bouquets were sent to the room with sympathetic messages from onlookers and industry acquaintances. In the afternoon her makeup team arrived, and then there were phone calls and couture dresses sent by hopeful designers, and the hum of the press outside her window, and somewhere, quietly, there was Leo, making his way from Berlin to the hotel Win's people had picked out. It lay high up in the cliffs, lavish, private, and delighted to have them.

"I'm sorry for the short notice," Win said, and then: "You cut your hair."

He ran a hand back over the buzz cut. It was almost startling to see Leo without the wild buffer of his hair. It brought all the lines of his face into high relief.

Win's publicist, Marie, had once described Leo's face as "well made." Severe bone structure, a satisfied mouth, those clear, dark eyes. He was tall and his silhouette was clean, and he moved like he was on his way to claim something and in no rush to get there.

"I thought it might add something to the story," he said.

They looked each other up and down. In the rush of media attention and damage control, she'd forgotten to prepare herself for seeing Leo again, for the first time in eighteen months or longer. He looked as good as he always did—older, perhaps, without the hair.

"You can touch it if you want," he said.

Win reached out and thumbed over his skull, from his temple to behind his ear. To her surprise it felt soft, the shorn hair running in smooth lines, like the coat of an animal. She ran her fingers back up against the grain.

Her assistant, Emil, came hurrying over to them from the check-in desk, pressing a key card into Leo's hand and throwing a look over his shoulder like he was being hunted.

"We should get moving. They spotted Leo coming in."

Win looked away from Leo, past the staff and security scurrying back and forth, toward the glass doors of the lobby. She couldn't see anything from this angle, and the hotel would try to keep paparazzi off their grounds, but she could hear it: a low rumble of excitement and chatter competing with the sound of the ocean. It was almost sunset. They were going to be late.

Win turned back to Leo. "Are you ready?"

"Yeah, I've been practicing in the car." Leo cleared his throat, letting his voice drop low, frowning sternly. "No comment. No comment. Yes, the sex is amazing."

Win laughed. "Your delivery needs work."

The car windows were tinted, and the doors were locked before the SUV peeled out through the hotel gates. In the waiting crowd of photographers there was a frantic struggle to get the best view. The trick was to let them catch a glimpse of him without revealing too much. It wouldn't look good to hand them Leo on a plate right away; there had to be at least one secret date first, like they were trying to keep it quiet. The rumors had to start as whispers, before they orchestrated a storm.

The SUV was obvious enough, pulling out of the drive, and they picked up a fast tail of paparazzi. Some followed in cars, others on motorbikes, trying to swerve up the side of the car, one man steering and a second brandishing the camera. Emil sat in the front seat, arguing in French with the driver about the best route with an arm poised, rapier-like, as if he wanted to take hold of the wheel. Leo sprawled next to Win in the back with one big hand splayed out on the seat between them, laughing a little when the car lurched sideways to avoid an approaching scooter.

Win watched him, mouth curling up despite herself. "You okay?"

"Fine," Leo said. "I'd forgotten what your life was like."

"They're here for you, too."

"Nah, they're not," Leo said, but he looked pleased, switched on, and Win didn't worry too much about him losing his cool. Leo was used to attention, as well.

Win checked her emails again. There was still no word from Patrick. Up until two days ago her agent had contacted her almost hourly, delivering an endless stream of updates and negotiations from Paramount. Less than a week ago he had messaged her: This could be the big one, Whitman. Since Nathan Spencer's public meltdown, there had been nothing but vague reassurances, platitudes that were far from comforting.

Marie had sent through the schedule for Win and Leo's orchestrated summer fling. All across the Riviera preparations were being made for them: white cloths thrown over tables, vineyard walkways raked clean, wilting roses and oleander clipped back from every trellis. The hotel had ordered a crate of Win's favorite Sancerre and the expensive whisky people thought Leo liked. On the weekend they would attend the Zacharias Chavanne party, and the whole time they would play happy and in love, making it clear that Win wasn't heartbroken, until the summer was over and people had forgotten that she'd dated Nathan Spencer at all, let alone their catastrophic breakup. With Leo next to her, it would be obvious that Nathan was just a blip, a fleeting distraction, nothing compared to the tumultuous, on-again, off-again love affair of Whitman Tagore and Leo Milanowski.

There wasn't much dignity in faking a relationship, and somehow even less so with Leo. He was too familiar with the industry; he liked fooling people too much; he'd known Win through all of her break-neck early twenties, and every time he looked at her it was like he was remembering them. But there wasn't time for shame. It had ceased to surprise Win that people cared about what she did off-screen, and with whom she did it. She couldn't just let her work stand for itself. She had to prove herself an asset, someone people would be excited to watch. As Marie had always said, real or fake was not the point. People just wanted to be entertained.

So it felt good to have a plan, to have all the players in place. The car swerved again as an overtaking SUV nudged too close to them, its driver trying to catch a shot through their windshield as it passed. Leo let out a rough bark of a laugh.

"Dating you is an extreme sport," he told her. "You should sell tickets."

"It's not always this crazy."

Leo gave her a look that she remembered deep in her bones and said, "Liar."

By the time they got to the planned coastal spot, there were only four cars still with them. It made it easier to pretend that they were alone, out for an evening stroll on the beach and apparently oblivious to the photographers lining the cliffs. Leo took her hand as they set out over the rocks, his face solemn and tender as if Win were a wounded bird he had rescued. There was a flutter of camera shutters as their hands met.

At this time of year, the Côte d'Azur was a smooth wash of jewel tones, the deep, smoky blue of seaside air, the ocean spread out like a glossy carpet, the honeycomb of cliffs and pastel-painted houses high above in the tangle of greenery. The sand was pale and silvery, warm to the touch when Win kicked off her heels, even as dusk caught fire across the water and the sun began to set. The view was exhausting.

"We've been to Saint-Tropez before, right?" Leo asked.

It took Win a moment to remember it: five years ago. A rival had beaten her to a role and unleashed a tide of rumors that Win was in a jealous rage over it; Win had needed to prove she had her mind on other things. She and Leo had spent most of the trip on a yacht anchored several bays over. She raised her hand without thinking, skimming across Leo's shoulders, warm through his crisp shirt.

"You got so badly sunburned."

She could feel his shoulder blades shifting as he walked. There was something feline about him sometimes, rangy and strong like a big cat. He'd told her once that Thea, his stepmother, had called him Leo the Lion as a child.

"Penny for your thoughts," Leo said.

"I get a higher asking price these days," Win told him. Leo smiled and looked out to the ocean, sliding his hands into his pockets. It was always harder, if they hadn't seen each other in a while, to renegotiate the boundaries of touch. It took Leo longer to settle into it, to remember that he was allowed to pull her close if he wanted. She leaned against his shoulder and he took the hint, drawing her in with an arm around her waist.

"Tell me how you've been, anyway," he said. "Aside from the asshole ex-boyfriend."

Win flinched. "Leo."

"I said *aside* from him."

Her jaw clenched. She didn't want to think about Nathan. She'd spent the last two days thinking about anything else—Leo, Saint-Tropez, her upcoming press tour, the deal with Paramount. Every now and then in the back of her head, she heard Nathan's drawling voice. *It's not as fun as you'd think, being with the most famous woman in the world. Imagine screwing a dominatrix without the sex. Eventually you're just always getting whipped and never getting off.*

"Whitman," Leo said, and Win drew a breath.

"Fine," she said. "Work's good. I'm pretty busy, I don't think I'll get a vacation this year, but—"

"This doesn't count as a vacation?"

Win tilted her head up to the cliffs, the glint of sunlight on lenses. The

8

photographers would get only candid shots, zoomed in from a distance, occasionally blurry or hidden by outcrops of rock and greenery—but the buzz would be enough, and Marie had already planned phase two for tomorrow. A flashbulb lit up as they both watched, like a signal from a far-off island: *Hello.*

"Don't look at them," Win said.

Leo turned back to her. "I take your point."

"Thanks for coming so fast," Win said. "I wasn't even sure you'd be in Europe."

"Berlin," Leo confirmed. They had to climb over a section of beach partially blocked by rockfall. Leo jumped lightly down and reached back to catch her hand, guiding Win over uncertain ground. *Click, click, click.*

"Raving?" Win asked.

"Meeting with some gallery owners," Leo said, then admitted, "which is basically the same thing there."

"Are you finally starting on the studio? I thought you wanted to set it up in New York."

"Oh, I don't know," Leo said, pressing two knuckles against his eyebrow. "I've thought about New York, but maybe somewhere on the West Coast...My dad's been asking me to look at some design plans for a new boutique place in Austin he's working on. He wants me to ship him the usual statement pieces for the lobby, you know, something he can pretend is avant-garde."

Six years ago Win had spent an afternoon with Leo trailing through a series of galleries in Miami, while Leo picked out paintings he thought would help revamp one of his dad's resorts. Leo had been determined in a way that was unusual for him. He put together a hefty list, with suggested pairings, color palettes, and ways to highlight the artists. Four days later Leo showed her the email he'd received in response, a thank-you from an assistant on his dad's design team, except she had forgotten to cut out the rest of the thread before forwarding it to Leo. His father had written: Pick a couple of the fancier ones and tell Leonard thanks.

"But here I am," Leo said, and they paused on the sand, holding each other's hands and gazing into each other's eyes. Leo's face was satisfied, like he'd designed the romantic moment himself. Win supposed he'd helped. "You saved me. Here's our stop," he added, and nodded at the chalk X Marie had marked for them on a large rock. They tumbled down together, laughing and tangling their limbs around each other in case anyone was recording video—someone probably was—until they were sitting side by side, staring out at the pink sunlight on the bay.

"I hadn't heard from you for a while," Leo said.

"I know, I'm sorry," Win said. There had been only a handful of messages over the last year, reaching quickly for him as though he were a friend she passed in the street with no time to talk, nodding without breaking stride. Normally they didn't leave it so long between seeing each other, but the past year had ripped past without Win even realizing it. Her projects had been back-to-back, and in between she was grappling with Nathan, trying to appease a man who'd begun to resent her. The wind caught at her hair, and Leo smoothed it back behind her ear. She smiled up at him. "What did I miss?"

"Ah, the usual." Leo glanced to the side, rubbing his nose with one square knuckle. "Charity galas, gallery openings. I passed out in a sweat lodge. Had visions of an archangel coming to rescue me, except she was Indian? And had this really rough London accent? Banging body, though—"

Win raised her hand to smack him on the arm, cackling, and he caught it, drawing it toward him.

"Actually, this is good timing for me. Gum's been threatening to fly out for a boys' weekend, and I was running out of excuses." He toyed with her fingers like he was remembering them, rough fingertips tracing over her manicured nails.

Geoffrey Milanowski was Leo's suit-wearing, chain-smoking older brother. He'd taken to corporate heirdom more eagerly than Leo and disgraced himself several times in the process. Gum—as Leo insisted on calling him—spent most of his time in New York, sleeping in his clothes and squinting at paperwork he didn't understand. He had a string of one-sided professional feuds, a perennially unfinished MBA, and very few friends. Gum wasn't a household name like Leo, but he was well-known enough that if a cop pulled him over on Route 101 and failed him on a breathalyzer test, the world would hear about it. And had.

"I love the guy, but Dad will just accuse me of enabling him again. I can always tell when he wants to go on a bender. *I haven't seen you for six months, mon frère, it's time to blow off some steam.*"

"Six months, really?"

"He worries about me," Leo said. "If I don't reply to one message, it's all *Leonard, you've become a recluse!*"

Leo put on a special Manhattan whine to imitate his brother. Leo himself had the sort of voice you couldn't put your finger on, because he'd lived between countries for most of his life and never settled into a standardized accent. He sounded like a Londoner and a Brooklynite and a cosmopolitan French prince all at once; it was part of why his public appeal was equally strong in Europe and America. That and the cheekbones.

Win curled her fingers against Leo's palm. Behind them she could hear the faint, far-off cries of a paparazzo calling their names. "Put your jacket on me?"

Leo shrugged his battered leather jacket off and settled it around Win's shoulders. It smelled like his cologne, and like airplanes, and a little like coffee. She looked up, and Leo was looking back at her. The air was still warm from the day's pounding sun, but it was evening now, and she could feel Leo along her side, at all the places their skin almost touched. His jacket was warm, too, like she'd stepped into the heat of his body.

"We're not doing the kiss until tomorrow," she said.

Leo didn't laugh, as she'd thought he might. He reached up and touched her cheek, long fingers sliding gently over her jawline. She didn't speak. The photos would be better if she didn't. He tapped two fingers against her mouth and said, "Understood."

They watched the last gulls of the evening career through the sky. Marie texted Win when she was sure enough photos had been taken, and they climbed back to the waiting cars.

"Any word from Paramount?" she asked Emil, once they were safely behind the tinted windows.

He shook his head, fingers flying over his phone screen; he was coordinating with the team at Chanel, with whom Win had just signed a contract to head up their next campaign. Win didn't press further. It always pained Emil to be the bearer of bad news.

Perhaps they would never hear about the role again. The film she and Patrick had been fighting for was a new adaptation of *The Sun Also Rises*. Win was in the running to play the female lead. It was an intense prestige project, with an electrifying script and big-name director attached, and the plot itself refocused on her character's storyline. Her dialogue simmered, and Win had wanted the role immediately. But the movie was also Oscar-bait, and the producers were known for their skittishness. They were already nervous about the idea of casting a British Indian woman in the lead, and the additional threat of a scandal would have them scurrying from her as fast as they could. Now Nathan had placed Win at the center of the ugliest celebrity breakup of the summer.

But, Win reminded herself, nothing had come of it yet. She hadn't been axed; no word from Patrick meant he was still working on it, and she was determined to do everything she could to alleviate Nathan's damage. With Leo on her arm, it was simple enough to pull focus. Nobody could resist the glamour of a love story. Their trip to Saint-Tropez was proof, to the producers and to the world, that Nathan's dramas were all of his own making and that Win had long since moved on.

Win and Leo shared a cigarette on the way back to La Réserve, a snake's tail of black SUVs riding along in their wake. Emil kept himself busy and pretended unconvincingly not to notice the smoke.

Win said, "Don't tell Marie."

"I'm sure her informants have already let her know," Leo said.

"I resent that, Leo," Emil said. "I haven't seen a thing."

Emil had wanted to be an actor, he once told Win, and played the newspaper boy in his college production of *A Streetcar Named Desire*. He spent the first half of the run happily categorizing the props, talking down their Stanley from the edge of despair after a costar called him "Marlon Brando with eczema," and responding to a determined missive from the dean to cut the nudity, and realized that he was much happier offstage. He handed his part over to his boyfriend and never looked back.

The professionals outside La Réserve had been joined by starstruck French teenagers, screaming Leo's name and holding up their phones with shaking hands. Win and Leo played tipsy and flirty, as though they'd been drinking champagne in the car, and Leo waved at a couple of fans with his arm around Win's shoulders, drawing her back against him. She reached up to slip her fingers through his. Everything felt familiar. His big palms, the showy rings on his fingers, and Marie waiting for them when they tripped into Win's penthouse suite.

"Hi," Win said. "I think that went pretty well."

Marie nodded. "We got some good shots. You're trending on most platforms." She came closer and sighed. "Oh, you were smoking."

"She didn't inhale," Leo said. Marie turned to him, taking in his buzz cut with pursed lips.

"Leo," she said.

"Marie."

"I've got the yacht confirmed for eleven o'clock tomorrow," Marie said to Win. "I've tipped off some paparazzi, they'll be ready to tail it. We're going to wait until we're away from the coast to do the kiss, I want it to look like you're alone."

"You going to mark another spot for us?" Leo's tone was mocking.

"Yes," Marie said, giving him a cool look. Leo and Marie had never actually fought, but they often seemed on the cusp of it. He'd made a lot of trouble for Marie in the past—she could still only mention the Met Gala incident in a guttural hiss—and in turn Marie had wrangled Leo into a lot of stunts he hadn't wanted to do. Their antagonism was well-founded, even before you got into their disagreements on what was good for Win's image.

"I'm going to get an early night," Win said. "Sorry we didn't have time to eat."

She hadn't eaten much recently, the upheaval of the last few days combined with a low anxious pit of nausea in her stomach throwing her off her meal plan. She would have breakfast tomorrow, maybe out with Leo on the terrace. Her eyes were strained, her shoulders heavy. Sleep, then food.

Leo released her hand; she had forgotten he was still holding it. He moved in closer to her, and she tilted her head up instinctively. Then she stopped.

They were hidden away in her suite, and the hotel was discreet and expensive enough that staff wouldn't leak updates to the press. There was no need to kiss good night.

"Have a nice evening," she said.

"No other warnings?"

Win shrugged. "The usual. Don't pick anyone up in the bar. But I think you're going to bed soon, anyway." There were faint shadows under his eyes, and Leo had been traveling all day as well. A week of raving in Berlin: she was pretty sure Leo would be asleep before midnight, and told him so.

Leo reached out and tugged a strand of her hair, as though testing the give. "You think you've got me all figured out."

"It's been seven years," Win said. "You can say goodbye to your secrets, Milanowski."

Leo's mouth opened, very briefly. He seemed to decide against what he had planned to say. "Sleep well," he said, and turned, hands shoved into his pockets, shoulders curling in.

Once she was alone, Win kicked off her heels and pulled out her phone. Emil had switched the SIM card two days ago and pared down her contacts to less than ten. There was a rambling voice message from Shift, her best friend, which Win listened to while she took off her jewelry. Shift didn't say anything about Nathan, just talked about the rain in Montreal and how her boyfriend Charlie had missed the delivery of her new audio mixer and wasn't even sorry about it because he'd been in the backyard at the time teaching the neighbor's dog to count to five.

It was nothing that required an immediate response. Win switched the phone off and stumbled through the door to the wide bed that was waiting for her, silk sheets, the French windows of the balcony left open and the sea air fluttering through gauze curtains. She collapsed onto it with her laptop, scanning idly through social media, watching the first stirrings of hysteria grow. When she finally slept, she slept restlessly.

CHAPTER TWO

Since she was twenty years old, Win had been two different people, living two different lives.

The first person was the Win who had, give or take some adolescent angst, always existed. Win grew up running wild with her best friend in North East London and then, determined to make a name for herself, grew decidedly less wild. She worked fourteen-hour days in the rain or dark. She had an acidic gift for mimicry, a complicated relationship with her mother, and a bad temper. This was the Win who attended late-night crisis meetings with Marie and spent hours alone with a script trying to talk her way into character. As a teenager, this Win had wanted two things very badly: for her father to get better, and to be given the chance to make it as an actor. She got one of them.

The second person, the second life that Win lived was as Whitman Tagore, international movie star, youngest woman to win a Leading Actress BAFTA, and venerated in both London and Hollywood. Win and Marie had spent the past seven years perfecting Whitman Tagore, testing her angles, honing her glossy edges, working and reworking her flaws. By this point, she was a masterpiece.

Whitman Tagore was never tired. Whitman Tagore was never angry. Whitman Tagore was never wasted. She worked hard, but she didn't do anything crude like sweat off her makeup, starve herself for a role, or take pills to keep herself awake. Most of all, Whitman Tagore was calm. She did not blink when cameras flashed in her face. She did not respond when talk show hosts speculated about her sex life. She could be emotional, but only when it became her; she could cry prettily as she accepted an award, but she could not sob in the back of a taxi. She could admit experiencing racism and sexism at the hands of the film industry, but she could never accuse a specific man of harassing her. Beneath the folds of this calm no move was uncalculated, no facial expression unplanned. Marie had written the mantra. *Stay calm. Don't panic. Stick to the narrative.*

There hadn't always been two Whitmans. For a while, she had hoped that Win would be good enough for the world. But the split from her real self that she kept closely guarded and the self she presented to the public was not gradual. It happened all at once, seven years ago. A Sunday. It was the day Josip sent the recording to the *Daily Mail*.

Win had been in America, sliding from bit parts in ensemble comedies to sidekick roles in romantic dramas. She didn't have a name for herself yet, but she was creeping slowly into the public consciousness, the newcomer Indian actress with deadpan delivery and a skill for stealing a scene even when she was the character with the least lines.

It had been jarring, to see herself described as an "Indian" actress. Win had grown up distinguishing between British Asians like herself and real *Indian* Indians like her parents and extended family. Becoming well-known in America meant allowing that boundary to slip away. "Yes, we don't want people to put you in a box," her agent Patrick agreed, "but we also don't want people to feel confused by you." *British with Indian heritage* was too long and clunky, and Americans didn't use the label *British Asian*. *British* on its own left people feeling deceived, like there was something she was trying to hide. Let it go, Patrick advised her. You're Indian, but you grew up in England and you have a white first name, so you're not *too* Indian. They can call you what they want as long as they're casting you. Just don't let them make you do the accent.

At the time she was in New York for a series of meetings with Patrick and a director they had been pursuing. Gigi Waits had just received her first Oscar for Best Director, the second woman to ever do so, and she was known for scooping up lesser known talents and transforming them into overnight stars. Her expectations as a director were well-known: Her cast should be disciplined. They should be happy to redo the same scene forty times without pause. They should be prepared to spend hours simulating hysteria. They should be ready to learn languages, instruments, fighting styles—and quickly. Win was desperate to work with Gigi, who would push her and strain her and bring the acclaim and success Win needed to turn a few fledgling achievements into a career.

That Sunday, Win and Patrick were invited for brunch at Gigi's loft in the East Village, and it was in the cab on the way over that Patrick's phone started ringing. Win never found out who was on the other end of the line—an assistant maybe, or a gloating rival. Whoever it was, Patrick's face dropped as if someone had died. He stared at Win in disbelief. Win must have looked confused, but a part of her, somehow, knew that Josip had done something terrible.

The voicemail that her ex-boyfriend sent the *Hollywood Reporter*, in exchange for an undisclosed sum of cash and a boost to the sales of his band's new album, had been recorded three weeks earlier while Win was still in the UK. When Patrick played it to her in the back seat of the taxi, she could barely recognize herself. She didn't remember saying those things. She only remembered calling Josip very late at night, alone in her flat between a flickering streetlight and an empty highball glass.

What are you supposed to do when your boyfriend of a year goes to a club with another girl, grinding close and smirking as they kiss, her hand already disappearing into his jeans? Do you pretend not to believe it? What about when you try to confront him and he doesn't speak to you for four days? Are you supposed to just take the hint and let him unstitch himself from your life? What if you haven't slept because of your filming schedule and you're on a no-dairy-no-sugar diet, so your only indulgence is vodka sodas? What if you look the girl up online and she seems to be everything you're not—laid-back, fun, unfazed? Doesn't it make sense to pick up the phone and wait for the inevitable beep?

Nobody heard any of that, though. They only heard Win's dark, vicious snarl on the voicemail, the cruel twist of her words as she swore to hate Josip for the rest of her life, the half-sneered jeer about his terrible music, how he was going nowhere and fast, how she didn't and had never needed him.

The recording spent two days on the front page of every gossip site in the UK, and at least half of the American ones, too. Josip was the lead singer of a mediocre Illinois rock band with a few lucky singles, but he was handsome and he knew how to command attention. It was what had attracted Win to him in the first place; now, it attracted a pack of late-night talk shows all too happy to laugh about crazy ex-girlfriends and give his album a plug in the process. Win's status was transformed from the interesting new girl to an international joke.

She would listen to the voicemail hundreds of times in the coming months. Presenters quoted it to her at interviews. Late-night hosts played it for their guests, who laughed merrily along. For a while a meme made the rounds where people performed it in their best weeping diva voices, fake mascara tear stains smeared across their faces, and "Hey, asshole, I'm just calling to tell you to go fuck yourself" became the standard opener for all ironic whiny tweets. She forced herself to replay it late at night, when she wanted a reminder of why she could never let it happen again.

"It's all right," Patrick said in the taxi, although he wasn't making eye contact. "It's just a voicemail. It's not like you did something illegal." It was the first time he had lied to her.

Gigi didn't even let them in the building. "My actors need to have self-control," she was quoted saying a few days later. "I'm not interested in working with divas." She never spoke to Win again, and Win's role was unceremoniously given to someone else. Other roles she had been chasing folded, too. She and Patrick went from rushing between ten meetings per day to barely rustling up three in a week. Party invitations were revoked. Callbacks were retracted. The only people who wanted to talk to her were entertainment journalists who called incessantly and left simpering messages explaining that they just wanted *her side of the story*. A hive of photographers sprang up in front of her hotel, hoping to catch a glimpse of Whitman Tagore wading through the burning wreckage of her short career. That was why Marie came to her hotel, the first time they met. They held the meeting in Win's suite to save her from having to step outside.

The first question Marie asked was if Win had spoken with other publicists. Win felt suddenly embarrassed to tell the truth: no, she had not. Before that week she had never considered needing one. Publicists were for reality TV stars scrambling for likes and views, or for influencers looking to sidestep the tough climb up to fame. Win was an actress. She was a professional. She almost said no when Patrick handed over Marie's business card. Then a photographer called her a crazy bitch as she was getting into her taxi, and Win decided some principles weren't worth dying for.

"I've looked into a couple," she told Marie. "You're the only one I've met in person."

Marie nodded. "That's good. It's best to speak to as few people as possible, during a crisis period."

A few weeks before, Win would have dismissed the idea of calling this a crisis. It seemed so petty. A stumbling relationship, infidelity, an untamed outburst. Now, Win only needed to switch the TV to an entertainment channel to confirm Marie's assessment.

"What we need," Marie said, "is to throw you back out there. Right now, this voicemail is all that Americans know about you. You're just this crazy British girl who's come out of nowhere. We need to show people another side of you. And that side has to be much more interesting."

Marie's idea was to send Win off to a glitzy party looking fabulous and untroubled. She would wear pale colors, and her hair would be down. She needed to look young, innocent, and carefree, like the sort of girl who only ever raised her voice to shriek in delight. She would smile with a self-deprecating sigh when questioned about the voicemail, but she would not go into details. She would attend with a date.

"I can pull in a favor and get that new French model from Balmain," Marie said, as if she were suggesting a rental car. She swiped through something on her phone. "Oh, but he's shorter than you. Better not. You need to look like the weaker one in the relationship."

Even in those early days, Marie was unabashed in her strategic management of other people. She didn't have a problem explaining her thinking to Win, no matter how uncomfortable the truth might be. Once, a few years after all this, Marie had scanned an article about an actress's son and said, "That child really limits her likability," with no inflection at all.

"Oh, how about this," Marie said. "The Horizons Group is launching a new hotel in Brooklyn tonight. It's going to be a very public event, lots of New York celebrities. Plenty of press."

Win, who had been dogged by the press and sneered at by New York celebrities for the past week, said, "That sounds good."

"I haven't told you the best part yet," Marie said. "The Horizons Group is owned by Bernard Milanowski, and he gets one of his kids to come to every launch. This time it's the youngest son—Leo."

Win had heard of Leo Milanowski before. The playboy son of a millionaire hotel mogul and a reclusive ex-supermodel. Rarely seen without a cluster of socialites around him. Caught between America and the UK, and famous for being famous in both.

"I have a source in Bernard's office who says they're still hunting down a date for him. Bernard wants someone who will make a splash, drum up more attention for the hotel, you know." Marie looked at Win. Sometimes Win wondered if Marie had tiny crosshairs printed on the back of her eyes. "They want someone people will be desperate to see."

As Win dressed for the party that evening, she watched Whitman Tagore appear in the mirror: the heavy dark hair, the high cheekbones, a winding silhouette and huntress shoulders. She practiced playing herself as a role, keeping her real self hidden. She practiced her smile. "Don't look so pleased with yourself," Marie said, and so she switched to the wide-eyed, agog expression of posh London girls that she and Shift used to laugh at. She was Whitman Tagore, who wanted nothing more than to go to a party with a spoiled It boy. While she slipped into her heels and pulled on a cape of pale silk, Marie briefed her as though she were a soldier about to go into the field.

"There's a line of press as you walk into the building. They will be hard on you. Maybe the other guests, too. Milanowski won't pull anything at his dad's own party, but he won't defend you, either, if things get tough. It's okay. Just keep calm, and keep smiling. Stick to our narrative."

Win met Leo for the first time in the back of a black sedan. There was less fanfare than she had been expecting, no elaborate greeting, no stilted introduction from Marie or one of Leo's entourage. As she slipped into the car, he said, "Just ask the band to start later."

He waved at her and mouthed, *On the phone*, as if Win couldn't see the cell phone tucked under his ear. Leo Milanowski had a strong, handsome face, a sharp jawline dappled with stubble that seemed designed to frame his mouth, and disarmingly long eyelashes. He wore what Win guessed was a very expensive suit with negligent ease, and he looked bored and a little sleepy, like a commuter on the tube, as though he hadn't noticed the lush leather interior of his surroundings or the actress sitting beside him.

"No, I won't be there for long," Leo said, running his fingers idly through the hair that curled over his forehead. "Just need to shake some hands." He laughed at something the other person said.

He stayed on the phone for the whole drive, leaving Win to watch Manhattan slide past them in silence, unsure if she was annoyed or grateful for the peace. She resisted checking her phone too often; recently it had only brought her bad news. She stared out the window and tried to relax.

When they stepped out onto the street, there was a storm of camera flashes. At the sight of Win and Leo, the thicket of paparazzi surged forward, the assembled line of security barely holding them back. They were all calling her name.

Leo leaned in so his mouth was almost touching her ear.

"Hi," he said, "hand on your back, or arm in arm?"

"Excuse me?"

"I'm a hand on the back guy, personally, but it's your call."

They were talking out of the sides of their mouths, with security waiting around them. Win remembered Marie's comment this afternoon. She needed to appear vulnerable, pitiable. The weaker one.

"Why don't you come closer?" she said.

Leo gave her a quick, assessing look, then put his arm around her shoulders, pulling her against his side. She turned her face toward his chest. He was very warm, this close, and when he ran his fingers gently through the hair falling over the nape of her neck, she didn't have to fake the shiver.

They walked into the party like that, arms around each other and turned away from the flash of cameras. When she peeked up at him, Leo's face was quiet and calm, almost possessive. He was a good actor, too, she realized.

In the lobby he uncurled his arm from her shoulder.

"No offense," he said, "but if I was you, I probably would've stayed at home."

Win smoothed down her dress and patted her hair to make sure it was still in place.

"Unfortunately, staying at home was not an option."

"Tell me about it," Leo said.

They sized each other up, an odd moment of stillness in the middle of the party. It wasn't the usual up-and-down look Win was used to from potential love interests; it was more calculating than that, more thoughtful. Win wondered what the possibility was of Leo selling his Whitman Tagore story to the press. She wasn't sure what Leo was thinking.

The walls of the lobby were decked out in graffiti paint (the graffiti artists, Leo told Win later, had been flown in from Paris and Rio de Janeiro, and their designs had been vetted by a team of six executives before they were allowed to start painting). Below the chandeliers, whose bulbs flickered to create a seedy, urban effect, guests mingled and waiters toting trays of champagne circulated among the crowd. The golden reception desk had been dented and artfully tarnished to give the illusion of decay.

"Edgy," Win said, surveying it.

"Thaaaat's Daddy," Leo said.

People had already begun to notice them. Back then, Leo's fame far dwarfed Win's, so he was getting most of the curious looks and hopeful waves, but there was a ripple running through the crowd, too, a snarky, sideways lowering of voices and narrowing of eyes, and Win knew that was just for her.

"You could pretend to faint," Leo said, keeping his voice low so only she could hear him. "That would get us both out of it."

"No," Win said. "I'm fine. I am having a *good* time."

The corner of Leo's mouth twitched, but he didn't argue. He offered his hand and Win took it, linking their fingers together. She leaned against Leo's side, like she was overwhelmed and needed him to protect her. It felt strange to be acting in real life; Win kept wanting to apologize to him. But Leo only looked entertained.

"Let's go get some drinks," he said.

"Strong ones."

They stuck together. Leo declared himself "unmoved" by the rest of the guests, and Win was tense the entire time, focused on her resolve to be as Whitman Tagore as possible: open, harmless, calm. After a week inside the media firestorm, she was constantly expecting attack, and it was only Leo's hand on the small of her back that kept her from her instinct to cut and run. Leo seemed to notice. When a probing New York columnist was getting a little too familiar for comfort, he leaned into her ear and said, "Honey, can I steal you for a moment?"

Win couldn't thank him properly, with so many people around, but she could return the favor when she saw him cornered by a grabby trustee. She caught his arm with affected urgency. "Darling, your father needs you."

They ran into Bernard Milanowski in the smoking lounge. Bernard had the same discerning stare as Leo, the same demanding jut of his chin, except Bernard expected obedience, not attention. He gave Win one abrupt, comprehensive look, and nodded at Leo. Win tensed and straightened without thinking. A second later, she realized Leo had, too. He let Win respond monosyllabically to Bernard's prosaic questions about how they found the party while he stared distantly over his father's head.

Win knew Bernard had only invited her as bait for the press. She got the impression he found her presence to be a distasteful necessity, like having to tip a maître d' to get the best table. After he excused himself, Win and Leo let out twin sighs of relief.

"I'm not a cliché, by the way," Leo said, as they escaped to the balcony. "I don't hate my dad. I just don't care for him."

"You're very complex," Win agreed. She turned as something caught her eye. There was a waiter a few feet away with an empty tray tucked under his arm. He was leaning against the railing with one hand hanging carelessly at his side, his phone angled toward them as if by accident. Win couldn't tell if he was taking photos or filming. She nudged Leo very gently, nodding in the waiter's direction. Leo kept his face casual as he glanced over his shoulder.

"He could probably get fired for that," she said.

"Well," Leo said, turning back to her, "let's make it worth his while."

Win's breath caught as Leo waited just long enough to give her the chance to tell him no, and then he pressed forward against her in a sudden, lilting kiss. His mouth was warm. She could feel his chest against hers, the press of muscle on silk. Win brought a hand up to cup his cheek, which was cleared of stubble but still faintly rough, and she felt his grip tighten on her waist. People would be looking.

Leo broke off, and she let her hand slide down to his neck.

"Too much?" he murmured.

She almost laughed; it was almost funny. She'd popped one foot up when he kissed her, not on purpose but instinctively, and she brought it down now. She could imagine the director in the corner, shouting, *Cut!*

"We got it," Win said.

Leo eyed her, making some judgment that she couldn't track or decipher.

"Whitman Tagore," he said. "Would you like to share a joint?"

Even six months later, by then a diligent pupil in what Leo called Marie's House of Shame, Win couldn't believe she'd risked it. She didn't know Leo then, and if he'd wanted he could have destroyed her with one well-timed photograph catching her in the act. Win knew better than to put her faith in handsome strangers. But that night she looked up into Leo's secretive, smiling face and realized that an evening that should have been an ordeal was turning out to be the most fun she'd had in weeks.

The rooftop was not quite finished, Astroturf half rolled down, wheelbarrows and tools still kicking around. Leo and Win slipped out of view of the open door and over to the edge. There was no sound or sign of the party. Leo's weed was strong but friendly, relaxing Win's shoulders further.

"How many of these do you go to?" Win asked, and Leo considered, taking another hit.

"One or two a year. My siblings and I trade them off," he said. "We used to go together but one time my brother brought this really shitty acid, and me and my sister nearly drowned in the champagne fountain. Gum freaked out and tried to do CPR on a statue. Dad said we were a bad influence on each other, so now it's one kid per launch."

Win wheezed with laughter, tucking her nose against Leo's shoulder. She always got touchy when she was high, but he didn't seem to mind, slouching obligingly so she had better access.

"Then for a while I brought my own dates," Leo continued. "But when I was eighteen I was seeing this German pop star—"

"I had a German boyfriend when I was seventeen," Win said, remembering him fondly. "Germans go hard."

"Germans go hard," Leo agreed. "And we, uh, we snuck off to have sex in the lift and we hit the emergency stop so no one would know, but we didn't notice when they fixed it and the doors opened in the middle of the party . . . Dad was not happy. So now I don't usually get to pick my own dates."

"How have I not seen photos of this?"

"Oh, Dad has five different law firms on retainer for shit like this. There was my sister's motorbike period, and the time I got uppers mixed up with poppers, and another time at the White House Correspondents' Dinner where they decided for some reason it would be a good idea to have a separate party for anyone underage. Politicians' kids are fucking crazy, there were these two senators' daughters passing me between them—"

"Oh, it's been a hard life," Win said, but she couldn't stop laughing. They exchanged quick, pleased glances, testing each other out, liking what they found.

"Well, you've had a normal childhood," he said. "I don't know many people like that. It's mysterious."

"Very mysterious," Win agreed, and told him about the raves she and Shift used to go to and the window in her family home she used to climb back through until her mum wearily told her that she might as well just use the front door. Leo had lived in London on and off for years, but he didn't know the curry houses in Aldgate where Win and her father used to go after school, or the house parties in Brixton out of whose windows Win had thrown up only a few years earlier. Hilariously, he thought he might have seen Shift play one of her early Dalston nightclub residencies, two years ago now: "That's my best friend!" Win said, pounding on his shoulder in glee.

"Maybe we were both there," Leo said, and gallantly offered her the last hit.

They swanned back to the party, Win's hand clasped lightly in Leo's, ducking around models and moguls. People were still staring at them, but now the whole thing felt ridiculous, Upper East Side snobs slumming it in Brooklyn, pretending to rough it while they sneered at the disgraced Whitman Tagore. It made her laugh, and Leo laughed, too, without asking what the joke was. Win felt high and satisfied, as though she could reach through the mess and noise to create the party she wanted, all the danger of the evening made impotent like a defanged snake.

The next morning, it was the sheer volume of photographs that shocked her the most. They had been immortalized in film at every moment of the party: Win and Leo catching eyes over another guest's shoulder. Win and Leo dissolving into laughter at some forever-private joke. Leo tucking his chin over Win's shoulder as he excused her from a discussion with one of the Horizons investors. Win and Leo sequestered away in secretive corners, looking as if they were whispering things too intimate to repeat. And of course, the kiss. His hands in her hair, the kick up of her heel as she leaned into him. Afterward she had bitten her lip and smiled, and their waiter had caught that, too.

Win went through the fourth, seventh, tenth gossip article about them. They looked unbelievable together. She thought suddenly that it was downright selfish of Leo not to be a real actor. Directors dreamed of this kind of chemistry. She only stopped clicking when her phone rang.

"Marie," Win said. "I need to talk to—"

"I have him on the other line," Marie said. "Did you see the *Post*? I'm sending you a link to the front page right now."

Under an overly excited headline, the main shot was of Win and Leo waiting for their car. There had been a brief shower of rainfall, and security was too preoccupied with the photographers to bring them an umbrella. Instead Win held her silk cape up for both of them and they huddled under it together, Leo's hand wrapped around her waist, his eyes sparkling between camera flashes. The caption below the photo read:

> Whitman Tagore and Leo Milanowski leaving the party. Exactly how long the dream romance has been going on is unclear, but by the look of these pics, these two know each other...shall we say...intimately. Looks like the witch has jumped off her broom and into bed.

Below the article, comments were reeling in on an endless feed.

> omg whitman tagore and leo milanowski!! im SO WEIRDLY into this!

> ugh that dress is giving me LIFE

how long has this been going on??

is she trolling us?

sucks to be josip lol

couple of the year tbh

"This is a big deal," Marie said. "If we play it right, it could totally eclipse the voicemail. It could do more than that—it will make people love you. All we need to do is give them more."

Win laughed. She hadn't thought it would be this easy. Just find another boy and make him like you, and the world will follow suit.

"Hey," Leo said once Marie had patched him through. "Your assistant is pretty intense."

"She's not my assistant."

Leo made a disinterested noise; he was harder to read over the phone, when Win couldn't follow his body language and his cue. "What can I do for you, Whitman Tagore?"

She tried to sound nervous, in case that might appeal to him. "I'm just— I wanted to say thank you."

"You're welcome," he said. "Although, you should probably say what you're thanking me for—was it thank you for the *Post* or thank you for *BuzzFeed*?"

"You've seen the pictures," Win said.

"They were hard to miss."

"Well—thank you. For all of it. I had a really good time with you."

"Likewise."

There was a pause. Even without him in the room, she could feel his amusement. He was enjoying holding back, waiting to see what she was going to say next.

"Leo." She made her voice breathy, like she was pent up with excitement rather than determination. "I don't know what it is about you. I'd really like to see you again."

He laughed. "Is that your best line? Did your assistant write it for you?"

"She isn't my assistant," Win repeated, irritated.

"Try again," Leo said. "I want a better story."

"Okay, I don't know what it is about *us*. But people like it. I think we have..."

"Chemistry?" Leo suggested.

"I was going to say stage presence."

He laughed again. "So what are you asking me for?"

Win paused. When she first started acting, it was because she was good at it, because it was where she felt best in the world, inhabiting a character and making them real. Her father had loved that about her. He'd told her that she had a gift and that she shouldn't squander it. She was sure that this—investing in herself as a brand, making people care about her personal life and not her work—was not what he'd meant.

But it was becoming clear that her work wasn't enough. And if she didn't want to squander her gift, if she wanted to stay true to her ambition and her father's belief in her, she would have to make sure that she got the opportunities she needed. To do that, she had to be liked. With Leo, she would be loved.

Win took a steadying breath. "I want us to pretend to date. I want to be seen with you, and I want us to look good."

Leo was silent for a moment. If he was impressed with her honesty, he didn't admit it. Eventually he asked, "And what's in it for me?"

"You seem bored," she said. She thought of Leo's lazy gaze drifting around the party, the way his focus had narrowed in on her. Leo seemed to like playing games. Maybe he would accept her as a teammate. "I thought you could do with a project."

Leo laughed again, short and delighted this time, like she'd caught him off guard. "I'm flying back to London next week for my friend's gallery opening. You can have me for eight days. How's that?"

"I think that will work," Win said. She sank back into her chair. She was smiling. "As long as you put on a good show."

"If you show me a good time," Leo said, so that Win could hear him grinning over the phone, "the rest of the world will have a good time, too. I promise."

Annoyingly, he was right.

CHAPTER THREE

The days that started with Marie instead of Emil were never good. The morning after Leo arrived in Saint-Tropez, Win was out of the shower and applying her moisturizer when Marie knocked on her door and came in, face hard.

Win was immediately on guard. "What," she said.

"Nathan Spencer went off on last night's show," Marie said. "It's been doing the rounds online all night. You can watch it, or I can just tell you which questions to expect."

Jada and Matthew, Win's hair and makeup team, paused laying out compacts and curling wands. "You want us out, honey?" Matthew asked.

Win made a face, smoothing cream down her jawline, over her décolletage. "Better not, we're already running late. You've seen worse," she said, and Jada winked at her.

Marie propped a tablet on the dressing table and hit play. Win glanced at it and then back to Matthew as he moved in, brandishing concealer like it was the answer to all their problems. Nathan was surrounded by his usual panel of celebrity guests, loosely organized into teams, even more loosely organized into the idea of a game. He wore a dark suit, and his eyes were glittering.

"I mean, speaking of celebrity romance," said a young guy whom Win recognized as having just transitioned from a soap opera to a

Victorian BBC drama, "we've got to— Are you still pretending not to know what we're talking about?"

"I'm sure I don't know what you mean," Nathan said. "Little old me and my little old nondisclosure agreement, we haven't got a clue—"

"Oh my god," another guest said, manicured red nails pressed to her mouth. "An NDA! That's the big guns. That's how you know you've messed that relationship up."

"Actually, I object to that," Nathan said. Win didn't need to look at the screen to know what he'd be doing; eyes sparkling with that laddish mischief that so endeared him to viewers, waggling a finger in jest. "I didn't mess anything up enough to deserve an NDA, that was brought out on our first date."

Jada hissed, fingers gentle on Win's hair. Win said, "Oh, for fuck's sake." She tilted her chin up when Matthew nudged her.

"Wait," Marie said grimly.

"Guess that's the price you pay, innit?" the first guest said. "When you're dating, like, the most beautiful woman in the world—"

"You pay a lot of prices, is the thing," Nathan said. "First it's the NDA, then it's being told where to go, what to wear, what to say. You end up having her publicist on speed dial, instead of her. Then you get told that certain things about you don't suit her image, and you have to change them, and you start to realize you don't even recognize yourself, let alone her, and when even her mum thinks it's a bad idea—"

"Oh my god," the latest *X-Factor* winner yelped. "Really?"

"Oh yeah, mate," Nathan said, laughing. "It makes sense for the mum to be a bit more involved. Every guy's a prospective son-in-law, you know. But she warned me off. Said that I was a nice kid and *my daughter's media machine will eat you alive, dear boy.*" This last was delivered in a cartoonish, head-bobbing imitation of Pritha's accent. Win didn't think Pritha had ever used the words *dear boy* in her life.

There was a general round of gasps, and he held his hands up, still smiling enough to make the whole thing look like a grand joke. "It was a bit like getting a bad diagnosis from your doctor. Did what I was told, didn't I. I bolted."

"Looks like she's not exactly pining, mate," the first woman said, and the audience went, *Ooooooh.*

Nathan was still laughing but his eyes were hard. "Ah well. Signing NDAs is probably the only thing keeping life interesting, when you've got no other talents to speak of—"

"Someone's jealous," the *X-Factor* winner said.

"Sorry, I forgot," Nathan said. "He's an artist, right? *Daddy, will you buy me another gallery?*" and the audience fell apart with laughter.

Marie paused the video. "Then they start talking about the most spoiled people in show business, but he doesn't bring you or Leo up again."

Something yawned, hungry and lonely, in the pit of Win's belly. It was as though Nathan and Pritha—clearly conspirators—were leaning over her shoulders, Pritha's disdain in one ear and Nathan's disgust in the other, and Win cold and stranded between the two. Jada and Matthew were watching her closely, faces sympathetic. Under their scrutiny and Marie's keen gaze, Win drew herself upright. "Has anyone spoken to my mother?"

Marie hesitated. "I wanted to talk to you first. I'm not sure if you want to talk to her or let me—"

"I don't have time for this now," Win said, and pushed the tablet away. "You call her."

"Whitman—"

"It's fine." She shook her head. "Are we saying anything?"

"It looks better if you stay quiet," Marie said, "at least for now. I'll leak some insider quotes about how you're too caught up reconnecting with an old friend to care." She looked back at the frozen image of his smile. "I give him two years." Marie had an uncanny ability to calculate a celebrity's use-by date, the moment attention would shift and they wouldn't know how to hold it.

"What about Paramount?"

"Patrick has a breakfast meeting with them in LA. I'm on damage control. If it goes away quickly, it won't be a big deal. You and Leo will need to put on a good show. We should get the first kiss on the yacht."

"We can do that," Win said.

Marie had an entourage of famous friends queued for the yacht, and outside the sky was flooded with sunlight, swept like a carpet over the bay. While Matthew and Jada were finishing her hair and zipping her into the day's outfit, Marie called Win's mum in another room. After that Win's phone buzzed a few times, texts from Pritha that read Call me please and then Whitman call me now, until she gave her phone to Emil.

"Only important work-related stuff, please," she said.

"On it," Emil said. Win loved him at these moments, brisk and businesslike, uninterested in the messy details. He'd always been able to sympathize with her about Pritha—Emil's parents didn't understand his job, either, wanting him to come home ten times as often as he did, and as the child of Haitian immigrants he understood the kind of gap between parents and children that spanned more than just years. Win let him blame his absences on her, his overbearing boss. More than once she had wailed, "Emil!" in her best diva voice to give him an excuse to cut a video chat short. In return he had no scruples about helping Win avoid the calls that she really ought to take.

"Is Leo ready?"

"Well," Emil said. "He's dressed."

"Just send him in," Win said.

Leo was sporting a linen shirt, boyish blue jeans, and that sly look he got when he knew she was in trouble.

"Ah, the monster herself." He leaned down to kiss her cheek, and

Win jerked backward, eyes narrowed. Sometimes it unsettled her when Leo touched her in private. She didn't know how to react. She always felt too hot. "You look radiant this morning. No one would think you'd been up all night, eating hearts, oiling up the media machine—"

Win put two fingers to her temple and massaged. "Leo—"

"You have really shitty taste. I think this is worse than that girl I dated," Leo said, flinging himself into a chair. "What's-her-face."

"Kristina."

"Yeah," Leo said. "Definitely worse than her."

"She set fire to your car, Leo," Win said.

Leo made a dismissive gesture. "So what?"

"I mean," Win said, "she threw a brick through the window, and then she *set fire to your car*, but sure, make fun of me—"

"Hey," Leo said, grinning, "at least she wasn't mean about my mum."

"Technically, if my mum wasn't so judgy—"

"Aw, don't you start on her," Leo said. "She didn't deserve an impression."

"My mum's a judgy bitch about you, too, you know."

"I know," Leo said. "That's my type."

Win seized a hard little embroidered cushion and hurled it at his face.

Leo caught it, laughing. "C'mon, Whitman, don't be like that—"

He took Win's hand on the way to the elevator.

"I'm just saying. Wasn't some of that stuff a bit...overboard? The son-in-law thing? The *accent*?"

"Yeah, but what do you want me to do, Leo?" Win said. "Release a press statement calling Nathan Spencer racist? People will say I'm playing the race card because I'm mad that he talked shit about me."

Leo gave her a disappointed look that she had seen several times before. It wasn't the first time he had been eager for her to denounce someone for an off-color comment. He had too much belief in her and thought that with a little push she could change the world; he also had no real idea of what the consequences of that push would be. He was naive enough to think that Win would be given the same respect as him, if she only spoke up.

"But what if you're playing the race card because he was racist?"

Win shook her head. "If people care about that, they'll figure it out on their own. Nobody needs to hear it from me. They're too busy hating me."

"Oh, people love to hate you," Leo said, drawing her in close, ready for the elevator doors to open. He swung his arm around her neck, and Win tilted toward him in a gesture of intimacy. "I just mean it's okay to hate them back. Especially an asshole like that."

"Of course I hate Nathan," Win said. "I just don't think it would help anything to say so."

Then they were out on the hotel steps and walking into the glare of flashing cameras, Win's bodyguards a circle around them. Win deployed her devil-may-care smile, while the paparazzi yelled questions at her about Nathan and her mum and whether she controlled all her boyfriends like this.

"Leo," one guy yelled, "hey, Leo, did you catch *Lad Rags* last night?"

"Nah," Leo said. His arm hooked around Win's neck, drawing her in closer. Win turned, her nose brushing his jawline, and Leo gave the paparazzo the slow, cocky grin that got him plastered over front pages. "I've been busy."

Behind the tinted windows of the car he let her go, leaned back, and waited. Win put her hand over her mouth, hiding her smile.

"All right," Marie said, lips twitching, "that was pretty good."

Leo stuck his feet up on the opposite seat with aplomb.

Win reclaimed her phone from Emil and texted her mum: Now who's in the magazines?? Everything fine, talk to you later, love you xx. Then she let Leo make fun of Nathan all the way to the harbor.

Seven years ago, the interest in Leo Milanowski and Whitman Tagore hadn't died when the novelty of their relationship did. After their first date at the Lattimore Hotel, every day they spent in each other's company attracted more crowds, more headlines, more feverish online speculation. The press was wild for them. Everyone was wild for them. Whenever they were together it was like they were disgraced politicians, or the Beatles; cameras followed them everywhere, and Win learned to enjoy performing for them. Her fame had shifted again, from the serious-eyed teenage actor the *Guardian* had called "the first wholly original talent to arrive in British cinema in a long time" to the American meme, a stand-in for hysterical ex-girlfriends everywhere, to this: Hollywood's darling, a romantic fantasy roaming city streets, careless and beautiful, caught close in Leo's arms. She couldn't look away from him, and nobody else could look away from her.

In that first week in New York, they veered from nightclubs in Manhattan to upstate wanders through apple orchards, from lunches with phone number–sized bills that Leo threw his card onto without interest to late-night runs to the bodega, the two of them hand in hand, dodging the paparazzi and screaming with laughter.

Win supposed it should have been exhausting or dull, but Leo was neither of those things. Instead, he flung himself into every scheduled activity with a kind of laconic glee that kept her constantly awake. Leo would derail plans if he could, but he never ruined them. He took great pleasure in making things difficult for Marie, but after the first night when Win caught his attention, he saw her as a coconspirator, someone who could be talked into fun, someone whose concerns should be taken seriously but not absolutely.

They weren't particularly similar people. She disagreed with him all the time, and he was more than happy to fight back. It seemed to make it better, not worse, like the juddering energy between them was lighting them up, like they were emitting their own spotlights.

"If you seriously think," Win had said as Leo helped her into the creaking wooden Cyclone car on Coney Island, both of them acting like they hadn't noticed the group of teenagers below screaming their names, "that privacy is a luxury and not a right, you must be either a self-sabotaging moron or the world's most ridiculous narcissist."

"Aw, Whitman," Leo said. "I can't be both?" He put his arm around her as they jerked into high gear, and by dinner, there were photos of them both flashing peace signs at the roller coaster camera all over the internet.

Two days later, on a private walk in the Hamptons with paid paparazzi cropping up every half mile or so, Leo argued, "But you can't control what other people think of you. That's just subjectivity at work—"

"That's completely different!" Win said. "People can decide whatever they like about me, but they don't need unlimited access to my personal life to make the decision."

"They don't have that," Leo said, and shrugged out of his leather jacket, tucking it around her shoulders. She gazed up at him. There was a man twenty feet away scrambling over a boulder to get his shot, and Win kept laughing, unable to get over how silly the whole thing was, but all that meant was the photos splashed over tabloids the next day gloated over her happiness, their infatuation with one another. TEENAGE DREAM, the headline screamed, though in actual fact Win and Leo were both twenty then, separated by a season.

Somewhere along the line, the kisses started to linger. They began to take on an unscripted quality. Win told herself she was taking the initiative. She was an actor, getting into character. She let herself look longer and longer at Leo, the width of his shoulders, his big hands, the secretive curve of his mouth. Whenever she looked at him, he was always looking back at her.

"I can allow people subjectivity without having to give up my privacy," Win said as they leaned opposite each other in the hotel's lift. It was fairly common knowledge that Win and Leo had booked into a suite in East Hampton; no one seemed to notice that there were two bedrooms up there. "That's not fair."

Leo shrugged. "It's not fair that I've got money and other people don't."

"Please," Win scoffed. "You think the way to make that fair is to smile nice for the paparazzi? Why don't you give away all your money, rich boy?"

"Oh, my father wouldn't like that," Leo said, laughing now. "You just have to remember it doesn't matter what people think."

"Maybe it doesn't matter for you," Win said. "But that's because your career doesn't depend on it."

Leo was fixing them drinks from the private bar, but he paused to look at her.

"You're talented, Win. I don't think your career depends on what random people say about you."

He seemed to believe it, too. Win didn't have the heart to argue with him, even though the episode with Josip and her voicemail had taught her exactly how wrong he was.

But Leo had been born into fame. He had always lived his life doing whatever he liked and still being adored, whether he was falling drunk out of cars or attending charity launches. He only had a handful of people that he needed to please: his father, his mothers, and his siblings. It would take much more than a nasty breakup to harm their legacy. The press could forgive Leo for things that would have them baying for Win's blood. Leo courted public opinion as a mark of respect to his family brand, but he had no producers to impress, no directors to charm, no casting managers to convince that he had the right image for a role. His dreams, if he had any, were unlikely to collapse at his feet.

Patrick had told Win seriously when he signed her that he believed she could make it to the big leagues; in the same breath, he warned her to expect significant pushback. Win didn't need him to fill in the gaps. It wasn't like Hollywood was full of Indian movie stars. Almost none had made it past the sidekick computer geek role. If Win messed this up, she wouldn't get a second chance, and it wasn't unreasonable to expect that Hollywood wouldn't take a chance on another Indian heroine for a long time after that.

It wasn't enough just to work hard and stay true to herself. People needed to like her. They needed to like the Whitman Tagore act that she performed for them, because that was what made them want to see her movies, and she needed an audience so she could keep doing what she loved. When they saw her and Leo living a fantasy romance, they loved it, and they wished they were her, and they could relate to her at last. Even though she didn't look like them. Even though she wasn't white.

Leo had always thought she should talk about it openly. If Win wanted, she could become the spokesperson for her generation, fight the good fight from inside the ranks. She had tried to explain to him the tightrope act of making vague political statements or tacitly acknowledging the existence of a power imbalance while avoiding anything more specific, anything based on real experience. It would be seen as complaining, playing the victim. White directors would be afraid to work with her, and white audiences would feel alienated by her. Leo could be exhaustingly self-righteous in response, but as part of Marie's cleanup team, he came in after the crisis. He missed the long, tense weeks when a director was messing Win around or a thousand different people on social media came up with a sly new campaign against her. He was there for the explosion and he wanted to fight fire with fire; he didn't see that most of the time, it was more like she was drowning and needed to tread water.

Win kept the focus on her career. She was playing the long game. She developed a skill for ignoring her frustrations.

Five days after Win and Leo met, screaming groups of fans and paparazzi had become a reliable constant. Leo drove her home after dinner at Via Carota, mostly so that the paparazzi could get photos of him kissing her goodbye in the hotel lobby. Win leaned into him, closer and closer, until the kiss was too much, turning messy, turning hard, turning demanding. She'd had two drinks with dinner and nothing to explain the hot jerk in her belly. Leo ran his fingers through her hair and over the nape of her neck. In her ear, he said, "It looks better if I go upstairs, anyway."

They went upstairs.

In Win's hotel suite they sat on either side of the dining table. Win folded her hands in her lap. Leo leaned back, legs spread.

"So," Leo said. "Let's discuss."

"It might ruin our working relationship," Win said. "And our working relationship is returning impressive results."

"That's very true," Leo said. "On the other hand, abstaining might also ruin our working relationship."

"Oh?"

"The curiosity," Leo explained. "It'll eat you up inside. You'll pine away for me."

"And if I sleep with you, I'll be cured of any need for a repeat? Is that your usual guarantee?"

Leo laughed, pleased with her. Win was pleased, too. The table wasn't as good a boundary as she had hoped. They were leaning closer and closer over it. She'd caught his hand and was touching his fingers one by one, watching them curl like he wanted to grab her and was just barely holding back.

"Your publicist will be very cross," Leo said.

"Is that a plus or minus for you?"

"I'm just making sure you have all the information."

"We would have to be careful," Win said.

"That's boring," Leo said. "You be careful for both of us."

"Okay," Win agreed, and crawled over the table.

She'd thought she would be measured; she felt very grown-up, after the slow anticipation of a week's foreplay and their conversation. But Leo caught her up in his arms hard enough that Win realized he had been holding himself back, that his performance had been just that, a performance, and now he was offering her something real. She wanted it with a fierceness that surprised her. She wanted to fight him, to push him, to see what else he'd been hiding from her.

The first time, they barely made it to the next room and gave the bed up as a lost cause entirely. Leo kissed her messily against a wall, and that seemed good enough, her fingers digging into his shoulders and her legs up around his waist. The second time they made it to the couch, where Leo pulled her into his lap and settled her with her mouth against his shoulder, writhing against his fingers, cursing him out and finally saying, broken, like she was annoyed about it, "Please."

"There we go," Leo said, and lifted her up.

The third time was some hours later, deep in the heart of the night, the window flung open for air and traffic blaring far below. Win's wrists, pulled above her head, were caught unthinkingly in Leo's hand as though he just wanted to keep her safe. Leo moved slow. Breathing felt strange and hot, like each deep drag of air lit up every part of her body.

In the morning they reached for each other before their phones, elated with their own good idea, pleased with themselves and laughing breathlessly as Leo toppled her underneath him again. The day was busy, packed with a fashion show downtown and a nightclub uptown. Win was high on success the whole way through it, playing two games, one for the public and one for her and Leo. They overlapped, but they weren't the same. When she danced with him at the club, he murmured, "Still curious?" in her ear, and they left earlier than they should have. It didn't matter. The next day there were photos of them splashed across the *New York Post*, tumbling still kissing into a waiting cab. CAN'T GET ENOUGH, the headline said. Win read it in bed with her coffee, smiling as she flipped through the photos and listened to Leo in the shower.

Then Patrick called. She hadn't spoken to him for a few days, and she was panicking as she picked up. "Is everything okay?"

"*Over and Over* starts shooting on Monday," he said, meaning Warner

Bros.' next big rom-com, already tipped to be a blockbuster. "They want you."

Win made a face, turning the page of her paper. "I don't know, Patrick. I've had enough of being the sidekick. I think this stuff with Leo Milanowski is working. Something better might turn up soon."

"Whitman," Patrick said, "are you watching any news besides your own? Katie Berger dropped out. They want you for the lead."

By the time Leo was out of the shower, Win's flights to LA were already booked. She flung herself across the room and into his arms and said, "You're gold dust, I swear to god," while he swung her around.

"So they tell me," Leo said. "I think your ascending star was probably just a matter of time, though."

Win looked down into his smiling face and heard him say again, *You'll pine away for me.* She saw then that in Leo's lazy arrogance and good humor there was real danger; that if she allowed herself to tumble like this into his arms, that if she shared her confidences and her bed, a very productive working relationship would crumble. Leo had accelerated her career like nothing else, and she liked him, very much. She did not want to ruin everything by loving him.

It was the right thing to do. That morning, after Nathan Spencer's on-screen rant, Win was grateful all over again that Leo was still around, dipping in and out of her life when she needed him. If they had fallen into the messy trap of costars slash lovers, it probably would have ended in disaster years ago. It was better for both of them if the relationship stayed professional. The idea of something real was a lacuna of hesitation and desire; unpredictable, unplottable, never something Win could depend on or be sure of. Leo was too important to risk losing. Everything was safer this way. When Leo held the car door open for her at Saint-Tropez harbor, his hand was thrown out like an invitation.

CHAPTER FOUR

The yacht was already full when they arrived: cabin staff and a captain, and then the group of pretty young things Marie had arranged. They were led by Riva, fresh from headlining Lollapalooza. She was in Saint-Tropez for the Zacharias Chavanne party, too, and she had brought her new boyfriend and a group of hangers-on to join her for the week. Win slipped into the motions, clutched their hands, cooed over them, and returned their compliments.

Win liked Riva. She saw her every couple of months because they were often thrown together at events, and every so often they met in the same high-rise hotels and read fashion magazines together by the rooftop pools. *Like two brown Carrie Bradshaws*, Riva had said. It was easy to be friends, and Win didn't mind the company of Riva's entourage.

Riva shrieked and hugged Win while her boyfriend Bart stood looking bland and handsome. Margaritas were handed around, fresh and sour, salt stinging at their lips, silver buckets filled with bottles and ice, heeled sandals scattered across the deck where Riva's friends had slipped them off. One of the girls had brought a little Yorkshire terrier on board that came to yap gleefully around their ankles. Win's mood was clearing. Out here she felt untouchable. Nathan's barbs couldn't land. The heat settled close and sinuous over her, twining around her shoulders, and the hollow of Leo's throat gleamed with sweat.

Riva tripped back to them, holding her hand out to Leo. "We've met before, I think."

"Have we?"

"In LA last summer?" Riva said. "I think you might have known some friends of mine."

Leo put two knuckles up to his eyebrow, as if to soothe a headache. "Are you sure?"

"I think it was you. Some outdoor party?"

"I feel like I would have remembered that," Leo said. It came out like a compliment, and Win wasn't sure why Leo seemed so uncomfortable. Riva clicked her fingers.

"No! It was at South by Southwest. You were at one of the after-parties. I think you let me paint your face."

"Oh." Leo relaxed. "Well, that sounds like me."

"We've never met, but I think we have friends in common," Bart said, joining his girlfriend and attempting to give Leo a sturdy hand-shake. Leo's eyebrows went up; he let go as quickly as he could, and Win coughed so she didn't laugh. Bart was making a fatal error. Leo liked nearly everybody, as long as they didn't try too hard. "I just spent a weekend in Belize with Robbie Hayes."

"Oh, how is he?" Leo said, and explained to Win, "Rob and I met in London, he's one of the crew there."

Marie leaned forward with studied nonchalance.

"The Radio 1 DJ? I'm surprised he hasn't made you a guest on the show."

"I don't know him that well," Leo said, and gave Marie a very inno-cent look. "I'm sure he's got more than enough people to talk to."

Marie scowled. It wasn't worth anyone's life, trying to talk Leo into an interview. She strode away, probably to book Leo in for a surprise chest wax back at the hotel.

"Rob said you were in Berlin," Bart continued. "Looking at studio spaces?"

Riva looked interested. "You're setting up a recording studio?"

"No, it's for, uh, visual art," Leo said, twitchy as though he'd been caught out. Win shifted closer so she could lean her shoulder against his. "It's just this idea I've been tossing around, like, a collective studio. People could come in and out, and we would cover materials, and there'd be fellowships for people who couldn't afford their own space, and we'd do a quarterly showcase or something."

"That's cool," Riva said, impressed. "You're doing it in Berlin?"

"Oh, I'm not really sure," Leo said. "I haven't worked out the logistics yet."

Leo had been *working out the logistics* on his studio for about as long as Win had known him. She suspected that the project was just too solid for him to start, too much of a commitment of time and energy. Leo liked to throw himself into something for a few weeks at a time, devote all his attention to one thing and then move on, whether it was starring in a music video for some indie band or pretending to be Win's lovelorn boyfriend. It was part of why they worked so well: Win needed him to give his all for very distinct periods of time, and Leo enjoyed a campaign.

"I have a friend who runs an artists' collective in Austin," Riva said. "It's small but they've put out some really cool stuff. I could hook you up, if you want."

"Sure, that sounds good," Leo said, but he didn't mean it. If Riva gave him a number, he would never call. Win had long since given up encouraging him to pursue the studio idea. Being reminded that there were people eager to see Leo succeed only seemed to make him more wary of starting. Leo was used to being a golden boy. The potential for failure troubled him.

The sun didn't let up, and every empty glass was replaced with a full one. Win didn't know where the boat was going; down the coast, she thought. There were Jet Skis ready for later, and a couple of the girls were already climbing on them, passing a champagne bottle between them as they took turns standing up on the seats. Riva controlled the music, and every new song was met with an elated whoop, sun-soaked voices crowing along with each chorus.

After a moment's consideration Win slipped her dress over her head, discarding it behind them on the red-brown wood of the deck. Today's bikini was a deep tangerine. Leo stayed quiet while she adjusted the straps and then lay down next to him. He handed back her drink.

Win was pleased. Leo leaned in and said, "Can I get you some more sunscreen?"

"Thank you, I'm all set. It's kind of you to offer."

"Anything I can do," Leo said. "This"—he tucked one finger under the thin strap of her bikini—"doesn't look like it's protecting much."

"Well, if you're very worried," Win said, and turned, holding out her hand. Leo paused and then laughed. He unbuttoned his shirt, handed it over, and Win slipped into it, white linen hanging demure off her shoulders. They watched each other, grinning.

"Oh, he's gallant," Riva said. "You looking at this, Bart?"

Bart was concentrating so hard he was almost frowning. "Whitman's an interesting name," he said, as though trying out some gallantry for himself. "Is it Indian?"

Leo's mouth twitched like he was trying not to laugh.

"No," Win told Bart, "my dad named me after Walt Whitman. I'm sure it felt like a good idea at the time."

"Ah," Bart said, "an *artiste*."

Win shook her head. "He was an English teacher." Leo's fingers brushed against her elbow—the briefest, warmest touch.

Their conversation was interrupted by Marie, calling Win's name from the cabin of the boat.

"Better not keep her waiting," Leo said. "I'm amazed she's left me alone with you for this long. Maybe I'm winning her trust."

"I wouldn't count on that," Win said, draining the last of her champagne and handing him her empty glass. He twirled the stem between his fingers.

"Oh, come on," he said. "You know better than anyone how I grow on people, Whitman." Win ducked inside the cabin, out of range of the sun and Leo's wry mouth.

Win's mother had called six times, Marie said, holding Win's phone out. Emil was glaring over her shoulder, clearly annoyed that Marie had hijacked duty of care for Win's phone. Win could tell from the icy atmosphere that they had been arguing. She wondered how Marie had come out on top; probably threatened to have him ferried back to the mainland in a dinghy if he didn't comply.

"You need to contain this," Marie said. "A messy family situation is the last thing we need right now."

She had clearly decided Win didn't require any more soothing. Marie's brutality knew no bounds: family, pets, and buried personal history were all fair game. She'd once told Win off for bringing a battered copy of *Pride and Prejudice* with her on a plane. It made her look basic, Marie said. At the very least, couldn't she read one of the less popular Austen novels? *Mansfield Park* would give her more depth.

"Marie, I need a word," Emil said, out for revenge for the phone theft. "Your schedule has five major conflicts." Marie sighed and followed him out, leaving Win alone. Win swallowed. She called her mum.

"Oh, I've got through," Pritha said when she picked up. "Hello, Whitman."

The sound of Pritha's voice washed through Win, and all at once she was home again, back in their old house in North East London with Pritha peering at her from the armchair. Once, when they were trading war stories, Win had asked Riva if she ever felt isolated, or homesick for her own identity, the parts of herself she had to leave behind in order to fit in at industry parties and awards shows.

"Girl, yes," Riva had answered. "It's why I haven't given in and moved to LA, you know? It's important for me to be with my community.

Not just other MCs on the scene or whatever, but, like, my parents and my sisters and my school friends and aunts and grandparents. Everyone who knows me, everyone who remembers who I was and where I came from. Then when I go home I can be myself again."

Win had nodded along, thinking only of this: her mum's low voice, her hesitant pauses, the crackle of the phone line, as though Riva had a chorus and Win had an echo. Most of Win's extended family was in India, and neither Pritha nor Win had visited them since Win's father died. Sometimes Pritha's accent was the closest thing she had to an anchor.

"Whitman," Pritha said. "Are you very angry with me?"

Win had been angry this morning, but that was a few drinks away now. *Don't you start judging her*, Leo had said. Nathan had been cruel to Pritha, too.

"Mostly I'm wondering if you congratulated Nathan when we broke up. *Cheers to escaping my daughter's machine.*"

"I remember that conversation," Pritha said. "It was a long time ago, when he came for dinner that night. We had all that wine. I think I was mostly teasing, anyway."

"I don't remember that conversation."

Pritha hesitated. Then: "You were in the bathroom."

"Ah," Win said. "So you weren't drunk enough to forget that."

"I don't think I said he'd get eaten alive," Pritha tried.

"No. I'm sure your phrasing was much more subtle."

"Well," Pritha said. "I liked Nathan. He was very polite to me."

"I know."

"It's ridiculous that this is even an issue," Pritha said. "I said one thing six months ago, and suddenly you turn it into a national scandal."

Win flinched. "I'm not enjoying this, either."

"You seem happy in the photographs," Pritha said.

Win couldn't respond to that. She stayed silent, rather than try to explain something that Pritha didn't want to understand.

Then her mum said, voice low, "But I'm sorry if I've caused you any trouble."

"You're no trouble, Ma," Win said.

"Well." Pritha drew in a breath. "I'm sorry if I hurt you."

Win wanted to cry. She remembered all that her mum had been through in the past few years, the sudden unwanted attention after Win's big break, having to snatch conversations with Win between flights to LA and Buenos Aires and Sydney, and then the news of her diagnosis, her surgery and stuttering recovery. It had been terrifying, too similar to those long, hopeless months with her dad. If it hadn't been for Shift, who flew back from Canada to help look after Pritha, and Leo, who called Win every other night without fail, long past the point where she thought he would lose interest, Win would have broken down. Pritha herself had taken the diagnosis with no great reaction, like a ticket for speeding, and mostly complained about the amount of work she'd missed. At least now her mum was back at the office, where she was happy. Win straightened in her seat.

"Okay. Thank you. Are people saying things to you?"

"No," Pritha said, "nobody I know watches such silly shows," and Win rolled her eyes, relieved and annoyed at once. She moved on and asked about her cat, whom Pritha was looking after while she was away, and about her aunt, making conversation until she could hang up without feeling guilty.

Out the cabin window was Saint-Tropez's aquamarine sea, scenes of luxury, yachts and fast cars beneath an impossible sky, exactly as she'd always imagined when she was seventeen and hungry. She looked back down at her phone. There was another voicemail waiting for her from her best friend.

Shift's message was short and sweet. "Hey, babe! Just wanted to let you know that I'm on my way back to London, where I'm gonna murder Nathan Spencer and swing him by his man-bun from the Tower. It's going to be awesome, very neo-Tudor. Love you, byyye."

Win was still laughing when she called Shift back.

"It's not funny," Shift said. When she was angry she lost the dry, measured tones she had picked up living in Canada and became a London teenager again, swinging off the straps on the tube and passing a can of tepid cider back and forth while she ranted at Win about their newly forbidden school musical production of *The Vagina Monologues*. "I hate that guy. I genuinely am going to kill him for you."

"You say the sweetest things," Win said. "I'm okay. Leo's helping me handle things."

"Yes, I've seen. I'm stealing that shirt you were wearing yesterday, by the way."

Win was almost touched. "I can't believe you're following my press."

"I'm just keeping an eye on things."

Shift didn't need to explain what things. She had always been cagey about Leo. She didn't dislike him, but she didn't trust him, either.

Leo had, however, introduced Shift to her boyfriend. Charlie had been best friends with Leo's brother Gum since their school days. Charlie worked as a model in the US, and a few years ago, Win and Shift had happened to be in Chicago at the same time as Charlie and Leo. They'd gone out for pizza together, where Win and Leo watched as Charlie and Shift leaned in close and then closer, shoving at each other's shoulders for the chance to touch. The night culminated in Shift teaching Charlie three power chords on her electric guitar before they sang a heartfelt duet of "Bat Out of Hell." Charlie and Shift had been together ever since.

The problem was that Shift saw a lot more of Leo's brother than she did of him. Gum meant well, but he was a jealous friend, clinging to Charlie, and he had failed entirely in trying to impress Shift with his New York credentials and corporate bluster. Shift tolerated Leo as just another Milanowski, a remnant from her boyfriend's indolent youth. And even from the start, Win had known Shift didn't approve of *The Win and Leo Show*.

"You know I don't give a shit that you're faking it," she told Win for the hundredth time. "It's just—sometimes it looks *too* real. I worry about you."

"I'm a good actor," Win said, also for the hundredth time. "So is Leo. We're on the same page."

Shift made a noise like she wasn't convinced. "Is he still throwing himself at you every half second?"

"Leo likes to flirt." Win shrugged. "I do, too. So do you, actually. I think Charlie is the only one of us with any modesty, and he's the literal runway model."

"Oh, Charlie Schmarlie," Shift said, then paused. "Actually. About Charlie."

Win felt a frisson of unease. It would be hugely inconvenient if Shift's relationship self-combusted in the same week as hers. "Is everything okay?"

"Yeah," Shift said. Win could hear Shift smiling in that very particular way that made her imagine Shift wandering about her Montreal house, phone tucked between her cheek and shoulder, carrying stacks of records, or DIY pieces of recording equipment. "It's good. Really good, actually." She laughed, sounding almost embarrassed, and said, "Charlie proposed."

Win gaped. "What?"

"I know," Shift said. "Little idiot. Uh, so, I guess I'm getting married?"

"*Shift*," Win said. "Congratulations! You need to open with this stuff, I just moaned about my bullshit for—"

"It wasn't bullshit," Shift said, "and you weren't moaning. But, yeah, it's—it'll be nice. Mostly I just wanted to check that you'll be my maid of honor, right?"

"Of course," Win said. "I'd be offended if you asked anyone else. Shift! When did it happen?"

"Yesterday," Shift said. "We were hiking and then he got down on one knee and I thought he was fixing his shoelace, so I kept walking and he had to call me back."

"Oh my god. And the ring?"

"Has *two hearts, four hands, one love* engraved on the inside. Fuck me."

Win was cackling. "Do you have any ideas about the wedding yet? No, Charlie has the ideas, doesn't he? I bet he has a binder."

"He has a Pinterest page," Shift said glumly, "and he wants to go through the whole thing with me. But we haven't worked much out yet, except that we're thinking December."

"Nice," Win said. "That gives you eighteen months to plan it—"

"No, this December."

Win blinked. "As in five months from now?"

"Probably only four," Shift said, "we're thinking early, before everything gets taken over by Christmas."

"Wow," Win said.

"I just don't want to do a long engagement, and the longer we draw it out, the more carried away Charlie is going to get. And I . . ." She sounded almost shy. "I don't really want to wait eighteen months. If we're going to do it, we should just do it, right?"

"Right," Win said. Her mind was racing. With any luck she would be working on *The Sun Also Rises* by then, which was already overlapping tightly with the press tour for *All Rivers Run*, her latest film, due to come out in late December. She'd probably be working right up until Christmas. Then Patrick had mentioned that she was on the short list for a spy thriller whose script she'd loved, with an Oscar-winning director attached, and—

"I'm sorry it's not a lot of notice," Shift said. "But it's not going to be a huge thing."

"Right, yeah," Win said. "I'll definitely try my best."

Shift hesitated. "But you're the maid of honor."

"Shift, I know, but you haven't given me a lot of time to work with,"

Win said. "I'll talk to Patrick, but I think I'm going to be busy pretty much all the way through the year."

"It'll be two days of your life. What, you don't get weekends?"

"I hope I'll be able to come for more than two days," Win said, trying to keep her voice gentle. "But you know what my job is like."

"I know." Shift sounded tense. "But this is important, Win."

"I want to be there," Win said. "I'm going to do my best."

"You have to be there," Shift said, and to save time, Win said, "Okay, well, I will." There was no point arguing when she wasn't even sure if it would be a problem. She changed the subject to ask how Shift was going to break it to her dad, who actively disliked Charlie and insisted on calling him "your friend Charles." Shift sounded happy enough when Win got off the phone, heading back out onto the deck and rubbing her hand across her eyes at the newly harsh glare of the sun.

The group had scattered across the yacht, leaving a trail of discarded Louboutins and empty bottles. Someone had started a poker game, and there was a pile of banknotes in the center of the couches, a fluttering mix of euros and dollars and pounds, weighed down with an empty cocktail glass. Platters of food appeared, although no one seemed much interested in them. The Jet Ski girls had stolen a plate of steak and were feeding it piece by piece to the dog. Bart sniffed, rubbing the heel of his hand under his nose, and someone cranked the music up louder, bass and bursts of brass bouncing between the sea and the sky. Riva made sympathetic eye contact with Win, clearly expecting that she had been dealing with the fallout from Nathan's rant. Leo tilted his chin up at her, a silent question.

"Where'd you go?" Riva asked. "Is everything all right?"

"It's fine," Win said, glad Shift had given her a good excuse. "Actually, my best friend's getting married."

"Charlie proposed?" Leo said. "I thought he was going to wait for Christmas. Gum told me he wanted to do some gag about mistletoe."

"Well, apparently they're getting married this December," Win said. "So maybe it's adaptable."

"Oh, winter weddings are *so romantic*," one of Riva's friends said. "Did you go to Henry's last year, when he married the Italian princess? They had real hot springs at the reception, it was back when I was dating that footballer." She stretched with a satisfied purr. "We were in there for hours."

Only Leo met Win's eyes across the crowd. He knew better than most how impossible her schedule would be. But she didn't need Leo's sympathy. She needed him for something else, and glancing out at the sea and the small motorboat of paparazzi with long-range lenses— hidden enough behind the froth of white foam and rocky outcrops for it to be conceivable that Win and her team wouldn't notice them—she reminded herself what it was.

She swiped back her champagne glass, strolling toward the bow of the yacht. Over her shoulder, she called, "Whenever you're ready to pay me some attention, darling," and ignored the muted chorus of whoops from the group.

Marie had taped down a discreet marker, and Win stood on it, gazing out across the blue water. It was a perfect day. She wouldn't be surprised if Marie had arranged dolphins.

Leo stood close behind her. "You want to do the *Titanic* thing?"

"I've been on a boat with you three times," Win said. "And every single time you make that joke."

"One day you'll say yes," Leo said.

Win loved her job. She was a good actor, she was good at assuming a new character, and she didn't put nearly as much effort into this as she did her actual roles. She didn't need to. It was always easier to sell to people when it came packaged as real life. But she still had that giddy, pleased feeling that she was doing something real, making herself someone new. She couldn't control Shift's wedding, or Nathan's mouth, or her mother's opinion of her, but she could control this.

"Take your sunglasses off," she said, "and look at me."

Leo pulled them off. After a moment's thought, he took Win's, too, and tossed them both aside. They stood on the deck together, exposed.

Win said, "You having fun?"

"That guy Riva's dating is one of the most boring people I've ever spoken to."

"I've met four of her boyfriends and they're all like that," Win said. "She says that she doesn't want to date someone famous, but they have to be rich or she worries they're only with her for the money."

"I hate it when people worry about that," Leo said. "So what, they like money. They're still being nice to you."

"Very wise."

"Anyway, not everyone has the advantage of your selection committee," Leo said, and put his hand up, stroking her hair. The sea winds were already tousling it out from its braid, sending it wild and wavy over her face. "I was wondering, this morning, after that video. What was the appeal there, with Spencer?"

Win's mouth twisted. "He wasn't always like that. Obviously. He could be really charming, and we had a lot of fun. He was the one who wanted to meet my mum in the first place." She hesitated, then said, "I don't know. He was— Look, I was really into him, it wasn't like you and me—"

"Ouch," Leo said.

"You know what I mean," Win said. "The thing is, it's not like we weren't both profiting from it. Nathan was down to earth, which made me look down to earth, and he was getting a lot of meetings with producers about new shows and opportunities. But he—he didn't get that I have my own public image and he wasn't always...good for that." She could feel her throat closing up. She'd liked Nathan. For a while, even as he tried to wear her on his arm like a backstage pass, she'd liked him a lot. "Then he finally told me I was a control freak, and I was making him look...weak, or something."

Leo wrinkled his nose. "Standard bullshit, then. Never trust a white man."

"Ha," Win said, in lieu of actual laughter. "Sorry, I forgot I was talking to the One True Good Man." Leo loved to tell her who not to trust, who to avoid, and who wasn't worth her time, and these people were inevitably men like him. He tried very hard not to count himself among the pack. "Anyway, then, you know, he . . ."

She made a gesture that meant *told the world I was a frigid, controlling prude so I had to come to you for damage control.* Nathan's words still stung, even when the breakup didn't anymore. Win pictured his statements like a reverberation, wave after wave of people having their worst assumptions about her confirmed.

Leo stood close, his face turned down to her, almost worried. He ran his fingers lightly over her shoulder, the warm linen of his own shirt, and Win admitted, "I haven't had a lot of sleep the last week or so."

"You just say the word," Leo said. "I'll get you a bed. You can sleep for hours."

"That's all right," Win said. "The press will already have the kiss. We can't give them too much. They'll get spoiled."

"Hey," Leo said, and gave her a long, considering look. "I wasn't going to let the press in, either."

Win opened her mouth, something prickling at the base of her spine, when someone across the deck dropped their glass. She remembered what they were meant to be doing. "Move a little this way," she said, and shuffled them until they were tilted toward the open sea; a clear shot of Leo, and Win's good side. The movement brought them closer, and Win reached out with one hand to curl her fingers through Leo's belt loops.

Then she waited. She had maneuvered him this far, but it was important for him to make the final move. From the taunting way he was holding back from her, she could tell he was enjoying it.

"Whenever you're ready," she told him.

"There's no exercises you have to do first? Warm-ups?"

"I'll be okay," Win said, and Leo took her chin in his hand, tilting her up. They kissed as easy as breathing: once and then again, Leo's mouth hot and guiding on hers. There was margarita salt on his bottom lip. Win licked it away and swung in closer to him. He got one hand on her waist and pulled her in, his palm low on the small of her back. Win let herself touch him the way she'd wanted to, her hands on Leo's flat stomach, the curve of his chest, sliding up until she could wrap her arms around him.

Leo tilted her back so that she had to cling to him to keep upright, and kissed up her neck. When he got to her ear, he murmured, "Marie going to say when?"

"No, just, you know—enough," Win said, arching up against him but not quite grinding. They needed to keep it light, not dirty enough for the press to turn ugly.

"Then you say when," Leo said, and pulled her in closer, deepening the kiss. It was as though the sure press of Leo's mouth could cut through all the murk and confusion of Win's days and make them subside into something uncomplicated and good. He knew how to touch her, and had for years. His fingers tangled in her hair just to the point of strain, and she gasped, clinging to him. They always kissed longer than you'd think: enough time to give the cameras a couple of good angles.

Win let Leo kiss her until her mouth felt bruised and swollen and she'd caught herself digging her nails into his shoulders three times. She said, voice gone rough, "That should be enough."

Leo's fingers brushed against her jawline when they broke apart, and they eyed each other, careful. Win didn't know what her face looked like. It felt hot.

She asked for the boat to move on to the secluded cove, where they could have some genuine privacy. The moment the engines went off, she climbed up on the railing, looking at the blue below, leaving Leo's shirt in a neat heap behind her. Then she dove.

The water closed up over her as though she belonged to it, and for the first time that day, there was quiet. She took two long strokes through the dark and surfaced, shaking her head like a dog and preening, stroking her fingers through her damp hair, waiting for Leo to come lean over the side and laugh down at her, which he did.

"Are you coming in?" she called up.

"I'm right behind you," Leo said.

CHAPTER FIVE

Leo wanted to take the jet across to the racecourse at Cagnes-sur-Mer, but Win vetoed it as unnecessary. She was feeling more sure of herself. The heat had broken last night and a heavy Mediterranean rain had fallen, blurring the bright lights of Saint-Tropez and bending palm trees gently backward under its weight. Win had listened to it drum against the French windows and mingle with the crash of the waves below. Leo slept through the entire storm dreaming, he told Win confidentially, that he was being chased through the woods around Lake Tahoe by a man with tiny hands and huge teeth. When they stepped out of La Réserve, he glanced around at the wet pavement and umbrella-laden paparazzi and said, "Oh, did it rain?"

Marie eyed him incredulously.

Win had woken up feeling cleansed, leaning out of her windows in the early morning and drinking in that electric-blue smell of damp paving stones, pearly sunlight, and the ocean. Their yacht trip yesterday had worked as intended. Shots of Win and Leo had done the rounds overnight, and in light of them Nathan looked like a bitter has-been, sulking because he'd lost out to Whitman Tagore's one true love. (Win had once seen T-shirts circulating with a picture of herself and Leo on the front and the words TRUE LOVE WINS. She wasn't sure what their love had supposedly won, besides the pun, but Leo bought twenty and spent the next six months shipping them to her one by one, wherever she was in the world, with a hastily scribbled note. *Just in case you lost yours!* said one, and another, *For your next red carpet??* The last one came with a note that read *I'm all out of jokes because Gum has been explaining his investment portfolio to me for 45 mins and I'm actively losing brain cells with every second. Come rescue me again soon.* She'd thrown out the shirt immediately but kept the note, for a while.) Fan speculation was moving back to whether she and Leo were endgame, and this morning Marie had sent her a wink-face emoji with a forwarded tweet that read: She's so much more real when she's with Leo. He really humanizes her.

They had rented a private box at the racecourse for the day, high up and secluded enough in the stands that they might not have been noticed, if Marie hadn't already queued up a series of carefully scheduled tweets from various dummy accounts. Win stood at the front railing watching ripples go through the crowd. As people started to turn and point, she went back to her seat, where Leo was already reciting a complicated cocktail recipe to their waiter.

Marie had two windows open on her laptop; one was Twitter, and the other a list of horses and their odds and best times. She had once told Win quite offhandedly that she would probably be a gambling addict if she had the time for it. It made a lot of sense. The only thing Marie liked more than a surefire win was a well-calculated risk.

Emil appeared with an attendant by his side. Win touched Marie's arm.

"Care to place a bet, mesdames? Monsieur?"

"Ah yes," Marie said, still frowning at her screen. "Let me put fifty on Crown of Thorns."

"Adventurous," Leo said, without looking up from his phone.

Marie glanced at Leo with vague annoyance. "And the bald monsieur will put a grand on Jean Paul II."

Leo huffed an appreciative laugh and waved his hand at the attendant's questioning look. "Sure, yeah, why not." He flashed his teeth at Marie. "I'll give you a cut when I win."

"So kind," Marie said, and turned back to her laptop. She was already bitter at Leo today. She had been irritated by the early morning runs he insisted on taking out in the hills, where she couldn't keep an eye on him. Then Leo refused to talk to the press, and declined one interview in particular that had been scheduled for tomorrow morning.

Marie wanted him to pretend to be caught out, cornered on camera by a persistent (and scripted) host, who would ask questions about Win that Leo could palm off with wry, enigmatic answers. Win had already warned her not to bother. Leo hadn't agreed to an interview in a long time. He didn't like being questioned by strangers, and he was so used to people apparently knowing his business that he struggled to filter out things that were better left unsaid. He had cursed on day-time television, leaked the album titles of friends on the radio, and once, taken by surprise and quite high at Coachella, had appeared on a livestream weeping at the beauty of the sunset. The first time Win and Leo spoke after their fling in New York was a direct result of Leo's disastrous interview technique. It was seven months after the Josip scandal, and she had been busy: her first Golden Globes nomination, a spate of exciting new roles. She had become used to exchanging only occasional texts with Leo, until he called her early one morning. Her heart felt a little unsteady, but she kept her voice cheerful and agreeable when she picked up.

"Whitman," Leo said. His voice was hoarse, like it had been scratched up by the satellites connecting them. "I need a favor."

Some months before, Leo had been asked to appear on a popular late-night talk show as part of their Father's Day special, and agreed because he had nothing better to do. He'd then forgotten about it until the day before the interview, when his father found out and gave him a lecture about Leo's "responsibility to the family brand." Leo had gone out drinking with his brother and turned up to film the segment hungover and still furious. He told the presenter and a host of cameras, slouching in his chair and scowling, that it was hard to tell funny Father's Day stories when your dad was such an asshole, and that any scraps he'd learned about being a good person were all from his mothers. His father took no interest in any of his children, Leo explained, running a dismissive hand through his hair; Leo was simply the only one who'd noticed.

"Shit," Win said.

Leo swallowed; she heard the dry click of his throat over the phone. "Listen, it's— Obviously my father will be furious, but it's really going to upset my brother. Gum idolizes our dad. The producers are refusing to reshoot the segment, let alone pull it. They said that unless I can give them something more interesting, they're airing it."

"You need a favor," Win echoed.

"I know this is so shit," Leo said, "but I wondered if maybe I could give them something about us. If we could do the fake relationship again. Everyone ate it up, and I know it's crazy, but maybe if we announced that we'd been dating secretly ever since or—or even, well, an engagement would probably work—"

"Jesus," Win said.

"I know," Leo said. He sounded miserable. "I didn't want to ask, but I can't think of anyone else who can help."

"Look." She drew in a breath. "It's not public yet, but I'm...I'm seeing someone, actually."

"Oh, hey," Leo said, startled.

"So I can't really— I mean, it wouldn't be fair to Dermott," Win said. "And I think it would come out pretty soon, or it would look like I was cheating on you, or..."

"Right, yeah," Leo said, with a bright, false tone to his voice. "No, obviously that won't work. Okay, well, forget I asked. Thanks anyway, Whitman. Tell Dermott I'm jealous of him."

He was obviously trying to be cheery, trying to let her escape without making her feel bad, and perhaps that was what made Win make her decision so suddenly. There was certainly no sensible reason for it, except that Leo needed her. Leo had helped her back in New

York, even though there hadn't been much in it for him. She could help him now.

"Wait," she said. "I could give them something else. You said it's a Father's Day special? I could talk about... my dad. My memories of him."

"Win," Leo said. She felt it like a touch, low and gentle at the nape of her neck. She shook her head and plowed on.

"People always want to talk about him and I haven't seen any reason to before now. I didn't want to be ..." *A sob story*, she thought, but Leo didn't need to hear that. She cleared her throat and moved on. "It's not important, but I haven't spoken much about him before. I know it's not the same pull as a story about you and me, but do you think they'd take it as a replacement?"

"I can't ask you to do that," Leo said.

"You're not asking," Win said. "I'm offering."

The talk show accepted it. Win filmed a twenty-minute segment where the host asked her grave, probing questions, and Win forced her shoulders to relax and spoke about her dad. She told the host, and all the people watching later, about her dad's quiet, happy life, about his small family and his teaching and the students who adored him. She told them how he had lifted Win onto his shoulders and whooped when she'd gotten the starring role in a theatrical adaptation of *The Secret Garden*, running in circles round the car park. She answered questions about his illness, his death. They talked about the funeral. She was impatient with the way her throat closed in on itself, the prickling spring of tears to her eyes, but she also knew how it looked. Her obvious emotion would make for excellent TV, and Leo would be safe.

The segment clocked up millions of views on YouTube. It wasn't bad press for Win, though it wasn't the press she would have chosen. Her Golden Globes nomination had been complicated—a nod to her talent, which set her aside from the pack but also triggered a new wave of suspicion about her ambition, her ruthlessness. But in the TV interview, she came across as honest, authentic in her sentiment and her memories. She allowed herself to be an object of pity so others could coo over her bravery and hold their hands out in comfort as if they knew her. She won over a lot of new fans. Her mother had disapproved.

She got a signed confirmation from the producers that Leo's footage had been deleted, and she had it express mailed to him before she left the studio. She got his text before she went to bed: Thank you. Whatever you want, whenever you want it, I'm all yours.

It still took her some time to realize he'd actually meant it.

By late afternoon the heat had returned, making their wineglasses sweat and the soles of Win's wedges stick to her feet.

Leo suggested they go to the balcony, for the breeze. Marie waved her hand no before Win could reply. Win knew she wanted to limit the amount of free shots they gave away, especially to the public, who could take pictures on their phones and have them online in seconds. There was no relief to be had.

Between Marie's incessant typing on her MacBook and Leo's arm thrown loosely around her shoulders, Win felt dazed, as if she were floating over the crowd in a sheer, shimmering bubble, drifting through the clouds of dust beneath the hooves of the horses, and out over the open sea. The thrum of the crowd and the races began to echo and catch high up in her temple. When they finally returned to the cars, Emil had security clear the area of photographers so that Win wouldn't have to smile for them under her sunglasses. She settled gratefully into the air-conditioned back seat.

It was only when they pulled up to La Réserve that Win realized she'd fallen asleep with her head resting against the tinted window. Leo squeezed her shoulder, helping her out of the car, his face close and concerned for a flashing second. The sun seemed very bright. It was hard work not to tip against him.

Coming through the gold-plated doors, Marie caught up with Win, Emil hurrying behind her.

"Patrick called," she said.

"She needs to rest," Leo said, commanding enough to make Emil jump, but Win cut over him.

"No, I don't. What did he say?"

"Paramount wants to talk."

Win's shoulders straightened; she pulled herself upright, ran a hand through her hair, and smiled at Emil, who was already offering up her phone. "I'll need you with me."

"Of course," Marie said.

"Win," Leo said, "why don't we get dinner first?"

"They've already been waiting for half an hour," Marie said. Win let go of Leo's hand with an apologetic shrug of her shoulders. He would forgive her. She had a cold brew brought up with them, which woke her up, though the coffee curdled in her stomach.

The news from Paramount was positive. They had not given Patrick their word yet, but their people had started pulling the paperwork together. The majority of the discussion was between Patrick and two of Paramount's lawyers, who were hammering out the terms of Win's contract. By the end of the hour-long call, it was implied that they could expect an offer in a matter of days. Win knew she should be careful with her expectations, but she couldn't help texting Shift a celebratory string of exclamation marks and will you hate me now I'm gonna be a Hemingway heroine??

"The Spencer issue is unfortunate, of course," the producer said as they were wrapping up.

"We're handling it," Marie said. "Whitman's name has been trending across Europe and the UK for the past four days continually, and in the US for at least a few hours every day. Nathan Spencer appears in less than 20 percent of the content. Maybe he hasn't moved on, but Whitman has, and so has the rest of the world. With Leo, people can see what she's really like."

"Yeah, Milanowski is a hit," the producer said. "And we love to see you looking so glam. It's always been my favorite side of you, Whitman. Kind of an exotic Sophia Loren."

"Thank you," Win said, forcing herself not to bristle. "In the meantime, we're expecting the whole Nathan thing to blow over in a few days."

"I'm glad to hear it," he said. "I think we have a better view on your suitability for the role. Don't let us down, now."

Once Paramount hung up, Patrick debriefed her on everything that was to come. The first rehearsals and shoots for *The Sun Also Rises* would start in mid-September, and were expected to carry on, with occasional breaks, for the following three months. Into those breaks she would have to fit the press tour for *All Rivers Run* and the Chanel campaign. Chanel wanted a few commercials plus photo shoots and making-of videos, Patrick explained; most of it could be done in one week in October, but she might have to fly back and forth between shoots for a while. Patrick had been in further talks with the director of the spy thriller, too, which he was excited about. He was, however, pessimistic about her chances of making it to Shift's wedding. He said he would see what he could do.

They were finally done by ten thirty. The dreamy, heat-sick feeling of the day had faded into a bone-deep exhaustion and mild nausea, like a hangover. Win went straight to the balcony, throwing the windows open and stepping into the dark blue of the night. She wished she'd stolen another cigarette from Leo. She wished she'd reacted to the "exotic" comment. She wished getting what she wanted didn't so often depend on keeping her mouth shut. Neither Patrick nor Marie had mentioned it in the debrief, and now Win felt tense with a frustration she couldn't voice.

The door of the suite opened behind her, and there was a murmur of voices and the sound of the door closing again as Marie left. Win breathed out, then jumped when someone rapped on the window behind her.

Leo raised his eyebrows through the glass and held up a pizza box.

"Oh, god," Win said, almost collapsing into Leo as he stepped outside. "I could kiss you."

"You're just in the habit of it," Leo said, flipping open the box and offering it up to Win. She reached for it, but the smell of grease and melted cheese hit her first, and before she could help it, she shuddered, a roll of revulsion in her stomach.

Leo frowned. "Are you sick?"

"No," Win said. She put a hand up against her forehead, and realized for the first time that she was damp with sweat. "I think it's just sunstroke. Give me a second."

Leo set down the box and disappeared back inside. She could hear the low murmur of his voice on the phone, his words lost in the crash of waves below her. She checked her phone while she waited; Shift and Charlie had sent her a video of them setting off a dozen party poppers in their living room in excited reaction to the Paramount news. The streamers settled in Charlie's golden curls.

When Leo returned, Win asked, a little guiltily, "Can we smoke?"

Leo laughed. "Yeah," he said, and pulled his tobacco pouch out from his back pocket. Win watched him, idle and quiet, while he rolled the joint, his long fingers, his quick movements. He ignored her reaching hand when he finished, tucking the joint behind one ear. "I have something better, too." He picked up the box with one hand and held the other out to her. "Come with me."

Win considered him. "I shouldn't really smoke outside. And we'll have to tell my security—"

"It's taken care of," Leo said. "Come on."

He led her out of the suite and back into the elevator, but instead of heading down, they went up, and the doors opened onto the roof. It was even better than the balcony, with a salty breeze coming in from the coast. Beyond the loungers and folded parasols was a rooftop pool, larimar blue and glowing in the soft underwater lighting. The water rippled in the wind. Saint-Tropez looked almost cozy against the dark hillside, dressed up in dark velvet and sequins of orange light. It was reflected, a second city, on the inky surface of the sea.

Leo tossed the pizza box aside and straddled one of the loungers, beckoning Win to him. She sat cross-legged in front of him and took the joint when he offered it up to her, tilting her head down so he could light it. He tucked her hair behind her ear, out of the way, and Win took in a deep, indulgent breath. Leo was smiling, crooked in the corner of his mouth, and the lounger was still baked hot beneath them from the day's sun.

"Where is everyone?" Win asked.

"It's closed to other people. Tell me about the Paramount meeting."

Win took another drag and then handed him the joint and told him, running through the details, the tight timeline, the issues with Spencer, the good news. The moment was the kind of familiar that hit her right in the chest, sitting in some quiet hideout Leo had found for them, talking through her decisions. Saying it aloud to Leo made a situation make sense, helped her work out what she actually wanted. When they were apart she would call him sometimes, listen to him saying, *Wait, one sec,* and the noise surrounding him would subside as he closed a door between Win and the rest of the world. But it was better like this, Leo's face intent on hers, the weed setting in and her muscles slackening.

"It went well, then," Leo said.

"Well enough," Win said, and picked up his hand, setting her fist in the center of his palm, sleepy and stoned. Leo slipped his hand out and pressed it starfish-style to her face, pushing her gently away, both of them giggling at each other.

"Cards?" Win said, because their knees were overlapping and she was edging closer to him.

"You're dangerous when you're high," Leo told her. "I think we should cool down first."

He undressed and ran for the pool before Win could really process it, arms pointed neatly as he dove. She trailed after him, slow, watching. His skin looked green under the water, and when he surfaced, drops of water were running down over his buzz cut to his collarbone. Win could only see his chest now, the rest of him distorted under the water. If she focused, she could just make out the V of his hips, the black line of his briefs. Win dipped a toe in.

"Don't be a baby," he said.

She'd left her heels downstairs, so there was nothing to delay the slide of the zip down her back. It was a thin, gauzy sundress that fell neatly off her shoulders, and Win had expected to feel cold, but it only felt good, like shedding unnecessary skin. Leo had made it to the far end and stood in the shallows, his back against the wall and his elbows up behind him over the side of the pool. He was watching her.

"If you'd warned me, I would have brought a swimsuit," Win said. Her bikini wasn't any less revealing than her underwear, but somehow she felt more exposed like this, in lacy black with Leo's gaze tracking across her.

"We're old friends, Whitman," Leo said. "No need to be shy." His mouth was crooked in the shadow of a grin.

Leo always wanted her company in such a frank, straightforward way that she could give herself over, into his hands, before she even knew what she was doing. She half considered running off, with the pizza and all the clothes, to leave him stranded up here. She had done that to him once before in LA, but he had only shrugged and met her at the hotel bar in his soaking swim shorts, running a wet hand affectionately along the back of her silk shirt. It was hot and stuffy in her room tonight, and the water seemed fathoms deep. She dove.

It was much colder than expected. She came up cursing, running her hands through her soaked hair in shock and kicking her feet to stay above water. Leo was moving closer, gliding through the water with wide, effortless strokes. He swerved around her, swam sideways behind her shoulder, and headed back up the pool again. She watched him, focused and intent. She remembered that if a shark came after you in the ocean, you were supposed to punch it.

"Feel better?" he asked.

"Yes," Win admitted. She started swimming, slow and distrustful around the edges of the pool. They were circling each other.

"This reminds me of Miami," Leo said. "Poolside at midnight. The only thing missing is a tattoo gun."

Win laughed. It had been so long ago—back when she was on the short list for her starring role in the *Reckless* action series, a secret-agent superhero franchise that would consolidate her staying power and give her a decent five years of regular premieres and a fanbase to match. But Patrick heard that the casting manager thought Win was too straight-edge for the job: *prudish* was the exact word they had used. She had needed to prove she could be cool. Leo, when she called him, thought it was hilarious. But sure, he said. He was ostensibly in Miami Beach for a cameo in a music video, but mostly for a string of parties, still in his fast-car bad-boy phase. Why didn't she come out and join him?

They spent a week racing around town, drinking beer out of cans and crushing them underfoot, making out against the walls of night-clubs in South Beach, molly under bright lights and seedy mornings with Bloody Marys and sunglasses against the paparazzi flashes. Leo announced his intention to get PROPERTY OF WHITMAN TAGORE tattooed on his chest, and pitched a huge fit when Win refused to get a matching one. They argued for so long that their tattoo guy passed out.

It was a relief to let go, even in such a calculated way: to take what she wanted, to slam shots and make obscene gestures at photographers, to unleash the anger and boredom she kept so closely contained. Leo called it the Win Gone Wild tour. Finally, the producer called. Win put him on loudspeaker while Leo and his friends played pool and the clamor of the bar was loud in the background. "All right, all right, we get it," he said. "The part's yours, baby, when can you get here for the first table read?"

She could still remember the thrill of triumph. After she hung up she had raced across the bar and flung herself up against Leo, looping her arms around his neck and kissing him. It wasn't the first time they'd kissed that week, but this time there weren't any cameras around.

They pulled back and looked at each other.

Win said, "Better not."

"The pining," Leo said. He didn't clarify who was in danger that time. "You're probably right." She'd had to leave the next morning, so she and Leo had left the bar and gone back to the villa they'd been staying in, stretched out in the backyard, and played long rounds of Sixty-Six, the card game Leo had picked up in Switzerland as a teenager. He'd taught her late one night in New York. They'd been fascinated with each other, making excuses to stay up. "We used to play this in dorms," Leo said as he shuffled, "after poker got banned because some kid put up half his trust fund."

"You're like an alien species," Win had said. She kept having to wrench her gaze away from his hands, his mouth. The next night they would discover a good alternative for stretches of unoccupied time—Leo's hands, his mouth—but in Miami, she realized the cards were safer. Now they played between shoots, while Marie was still organizing their next location, in hotel bars after long days, in the early mornings before the car arrived or when Leo was watching her a little too closely and Win's thoughts kept circling back to those nights in New York. Leo kept a note in his phone, a long spiraling list of scores.

She wondered if he'd brought the cards up to the pool with them tonight. They could play sitting cross-legged in their underwear, dripping on the heat-baked concrete, Leo's throat cool and the smell of chlorine rising off him.

Win struck out for the deep end and dove under again, reaching out to brush the bottom of the pool with her fingertips. She could just catch Leo's silhouette, blurry in the pool lights. She pushed her feet against the tiles and propelled herself upward, bursting out of the water again and sending waves out around her.

"Show-off," Leo said, drifting past her. She could see the solid line of his shoulders, his narrow waist, and then she let her eyes slip away. She didn't know how much of her body was visible under the water. When he reached the other end of the pool, he dragged the pizza box over and flipped it open. Win tried not to think of it as bait.

"I have a proposition for you," Leo said.

"Oh god," Win said. "You're not going to suggest we get engaged again, are you?"

"No," Leo said, and gave a high, barking laugh. It was a startling contrast to his usual low laughter, and Win twisted in the water to look at him. "Why would you say that?"

"I was kidding. I can't let you forget your youthful idiocy."

Leo rubbed the back of his neck, shaking his head. "No," he repeated. "Obviously not. I wanted to ask you to be my date."

That piqued her attention. "Does your sister have another premiere?"

Unlike her relatively aimless brothers, Hannah was the only junior Milanowski who had carved out a genuine career for herself. She produced intricate documentaries with obscure subjects, like Canadian fishing towns or radio telescopes in the desert. Hannah was reclusive, happier behind a camera than in front of one, and she tended to wilt under the spotlight. A few years ago Win had run into both siblings at a Sundance after-party. It was the year that Hannah's short film was panned by critics, and she'd been almost certainly about to cry in front of the cameras before Leo grabbed Win's hand, begged a favor, and they crashed the interview, playing drunk with their arms wound around each other. Hannah had made her escape unnoticed. Marie had not been impressed.

"No, Hannah's in Thailand," Leo said. "She's tracking down witnesses for some true crime documentary. I meant to the wedding."

"Shift's?"

"What, you thought I wouldn't get an invite?"

"No, I guess—I hadn't started thinking about dates yet."

Leo shrugged. "I figured since we'll both be there, we might as well go together. Saves me from having to make small talk with whatever hot new talent you dredge up."

"My dates are always carefully selected through a matrix of prestige, attractiveness, and conversational ability," Win said. Leo laughed, but he was still waiting for her answer. She stretched and struck out toward him on the far side of the pool. He listed away when he saw her coming, watching her and paddling backward. Her bra was soaked through, near transparent. She slung her elbows up on the edge, and Leo shook his head, gaze slipping away. She took a slice of pizza for herself.

"I don't know," she said after she'd swallowed. "I mean—yes, if it all works out, of course I'll go with you. I'm worried about finding the time for it."

"Ah, c'mon," Leo said, his shoulders relaxing again. "You're the big movie star. Just pull a diva moment, you can take a few days off." He held his hands up when he saw the look on her face. "I know, I know, you have this big planned schedule and everything's crazy all the time, but come on. It's your best friend."

"I know who it is," Win said. "It's fine. I'll sort it. Let's stop talking about it now."

"Okay." Leo changed tack. "It looks like Gum's going to be the best man. He keeps calling it Charlie's last hurrah and he says it's a joke, but I'm starting to worry it's not? It's going to be a nightmare."

Win laughed but didn't respond. She knew how responsible Leo felt for his older brother. When Gum was arrested for drunk-driving in

Santa Barbara, Leo had sped up the news cycle by appearing in a series of dazzling shots cavorting with Win around Morocco's Atlantic coast while she filmed the second *Reckless* movie. Truthfully, they'd barely seen each other. He'd been distracted and worried, fielding endless calls from his family members, Gum calling tearfully from rehab, and Win was busy with twelve-hour days on set. She remembered watching him drive out to meet her in the desert, his skin burnished by the sun, his boots heavy with sand.

She finished her first slice of pizza and helped herself to one more, trying not to think about what her nutritionist would say. She couldn't remember the last time she'd eaten like this, hot cheese and grease and the weed sharpening every flavor. The air was warm and smelled distinctly of Saint-Tropez, palm trees and clean asphalt and the rich drift of gasoline from the sports cars as they raced through the hills.

"It would be nice to go to Montreal," she admitted to Leo. He was gliding up the pool again. Soon he would be right next to her. "I haven't seen snow in a long time."

"We can drive to the Alps tomorrow, if you like," he said.

"You can suggest it to Marie," Win said. "I think it might conflict with our reservation at Château de la Whatever."

"God forbid," Leo said, but didn't push it. Win could feel herself becoming melancholy, and was irritated by it. Now he was close enough to give her the searching Leo stare, the one she'd had so many times before: in LA, when he was trying to talk her into ditching a party to go make their own fun; in Paris at New Year's, when she said she didn't believe in resolutions; in Singapore, when he suspected her of cheating at cards. Tonight she wasn't in the mood for scrutiny.

"I think I'm done," she announced. Leo didn't argue. He followed her out of the pool and handed her a clean towel.

They were quiet on the way back down. Win couldn't stop yawning. Her head was drooping, weighed down with wet hair. She wondered if she could let herself go to sleep without showering. She had an impulse to apologize, as if she'd somehow let Leo down.

"Sure you're okay, Whitman?" he said, when they were almost at her door.

"Just something a producer said. It's good, though, they like me." She didn't want to get into it tonight. Too much fuss over one word, and it would be easier to hold her own once contracts had been signed. Leo would take it seriously, offer to spread mean rumors, wonder if maybe Win should turn down the role altogether. He wouldn't understand that biting her tongue was dull necessity, rather than indifference.

Once, nearly four years ago, Win had gone to an industry party and met a guy. Leo had been jetting around with a model who loathed Win, and Win herself had been sequestered in the West Village preparing for a role. Neel lived between New York and Mumbai; he was a journalist, and some of his longer pieces had been optioned for film. He and Win ended up spending most of the party on the balcony, not unlike the one at La Réserve, above the roar of Manhattan traffic instead of the sea.

Neel had a girlfriend in Mumbai, and Win had a movie to shoot. It was one of those strange, prickling nights, the tension between them as understood as if they'd said aloud ruefully, *Ah well, maybe in another life*. They didn't kiss, but they leaned in close, the conversation jolting with energy. He touched her wrist, her shoulder. She knew she was looking at his mouth too much. They swapped stories in the way that first-generation immigrants do, familiar in their incongruity, Win's mother's blank distrust of her career and Neel's disdain for the white yogis preaching spiritual awareness out in LA.

Win had thought the balcony was private, but it wasn't, and the next day there were photos of Neel and Win together, leaning close, hands touching. What surprised her most was the tone of the head-lines: settled, smug, a little bored. Only a few were outright racist—BOLLYWOOD BEAUTIES, read one; IS MAMA MATCHMAKING? demanded another—and most of them seemed almost pleased, as though at last Win had done something conventional. She'd texted Neel to apologize for the fuss and ask him whether he wanted her to reassure his girl-friend that nothing had happened. It was a pleasure, he replied, and no problem, Mahani is very understanding. They really want you to shut up and settle down with an Indian guy, huh?

It was a weird jolt, to be understood so clearly. To have someone put into words what Win mostly experienced as a nameless, simmering undercurrent.

"What happened to that one journalist guy," Leo said when they met a few months later. The supermodel had ditched him unceremoniously once fashion week season was over, and he had shown up on Win's set to play cards in her trailer and lick his wounds.

Win said, "Oh, that wasn't a thing. People just got excited that I was finally back in my own lane. Settling down with an Indian guy at last."

Leo laughed. "God, that's so reductive. You weren't even born in the same country. It's almost funny, isn't it?"

"Well, not really." Win waved a hand when Leo went to apologize. She hesitated. "The worst part is—I had a really nice time with him," she said. "He got it. I didn't have to explain things to him. It was like . . . recognition."

"Well," Leo said. "You're Whitman Tagore. If you want something like that, I'm sure you can get it."

"Ha. Thanks," Win said, and laid down her cards. "Your shuffle."

She never saw Neel again, more by happenstance than deliberate avoidance. She didn't mind it—she was used to dealing with these things alone, and the click of recognition she had felt with him was a passing thrill, something she had enjoyed but could live without. But every now and then she wished she had someone else to call, to get a second read on a word like *exotic*, to understand her discomfort without needing an explanation. Now she couldn't even properly remember the producer's phrasing, his exact words. Was it a compliment? Was she overthinking it?

They lingered at the door of her suite, wet hair dripping onto the plush carpet. Leo leaned against the doorjamb, halfway through a yawn when something came to him. "Oh, shit. Listen, I forgot to tell you—I got a weird call this evening."

Win tensed. "A journalist?"

"No, it was…" He paused, looking almost embarrassed. "My mums, actually." *My mums* was how Leo referred to his mother and her wife, who'd been together since Leo was a child. "There's some kind of disaster going on with their friend Anya—don't worry, disaster for them usually means somebody's shih tzu got quarantined for sneezing at customs."

"Ha," Win said, trying to conceal her relief.

"The thing is, Anya's already down here for work, so they want me to meet up with her on Saturday."

"Of course," Win said. "Just let Emil know what time you're going."

Leo nodded. "Right, I was just going to duck out for an hour, but— she wanted me to ask if you'll come for brunch? She said she likes your aesthetic."

Win cocked her head to the side. "You're becoming very demanding."

"I've always been demanding," Leo said. "You're just finding me harder to resist."

"Maybe I'm just trying to keep you sweet and pliable," Win said.

"Whitman," Leo said, as if offended. "When have I ever not been sweet?"

Unspoken between them: Win already owed him much more than this. Through the years their respective debt to each other had become tangled and overlapping, so it was hard to keep track of who was in the black and who was in the red. Win remembered the relief she had felt when Marie turned to her, just before their jet was due to depart for Saint-Tropez, and said, *Leo says he'll be there.* It was best to assume that a favor was always deserved.

"We'll make it work," she said.

"Thank you," Leo said. "I'll give Emil the details. Good night, Whitman."

"Sweet dreams."

"I expect so," Leo said. Win laughed, and closed the door. She pictured him wandering back to his own room, changing into a dry shirt, collapsing into bed, and falling asleep without effort. When they'd shared a bed in the past, he always drifted off first. In sleep all the sharp lines of his face seemed to retreat, and he looked soft and pink-mouthed like a boy.

She didn't have a shower. She lay on her bed. She thought about Leo's shoulders cutting through the water.

"Jesus," she said, and put her hand between her legs.

It was easy, most of the time, to flirt without letting the steady flicker of attraction between them leap up and catch. They used each other instead, flaunted the other on their arm when they needed a story, created new personalities and narratives and lives. Slowly, Win had realized that Leo was on her side, no matter what she asked, no matter how ridiculous he thought her latest project was. Leo was flippant and spoiled, but he was also loyal. He remembered what she'd done for him. Sometimes she thought he loved her for it. And he showed up every time she called.

Sometimes she didn't have to call. When she was conspicuously snubbed at the Oscars several years back and Hollywood was rubbing its hands in glee, she opened her hotel door and found Leo lounging in the frame. He was sleepy-eyed and faintly hungover, and he said, "I heard you were in town. Do you want to go for a drive?"

There were hundreds of blogs detailing their impromptu road trip, catchy *New York* magazine write-ups about their "effortless sexiness" and Tumblr compilations of every Instagram photo and paparazzi shot. Win and Leo in Leo's convertible flying through Tijuana; Win doubled over with laughter and banging her Corona on the table to prove a point in a forever-looping GIF; Leo squinting out at the Gulf of Mexico, captioned Which way to Alaska? But what Win mostly remembered was lying awake swatting mosquitoes and talking drowsily as they outran awards season and the winter. "You'll get them next time," Leo said. He was always so complacent in his belief in her. Most of the time it annoyed her, like he didn't understand what she was up against, and then once in a while it would hit her hard, the lazy way he stacked all of his bets on her, his quiet faith.

The world thought Win had the perfect love story with the perfect man, passionate and devoted, always breathless, always in the honeymoon stage, stormy and on-again, off-again but still that strange, magical thing: true love. But Win had something better than that. She had a friend, and a secret.

CHAPTER SIX

Nathan Spencer was scowling outside Dukes. He had stumbled coming out the door, a glass still in hand. He took one last, long gulp of wine, and hurled it at the camera. The footage cut out at the moment of impact.

The gossip was that Nathan had stormed outside in a rage, following a tantrum at the bar and an attempt to drink beer directly from the tap. After throwing the glass, he vomited into a storm drain (there was footage of that, too, but Marie declined to play it), and then one of his friends bundled him into a taxi.

"Is this bad for me?" Win asked.

Marie held up her hand and tilted it, fifty-fifty. "It looks a bit like you broke him. But mostly it makes him look unstable. It discredits anything he's said before. Clearly he's not thinking rationally."

Win leaned back and exhaled. It had been a successful week of parading Leo up and down the coast. The public was back on her side. Her image had been revitalized. The first thing that came up when you googled her was a barrage of excited rumors about *The Sun Also Rises*. The Chavanne party was tomorrow, and after that, Win and her staff would be able to pack up and return to their real lives.

"We should dial it back a bit today," Marie said. "We don't want you sharing the same front pages. He's imploding because of what he did, not because of what you're doing."

"I like that," Win said. "So what, we just hide inside all day?"

It wouldn't be the first time. Sometimes mystery worked better for Win and Leo, their hidden life like a hot, thudding pulse that everyone clustered around.

"Yes," Marie said, at the same time that Leo said, "Except for brunch with Anya." They glared at each other.

"It's just a casual meeting," Win said. "We could do it quietly."

Marie looked unconvinced, but Win had the final say, and she was loath to go back on her promise.

"It can just be us," Leo agreed. "We'll sneak in through the back. No entourage. We can even give Emil the morning off. Unless you want to come?" he added. "Anya spends all her time surrounding herself with handsome young men, she'd be delighted."

"Tempting," Emil said. "Unfortunately I already spend all my time surrounded by demanding older women."

Marie looked up, sharp-eyed. "What's that?"

"He's so brave," Leo said to Win with admiration as they left. "I hope he's still there when we get back."

Anya was staying at Luna Beach, and they met her in the restaurant on the sand, hidden away from cameras and patrolled, in the distance, by stern-faced security in suits. When Anya saw them approaching, she set down her magazine and smiled, standing with arms outstretched. She was a broad-shouldered woman in her late fifties with close-cropped dark hair and a prominent nose. Standing like that, she looked like the figurehead of a ship.

"Look who decided to turn up," she said. "Late as usual."

"You know I like to keep you on your toes, Anya," Leo said.

"You remember Tomas," Anya said, gesturing at the man seated next to her—dark-haired, with horn-rimmed glasses—who raised his hand to them without rising.

"Hello, Leo," he said. Win realized he was younger than she'd first thought, maybe thirty-five at most. When Leo reached out his hand, Tomas took it, held it to his mouth, and kissed it as if Leo were a lucky dice roll.

"Tomas," Leo said. "How's the PhD?"

"Oh, you know," Tomas said.

Anya tutted. "He's a master in his field."

"My angel is supportive as always," Tomas said.

"And hello to you," Anya said, pushing Leo aside so she could get to Win. "Oh, you're so tall. Are you taller than Leo?"

"She's wearing heels." Leo slid into his seat and reached for a menu as Anya drew Win into a tight hug.

Meeting people from Leo's family circle was always strange. Win was used to wealth in a new money sense, professional success signified by the use of private jets and luxury suites. The people Leo had grown up with operated on an entirely different wavelength. Wealth was inherent to them, and it spoke with unfeigned confidence of second and third homes on the coast, secure spots at elite universities, fresh-cut flowers, stocks and bonds, housekeepers who were *part of the family*. Leo thought of himself as an honorary guest who showed up only when his presence was requested. But though he might hide his membership card when it suited him, Win knew it would never be revoked.

"You must be nearly six foot," Anya said, examining Win.

"I enjoy your movies," Tomas said. His voice was deep and sunbaked. "You have a very commanding presence."

"Oh," Win said. "Thank you."

"You're welcome," Tomas said. He tapped two fingers against Anya's side. "Antalya, the mimosas."

"Oh yes," said Anya, flagging down a waiter. Win slid in next to Leo, who raised his arm to wrap around her shoulders, tucking her against his side. Tomas eyed them with relaxed scrutiny.

As a crystal glass was set in front of her, Win said, "I'll just have orange juice, thank you."

Their waiter nodded, but before he could move on, Tomas reached out to touch Win's wrist.

"My darling," he said. "We all work so hard. We're in Saint-Tropez. You need to drink the mimosa."

"Yes, Win," said Leo, leaning back so he could watch the interaction in full. "You're upsetting Tomas."

Under the table, Win pinched Leo's thigh through his jeans. He pinched her back, through the thin cotton of her dress, digging into the softer flesh around her waist. She stuttered out a gasp, turned it into a cough, and nodded.

"Maybe just one."

Anya clapped her hands and said, "Good girl. Leonard, I'm so glad you're finally over that ridiculous sobriety phase."

"It wasn't a phase. It was a . . . brief period of abstention."

"That is the definition of a phase," Anya said. "Your mothers were worried about you."

Leo said, "Anya's not forgiven me for refusing to do shots with her at the Royal Opera House last year."

"Especially," Anya added, her rising voice indicating she had been nursing her resentment for some time, "when only two months later you were raising all sorts of hell in Los Angeles, with that group of—"

"We were not raising hell," Leo said sharply. Win wondered if this was a sore point. Leo couldn't stand his mothers' disapproval, and he might have somehow upset them in LA.

"I was just detoxing," he said, calmer. He added to Win, "I met this guy at an ashram in Kerala—"

"Oh, I don't need details about you finding yourself in India, thank you," Win said, and Anya laughed from her throat and added, "Yes, do shut up about it." Leo returned to his drink with a sardonic grin.

"Anyway, darlings," Anya continued. "I have a confession to make. I didn't just bring you here for mimosas."

Leo made a strangled sound, clasping one hand to his heart. "Anya. You shock me."

"Now don't be cruel," Anya said. "We are undergoing something of a crisis. It's about the magazine."

Leo had told Win about *Ci Sarà* on the ride over, a luxury travel quarterly that Anya had been editing since she left *Vanity Fair* three years ago. It was a pet project that was beginning to make a reputable name for itself. Tomas and Anya's whole life was a big vacation anyway, Leo said, so it made sense to profit from it.

"We had already put together a wonderful selection for the fall issue. A romance theme, to round off the summer. We had the cover stars lined up: a certain young pop star and her certain young beau, modern love in a classic climate, and so on. Anyway, the whole relationship has crashed and burned, as these things are wont to do, and so the shoot is off. That leaves me with the sets, the gowns, the photographers, and all that's missing is our star couple." There was a pregnant pause. "And, darlings, you know that I would never normally do this, but wouldn't it be so perfectly serendipitous, the two of you just happening to be here and so young and gorgeous and in love—"

"Oh no," Leo said, with mounting dread. "You know I don't do interviews, Anya—"

"I'm not asking you for an editorial, Leo. Just a few nice shots, something tasteful. I don't even need a quote. Everything's arranged, and it would only take a day. You wouldn't have to leave the Riviera."

"We're very busy," Leo said.

"Yes." Anya smiled. "I've seen your press."

"It could be a good opportunity," Win said. "I have a press tour coming up, and it wouldn't hurt..." She trailed off. A spread of Win and Leo wrapped up in each other in a heady European glamour shoot would be good foreshadowing for *The Sun Also Rises*. In a big-name publication like *Vogue* or *Cosmo* it would have been too on the nose, but a high-end, more artistic magazine like *Ci Sarà* would strike just the right note between enigmatic and provocative. It could keep the dream of their summer romance alive into the colder months of the year.

"I don't know," Leo said. "When would you want to do it?"

"Well, darlings, we're on quite a tight deadline," Anya said. "The venue is booked for tomorrow."

"We have plans tomorrow evening," Win said.

"Of course, you must be attending the Chavanne party," Anya said. "But we'd start early and wrap up with plenty of time for you to get back to town."

"I'll have to speak to my publicist," Win said. "Can you give us until this afternoon to confirm?"

Anya clapped her hands. "Of course. Just as soon as you can let us know."

Leo groaned. He ran his hand up Win's neck and into her hair, as if he wanted to tug it, but he only curled his fingers through, making Win tilt back without thinking, almost a shiver.

They sailed back to the hotel a few hours later. The cars took them through the garage to the back entrance, where they could enter without being seen. In the elevator she didn't bother pretending Leo might go back to his room, and just sent them both straight up to the penthouse, where Leo collapsed onto her bed with a relieved sigh while Win hunted through the bar for more champagne and orange juice.

"That was fun," she said.

"Yeah, they're good," Leo agreed. "Tomas has been with her forever, it's like a never-ending honeymoon. Thea and Anya went to art school together in the seventies, but I guess now they're just part of a...an...a..." He waved his hand around, giving Win an expectant look.

"Amalgamation," Win suggested.

"Yes! An amalgamation of friends," Leo said. "They're old and married and stuff, and Thea and Mum don't know who belongs to who anymore."

Leo's mother, Gabrysia Milanowski, was the kind of celebrity who'd captured a moment and didn't need to do anything else to be remembered forever as the face of the eighties. She had grown up in Poland, moved to London when she was sixteen, become an international supermodel by eighteen, and retained an airy distrust of the world through it all. She married Leo's father in her early twenties, and a mutual and unsurprising divorce followed several affairs on both sides, concluding with a generous alimony settlement that would keep Gabrysia stocked in couture and pinot noir for the rest of her life.

Leo was only two years old when Gabrysia agreed to sit for an artist friend of a friend who was doing a portrait series on divorcées. Thea decked her in green paint and ivy leaves and sat her behind a work desk like a modern-day Titania. They were engaged six months later.

He'd told Win that he didn't remember life before Thea. On a family trip to Toulouse, when Leo was six, Thea had told him that when she was a little girl, she'd lived just down the road. Leo had sighed. *I wish I knew you then*, he had told her, *and we could have lived together*. It was still one of his mother's favorite stories.

"Why don't you call Thea 'Mum,' as well?" Win wondered, taking another sip of her drink. "If she's been part of your life for so long. Or is it too confusing with . . ." She trailed off.

Leo smirked at her. "Are you being homophobic?"

Win threw a cushion at him, and Leo laughed.

"I used to call her Mum," he said. "I just pointed when it was unclear. Then when I was a teenager, she had one of her hippie phases and insisted that I call her Thea. She said that there were a billion mums in the world and only a couple hundred thousand people called Thea at most and it was important to claim *individuality*. By the time she got over it, I was in the habit. Sometimes I call her Mum. I don't really notice." He yawned, stretching back against his chair. "It made me feel very grown-up when I was fifteen, anyway."

"I bet," Win said. "When I was fifteen, Shift and I started calling all our teachers by their first names, to promote equality. We got detention for a month."

Leo cackled. "I can just imagine angry little Whitman Tagore in detention."

"I bet you never were."

"No," Leo acknowledged, kicking his legs out. "I usually talked my way out of it. It's a pity we didn't meet when we were teenagers," he added wistfully. "You could have corrupted me."

Win laughed. "In what fucking universe would we have met when we were teenagers?"

"It could have happened!"

"I didn't take many first-class trips to Switzerland," Win said. As a teenager she had been suspicious of strangers, still raw from her father's death, rude and uninviting. She flipped people off on the street and knew the best places to jump the barrier and ride the tube for free. She had felt on edge everywhere she went, and to make up for it she walked at a quick clip, so she was never anywhere long. Leo would have been pampered, slouching, confident of his welcome wherever he was. Win wasn't sure he would have been able to keep up with her.

"And look at you now," Leo said. He bared his teeth. "Come on, it would have been great. We could have had a tortured teenage romance."

"You wish," Win said. Privately, she thought that perhaps she would have been fascinated by him despite her own better judgment, an itchy sort of interest she wouldn't have been able to quell.

Leo gave it up. "Oh well. Are you really going to make me do a photo shoot?"

In lieu of answering, Win held up her phone. The last three messages from Marie were still visible on her lock screen:

THE Anya Willoughby? Ci sara??

a bit last minute but i think we can handle it

can she get us a contract by e.o.d?

Leo groaned. "She's going to dress me up in leather, I know it."

"You can say no, if you want to," Win reminded him.

"To you I can," Leo said. "But Anya will not be refused. And my mums would never forgive me."

"Done deal, then," Win said, and forwarded Anya's phone number to Marie. Leo would get over it by tomorrow. For all his grumbling, he liked photo shoots. They appealed to his love of showing off. She watched him lean back on her bed with almost absentminded interest, the way his T-shirt rode up and bared a dark trail of hair over his stomach.

"So you've been raising hell in LA? It didn't come up in Marie's Google alerts."

"Oh no," Leo said. "I was just in California for a few months."

"That's longer than you usually stay anywhere." She handed him a glass. "What was it, the art? The company?"

"What? No," Leo said. He frowned. "Oh, the art, sure."

"Leo," Win said. She stifled a giggle. Toward the end of brunch Anya had ordered them a round of Bloody Marys, the effects of which were still setting in. "Why are you being so—"

Her phone started ringing.

"Oh," she said, looking at the screen. "It's Patrick."

When she picked up, Leo sighed and flopped backward on the bed, narrowly avoiding spilling his mimosa all over it. "I don't care for Patrick," he said.

"Hello," Win said, ignoring him. "Shit, did Paramount see Spencer's breakdown?"

"No, no, it's the opposite. I just got word from their people. They're sending me their offer as we speak."

"*Patrick*," Win exclaimed, falling back onto her armchair. "That's incredible." She glanced over at the bed. Leo had put his glass on her bedside table and curled on his side, eyes closed. She wondered if he was actually asleep or just trying to give her the illusion of privacy. It was sweet but unnecessary: Win was used to having all of her conversations with an audience of at least two people.

"I'll read over the summary this afternoon, but it looks like they're going to meet your quote," Patrick said. "They suggested we all talk at eight a.m. Pacific—that's five p.m. in France."

He hung up without much fanfare. Patrick was averse to premature celebrations. It would be months before they'd know if their instincts had paid off. *The Sun Also Rises* might turn out to be a flop. Win didn't think so, though.

She set her phone and her drink down, rubbing her hands across her face. It had worked. Everything was working.

"God," she said.

Leo hadn't stirred. He'd kicked his shoes off without her noticing, but aside from that he was fully dressed. His chest was rising and falling evenly, and his head was tucked in, chin curling downward.

Win felt like she was cradling the good news in her hands, a warm ball of light. She felt validated for the first time since the breakup. It was proof that every accusation Nathan Spencer had leveled at her in front of a host of delighted cameras—*control freak, workaholic, narcissist*—had been worth it. It was worth being called all of those things, if she got to feel triumph like this. She had a sudden impulse to call Nathan up and tell him. But Leo was right in front of her. He had never needed convincing.

She lay down on the bed next to him, with a good gap of space between them. The dip of the mattress made Leo's eyes squint open.

"Everything okay?" he murmured.

"Good," she said. "Really good."

"Mmm." Leo sighed, eyes closing again, and Win thought he was asleep until he said, "I wish we *had* known each other as kids. I was lonely sometimes. It would have been good to have you."

Win didn't respond, and Leo drifted off again. She'd rest for a little while, let the mimosas wear off, take a shower and prep for the call. The room was filled with a sultry afternoon heat, and the familiar sound of Leo's breathing. Win closed her eyes.

It was sweet that he meant it, that he thought the connection between them would have snapped as taut and immediate as ever. That if they'd met at sixteen when Leo was a rich white boy at a Swiss boarding school and Win was a British Asian girl from the suburbs of London with one weirdo friend and a dead dad, they would still have recognized one another as allies, as partners.

It was a nice image, but it was so divorced from the reality of their lives and the differences between them that it made Win wonder what else about her he'd resolved into such a nice, tidy image. Leo saw their lives so simply, he understood his own privilege so simply. He saw racism or money or power as monsters that you only had to name in order to banish, and once you had, your core remained unaffected, your heart still true. He saw their backgrounds as backdrops they could walk away from, rather than stakes in the ground that they had grown up around, that twisted them into the shapes they were today.

Talking to Leo was sometimes like shouting over a giant gulf that gaped between them that Leo thought was just a crack in the pavement. He thought he could lean forward and offer his hand and guide Win lightly across. But Win wasn't even sure she wanted to be on the other side.

The dry, awful taste in her mouth woke her up, and she opened her eyes, closed them again, opened them, squinting, each movement painful and sluggish. Her eyelashes felt heavy with grit, her eyelids glazed with sleep.

Leo lay closer, turned toward her now. He'd gotten slightly sunburned, the bridge of his nose pink. Win stared at him, too tired to move her head, sure that she shouldn't close her eyes again. They'd curled in close, though they weren't touching, their knees brought up, their bodies forming a loose horseshoe.

Everything felt golden and preserved, like they'd been dipped in amber while they slept. It would be easy to forget the time or day or year, easier still to roll over and move into the circle of Leo's arms, let him throw his leg over her hip and pull her in close. They'd shared a bed before: when they were in the same suite, dozing off in front of bad Mafia movies and Elvis films, waking up to a blue screen and a busy schedule; or staying at a holiday villa with a bunch of other industry people, where they lay awake analyzing everyone else in whispers that got meaner and funnier as the night went on. And, of course, that first week in New York, poured on top of each other, her nose stuck in his armpit, or his cheek against her stomach, working themselves into new shapes and molds so that even the moment of reaching when they woke up could be avoided.

There was a quiet knock at the door, and then another, accompanied by Emil calling, "Whitman?"

"Mrgh," Leo said. "Whassit."

Win gave a huge, bone-cracking yawn. She could feel a headache threatening, looming like humidity.

Leo blinked open his eyes. "We fell asleep," he said, sounding confused.

Win ignored him. She pushed up onto her elbows.

"Whitman, it's five o'clock," Emil said through the door.

"Shit." Win touched her hand, very lightly, to her forehead.

"Come back," Leo said. He stretched out an arm. She looked down at him, the light muscle along his upper arm, the soft drape of his shirt over his chest. She thought about falling back onto him and turning her face into the line of his throat. His eyes were half-closed like a snake's. He mumbled, "I need to talk to you."

"Shit, I'm late," Win said. Her brain had started to catch up with her now. She said again, louder this time, "*I'm late*. Emil, I'll be out in two seconds. Can you tell Patrick I'm almost there?"

"On it," Emil called back.

Win half crawled off the bed and stopped, when Leo took hold of her arm. He'd closed his eyes as though he'd fallen back to sleep, but his grip on her wrist was firm and sure.

"What," Win said.

"What," he repeated, opening his eyes properly and frowning up at her. He shook his head and let go of her wrist. "Sorry. I wanted to— I need to tell you something."

"I need to take this call," Win said.

Leo had pulled himself up now and was leaning toward her. There was something incongruous in his expression.

"Meet me for dinner after, then."

Win shook her head. "I'll probably be busy until late. I got that role we wanted."

"That's..." Leo rubbed at his forehead. They were both hungover. "That's great, Win, I'm really happy for you. Can you meet me when you're done? We could grab drinks somewhere."

"We're not going out today," Win reminded him. "We can talk tomorrow, we'll both be at the photo shoot all day."

"But so will everyone else," Leo said.

"Whitman," Emil called again.

Win stared at Leo a moment longer, then went and opened the door.

CHAPTER SEVEN

ey!" Shift said when she answered Win's call the next morning. "This is a surprise. I thought you were wrapped up in *L'Opera Leonardo.*"

Win was in the bathroom of a new hotel room, sitting in the wide green-tiled window seat above an enormous freestanding tub with high sloping porcelain sides. There were flowers everywhere, the air heavy with heat and the cloying scent of peonies.

"It's the intermission," she said. "I thought I'd check in on the wedding planning."

"God," Shift said. "Don't."

"What," Win said, as a flicker of hope sprang unbidden into her chest. "Is it a disaster? You could always postpone."

"No, it's actually going quite well," Shift said. "Charlie's already booked a venue, this fuckin' beautiful greenhouse, and my mum's visiting. We went out dress shopping. Win, I'm *enjoying* myself."

Win laughed. It was hard to imagine Shift in a wedding dress, though she'd worn one once, when they were seventeen and she'd dressed up as Miss Havisham for a Halloween party; filthy white from a charity store, combined with bright pink hair and combat boots. Win had gone as the messenger from *Romeo and Juliet* who died halfway to Mantua. They'd left the party early, taken a bottle of Sprite mixed with vodka onto the night bus, and rolled around and around the city, planning their magnificent futures.

She pushed open her shuttered windows to let in more fresh air. Their new hotel was near deserted, an old palace made into a secret luxury resort. They had closed the deal with Paramount. A photo shoot today, the Chavanne yacht party tonight, and soon the summer would be over and she could get back to her real work. Win ran her hand over the back of her neck, catching sight of herself in the mirror. There were bags under her eyes for the makeup artists to cover, and her hair lay limp. The woman reflected looked troubled, unconvinced.

"If I start calling you to worry about flower arrangements, I need you to come out here and kidnap me," Shift said. "Take me to a show. Take me to a *rave*."

"I promise," Win said. "But you're not worrying, are you?"

"No," Shift said, and sighed. "It's really nice. I'm happy. I'm just embarrassed. You're going to be there, right?"

"I think so," Win lied. There was no point having a fight about it until she knew for sure. "You'll know when I know."

"I hope I already know," Shift said, but she didn't linger on it. "How's the fame monster?"

"The monster and I are both doing well," Win said, gaze drawn out the window. The sea was so blue, with patches of darker depths out beyond the break of the waves. She let out a quick breath.

"What is it?" Shift said, with a sudden thread of concern. "Has something happened? I saw that Nathan was an asshole again, but you guys looked like you had it in hand—"

"Oh, we do," Win said.

"At least he's mostly just destroying his own life now."

"I'm sure he's okay," Win said. She hesitated. "I think something's going on with Leo." It felt good, articulating that nameless unease that had been growing in her, confirming that there was something new making her spine prickle. But it felt wrong, too. Like saying it aloud made it real.

"What kind of something?"

"I don't know," Win said. "A friend of his mentioned he'd been in LA earlier this year, and when I asked why, he wouldn't say. And he's been . . . clingy and then distant."

She thought of him, reaching toward her in the shadows of their accidentally shared bed. *I need to talk to you.* She hadn't been awake enough to pay attention when he said it; now she wondered what he'd wanted to tell her, just risen from a dream.

"Something's different. He wanted to talk to me privately yesterday. I think there's something he's not telling me."

"Did you talk to him?"

"No," Win said. "I was working."

"What about this morning?"

Win grimaced. "Well, we had to drive up here . . ."

Shift sounded a little amused. "And right now, when you have the time to talk to me?"

"Well, I'm . . . hiding in the bathroom," Win admitted.

"Okay," Shift said. "Why are you so worried? Do you think it's about you?"

"Yes," Win said. "He'd tell me anything else."

Shift was quiet. She said, "Win," drew in a breath, and then let it trail off.

"Come on," Win said.

"You're thinking it, too."

"A little." She thought of the way he'd looked at her in the swimming pool the other night, eyes dark, mouth soft, curving around her in slow circles that began to narrow. "I'm probably just being arrogant."

"You guys have spent the last seven years pretending to be in love with each other," Shift said. "Would it really be so wild if he actually was?"

Win ran a hand through her hair. "Yes. Yes, it would. Yes."

"Why?"

"Because we have an arrangement," she burst out. "Because this is what works."

"Other things can work, too," Shift said.

"Shift, come on," Win said. "Me and Leo are very different people. We argue all the time—"

"Like me and Charlie are so similar. Like couples never fight."

"But it's more than that," Win continued, talking over Shift. "Leo is the most important thing that ever happened to my career. If we got together and then messed it up, that would be it. I would lose it—"

"You'd lose him, not it, Win. He's a person, not a tool."

"I'm not being a bitch," Win said, frustrated. "If you asked Leo, he'd tell you the same thing. We're useful to each other. We're really good friends and obviously I care about him, but we're much better for each other like this than as a real couple."

"You've never even tried, though."

"It wouldn't be worth the risk," Win said. "Look, Leo's—funny and smart and hot, obviously you can romanticize the idea of us being together, but that's not what I need. I need—stability. You don't even like Leo that much, why are you advocating for him?"

"I want you to be happy," Shift said. "Do you think you'd be happy with him?"

"No," Win said. "I'm happy around him, but that's because I'm not with him. I don't have to worry about him getting bored. I don't have to sacrifice anything for him."

Leo got bored quickly. He made Win furious without even trying. Leo was one of her closest friends, but as her boyfriend he would have a power over her that she didn't trust him with. It wouldn't be staged dates and photo shoots and schedules: it would be real life, and real life with Leo was unpredictable. He thought he understood everything, or that everything was easy to understand and just as easy to explain. He would be furious at every backhanded comment, every "exotic" and "nontraditional," every Nathan Spencer look-alike mining her family for laughs on TV, and that fury would become Win's problem. Win's to soothe, Win's to explain why she could or couldn't respond, and Win was already so tired. She relied, very heavily, on being able to dismiss the people who dismissed her, and Leo would never let her look away.

Win lived in a house of cards. She couldn't risk what they had on the occasional impulse that flickered in her hindbrain when he bent his mouth to hers.

"Okay, well, look," Shift said. "No matter what, you have to talk to him."

"We've got the Zacharias Chavanne party tonight," Win said. "Everyone will be watching us."

"After that, then."

"Pretty soon after that the filming for *The Sun Also Rises* starts. And then my next press tour."

"He's not going to go with you?"

Win shook her head. "We don't want him to be too closely associated with my career," she said, summarizing long conversations with Marie while her thoughts raced on ahead. "If he comes on press tours for a film he's had nothing to do with, it looks like I'm not interesting without him."

"Okay," Shift said. "Then you have to make time to talk to him. You owe him that much."

They were both quiet. Win wished that Shift were there with her. It was sometimes strange that they had such separate lives now, when their teenhoods had been so intertwined. She couldn't think of an important memory that Shift didn't feature in: whooping and forcing the rest of the audience to their feet after Win's first starring role in a community theater production, or her shoulder pressed hard against Win's at Win's father's funeral. Win had taken Shift as her date to her first movie premiere in London, both of them shiny-eyed and raw with their own youth and pleasure. It hadn't been long after that, though, that Shift moved to Montreal to record her first album, and Win's dates started to be organized for her.

Win stepped up to the window, leaning out, and the coastal wind slapped her in the face. There was a strange lump in her throat, like she was giving something up.

"We might be wrong," Shift tried, as though offering Win something. "Maybe he just wants your advice on his next ridiculous haircut."

Win managed a laugh. "Sure."

Shift paused. "Leo's a big boy, Win."

"I don't want to hurt him."

"So talk to him," Shift said, "or leave."

"Well." Win let her feet swing back onto the bathroom floor. "I'll probably do both."

Leo clicked his tongue as they walked into the hotel ballroom. Even the technical setup—the cameras and screens, the lights being maneuvered into place and the great wardrobe rails tucked off to the side, coils of wires and empty packaging—couldn't hide the brilliance of the room. It was a cathedral of gold columns and a high soaring ceiling fitted with frescoes, angels and weeping women clutching round-faced cherubs. The floor was marble, and Win's heels were loud. She took a slow, wondering circle, with Leo on her arm, his expression remote and inscrutable. She discarded several opening lines, and in the end didn't say anything at all before the team pulled them apart for makeup and wardrobe.

They lined Win's eyes in gold and her mouth in a deep red, and teased her hair into something more artfully disheveled: "Bedhead," the hairstylist said, "but for a dark angel." They stripped her out of her clothes and put her in pale, expensive underwear, spiky threads of cotton feathering over her hips, her thighs, no bra but a backless pink silk slip dress.

Anya arrived with Tomas in tow, who settled in a plush chair in the corner and began mulling over his laptop, apparently undistracted by the chaos around him. Anya came over to look at Win. "Beautiful," she said, "but her eyeliner needs to be higher. Whitman, when the mascara goes on, blink while it's still wet—"

Win did. It left freckled dots of mascara under her eyes, and Anya nodded, satisfied.

"We'll do the bed shots later, put a coat on the poor girl, for god's sake," she said, though it wasn't cold. Win got to sit and have a smoothie while they tested the lighting. Leo showed up in a Lanvin suit with the jacket sleeves shoved up.

"They took ages on you," Win said, lowering her phone.

Leo made a face. "The trousers were too long, they had to sew them up."

Win laughed. "Don't they know your measurements?"

Leo threw himself into the chair beside her. "Apparently I look taller than I am," he said, and bounced up out of the chair with a guilty look when Anya snapped at him about rumpling the fit of the suit. He put his hands in his pockets, sulking like a kid. "She gets to sit down."

"*She* is wearing heels," Win said. Leo gave her a flash of a smile.

Win wished he'd keep grumbling instead, making himself ridiculous. They'd trimmed back his hair from where it was getting just slightly bristly, and the dark lines of the suit brought out his bone structure, made him look feral and handsome. Win turned back to her inbox. She was very careful not to think about the conversation with Shift.

"We're ready for you, sweethearts," Anya said.

Leo held out his hand. They'd spent time on more than his trousers, she realized; the dark circles under his eyes were gone, hidden by concealer. It made him look younger, made Win wonder how worn down he actually was.

Anya called out instructions that were half editorial direction and half film narrative, some vague story line about two mysterious strangers meeting and falling in love. Win slouched against a pillar and Leo leaned over her, his arm braced above her head, his face tilted down to her.

"Won't do interviews, won't act, but you're a professional at this," Win said as they posed leaning up against a pillar.

"This is more fun," Leo said. He took her hand, whirling her out as though they were about to start dancing. Win tossed her hair around a bit, kept her face turned to his and half smiled. There were people filming for a making-of video that would go up on *Ci Sarà*'s website. Marie was in the corner looking critical. Emil was petting a Tom Ford coat with a sneaky expression.

Anya said, "Win, could you give us some— Yes, perfect," as Win gripped Leo's neck with one hand and dropped backward.

Leo held her by the hips and leaned forward so she was in a dip, her hair a long dark cascade toward the ground. A couple of assistants ran over and tugged down her coat so that it fell low and bared her shoulders.

Leo's smile was calculating. "You're not wearing a bra," he murmured, keeping his mouth still so Anya didn't snap at him.

"Don't drop me," Win told him.

"I'm just commenting."

"Well, concentrate," Win said.

"You don't need to pinch, Whitman," Leo said. He didn't sound unhappy, only interested, his voice low in her ear, a little rough, the way he spoke just for her. Win put her leg up, knee against his hip, and Leo smoothed his hand over the thin silk. "I've got you."

They took more photos up on the roof terrace in new outfits. Win sprawled across cushions with Leo's head in her lap, another set taken of them gazing out over the view. Marie and Anya broke off occasionally to look at the shots, but neither Win nor Leo bothered to join them.

Win had seen hundreds of photos of herself with Leo, posed for shoots or on the red carpet or apparently candid paparazzi shots. Her own face looked back at her from magazines and billboards like a casual acquaintance, someone Win felt fondly toward without any real interest in getting to know. It had been a long time since a photo of her and Leo properly captured her attention—none, really, since that week in New York when Win first realized their chemistry.

Except, perhaps, one other, stuck with a magnet to Shift's fridge in Montreal. Shift had taken it the night they introduced her to Charlie. They were posing for the camera, but the photo wasn't a story for viewers to obsess over, just a private smile for Shift. Leo's arm was slung over Win's shoulders, and they both looked smug: their plan had gone well; Charlie and Shift were hitting it off. At the time it felt natural, but now whenever she saw the photo, at Shift's house or in the back of video calls, Win was always faintly uncomfortable, her stomach dipping. There was a line of empty bottles in front of them, and Win looked tired and happy. They could have been college friends, out after an exam. It was like peeking into another life.

Downstairs, Leo put on a new shirt and jacket and straddled a motorbike in the driveway while Win pretended to run down the stairs toward him in a long, dreamy Nina Ricci gown, bracelets jangling. While Win posed leaning against the motorbike with Leo braced forward like he was about to take off, Anya and Marie engaged in a low-pitched and furious debate. "My vision!" Anya cried, and "A waste of an excellent opportunity," Marie countered, before they went back to hissing at each other.

With her arm wrapped around his neck, Leo was at the perfect height to murmur in Win's ear. "If your publicist gets me in trouble with my mums, you're gonna have to work really hard to make it up to me."

"What's the problem?" Win asked.

Marie was adamant. "There should be a kiss." Her eyes were

gleaming, already, Win was sure, envisioning the page torn out lovingly and pasted to thousands of teenage bedroom walls or circulating endlessly online. Anya thought it would sully the "delicious sexual tension." Leo, one arm around Win's waist to keep her from falling, looked sleepy and uninterested.

"Okay, Marie," Win said. "It's fine. I don't think we need a kiss."

"Thank you, Whitman," Anya said. She looked very pinched about the mouth.

Leo nodded toward the guys filming. "Are they still shooting for behind-the-scenes?"

Marie gave him an astounded, approving look. Win pushed her sunglasses up to the top of her head and met his eyes.

He nudged her backward, so she was half lying over the motorbike handlebars, and leaned down to catch her mouth, his hand cradling her hip, thumbing at the gauzy material. Win wrapped one arm around his shoulders and let the other one touch his cheek, giving herself up to him. The grip of his hand in her hair felt like an anchor, but his mouth was soft, almost unsure, lingering like he was waiting for her to tear herself away.

When they broke apart, Anya was faintly annoyed, Marie had calmed down, and the photographer looked a little heartbroken that they would not be including any photographs she may or may not have just taken in the final editorial.

"One more scene," Anya said. Win was taken upstairs and dressed in strappy cutout lingerie. She draped herself across satin green covers, while Leo leaned on one corner of the four-poster bed, taking her in as if she were a prize he had long since earned.

CHAPTER EIGHT

Sparkling wine and roses, to mark the end of the shoot. Oat milk lattes in the cars on the way back, while Marie briefed them on the guests at the Chavanne party. A bowl of quinoa salad at La Réserve, bites stolen between swipes of Matthew's brush. Then pink Bellinis as they glided arm in arm onto the Chavanne yacht, and a revolving stream of waitstaff to refill their drinks as soon as they emptied. It was only when Win and Leo set their glasses down and escaped to the dance floor that Win was able to catch a breath, without anybody pressing the next thing into her hands.

This year's theme was Cherrybomb! and, as always, Zacharias had shown a dogged commitment to the aesthetic. Waiters with pouty red lips were dipping glacé cherries in vodka and hand-feeding them to passing guests. The upper deck had been turned into a cherry orchard complete with several full-grown trees. There were gilt-edged vending machines dispensing cans of something called Cherry Chavanne by the bar, and a mirrored wall to the dance floor was hung with pink lipsticks on gold chains. A few lip prints were already smeared across the glass. The boat was sailing up the coast to Château de Montfort, a renovated castle where the after-party would unfold. Win wished she could rest her forehead on Leo's shoulder without looking like she was already drunk.

"This feels like the first time we've been alone today," she said.

"This is a pretty liberal definition of alone."

They were surrounded on all sides by guests and their entourages. They would need to do the rounds later. There were a few important producers here, rubbing shoulders with the pop stars and actors and European royalty, everyone taking the opportunity to shake hands and pose for photos before the night got started. Zacharias Chavanne was wearing a three-piece suit, meticulously sequined with tiny glittering cherries, sighing about how gorgeous everyone was and adjusting supermodels' collars with pursed lips. Win's team had gone under-stated, a white minidress and a silk red bomber jacket that draped over her shoulders, a few sizes too big. Versace had sent Leo a tux with *Mon Chéri* emblazoned across the back in fluffy pink fur. People kept reaching out to stroke the words as they passed.

"It might be as alone as we're going to get tonight," Win said. She took a deep breath. "You wanted to talk to me."

Leo looked away. "I'm sorry for pushing. I know you were busy."

"I don't care about that," Win said. She waited.

"I don't think we should do this here," Leo said.

"Do what?"

"I—" Leo faltered. "It's just private. I don't want to talk when there's eighty other people in the room."

"We can go somewhere else." Win stepped back. "Let's go outside. It's quieter there."

Leo didn't look convinced, but he followed her all the same. Most guests were still circulating inside, and in the cherry orchard they could feel more alone than they were. Laughter filtered out through the leaves. The sunset cast them in glowing pink, and the air felt too soft, like the calm before the storm. They found a stretch of railing toward the stern of the boat and leaned over, watching the white path of waves as they cut through the water.

"I hate these parties," Leo said. "Why don't we just take a few selfies and leave?"

"I don't want to miss the fireworks," Win said, though she knew what he meant. It was a tiresome crush of false enthusiasm, the endless chorus of *ohmygodhihowareyou*, and only a matter of time before the coke-fueled pop stars and leering producers found them. But Win had looked forward to weathering it with Leo as they always did, exchanging amused glances over the shoulders of weeping boys, rounding up Riva and her friends, and sneaking off to one of the cabins below deck with a case of champagne, a bag of edibles, and a stolen tray of cake. Right now, Leo still wouldn't look at her.

"Do you remember that night at the Met?" he murmured.

Win shook her head. "God, don't."

"That was a good party."

He meant the night three years ago, when they'd run into each other at the Met Gala. Leo had come alone and Win had brought Adam, a comedian she was seeing at the time, but he'd wandered off to admire the exhibit and—Win suspected—smoke in the bathroom when Leo came over, friendly, to lean over the back of her chair.

"I like the outfit," Leo had said, smiling at her. The theme was Golden Ages, and Win was draped in heavily embroidered gold fashioned to look like armor, brocade plates around her shoulders and the suggestion of a shield slung over her back. Win stood up to hug him, taking in the clean hit of Leo's aftershave, the hint of stubble when he kissed her cheek. They were moving wordlessly away from the bright lights, where they could talk properly, when Jack Caplan, once a heartthrob and now a seedy older actor with a string of shiny twenty-year-old girlfriends, came storming over.

"Hey, Milanowski!" he called. "Milanowski! You think you can just fuck my girlfriend?"

Leo looked up, startled. Win rolled her eyes.

"Oh, come on," she said. "Leo wouldn't do something like that."

"Uhhh," Leo said. "What's your girlfriend's name?"

Win started to laugh despite herself, Leo grinning guiltily at her.

"You think it's fucking funny?" Jack said, voice ugly. "You think that's a really good joke? I'll show you a fucking good joke—"

"I mean, this is already pretty funny," Leo told Win, relaxed and amused as ever, which meant he missed it when Jack lunged toward him, fist raised, face dark with rage.

Win, who had been eyeing Jack with dislike, did not miss it. She moved forward on instinct and shoved him, hard and solid, one heavily jeweled ring catching in the flimsy silk of his toga-style shirt and tearing across his chest.

"That's enough," she snapped.

"This doesn't have anything to do with you, princess," Jack jeered. "Stay out of my way." He barreled forward again, but he was wasted and stupid and Win had spent the past two years starring in a superhero franchise, working out early in the mornings and late in the evenings. She took another step and shoved Jack again, and this time he stumbled backward, flailed for a moment, and then tripped right over the edge of a mosaicked fountain, falling with a heavy splash. Silence broke around them. Jack gaped up at her before his face twisted in rage.

"You fucking bitch," he said, and launched himself out of the fountain and toward her, at which point Leo swung smoothly in the way and punched him in the face.

There was no video ("Thank god," Marie had said, looking pale, at the same time Emil said, "Too bad"), but the incident was widely reported and discussed, especially when a photo emerged of Jack with the first beginnings of a black eye, dazed and furious, and Win and Leo blurry in the background laughing into each other's faces. More photos continued to surface over the next few days as Marie desperately tried to do damage control, revealing the truth of the night. They'd been so pleased with each other, high on adrenaline and their own daring, slouching through the party like they owned it, arms slung around each other. "You fucking idiot," Win had said, smiling up at him, "can't you keep it in your pants for, like, half an hour?" Leo had shrugged.

"Didn't know they were exclusive," he said, and put her hand to his mouth, kissed her palm, told her she was better than a knight in shining armor. Win never remembered to find Adam again. She didn't even think of him, spending the dregs of the gala swaying with Leo in a low-key slow dance, half messing around, half... not, with Leo's hands on her hips, Win's fingers hooked through his belt loops. Their mouths a breath apart.

The media was delighted. Win was a diva, she was dangerous, she'd grown up doing who knows what in the rough parts of London. She became the crazy voicemail girl again—unstable, untamed—except now she'd corrupted America's golden boy in the process. People were worried for Leo.

"This is highly embarrassing," Marie said. "If you'd just let Leo fight him on his own, we wouldn't be in this mess. I could have made it look like a romantic gesture." She considered, then added reluctantly, "It's quite an impressive black eye."

"That was a nightmare," Win said.

"I shouldn't have put that picture up," Leo said ruefully, because a week after the party, when the gossip was just starting to die down, he'd posted a photo of Win in her gold armor, looking directly at the camera, hand out like she was reaching for him, pleased and possessive, her eyes lined with black. He captioned it My hero. "Marie was so mad."

"You have no idea."

She didn't tell him about the private conversation between her and Marie, at dawn on the fire escape of the hotel, hunched over their coffees. *Is this something I need to worry about, Whitman?* Marie wasn't accusatory. It wasn't her job to dictate Win's private life, only to control how and when it was revealed to the world. Win's *no* was firm.

"One day she'll forgive me," Leo said.

"Well, you've been very well behaved this trip," Win said, and frowned when Leo winced. "Leo?"

It had gotten dark while they were standing there. Inside, a Runaways cover band had started up and were already being matched shout for shout by the crowd. The orchard was filling up with partiers eager for smoke and gossip. No one was sucking on cherries anymore—instead bottles of red liquor were being passed from group to group, tossed carelessly aside when they were empty, and Win had to lean in close to keep her focus.

"I don't know how to say this," Leo began.

"*Leo!*" a stranger yelped, not for the first time that night, but Leo swung around at the sound, and then the man was shoving himself between them, wrapping himself around Leo in a greedy hug. Leo hugged him back with startled, stilted affection.

"Alex?"

"Who else?" Alex said. He was a tall, wiry guy with straggly blond hair, underdressed for the party in a brown leather jacket and wide-framed glasses. Once he and Leo had untangled themselves, he turned to Win and held out his hand.

"Right," Leo said. "This is Win."

"Your date!" Alex said.

"Kind of, yeah." Leo glanced at Win. "Alex is a friend from LA."

"This is crazy, right? Like five people have already asked if I'm selling coke."

Win gave Alex a sharp once-over. He seemed to be a typical Silver Lake hipster. A little drunk, maybe, but harmless. She thought he had decided to flout the Cherrybomb! dress code until she noticed his worn T-shirt, a 1960s motif reading BAN THE BOMB. "I bet he's been complaining all night," Alex said, jerking his thumb at Leo. "*Oh, parties bore me. I don't care for fireworks.*" His imitation was so close to the real thing that it shocked Win into a laugh.

"He wanted us to take a few selfies and leave," she told Alex.

"Lenny," Alex said, mock distraught. "You never take selfies with me."

"You're not very photogenic," Leo said.

Alex sighed, resigned, catching Win's gaze and looking rueful. "It's hard when you don't meet his high standards."

"I wouldn't know," Win said, which earned her a laugh from Alex, but Leo was stony-faced. He had let go of her hand.

"What are you doing here? Who else is with you?"

"Hae got us invites from the label," Alex said. "The European tour starts in a week anyway, so we thought, why not? We only landed a few hours ago. Lila and Hae are still sleeping off the jet lag, you know what they're like. They probably won't hit the after-party until four a.m."

"Did you follow me out here?" Leo asked. Win tried to touch his hand, but he brushed her away.

Alex seemed taken aback by the question. "Of course not. We didn't even know you would be here. It doesn't really seem like your speed." He gestured around at the crowd. Beside them two girls were posing for photos, passing a diamond ring back and forth between their teeth. One of the trees had already been knocked over by a couple making out against it, and now they were rolling around in its wreckage, while inside the band screamed on and on. It seemed exactly like Leo's speed to Win, but maybe there were other sides to him, other Leos Win had never met.

"Sorry," Leo said, although he looked harried, as if Alex were an annoying fan, demanding something of him. "It's good to see you. We're just busy right now."

He put his arm around Win's waist. The gesture felt awkward, because, Win guessed, he didn't really want to do it.

"I get it." Alex nodded. "I don't want to interrupt any *secret Hollywood business*." He threw his hands up in a showy gesture. Win felt tension slip through her, iron in her spine, and she looked around reflexively to see if anyone was paying attention to them. Immediately she locked eyes with a smirking casting manager, a man who had labeled her a "high and mighty cockshrinker" a few years before. He wasn't the only one watching them. She forced her smile.

"I'll see you at the after-party, though?" Alex asked.

"Maybe," Leo said. "Or I'll call you tomorrow, okay?"

"Better call Lila. My phone's been dead for a week."

"Sure," Leo said as he basically stage-managed Alex off of the deck. He gave Alex a solid pat on the back that was almost a shove. Alex looked a little hurt. Leo turned his back, his arm tight and demanding around Win's waist, and started walking.

"Nice to meet you," Win said over her shoulder to Alex. Alex raised a hand, watching them fold into the crowd.

Leo pulled her another couple of meters before Win disentangled herself as unobtrusively as she could. Smiling, keeping her lips close together, she said, "Leo, what the hell?"

"Sorry." Leo pressed two knuckles against his eyebrow, drew in a sharp breath. "God. Sorry. I wasn't expecting to see—"

He was actually starting to look upset, and Win caught his hand in midair, linked her fingers through his.

"Hey," she said. "It's okay. Come on, let's go somewhere a little quieter." She pulled him through the crowd. Inside the dancing had gotten dirty, desperate, and hands came grabbing for them. Cans of Cherry Chavanne were rolling between their feet. They took a door on the far side and ran into Zacharias himself, leaning against a locked porthole and looking bored. "Babies," he was calling to a group of models, "babies, please, give the captain back and nobody gets in trouble." Beyond him were stairs, and the way down to a blessedly quiet lower deck where there were only a few other people, huddled in circles, the click of lighters in the dark. If they were lucky, they might have five minutes' peace.

Win turned to Leo. His restless energy had infected her, left her on edge, her heart racing. "Do you want me to talk to security?"

Leo let out a surprised bark of laughter. "No." He passed his hand over his face. He looked very tired. "No. Sorry. He's fine. I just wasn't expecting to see him."

Win hesitated. *Secret Hollywood business*, Alex had said. She steeled herself, then asked, "Does he know about us? The . . . truth about us?"

"I—no," Leo said. "Maybe he's picked up on some of it, but he wouldn't . . . You don't need to worry. It's not about that. It's just a little— I'm not sure about some of his friends."

"Sure about what?" Win said. Leo shrugged. They were quiet while Win tried to fumble her way through the confused fog of champagne and moonlight and her own apprehension to understand what was upsetting Leo. Finally she said, "I know you don't like lying to your friends."

Leo shook his head. "It's not that."

"You wanted to tell me something," Win said. Leo's lips were pressed tight together. He wasn't meeting her gaze. "Leo."

"It's . . ." Leo cleared his throat. "I don't know how to start."

That was when Riva came teetering down the stairs, calling their names. She was in a red leather two-piece and flanked on either side by long-legged, beautiful girls. She had to lean down to hug them, cooing as she ran her hands over Leo's jacket. Each of her friends wanted to hug Leo, too, and one of them demanded a round of photos, Win and Leo caught tight between them like rabbits in a snare. They smelled like expensive perfume and whisky and sweat. On the deck above them a fight had broken out, and Win could hear the grunts of men throwing punches and tables being upended.

"Uh-oh," one of the girls said, not sounding very concerned. "That's probably about me. We should go and stop them."

Riva went with them, all of them doing an admirable job of stalking upstairs in their heels.

"Leo," Win said, "just fucking tell me."

Leo was pale. "Look, I hung out with Alex and his band for a few

114

months earlier this year. We were friends but it ended weirdly and I'd rather not see them."

He looked away the moment he'd said it. Win watched him, waiting for more, but he only shrugged, staring out at the black sea. Upstairs Win could hear joyful cries of "Quentin, stop!" Win knew Leo was still holding back, and she had the sinking feeling that she'd let him down, and let Shift down, but she drew in a breath, taking his hand and pulling it toward her again. There would be time to talk later and tease out the real problem, whatever it was; there was always time to talk.

"All right," she said. "That sucks. But look, we don't really have to be at the after-party. We'll just get off the boat with everyone else, and Emil can have a car waiting. We'll be there for five minutes and then leave. We don't have to talk to your—friends. Alex said they probably wouldn't even get there until four, right?"

"Right," Leo said, nodding fervently.

"Everything will be okay," Win said, and put her other hand up to touch his wrist. She curled her fingers around his, resting their hands on the rails.

"Yeah," Leo said, and managed a stuttering laugh. "Are you reading my palm? Does it say so there?"

"I don't know how to do that," Win said. She wanted to distract him from his panic. "But maybe I'll read your gaudy jewelry." She slid her nail over the silver thumb ring Leo wore. "This says that you went to a fancy boarding school, and still attend reunions every couple of years, and laugh about it but secretly feel very fond of it. I bet you refer to the headmaster as a good old boy."

"Amazing," Leo said. His shoulders relaxed. "Truly your psychic powers are unparalleled."

"Thanks." Win touched the elegant gold ring that snaked up in a spiral from the base of his finger to his knuckle. "Here's your India trip for you. It opened up your life, it changed your world, and now you have something tacky to remember it by."

Leo managed a grin. "Actually, that's an old one of my mum's that I found a couple of years ago. I used to have a ring from India, but it turned my finger green."

"I'm sorry. That was a misstep."

"It's okay. Do you want to go to India together? Think how much fun you'll have telling me about all the stuff I'm doing wrong."

Win wrinkled her nose. "I'll pass." Going to India was tied up in childhood trips with her parents, the crush of hot cities and dozens of strangers waiting to greet them as family, and she wasn't sure how she'd fit Leo into those memories. Most of those family ties had dissolved now, anyway. Win couldn't remember her relatives' names, the places they lived. She took his other hand instead, touching the gold ring, and Leo turned his hand over and let her run her fingers over his palm, skimming down to touch the pulse in his wrist. His forearms were tanned. Her mouth felt dry.

"This one's nice," she said, touching the delicate silver ring that sat on his index finger. "Pretty."

"Hannah made it for me. She went through a metalworking phase."

Win tapped another ring that sat under Hannah's, a bronze band with a greasy pink gem pressed in the center like a dead bug. It glimmered like broken glass. "And this one?"

"Don't actually remember," Leo said. His voice was strange. Win looked up at him and swallowed; his eyes were fixed on her but something about him was closed off, as if he had pulled down the shutters to keep her out. "I think I picked it up in Vegas."

"Appropriate."

If Leo would just tell her what he was thinking, then at least she would be able to react. If it was a problem, they could solve it. If it was about the two of them, they could talk about it. If she knew what he wanted, she could give it to him, or let him down gently. But she wasn't used to Leo not talking to her. Leo was happy to piss her off and happy to fight with her; she wasn't used to being shut out like this. Her heart was pounding in her throat, fluttery and panicked.

There was another round of commotion on the upper deck, and then a shriek as someone—presumably Quentin—was shoved overboard. He fell right past Win and Leo, but the drop at this end wasn't so far and he landed in the water with a splash, coming up spluttering. His nose was bleeding and he turned back up to his adversary, shaking a pathetic fist. "Fuck you, Antoine!" he cried, and behind them the staff came pattering down to calmly fish him out, tossing down a life preserver.

"You really know how to pick a party," Leo said.

"You can talk," Win said. She realized she was being stupid, and turned back. "I just...I want you to know." She spoke slowly, like she was feeling her way across unstable ground, one foot scuffing forward before the other. "I know this is maybe not the right setting, but I want you to know, you can tell me anything."

Leo's voice was rough. "I can?"

"Yes," Win said, "and we'll sort it out, whatever it is, you and me." She looked up at him. "Sometimes it feels like everyone's either lying to me or telling me what I want to hear, but it's not like that with us. You showed me there are still people I can trust. You can trust me, too."

Leo looked stricken, turning away.

"Whatever you need, whenever you need it," she said, and Leo snapped back to her as though she'd tugged on a leash, his eyes dark. Win swallowed. "That's the deal, isn't it?"

Leo nodded, mute.

"Then everything's okay," Win said.

They stood next to each other in the dark beneath the pinpricks of the stars. Leo opened his mouth and closed it, frowned and tried again, and then gave up. Win's heart was beating, too hard.

"What?" she said. "What is it?"

Very quietly, Leo said, "Do you want to do the *Titanic* thing?" and above them, the fireworks took over the sky.

CHAPTER NINE

The faster Win got Leo out of there, the faster she could solve whatever was bothering him. But it was a slow, stately crush as they filed off the yacht, broken glass crunching underfoot and a weeping socialite behind them who demanded Leo's jacket to cover up the candle wax stains on her dress. He shrugged it off wordlessly.

There were golf carts waiting at the bottom of the hill to carry them up to the château, and Leo climbed into the first one they could reach, tapping his hand on the wheel while Win buckled herself in. Usually he would have wanted to race her, or hijacked the cart altogether and swerved them off into the grounds for a joyride. Tonight he was pale and tense, and they didn't speak until they lurched to a halt at the top.

"Where's the car?" he asked.

"It's waiting for us out the front, on the other side. We just have to get through the party."

Leo nodded grimly, and when they reached the castle, he treated these instructions as though they were a military mission, catching Win's hand tight and pulling her through the crowd. It was slow-going: the castle was a series of warren-like rooms with wood-paneled ceilings and marble surfaces, guests already draped over them like expensive furniture. It was hotter inside than it had been out at sea, and people were fanning themselves and dabbing at their brows as they waited for someone to bring them their next drink. Every room was already packed, everyone smoking and chattering and glancing over at Win like they thought she wouldn't notice. A hundred hands reached for Win's and Leo's sleeves, pulling them in, exchanging exuberant greetings.

"This is a nightmare," Leo said.

"Just relax," Win said. "We're almost out."

"Leo, Win! Wait up!" Alex caught up with them, now with a tall, stylish girl on his arm. Her eyes were lined into thick black points.

Leo faltered when he saw her. His hand tightened on Win's hip.

"Hae," he said. "I thought you weren't coming until later."

"Couldn't sleep," Hae said. "Whitman Tagore, it's *such* a pleasure." Win shook her hand warily; Hae had a self-satisfied look to her, with eyelashes that seemed to catch and release every time she blinked, and she wound her arms around Alex and surveyed Win like she didn't trust her.

"Let's go," Leo repeated.

"You can't go!" Alex looked heartbroken. "We just got here. And I think the others will be around, too—"

"The others?" Win asked.

"Our band," Hae explained. Her voice was lush Californian, raw gold. "Leo hung out with us for like, a year, he even came on tour—"

"It was just a few months," Leo said. "I'll catch up with you guys later. It's too crowded here, Win, let's just—"

"Yes," Win said. "Sorry, maybe next time. We really have to get going—"

"*Lenny!*" someone shrieked, and Leo took a step backward, his face blooming with horror.

Shoving her way through the crowd, a girl in faded denim shorts and a halter top broke into a run, wild blond hair falling everywhere, and launched herself at Leo. Win stepped quickly away from the line of impact.

Leo stumbled back, hands coming up to grab the girl's waist as she threw herself onto him. He said, "Lila," and his voice was strained like Win hadn't heard it in years.

"Where have you been, motherfucker?" she asked, climbing Leo like a tree. "You never check your goddamn emails—*oof*—" Leo had dropped her and tried to shake her off, but she clung on, her bare thighs tight around his hips, and instead climbed higher, trying to put him in a headlock. Leo struggled and the two of them went stumbling across the floor, the girl continuing as though there was nothing strange about this at all. "Hae and Alex got invites to this schmoozy yacht party—"

"Lila," Leo said, shaking himself about like a dog trying to lose a tick, "Lila, c'mon, get off—"

Lila flung herself upward, catching herself over his shoulder with a yelp. "And I said, *hello*, you know I get seasick, but I'll come to the after-party, and now *you're* here as well!"

Leo put his hands up in the air, flatly refusing to hold her up, and Lila shrieked again and slid further, saving herself with her arms tight around Leo's waist. She hung upside down over his shoulder, her cheek pressed to the small of his back. They were making a scene. A lot of people were staring. Win tried to smile as if she thought the whole thing was hilarious.

"Lila," Leo repeated. "Seriously, get off me," and he gave another determined wriggle and Lila said, "Oh, fine," and dove forward into a—mildly impressive—somersault, nearly kicking Leo in the nose in doing so.

She landed on her feet with a flourish. When she straightened up, she was still a head shorter than Win. "I'm *so* underdressed," she drawled, that nasal Californian accent like a skinnier version of Hae's.

"Leo," Win said. Leo turned to look at her, his expression frozen. There was an awful, hollow feeling expanding in Win's chest.

Before he could say anything, Lila turned to Win and stuck her hand out. "And you must be the girlfriend," she said, with a certain derision in her voice that made Win feel on show, seen.

Win took her hand and shook it. "That's right," she said, keeping her voice pleasant. "And you're . . . ?"

"Oh, babe," Lila said. She leaned in and spoke in an exaggerated stage whisper. "I'm the wife."

"Ha," Win said. For a moment everything was blurry and then it coalesced again, Leo's horror and Lila's cocky smile. "What?"

Then Lila stuck out her hand, wiggling her fingers. On her left ring finger was a tarnished bronze band with a filmy pink jewel, just the same as Leo's. Win blinked. She turned to Leo, who was clearly miserable, looked at his stricken face with his mouth half-open, looked at Hae and Alex, who were a mixture of laughing and guilty, and looked, finally, at Leo's hand, at his fucking ring, at the *ugly cheap ring* that he'd lied to her about, once aloud and every second before and after, like she didn't deserve to know the truth.

"Right." Win thought of her conversation with Shift and of Leo's desperate attempts to talk to her and wanted to laugh, hysterical and furious. God, she'd been such an idiot. Of course Leo wasn't nurturing secret feelings for her. Of course it was this: Leo being irresponsible, and untrustworthy, and selfish, and reminding her for the hundredth time why they would never, ever work.

"Win," Leo said. "Whitman, listen—"

"You can't remember, huh?" Win said. She tried to keep her voice level. It was important not to attract any more attention. "You picked it up somewhere in Vegas? I—" She stopped and laughed. It sounded brittle even to her own ears. "No, right, that makes sense."

"I think I won the rings, actually," Lila said. "Leo's got a terrible poker face."

"Whitman," Leo said. "Come with me—"

"No, you stay here," Win said. "I'm leaving." She turned and stalked away, keeping her face as composed as possible, pulling her phone out of her clutch with hands that were only slightly shaking. She couldn't find the exit and the car that was waiting; she swung a hard right, deeper into the innards of the castle instead, wanting only to be away, and alone.

Leo followed her, though she moved quickly and darted through enough doors and crowds of milling people that he took a while to find her again. By then she'd discovered a side room, dark except for one bare bulb hanging in threads of electrical wiring from the ceiling, empty except for the mess of party planning, deflated balloons and used confetti dispensers shoved into boxes in the corner. When he came in she turned away, focused on her phone call.

"No, I'm fine," she said. She was annoyed that Leo had come in time to hear her say so. It was true, but she thought it might be coming out defensive. "It's a massive pain, of course, but—yes, I know—"

"Win," Leo said as he closed the door. Win held out her hand, one finger pointed up, a polite *one moment please*. Leo's eyes narrowed.

"I'll find the car," Win said. "Yeah, that's him."

"Hang up," Leo told her. He was coming closer with intent; Win sidestepped him, skipped out of the way. "Win, c'mon, talk to me."

"Yeah, I assume he's here to grovel," Win said. Leo's mouth twisted. "Okay, look, I'll talk to you soon. Thank you. Thanks. Bye."

She hung up.

"Win."

"Yep," Win said. He was right there but she felt very far away. "Go on, then. Let's hear it."

Leo rubbed his hand over his face. He was like a child, Win thought, who didn't know what to do with attention once he'd claimed it.

"You've got about five minutes," Win said, tapping out a text message to Emil, "and then I'm leaving. I've got an early flight tomorrow, so—"

"What?"

"Oh, I'm sorry," Win said. "Did you want to hang around with your fake girlfriend and your apparently real wife? That's such a sensible thing to do, it should have occurred to me."

"Win," Leo said, and took a step forward, grabbing her hands. "I'm really sorry. I should have told you."

Win wrenched herself out of his grip. "You think?"

"I tried to," Leo said. "But it's complicated. I couldn't get you alone, and then there was all this other stuff going on—"

"Right," Win spat. "I forgot this was my fault."

"That's not what I meant," Leo said. "Come on, Win, look at tonight—I tried to get you on your own—"

"You told me that you didn't want to see the band because it ended weirdly," Win snapped. "Is that your definition of a wedding?"

"I shouldn't have said that," Leo said. "I was trying to tell you and it was— We kept getting interrupted, I panicked. I didn't want you to find out like this."

"Oh, you're such a gentleman."

"Just listen to me." Win wanted to look away and couldn't. Leo could get so serious so fast, could demand things of her that no one else could. "I got a call from Marie in the middle of the night that Nathan fucked you over and you needed me and then—you wouldn't talk about him—"

"What does Nathan have to do with any of this?" She took a step forward, set her hands against his chest, and shoved him. It felt good to finally shout, a month or a year or a decade's worth of frustration unleashed on Leo, who finally deserved it. "You lied to me!"

"I know! I know!" Leo turned, running his hand over his head, taking a few rough steps away and whirling back. "I just mean every-thing was weird, and you were upset, and I wasn't ready for it, and there was never a good time to tell you."

"We've spent every day together for a week," Win said. "Don't blame this on me. You know what my life's like. If you wanted to tell me, you would have told me."

"I should have," Leo said. He licked his lips. "I wanted to. I didn't want it to be like this. Really, I'm not lying, I didn't think we'd see her,

I didn't think it was going to be an issue. I wasn't thinking about her, I was thinking about you."

"Oh yeah, you're such a good guy," Win said, and leaned against the wall, arms hugged around herself. "Leo, you're married?"

"It's complicated," Leo repeated. His voice sounded like it had been dragged over coals. "The whole thing was so intense. I haven't even seen her in a couple of months, we barely talk."

"I just can't believe you didn't tell me," Win said.

"I didn't want to hurt you."

"Well, this will," she said. "You must know that."

"I thought that I could explain in a way that would, like—" Leo stopped speaking so abruptly that Win turned to look behind him, wondering if someone had come in and shut him up. But it was just Leo, his brow furrowed in the dim light. "Wait. *Will* hurt you?"

"How long do you think you can keep your secret marriage a secret for?" she demanded. "You're not this oblivious, Leo, come on!"

"What exactly are you angry at me about?" Leo's voice was strained. Win stared at him. "You know what."

"Yeah," Leo said, pushing off the wall toward her, "yeah, but— why, then?"

"You're going to mess everything up," she said. "The press are going to find out. No one's going to believe in our relationship if you have a secret wife. If anyone figures out it's a publicity stunt—"

"Holy shit." Leo let out a breath, and Win felt her whole body light up with outrage.

"Do you think I'm *jealous*?" she snarled. "I'm working, Leo! I'm doing my job! You're the one fucking about, you're the one who thinks this doesn't mean anything—"

Leo's expression was mutinous. "Am I?"

"Yes! I trusted you! How am I meant to be able to trust you for this stuff when you keep secrets that can fuck everything up?"

"Who were you on the phone with just now?"

"What?"

"On the phone," Leo said. "You were talking to someone about me. Was it Shift? Was it your mum?"

"No," Win said. "No, obviously, it was Marie."

"You're unbelievable."

"Oh, get over yourself," Win snapped. "This is a business arrangement, and I don't appreciate you acting like you don't know that."

"You don't appreciate it," Leo repeated, face dark with anger. "Jeez, Win, I'm sorry to disappoint you. I guess it's just hard for us normal people sometimes. It gets hard being fake about everything all day every day. Not everyone lives their life based on what it's going to look like on the fucking internet!"

Win gaped at him. That yawning, hollow, terrible feeling was eating further into her chest, and Leo was breathing hard, like it was something he'd wanted to say for a long, long time.

"You're right," she said. "You don't care what your life looks like at all. You're going to spend the next forty years being as spoiled and aimless as—"

"This isn't about what I want to do with my life."

"Nothing's ever about what you want to do with your life," Win said. She was rigid with the effort of keeping her voice level. "Are you mad at me for having ambitions? For going after them? You've been going on about your studio for years and you haven't even picked a fucking country for it. Sometimes I think you just talk about it to cover up how empty your life is."

"You got me," Leo said through gritted teeth.

"It's pathetic," Win said. "Your whole life is set up for you and you still can't do anything with it. You can have anything you want. All you have to do is take it, and you can't even be bothered to reach out."

"Fuck you, Whitman."

Win bared her teeth in a smile. "I think that's adultery now."

"I can do what I want," Leo said, stepping up close. "It was never part of our deal that I have to live by your robotic standards—"

"Then go live your life," Win said, "and stop messing up my plans. Just leave."

"No," Leo said, "listen. You can manage Marie and Emil and the paparazzi—you can manage Nathan and your *mum*—but I won't let you manage me."

"I think you've misunderstood something there, Leo," she said. "I've been managing you for years."

They stared at each other. Leo was trembling with rage.

In her hand, where she was still clutching it, Win's phone started to buzz. She looked down and saw Ma flashing up on the screen. Leo saw it too; his lip curled. *You can manage your mum.* Win wanted to hit something.

"Ma," she said, picking up and turning away from Leo; she was done with Leo. "This isn't a great time—"

"Whitman." It wasn't her mum. It was her aunt. "I'm sorry to call so late. But I think you need to come home."

CALIFORNIA ✈ LONDON

CHAPTER TEN

Kuffel Canyon, California, is a stone's throw south of Lake Arrowhead. Because of the thickness of the pines, it feels like there's a great distance between you and any other people, even though the woods are dotted with cabins and holiday homes. There's a small village on the south side of the lake, with a harbor, a rinky-dink amusement park, and a general store where you can pick up candy and fresh-cut watermelon. The store closes at eleven p.m., so every night that summer at around ten thirty, Lila and Leo and whoever else was awake would pile into her secondhand Ford Fiesta and cruise into the village. Most of the bars and restaurants stayed open late at that time of year, but the village still felt sleepy, and the cashier who rang up their purchases of green vegetables and Anchor Steam beer was usually yawning. Some nights the sky was clear enough that they could see the starry rim of the San Bernardino Mountains from the parking lot.

The band split the rent of their cabin fifty-fifty with their label. There were two bedrooms, one occupied by Alex and Hae, the other by the band's drummer, Jennifer. Officially, Lila slept on the foldout camp bed in the laundry room, and Leo had the couch. In reality the cabin was furnished like a kid's fort, every surface soft and roomy, full of cushions and beanbags and love seats, and they tended to fall asleep wherever they fell. More than once Leo had lost track of time and spent the night in the hammock on the porch. He woke up covered in insect bites and had to spend the next day taking ice baths in the porcelain tub.

Eighteen months before he came to Saint-Tropez, Leo had arrived in LA for the spring, because his dad had requested Leo's presence at the thirtieth anniversary party of one of his hotels. He'd also requested that Leo take a room there for the week, but Leo told him he already had a place to crash. Alex was a friend from New York who used to project kaleidoscopic animations on the walls of loft parties until he moved to LA to start a band. He came to pick Leo up from LAX, along with a girl wearing a ripped denim jacket and Birkenstocks. They were arguing at the arrivals gate. After Alex had introduced them, she grabbed Leo by the elbow and said, "Settle this for us, do you think this text is scary or sexy," and held out her phone to him. Leo was jet-lagged and confused. It took him several blinks to make a judgment.

"Both," he said, and the girl crowed in triumph.

"You're too good for Alex," she told him, hitting send. "You're mine now." Leo stretched and thought, *Well, why not.*

The party came and went, and Leo shook enough hands and drew in enough photographers for his dad to send him a grudging thank-you note signed, *With all due respect, Bernard Milanowski.*

"I'd say he's a dick," Lila said, "but I'd kill for your trust fund. You can deal."

Lila had lived in LA since she was twenty and had worked at a greengrocer, an anarchist pet store, and several vegan restaurants before her music finally started bringing in enough money for her to focus on it full-time. The band never hit the mainstream, but they had been featured on a few indie movie soundtracks, and they had a scrappy cult following across the States. She had also cowritten a love song that was passed down the line and reproduced into a one-hit wonder, and the royalties from that twinned with various other songwriting credits made her enough money to live on. She rented a room in a house in Echo Park with five other people and an outdoor kitchen. The floor was always sticky and her room was full of empty bottles, but Leo loved to wake up there, to hear the early morning sounds of her roommates around him while they lay curled in her bed.

When she told him that they were renting a cabin for the summer where they could write their next album, Leo signed up to join them before she'd even offered. He had spent the last two months drifting between Alex's and Lila's houses, and now he looked up for the first time and realized he had no plans to leave. His father was spending the summer at one of his resorts and was unlikely to need Leo. Gum was busy fumbling deals in New York, and Hannah had dropped off the radar since March. Win was filming back-to-back projects and had been seen holding hands with a panel show host, so nobody was looking for Leo. He disappeared with Lila into the woods.

"You can pay for groceries," Lila said. "And you can have my back when Alex starts messing with my lyrics."

In the early evenings when the air was cooler, they would take hikes into the pine forests or drive to the lake and swim together in the shadow of the mountains. Depending which beach they were at, they could sometimes see the watchtower at Strawberry Peak glinting in the darkness. This always made Alex paranoid, because he had read too many articles about government surveillance and was distrustful of lights that came on at night with no apparent function. He avoided cameras, security checks, and social media, and the rest of the band indulged him. Leo's online presence shrank down to his weekly video calls with Gum, who gave forlorn monologues on various feuds with more-successful businessmen and chastised Leo for the state of his personal grooming.

It was the sort of idyll Win would've rolled her eyes at. Lila rolled her eyes a lot, too, but she also took pure enjoyment from her surroundings in a way that Leo had only seen imitated before. She stayed up the latest and woke up the earliest. She wrote strange, yelping, sexy songs, and she played her own albums at her own parties. When she wanted

his attention, she would wave a hand in front of his face like he'd
fallen asleep. When he wanted her attention, he would reach out as she
ran past and hook a finger in the belt loop of her shorts to slow her
down. They took long drives together and climbed to the top of the
Pinnacles. Once when they were both sick, she flew her older sister in
from Orlando to look after them.

He'd wondered for a while what would happen if Lila and Win met.
But the possibility of it seemed so far-fetched, like trying to imagine
the boulevards of LA cracking open when the Big One hit. Unthink-
able. They moved in different orbits. In his own head he never let
them touch. He waited for Lila to ask about his turbulent relationship
with Whitman Tagore the movie star, but she never brought it up.
Eventually he brought it up himself, telling her unprompted about
their first week in New York, about their deal, about the way Win
made him feel useful and important but sometimes also claustrophobic,
like he was caught in a net.

Lila said, "You could just be like, *I don't want to do it anymore.*"

"But then I'd never see her," Leo said.

Lila shrugged, went back to painting his toenails, and changed
the subject.

The band returned to LA in the fall, with twelve completed tracks,
several garbage bags full of dirty laundry, and Leo in tow. Leo checked
his emails for the first time in months. He hadn't missed anything
important. He called Win on a whim at Alex's birthday party, barefoot out on the porch among the prickly pear and cigarette butts. She
wasn't entirely tuned in to the conversation, said there was a bit of a
shitstorm going on with one of her projects and *thanks but I don't think
so,* when Leo asked if he could help. He came back inside just as they
were lighting candles on the cake, everybody singing "Happy Birthday" at different tempos and with terrible harmonies. It was good not
to be needed, he told himself; it was good to go only where he was
genuinely wanted. Lila told him that the band was preparing to spend

the rest of the autumn on tour. Leo had never lived on the road before. He was curious.

They rattled off in a van, unspooling months of Leo and Lila rambling across the country together underneath a highway sky. He got used to the dim lighting of basement shows and motel showers. He developed competencies he had not thought possible. He learned how to take apart a drum kit and put it back together again, how to push-start the van, how to hit and hold a low C. He goaded Lila into writing a song about him that she would never record. They indulged each other. Lila picked fights with Alex constantly but with Leo she was lenient, unconcerned. Leo never had to parse his thoughts in his head before he said them out loud. It was cold on the East Coast, and they were forever finding new hidden places to sneak away together and get warm. They talked through sex, as they talked through everything.

Leo got used to a different scale of problem, no longer caring about international press scandals or navigating billion-dollar industries. Now a problem meant a motel owner catching them trying to sneak four people into a two-bed room, or beardy technicians talking over Lila at sound check, or neighbors yelling at them through the drywall to turn their music down. Lila snapped back at anyone who was rude to her and seemed surprised when Leo asked if he could help. "Just don't be a dick," she said. "What else are you supposed to do?" It was what Leo had always wondered, too.

By December they were deep in the Midwest, and Leo thought, looking out at cornfields and eating his drive-through meals, that he had found the real world at last. "Poor runaway Leo," Lila said, "like the Little Prince coming down to earth," but she took him wherever he wanted to go.

Once he woke up early because Win had messaged him. She'd mentioned him in an interview coming out the next week, no big revelations but a hint that they were still in communication, and wanted to warn Leo not to be surprised by an influx of messages when it came out. Marie thought it might get them trending for a while, and Win didn't want Leo to wake up and think someone had died or Gum had tried to sue the Rockefeller Foundation again. Everything's okay, she wrote, just more of the usual. Call when you're back in London. Miss you!

It occurred to Leo then that he ought to tell Win about Lila. She had always known about his past relationships, coming up whenever they spoke ("Not another performance artist," she would groan, "the last one livestreamed her appendectomy,") but Win had been busy and Leo had been asleep in Lila's bed, without much cause for talking. He considered it for a week, back and forth. Win's interview came out, and Hae read the part about Leo aloud in a silly voice while they were stuck in traffic on the interstate. Leo laughed along. He decided that no, Win didn't need to know about this. The decision gave his feelings a solidity they hadn't had before. He sometimes felt that Win knew more about him than anyone else, could feel her cool assessment tracking everything he did, so the very act of keeping something from her made it significant.

He communicated some of these thoughts to Lila, and concluded with "Anyway, I think I'm in love with you."

"Oh, Lenny," Lila said. "That's a little bit fucked up, but I love you, too."

They got back to LA just after New Year's. Leo stayed at Lila's place and spent his mornings cleaning her kitchen to the sleepy approval of her housemates. He kept himself busy, helping Alex set up a short film exhibition and organizing an elaborate homecoming party. He laughed and shrugged when Lila's friends asked him what he did for a living; it was LA, so living off your parents' assets wasn't rare.

In the spring Leo flew to New York for Gum's twenty-ninth birthday party. It was held in a rented-out nightclub in Chelsea, and he spent most of it locked in a back room with Charlie and Gum, who smoked furiously and performed live readings and rebuttals of his own hate mail. There were numerous VIPs at the party and a cohort of press outside the gates. Diving into the attention and crush of bodies felt like falling into a cold spring after spending hours in a sauna. While Leo had been playing house, Win's panel show host had turned into a serious boyfriend, and people were eager for his opinion.

In the absence of direction from Marie, Leo performed as a cocksure playboy: sure, he was happy for Win and the new guy; no, he hadn't heard of Nathan Spencer before; and no, he didn't care to comment on his own relationship status at this time. In his hotel room he googled Spencer in the middle of the night, and was immediately snowed under by photo after photo of Whitman Tagore and her new lover. He slammed his laptop shut with a shock of guilt. He went to sleep.

The morning after the party he half expected a call from Win; she normally checked in with him when he came up on her radar. Usually these were long, spiraling calls that got away from both of them, where Leo would look up absently and see that two or three hours had passed without either of them noticing. If she was filming, she would video call and prop her phone up against the mirror as the makeup artists went to work, talking to him out of the corner of her mouth, telling him off when he made her laugh. She waited until the last minute to hang up, as though speaking to Leo were a charm that needed to be drawn out for potency. But this time there was nothing. He would find out later that she had been filming in rural Scotland and mostly off-line. That was fine, obviously. Win lived strangely in his head. She didn't follow patterns, like a body of water that was always there but emptied and refilled erratically over time. He packed up his bags again and left New York with relief.

In LA, all his new friends were waiting for him in the backyard, burning hickory firewood in a pit in the ground. The stars were out, and there were plans to get up early the next morning and go whale watching in Monterey. Lila and Leo snuck up to her room and ended up having sex half-dressed on top of all the debris on Lila's bed.

"Welcome home, for real," Lila said, smiling hazy-eyed, and Leo had that feeling of wanting to be trapped in one place, wanting to dig his heels in. It didn't need to matter that he had no plans. It didn't need to matter that Win hadn't called. He wanted to be on the road again, wanted to sleep in the woods with Lila and be nobody, mean nothing to anyone except her.

If his mood had noticeably changed, Lila didn't comment on it. They got married in Vegas a week later.

There was no honeymoon, just a hangover the morning after, eating pancakes for breakfast at three p.m. Leo rapped his new ring against the plastic tabletop and Lila said, "Hey, does this mean I get half your trust fund?" They piled back into Alex's car together and took turns napping on the drive home. It took them a while to realize their mistake.

Lila took on a few different projects, songwriting and production, and came home late in the evenings. Leo wasn't sure where to be while she was gone. He started losing sleep, milling about the house in the early hours before dawn, and picking up books that he never read to the end. In the evenings he stayed up until she returned, and warmed up dinner for her, and they kept running out of things to say. He slept over at Alex's place a few times, and after a while he moved his things over as well. Alex's place was bigger, and it wasn't fair to Lila's roommates to have Leo there all the time, sloping about, buying the wrong kind of cereal and getting in the way. He could sense the disintegration as it happened, like watching crushed ice melt in a glass.

He didn't know what he had expected from the marriage. Were he and Lila going to buy a house together, have kids? Did he think he could just step out of his own life and disguise himself in Lila's? As if everyone would eventually just forget who he was, and let him go.

Finally Lila said it, brightly, the same way she'd announced a wrong turn while they were on the road. *Oops!* "I think maybe we killed it, Lenny."

"Yeah," Leo said. "I think that was my fault."

She patted him on the arm. "Look, everyone says you're supposed to marry your best friend, right?"

"Right," Leo agreed, and for some reason thought of Win. He knew then that he needed to leave.

He left LA in the first throes of summer, first to London and then, when that didn't feel far enough away, to Berlin. He kept himself busy scouting artists for his dad, and with the time difference it was easy to dodge Lila's occasional calls. He felt as though he'd spent a year in orbit, circling without ever touching down. Berlin at the start of July was like living between the first two dots of an ellipsis. The sun went down but the streets never cooled, and the rain fell like steam. Leo ate vegan pizzas and spent time with the handful of expats he knew and tried to ignore the itch of failure that had settled over him.

When Marie called him out to Saint-Tropez, she had not given him time to think, and Leo didn't want to think too much anyway. He buzzed his hair down low, blinking at himself in a bathroom mirror, while he waited for the private car that would take him to the airport. He felt clean and ready, made new. Win needed him again, and he would be good at this, he knew; he would be good for Win. It was the only thing on his mind.

That made things all the worse the night of the Chavanne party, after Win had put her hand over the speaker of her phone, looked at him coldly, untouchable, and said, "I can't deal with this right now." She disappeared, like Leo was an annoying fan, a problem beneath Win's attention. He turned on his heel and headed straight for the bar.

Lila was there, chewing on a straw, and her stricken face made him angrier.

"Hey," she said, "Leo, look, I didn't mean to piss her off—"

"It's fine," Leo said. Lila reached one hand out to his face but didn't quite make contact. "Let's get some shots."

"All right," Lila said, but she was still watching him. She waved the bartender over and ordered tequila. Leo passed on the salt and lime. Lila looked concerned, but nodded, and they did them straight, standing up at the bar. Leo signaled for another.

"Baby," Lila said. She looked unsure. "I'm really sorry, I was just excited to see you—"

"It's not *your* fault," Leo snapped.

Lila's eyebrows went up. "I know. I would have called if I thought you'd pick up the phone."

The first shot was lingering in Leo's throat, like smoke after a forest fire. "Yeah," he said. "I'm sorry."

Lila did touch him then, stroking a hand roughly over his head.

"Why didn't you tell her? I wish I could tell everyone. It would be my opening line at parties. I'd say, like, *My husband is in Saint-Tropez with another woman*, and they would all buy me drinks."

Leo took the second shot and ordered a third, which was a foolish thing to do. Lila watched him. The space between her question and his answer was growing.

He spent the night refusing to think about why he hadn't just told Win. Lila stayed subdued and guilty, sticking close to the bar and not seeking Leo out. Leo passed from guest to guest, finishing their drinks for them and telling anyone who asked that Win was in the next room, they had just missed her. He found some of the male models he'd met in Paris hanging shiftily about the bathroom, and took what they gave him, came back grinning, and dragged Alex out to dance.

The night blurred. The music took on a wilted, end-of-the-wedding tone, a few lone couples on the dance floor. He stumbled through the smoke and back out into the long driveway. Lila was behind him again. She put a cool hand to the back of his neck. There were cameras and photographers shouting, as always, though not as many as when Win was about; they hadn't worked out yet that anything was wrong, though Leo was sure it was only a matter of time. He let Lila lead him away and out of the crowd, past security and into a quieter area, just the waitstaff smoking and valets running past to bring out the cars. Leo couldn't remember where they were and handed Lila his phone so she could call him a cab.

"Leo," she said, "I think you should—you have all these missed calls from a Marie, is it—"

"Ugh," he said.

She patted his neck again. "All right." She waited with him until the car arrived. She'd once told him that she was at her most brilliant and functional at the end of a bad night out, while everyone else was relighting cigarettes and sitting cold on the curb.

"Hey, Lenny," she said, and straightened up, solemn-faced. "I really am sorry."

"All you did was tell the truth," Leo said. "Lila. *I'm* sorry."

Lila thumbed over his ear. "We're good. Talk to me sooner, this time."

She helped him into the back seat. Leo must have gotten the cab to drop him off a few streets away in the hope of avoiding the paparazzi, because he could remember stumbling down several graveled pathways before he found the hotel. His phone rang again, Marie's name and a picture of Cruella de Vil flashing bright on the screen, and he tossed it into a dumpster before he could stop himself. Later he would wonder if the press could get hold of it. Anyone might find it there, but he told himself he didn't care.

He managed to enter La Réserve through the garage, but once he was inside he got lost, not sure what floor he was on, wandering down corridor after corridor and holding his key card up to doors that seemed familiar, even though they all looked the same. He made it to reception eventually, where he sat waiting in a plush armchair while the concierge booked him an early morning flight back to London. He kept fishing in his pocket for his phone, and then remembering.

In London's misty dawn Leo got a cab from the airport back to Primrose Hill and the apartment he shared with his sister. Hannah wasn't there. They both saw their apartment as more of a crash pad and storage space than an actual home. The kitchen was a mess of coffee cups, empty beer bottles, orange peels molding on the countertops, and several copies of Gum's self-published autobiography (*Gums Away!*) covered in cigarette ash. He spent a laborious, grim-faced hour clearing as much of it as he could, stripped down to an undershirt and jeans, stalking out to the trash with garbage bags five times in a row. His mouth tasted sour and there was nothing to eat.

When he was done, he sat on his sofa and rubbed the heels of his palms against his eyes until his vision went blurry, little sparks going off in the corners of his eyelids. He needed to get a new phone. He needed to let his mums know he was in the city before they found out and got pissed he hadn't told them. He needed to listen to the inevitable tirades Marie would have left on his voicemail and see if there was anything he should actually care about.

He took a shower instead, and found some beer hiding at the back of the fridge. He watched a documentary about the ice caps.

September was long and extraneous. Word got out that he was in London, and people started coming around, the old crowd bringing over food and drinks and gifts and purposefully not asking about anything they might have seen or heard about him. His mother Gabrysia showed up and spent half an hour stacking the dishwasher badly and asking him leading questions that he ignored, sulky like a small boy. For the whole month he was so angry that it almost bored him. He woke up with his fists clenched. He felt stupid and abandoned. He started doing yoga again to try to calm himself down, but he couldn't hold the poses for long, sliding back down to the floor with a satisfying thud.

There were photographers hanging around, of course. They showed up gradually, a shuffling, smoking crowd on the pavement, talking shop to each other while they waited for him to come out. Leo didn't really care, and his friends were used to it. He wondered if the press had found out about the marriage. Twice he went to go outside and tell them, and then stopped himself, scowling. He gathered from his friends and the occasional glimpse of a magazine cover at the corner shop that Win was also back in the UK, and had gone silent, holed up in one of her homes on the coast. He'd thought she was starting some amazing new project this month. He told himself he didn't care about that either.

The first time he ventured outside properly was to visit Thea's studio—he still didn't have a phone, so she had, quite inventively, sent him an insistent postcard. On the way to his car there were stirrings of attention from the paparazzi and a clamor of calls.

"Leo, what happened? Did you guys have another fight?"

"Did she go back to Nathan, Leo? Did you fuck it up again?"

Leo glanced at them and yawned, unimpressed, as he unlocked the car. While he was climbing in, one of them called, "You're looking tired, Leo."

He tried to go out more after that. He went to a friend's gallery opening and came back mutinous; it was the kind of show he would normally have enjoyed, but he'd had Win's voice ringing in his ears the whole time. *You just talk about it to cover up how empty your life is.* He got a new phone with a new number. He checked his emails once, for five minutes, but there were about three thousand messages waiting for him, and he logged off again. Every time an unknown number called, he hit decline, but he had reluctantly saved Marie's and Win's numbers, and neither of them ever rang.

Gum came to visit, depositing piles of duty-free aftershave and cigars onto Leo's kitchen counter. Their father was concerned that Leo was nearing a public breakdown, and wanted Gum around to keep him from doing anything that would damage the Milanowski brand.

"How does he think you're going to help?" Leo asked, and Gum shrugged.

"Beats me. I think he just wanted an excuse to get me out of New York."

Leo was surprised how much of a relief it was to have someone to talk to. On the first night, they covered the marriage ("Very gauche!" Gum said), the fallout with Whitman ("A bitch!" Gum said), and Leo's current state of low-level fury ("Tiresome!" Gum said). He advised Leo to come back to the States, roll up his sleeves, and bury his troubled mind in the business. Leo, who could not think of anything worse either for himself or for the business, declined.

In an attempt to convince him, Gum dragged Leo to a series of lunches and unending dinners with various family acquaintances. Gum still believed that he had been born into wealth for a reason, and was trying to live up to it by becoming the spitting image of their father. Leo watched Gum falter through meeting after meeting, trying to be liked, trying to be the real deal rather than a hapless heir with an anxiety disorder and a complete lack of business sense. It was another life that Leo could have chosen, and it would have been even more pointless than bumming around LA with Lila. The idea that any of them could be worthy of their wealth seemed ridiculous.

All the time Leo's bitter mood circled them, present in every room. At the end of the week, Gum gave his prognosis: Leo was spoiled, the entire episode was trite, and he needed to get over it.

"Hannah says we're all spoiled," Leo said.

"I don't think she meant that to be an excuse," Gum said. He headed to the airport several hours later, leaving behind a bottle of Xanax, a vape pen, and a pile of tabloids, most featuring Leo's face. The note on top said: *You look like shit! Move on!!*

Leo flipped through them with a desultory hand. Flashes of his own face, sunglasses on under gray skies, mouth twisted down and disapproving, and then of Win, all her photos taken at bad angles and timings so that she looked tired, stretched out, worn thin. His gaze darted over the headlines: WIN'S BREAKDOWN; LEO'S GONE AND SHE'S OUT

OF CONTROL; and perhaps his favorite, THE EX FACTOR: LEO AND NATHAN DISH ON THE BISH. He thought idly about beating Nathan Spencer up, then threw them all out.

He'd been lulled the way he always was when his family were around, but after Gum's departure Leo was alone again. Win's silence felt deliberate and communicative, not a missed connection but a closed door. Over the next few days he did his best to follow his brother's advice, but it didn't take long for the anger to creep back in, insidious and nasty, whispering in his ear. *Did you think I was jealous?*

The year was closing in on October when Leo got stopped outside his apartment. He had his usual chaperone of photographers talking at him in an indistinct chorus, when one of them yelled out, "What happened at the hospital, Leo?"

He paused. "What?"

The paparazzo's eyes widened, like he couldn't believe his luck. "Is she on drugs? An eating disorder? Don't you know?"

Leo stared, opened his mouth for another question, but he'd stood still for too long, and they were circling him. Another guy stepped forward.

"Did you do something to her?"

Leo closed his eyes, then blinked them back open. "No. C'mon, guys, I have places to be." He shouldered his way through.

He only had to type Whi into the search bar before she came up in suggested searches. The second suggestion was Whitman Tagore and Leo Milanowski. The third was Whitman Tagore rehab. The headlines were much worse. TRASHED TAGORE. IN AND OUT OF HOSPITAL WITH WHITMAN'S SECRET ADDICTIONS. DRUGS AND DESPAIR: LIFE AFTER LEO.

He opened the first article, scrolling quickly. When he was done he read another, and another.

He stood up, hovering in the center of the room. He wondered what Marie was doing now. Then, determined and undone, he picked up his phone, and his keys.

EAST SUSSEX

CHAPTER ELEVEN

Leo didn't switch on the radio until he was out of London, by which time BBC Radio 1's afternoon show was already in full swing. During a music break Robbie himself texted Leo, just a string of exclamation marks and then mate i'm fucking honoured haha. Leo grimaced. His shoulders were tight, his spine a long bar of tension. He settled for glaring at his GPS.

"Iiiit's five-oh-seven p.m. and you're listening to BBC Radio 1," Robbie said as the latest pop track faded out. "Are you having a good day, Dunya? I'm having a good day."

"Just fine, thanks," Dunya, Robbie's producer, said.

"Other people aren't, though," Robbie said, his rich, plummy voice thrilling with delight. "If we pop back to our usual segment of 'Celebrity Schadenfreude'—"

"That is not what we're calling it," Dunya said.

"Of course we are, we're very cultured over here," Robbie said. "We've got the latest ominous whispers from Kensington Palace, but let's be honest, we still want to talk about Whitman Tagore."

"You've always had a thing for her," Dunya said.

"Who among us hasn't, Dunya? I've met her, and what a girl, very calm under pressure. But maybe no longer, huh?"

A message from Marie flashed up on his phone screen. *That's your cue.*

Leo settled his phone in the cradle and dialed the number she'd sent him. "I mean, this is a woman who's normally very open," Robbie was saying when they patched him through. "She lives in the public eye, a total charmer, and then all of a sudden—bam!—dumped by Nathan Spencer, big blowup with the on-again, off-again boyfriend—old mate of mine, by the way—"

"You just can't drop that in enough," Dunya said. Leo exhaled.

"And she disappears," Robbie continued, "holes up with her mum, keeps getting photographed going into the hospital looking dreadful, I mean, what are we supposed to think?"

"Well, we've got a surprise caller," Dunya said. "Speaking of your old friend."

"You're kidding," Robbie said, with cheerful faux surprise. "Leo Milanowski, as I live and breathe!"

"Hi, Robbie," Leo said, keeping his voice light. "Heard you were throwing my name about."

"It's been too long! You practically taught me how to pick up women—"

"Not that successfully," Dunya added.

"And now look at you, you don't call, you don't write—"

"I'm still getting over my hangover from your last birthday," Leo said.

Robbie cackled again. "What a nice surprise, though. Are we in trouble?"

"No, no," Leo said. "You guys are fine. But, you know, there's been a lot of strange things being thrown about, a lot of rumors and then just crazy, unbelievable— Can I swear on air?"

"Dunya would really prefer if you didn't," Robbie said. "For those just tuning in, it's BBC Radio 1 with me, Robbie Hayes, and I've got London's very own bad boy Leo Milanowski on the line. This must be your first interview in what, five years? Where are you now, Leo? You sound a bit fuzzy, are you out and about?"

"I'm actually heading down to the coast," Leo said, changing lanes.

He caught sight of his own strained face in the rearview mirror. God, he hated interviews.

"*Interesting*," Robbie said. "Doesn't Whitman Tagore have a house on the southeast coast? Doing a little visiting?"

"You could say that," Leo said, keeping his voice amused. "Actually, Win's been staying with her mum for a while, as I'm sure you already know, and I'm going to join them now. I've had some stuff on and needed to be back in London for a bit, but I'm looking forward to catching up with them."

"That's great, Leo," Robbie said. "But listen, shall we address the rumors? What about you storming out of Saint-Tropez last month after a big fight with Whitman, and you two haven't spoken since—"

"Look, first of all, just because Win and I aren't in the same room doesn't mean we're not speaking," Leo said, drumming his fingers on the steering wheel. "She's one of the most important people in my life, we're always in touch." He smiled, tight and unimpressed with himself. "There's these amazing things called phones..."

"All right, all right."

"But sure," Leo continued, "we fight sometimes, like most people. That doesn't change how much I—" He made a face. "How much I care about her."

"Dunya's gone all dreamy-eyed."

Leo forced a laugh. "A true romantic."

"Tell us, though, Leo," Robbie said, "like you said, there's a lot of crazy rumors going around and it's confusing for people and it *must* be frustrating for you."

"Yeah, it drives me nuts," Leo said, swinging off the motorway. "You're right, I don't do interviews a lot, but it's just gotten out of control, and Win's busy, you know, she doesn't have time to deal with this." He hesitated, aware that if the whole conversation was dangerous ground, then he was tiptoeing over a land mine right now. "But yeah, there's been some tough stuff happening at home. It's an illness in the family, actually."

"Oh no, I'm sorry to hear that."

"Thanks. Anyway, obviously Win wants to keep stuff private right now, and so do I. But because rumors have gotten so crazy, I thought I'd call and just like, on the record: she's not in rehab, she doesn't have an eating disorder, she's fine and so am I. We fight sometimes like any couple, but I'm heading down there now to be with her and her family and help support her. Same way she supports me."

He clenched his hands around the steering wheel.

"What a prince," Robbie said. "You're a cool dude, Leo."

"Oh, thanks," Leo said. "I try really hard."

Once the next song faded in, Robbie's voice settled into a more normal register.

"Thanks so much, Leo," he said. "My producer's losing it."

"Hey, thank you," Leo said, because Robbie was a nice guy and it wasn't his fault interviews set Leo's teeth buzzing like he'd bitten into foil. He glanced in his rearview. A big black SUV had just started tailing him.

"Look, man, it's been forever, let's grab a pint sometime. Bring your girl, if you like."

"What, so you can flirt with her again?" Leo said, although he barely remembered Robbie and Win meeting. He supposed it had been in London sometime, or maybe LA. Win would have been charming and Robbie would have tried it on a bit.

"God, I wish," Robbie said. "Er, tell Whitman good luck and well-wishes to her . . . family."

It would be intensely obvious to everyone, Leo thought, that Whitman's family was just her mum. But there wasn't much he could do about that, and even Marie had agreed that something vague about Win's mum was better than rehab rumors.

"I will," he said. "Thank you, mate." The word was unfamiliar in his mouth. A hot spasm of anger flickered through him. He hated lying, and he hated plots, and he hated Win for doing this to him.

A text from Marie was already waiting when he hung up: Good start. Leo threw his phone into the back seat.

It wasn't hard to find Win's mother's house, even hidden as it was on a stretch of hillside that crested the sandstone cliffs. In the last part of the drive, Leo had been able to see the sea, foamy and gray at this time of year, as a line on the horizon where the fields ended. Ordinarily, he might have missed the turn to her secluded driveway, but there was no chance of that today. A crowd of paparazzi had assembled outside the house.

The photographers noticed his car in ones and twos, reluctantly shuffling out of the way so he could inch past them toward the gate, trying to peer in past the tinted windows. They were clinging to the roadside and stood huddled together like penguins at the front gate. Beyond them Leo could see some of Win's security team, arms crossed.

The guard stationed outside the gate eyed the car with suspicion. Leo rolled the window down an inch, just enough that his eyes would be visible, but he was down on his luck because this wasn't a guard that he knew.

"No visitors today," he said.

"I'm not a visitor," Leo said. He could see the photographers straining forward to hear. "I need to speak to Whitman."

Win had bought this place for her mother several years ago, somewhere peaceful near the sea *where she can grow old and judge me in peace*, Win had said, in the last dregs of that evening at the Met Gala, when they'd found a quiet place to sit and Leo had been trying not to kiss her. He could just see the tilted corner of the thatched roof and the edge of a front porch. Someone was tapping at the back window of his car. He turned to see another camera lens, pressed hopefully against the glass.

"Tell her it's Leo." When the guard only narrowed his eyes, he added, "Please."

The guard stared Leo down for another long moment before he sighed and pulled out his comms device, whispering so Leo couldn't hear. Halfway through his sentence the speaker started burbling back, cutting him off, and he took a step back from the car.

"In you go," he said.

Leo released a breath. He'd only just started to inch the car through the narrow gates when the front door to the house swung open, and Win came out.

She'd washed her hair at some point today and it was nearly crackling with static electricity in the cool air. She was wearing an oversized sweater, neat jeans, and worker boots, and she came striding across the ground between them, her face lit up with hope. Leo got out of the car, and Win tumbled into his arms.

He smiled at her, took her face in his hands, looking at her closely like it had been years, not weeks, since he'd last seen her. She broke forward and pressed her face against his neck, hugging him tight, and Leo let his hand slide up her back, stroked her hair, turning his face down toward her. There was a storm of camera flashes behind them, scattering the oncoming dusk.

Win's hair fell forward, half hiding them both. In Leo's ear, her voice was low and pleasant.

"I'm going to fucking kill you," she said.

Leo took his backpack and walked into the house with Win tucked in under his arm, turning her face toward his chest as though she couldn't bear to be parted from him. The moment the door closed, she jerked away like he was painful to touch. There had been a moment, with her running toward him, with the hard weight of their bodies colliding, where Leo had thought she was genuinely glad to see him.

"It's amazing you haven't won an Oscar yet," he said.

"What the hell are you doing?"

"You're welcome, Whitman."

"You've got to be kidding me," she said. "You're expecting me to be grateful? For the latest way you've decided to fuck up my life?"

"Actually, you were managing that just fine," Leo snapped. "Unless all the rehab and eating disorder rumors were part of your grand plan?"

"I was handling them—"

"That's not what Marie said," Leo said. "She said you couldn't change the conversation without leaving your mum—"

"So now you're calling my staff behind my back?"

"I— Marie called me," Leo said, hesitating perhaps a beat too long, but Win's furious expression faltered slightly, so he supposed he'd gotten away with that. "Look, I'm here to help. I can fix this."

"By going on the radio and talking about how much you care about me?"

Leo stretched, long and luxurious, lounging back against the wall. "Oh, Whitman, you were listening? Don't make me blush—"

"You can't fix this, Leo. I'd kick you out except you've made it impossible for me to do that. You've trapped me."

"I've trapped myself," Leo snarled. "I was *out*, I was free of this whole ridiculous fucking sideshow. But I'm here now."

He could feel his stomach sinking as he said it, the full reality of what he'd done setting in. He'd thought Win would be a little grateful, at least. He'd been so angry, he'd half managed to forget how angry she was herself, and Win in a bad mood was one of the most infuriating things Leo had ever come up against. Now they were stuck here together, with photographers camped outside to watch them fall apart. And Leo was beginning to think that there was no crack in the wall, no escape from the lie he and Win had built up around themselves like a fortress. Lila hadn't saved him, and neither had LA or Berlin or London: here he was, caught again, with a coconspirator who didn't even like him anymore.

"If you think," Win hissed, "that this is going to make up for what you did—"

"I'm not trying to make up for anything. I'm not sorry for having a real life."

"Then why are you here?"

"You need me! And believe me, I'd rather be literally anywhere else, but you've made a mess of handling this and you need to fix it and guess what, Whitman, I'm all you've got! That's what happens when you don't let anyone in, you end up having to trust *me*."

"I will never trust you," Win said, with venom. "I'm never going to make that mistake again."

"Fuck's sake." Leo turned away, pacing in the dim corridor. He tried to look Win in the face and couldn't. Eventually he asked, "Is your mum okay?"

"Marie told you."

"Well, I'd already figured it out by then," he said. He dared a glance at her. Her face was tight and closed down, her eyes very dark. "Is it the—the breast cancer again?"

"Yes," Win said.

"Is she going to be okay?"

"Yes," Win said, razor sharp.

"Good," Leo said, and ran his hand over his head. "Good. Well. I came to help."

"We don't need your help," Win said, and pushed off the wall she was leaning against. She headed down the corridor, disappearing into the evening's growing shadows. "But you haven't given me any choice. Guest rooms are on the second floor. Stay out of my way."

The next morning Leo made breakfast. The kitchen was huge, and rustic in a calculated way like it had sprung straight from the catalog. It was still early, and the house was silent as Leo crept around collecting ingredients. It was one of those IKEA kitchens where everything was labeled, tins with SUGAR and TEA and BREAD written on them. When Leo opened the sugar tin, he found coffee instead, three half-empty packs of it held shut with rubber bands. The bread bin was full to the brim with Ritz crackers. Leo ate one leaning over the sink.

He hadn't slept much. He'd heard Win talking on the phone at some point in the night but couldn't make out her words. After that he couldn't fall back to sleep.

Now it was a fresh morning, the sky raw and pink like grazed knuckles and the world outside coming blearily to life. Leo could hear the hum and splutter of cars by the front gate. Most of the photographers out there had probably slept in them.

"You're awake."

Leo started, and turned to find Win's mother easing herself onto the stool at the kitchen island. She folded her hands over each other on the counter.

"Good morning," he said. He tried not to stare. She didn't look much like Win: she was shorter and rounder than her daughter, her hair cut into a curly bob. She wore a plain blue-and-white-striped dressing gown, which she'd drawn tight around herself, and she was eyeing him with unconcealed distrust. Perhaps *distaste* was a better word. That looked like Win. Leo forced a smile and held out his hand. "I'm Leo."

"I know," Pritha said. He knew her name, of course, but it unsettled him that she didn't offer it.

She didn't shake his hand either. After a moment he let it drop. "Do you want some coffee?"

"Tea," she said. "It's in the high cupboard."

Leo went to put the kettle on, certain she was still watching him. His neck was prickling. He watched the kettle until it began to boil.

When he brought her the mug, she nodded in acknowledgment and gestured for the salt jar, which was filled with sugar. She pulled over the iPad on the counter and started to flick through emails. Leo felt an unprompted tug of fondness, which had nothing to do with this strange, quiet woman and everything to do with the familiar crinkle of her brow. Then he rolled his eyes and turned away again, resuming his hunt for bread.

"Would you like some toast?" he asked.

She looked at him like she thought he was making fun of her.

"My daughter has made me a diet plan." She gestured at the fridge. "It's probably muesli again."

"Yikes," Leo said. He walked over to examine the timetable tacked to the fridge. It was color-coded and littered with comments like *give yourself a treat!* and *delicious!* It didn't look like Win's work, but like something she would hire someone else to do. Today's breakfast menu read *Green smoothie, almond yogurt, muesli—no added sugar*. He turned back to Pritha, raising an eyebrow at the mug of tea. She glared back at him.

"All right," Leo said. "Muesli it is."

He poured two bowls for them (BOWL, each of them read on the side). He was acutely aware of the silence, but Pritha didn't seem concerned. She had closed her emails and opened a card game. She glanced up and grimaced when he set the muesli in front of her. It was dry and floury, and they both chewed on it slowly and without speaking.

"Oh," Win said, in the doorway. She looked startled, as if she had expected him to be halfway back to London by now. "How are you feeling, Ma?"

"Fine," Pritha said, not looking up from her card game. "I think I'm going to have a new high score."

"Great," Win said. She swept past them to the fridge, pulling out a bottle of mineral water. Leo waited.

Finally she said, "You're still here."

"Have you checked Twitter?"

"I'm not interested, Leo."

"You should see this," Leo said, and took out his phone. He opened the message he'd gotten from Marie in the middle of the night.

He'd already watched the video. It was an American talk show, four beaming women sitting at a round table with a green screen Miami vista projected behind them. He ate his cereal while it played, and Win drew grudgingly closer, hugging a light arm around her mother's shoulders.

"One more time," one of the women was saying, "one more time, come on—"

"Oh, Janine, you softie," said another.

"Just once more," Janine said, and the show played back audio of Leo's interview.

"We fight sometimes, like most people," the recorded Leo said, his voice fuzzy over the phone line. He sounded easy, sure; the thread of discomfort with the interview in his voice had come out as seriousness, like he was discussing his future. "That doesn't change how much I— how much I care about her."

"See?" Janine demanded. "Oh, Kirsty, don't tell me that doesn't warm your heart. Look how he jumps to defend her honor. It's his first interview in *five years*."

"It is sweet, it's very sweet," Kirsty said. "Wow, though. I guess I'm just surprised that Whitman Tagore and Leo Milanowski have apparently lasted longer than a week, this time?"

"I think they're growing up," the third woman chimed in. "You know, Leo's matured a lot in the last few years. I think he's ready to stop being a playboy and start *committing* to the woman he loves. Look how happy Whitman was to see him, her whole face lights up—"

"Who are these women?" Pritha said.

"It's a random talk show," Win said. "It doesn't mean anything."

"It's all over the internet," Leo said through a mouthful. "And Marie says most of the morning shows will be covering it."

Win scowled at him. On-screen, Janine said, "And you know, I told you guys this, I have such respect for Whitman Tagore. There's a lot of rumors about her mother and, like, a lot of celebrities would just hire someone to take care of it, but she takes a step back, she doesn't care what people are saying about her, she only cares about her mom—"

Pritha snorted. Win, lips pressed tight together, reached forward and clicked Leo's phone so it went dark.

"You've made your point."

"It's working," Leo said. "That's my point."

"You haven't given me any other options," Win said, "and you've exposed my mother—"

"It would have happened sooner or later, regardless," Pritha said. She pushed her bowl away. "With your ... public position."

"This way we can control it," Leo said.

Win was quiet for a second. She had her hair pulled back, and she looked tired, Leo realized. The same frustrated expression he had seen on her a thousand times before. She took a step toward him, and he almost reached out to touch her, but she went past his shoulder for the handset on the wall and punched three numbers in a row.

"I'm coming out for a run," she said into the speaker. "All clear out back?"

"Clear," a voice crackled.

"I'm glad you two have already teamed up," she said, striding out of the room. "You can just give me your schedule for the week when I get back."

She was gone before Leo could say anything else.

"I'm going back to bed," Pritha announced. "Today is not going to be a good day."

Leo nodded. She struggled off the stool. When he held his arm out to help her, she took it, sighing. She let go of him once she was upright.

"Do you need help up the stairs?"

She gave him a long, discerning look. "I know that you're trying to prove that you are useful. I won't be able to help you. She doesn't trust me either."

"I'm not trying to prove anything," Leo said. "I'm just trying to help."

"All right," she said, like she didn't believe him. "I can manage the stairs."

He watched her shuffle away. Now he felt irritated with both of them, and he paced around the kitchen, unsure what to do. Maybe it had been a bad idea, coming here. He hadn't thought things through properly. The litany of articles about Win and hospitals and crisis had spooked him, and then the phone call with Marie planning his Radio 1 appearance had only made it worse. He'd wanted something to focus on beyond his own anger, beyond the realization that she'd never really cared about him. He'd wanted to see her again. He'd wanted the physical fact of her, the exact cadence of her voice.

For lack of anything better to do, he went back to his room. There was a cat curled up in the sheets where he'd pulled them back, old and surly with its eyes squinted closed. He sat down next to it and switched the TV on, flipping channels; a cursory flick through the entertainment news in case his face showed up, and then on to a bad cop movie he'd seen before.

The house felt close and confined despite its size. Without realizing it, Leo had been picturing Pritha as an invalid in bed with Win pious by her side, and Leo the hero arriving to save them both. Instead Pritha was an unknown quantity, and she and Win interacted as though they were colleagues working to defuse a bomb, never speaking more than necessary, professional and distant. Leo didn't fit here, but neither did Win or Pritha. He didn't understand what was happening.

After a while the cat woke up with a sleepy yowl, and picked its way down onto his lap. He scratched under its chin. It didn't have a collar. It was nameless and grumpy, turning circles over his knees trying to get comfortable. He stroked it until it batted its paw at him to make him stop. He watched it fall asleep.

Leo didn't wake up until somebody switched off the TV, and then he inhaled sharply, opening his eyes. The cat jumped from his lap and stalked off.

Win was in the doorway watching him, the TV remote in her hand. It must have rained while she was out because she was soaked through, and her cheeks were flushed pink from running. There was mud on her calves. He wondered how long she'd been out there.

"How many people know?" she said. "About the marriage?"

Leo scrubbed his palm over his face. "Hardly anyone. No one who talks to the press, anyway. Lila jokes about it, but I don't think she'd actually tell someone."

"And Lila knows the truth about you and me."

Leo stared at her. He felt off balance from the unexpected nap, not ready for another fight. "Yes."

"Wonderful."

"I never said I would lie to my friends," Leo said. "That's not part of our deal."

"Oh, your *friend*," Win said, and looked away, her lips pursed. "Well, maybe—if you're here. It might help."

He raised his eyebrows. "You figured that out?"

"Don't be a dick, Leo." She sounded more dismissive of him than she ever had before. "And this doesn't make up for anything. I won't owe you anything."

"Fine."

"I have work to do," Win said. "Marie's going to call us this evening. She's working out a plan, the best way for us to handle this. Try not to pick up any new wives in the meantime."

Leo scowled at her. "Are you sure you don't want to give me more-specific instructions? A script maybe?"

"You never stick to them anyway," she said, and her voice was bitter like black tea.

CHAPTER TWELVE

Marie called in from New York to summarize the coverage. Since Win had returned to the UK, there had been competing theories about her nervous breakdown: she couldn't handle the pressure of her career; she was too controlling and pushed men away (first Nathan, then Leo); and now, with the added fodder from Leo's radio interview, she was struggling with family issues that were threatening to push her over the edge.

Marie looked up brightly from her notes. "So there's plenty to work with here."

Leo turned to Win to share a look of disbelief, but Win was nodding, waving Marie on.

"Let's see this as an opportunity for you. We've always had to walk a difficult line between calm in the face of criticism and coming off as boring. This is a chance to showcase some real vulnerability. You're just like everyone else, and bad things happen to you, and you're surviving."

They would do away with the romantic photo ops and the luxury shopping trips. Instead, Win should appear distracted and anxious in public. They would dial back her makeup and hair and dress her in sweaters and leggings; Marie called it a "tired but hot" wardrobe. She would smile weakly in photos with fans, and Marie would arrange for her to be ambushed outside the hospital—not Pritha's real one, obviously, but a decoy clinic in a different town where Win could appear unfairly cornered and slip away into a waiting Leo's car. They wanted people to feel sorry for her rather than revel in her misfortune. They wanted young women to recognize their own fraught lives in her. They wanted her to be the strong but vulnerable hero, who did fall down but got back up again.

Leo's presence would signify an active support network behind the scenes, adding a touch of tenderness to avoid Win becoming rock-bottom pathetic. She hadn't been abandoned; she had just chosen to retreat. And the fact that she and Leo were still together made it clear that beneath this new veneer, stripped of glamour and laughter, the same Whitman Tagore remained. She was still beautiful, still fascinating, and Leo was still bound to her.

"Let's imagine your life turning to dusk," Marie said, sounding dreamier than Leo had ever heard her. "It's been a long summer's afternoon, and now everything is poised still and waiting. Like a new dreamscape for the two of you to wander through, hand in hand."

"You've *got* to be kidding me," Leo said, lip curling. He felt like the one sane character in an absurdist play.

Marie narrowed her eyes. "Not at all. I have a mood board if you need something to visualize."

"You're not happy about this," Leo said, because Win's mouth was tight with anxiety. "I know this isn't you—"

"Don't try to tell me what I am," Win said. She looked back at Marie on the video call. "You think this will work? People don't..." She paused, considering. "They don't really like it when I'm upset."

"Not upset," Marie said. "Vulnerable. Worried. Sad. They'll relate to all of that."

"Christ," Leo said. "What happened to not playing the victim card?"

Win gave him a cool look. "I'm not playing, Leo. My mother is ill."

"You're being a hypocrite," he said. "You won't talk to me or anyone else about anything difficult, not your dad or creepy directors or when

Nathan fucking Spencer makes a racist joke on TV, but suddenly we're telling the whole world how your life is falling apart and that's totally fine. You're not actually upset—"

"I'm not upset that my mother is ill? Thanks for another amazing insight—"

"I'm trying to help you," Leo snarled. "Marie just said that if I leave, people might turn on you again."

"Is she meant to be grateful for that?" Marie said, sudden and unexpected. "That she needs you here to make her palatable? If people would take her seriously on her own, or give her just a tiny bit of credit, or not make her work a thousand times harder than every other actress I work with . . . "

Win smiled, neat and bitter. "Yes, thank you, Leo. It makes me feel so good that I have to be dependent on some guy because alone I'm a bitch—"

Some guy stung. Leo said, "It's not my fault they don't!"

"Nothing's ever your fault, is it," Win said. "You're not like every other guy, right? How could anyone blame Leo Milanowski for anything? And you're calling me a hypocrite?"

Leo's face went hot, embarrassed. He felt some yawning desperation open up beneath him. It wasn't his fault that the same people eager to shove Whitman Tagore aside would make excuse after excuse for Leo. What did she want him to do about it? How was he supposed to take responsibility for something so complicated and ingrained?

Into the silence, Marie said briskly, "Your complaints have been noted, Leo. It's unfortunate that we're all in this situation now, but we just need to get through the next few months, and then I can phase you out for good. It might be time to push the independent woman angle, anyway."

"Agreed," Win said, and swept out of the room.

"I'm not going to do this," Leo said, voice strained. "I'm not going to be part of this."

Marie was uninterested, packing up her notes, glitching over the connection as though she was already turning her energy to the next problem.

"I'm curious," she said, looking up. "Do you really think this is so different from anything else you've done?"

They went outside. They took walks on the beach. Marie tipped off a few of her pocket paparazzi, and the next day there were photos splashed across the internet, Win and Leo hand in hand, heads bent close, leaning into each other as though they were the last couple in the world. Photos of Win sitting on a big gray rock, Leo kneeling before her as he adjusted her scarf. The photos hadn't caught the way Win had said, her mouth a breath away from his, "I don't think we need to get any closer than this."

They visited Marie's decoy clinic together in dark sunglasses with a host of suited bodyguards. They bought to-go lattes, ducking out of coffee shops hand in hand with their faces tilted down, expressions sad and unsure. Marie announced it would be better if Win looked raw, exposed, so the stylist team had left, and Win didn't bother hiding the deep shadows under her eyes. Once they were back behind the tinted windows of the waiting car, Win shoved away from Leo and took out her phone, messaging someone until they got home. Leo still wasn't cleared as a houseguest by her security, so every time they drove up to the gate, she had to lean over him and tell whoever was there, "It's okay, he's with me."

It made him feel like a sulky child, unimportant and neglected, like he was part of his dad's entourage again. He would have complained, except he was absolutely certain that Win knew and was doing it deliberately.

When Leo wasn't being shepherded on an outing, he wandered

around Pritha's house. Except for the framed photos hung in the hall, there was no real sign that Win or Pritha had anything to do with the place. He wondered what had happened to the home Win grew up in. A few pictures showed glimpses of it, a poky terraced house with ugly red carpeting and overflowing bookcases. Win's father appeared in some of them. He was usually pulling Win or her mother forward, arm hooked warm around their shoulders, bright-eyed and cheerful behind an old-fashioned pair of tortoiseshell glasses. He seemed incongruous to the misty, fragile past that had produced Pritha and Win.

Leo remembered Win having an aunt, but he'd never heard about any other family. It was hard to imagine Win blending into a large group of cousins, Win as a descendant from a long, sprawling line. She had always seemed marked apart to him, a stranger in every room she walked into.

As much as he could, Leo stayed out of their way. The house was big enough, the fridge stocked, the rooms full of diversions: a mini-gym in one, a massive entertainment center in another. It would have made sense for them to hire a housekeeper, but Leo never saw anyone else in the house, and most of the rooms seemed pristine from disuse. Meals were delivered once a week to be reheated, half eaten, and discarded without comment; nobody seemed to have much of an appetite. The only daily chore Leo could find was emptying and refilling the dishwasher. After two weeks he had yet to find any discernible system to the kitchen cupboards, so he just put things away wherever he felt like.

The rest of the time, he sat in bed and read gossip articles on his phone. His arrival had helped, as he and Marie had known it would. The tone had changed drastically; he suspected Marie had leaked more information about Win's mother. Now there were headlines like 'It's Me and Leo Against the World' and Leo Tells Win: 'I'm Here for You.' When he searched Win's name on social media, the usual jeering comments came up, delighted at her newfound weakness, but they were outnumbered ten to one by posts defending her. leave her alone i would die for her!!!! one girl wrote, fresh-faced and glittery in her profile picture. One long, earnest article kept appearing, shared thousands of times: Whitman Tagore Isn't Flawless. She's Real.

They went to supermarkets and bought ingredients for imaginary meals, taking selfies with overwhelmed cashiers. A fan wrote this sweet fuckin prince under a photo compilation of Leo buying Win coffee and racked up thousands of likes. Marie was very pleased. Win left the coffee next to her in the car, untouched, going cold, and ignored him whenever she could in favor of her phone, probably texting nasty reports about him to Shift or Emil.

It wouldn't look good for them to be caught making out, Marie said, but she wanted them to touch. They walked into storms of camera flashes with their heads ducked, Leo's arm wrapped close and possessive around Win's shoulder, Win wearing one of Leo's baseball caps tugged low over her eyes. He could feel the tension in Win every time he touched her. Her spine was rigid, her grip on him entirely forced. The moment they were out of view, she jerked away.

Win's career continued behind the scenes, an unstoppable force that ran ceaselessly beneath Leo's feet, like the rumble of an underground train. He'd gleaned from their debriefs with Marie that *The Sun Also Rises* was still on the cards, although delayed. All press appearances had been canceled, although it was unclear to Leo whether they had been axed to make time for Pritha, or just to bolster the idea that Win *wanted* to spend more time with Pritha. Chanel couldn't be delayed, and Win had agreed to go ahead with filming for their spring campaign as scheduled; Leo ended up being dragged along with her for the inevitable behind-the-scenes videos.

"I don't think the concept of behind the scenes applies here," Leo said, waiting for her in the kitchen.

"They could come and film me vomiting in the toilet," Pritha offered. "Or is that the wrong kind of backstage gossip?"

Leo watched danger flash across Win's face. He almost felt excited at the prospect of her screaming at them. It would be better than more icy silence. She looked up at him, as if she could tell what he was thinking. Her hair was falling out of its tie and she was scowling, and for an instant Leo forgot where they were, what they were doing; he wanted to flick her on the nose and pour her a drink.

"There's something else," Win said. "Riva Reed has been pulled in for the photo shoot. They liked us together in Saint-Tropez. Apparently they're going for some kind of witch coven aesthetic."

Pritha made a faint, disbelieving noise. Win ignored her. Leo said, "So?"

"So, she's been around us when we were...friendlier," Win said. "You have to be convincing. She'll notice if something's wrong."

"Why don't you just tell her? She's your friend, isn't she?"

Win didn't answer. Her gaze was unreadable.

"For fuck's sake," Leo said. "You don't trust Riva?"

"Someone taught me not to trust anyone," Win said lightly, and went out to the car before Leo could respond.

They had to drive farther up the coast for the shoot. It was meant to give the impression of deserted wilderness, Leo supposed, green fields, a rocky beach, trees whipping back and forth in the high October wind, but by the time they arrived, it was a busy hum of activity. There were half-built studios and several trailers. It reminded Leo of afternoons spent on shoots with his mum, and that one disastrous month interning with Marc Jacobs when he was sixteen. People with composed faces rushed past him dragging racks of dresses behind them. Win hung off his arm as they got out of the car and joined the mess; in the sudden flurry of campaign staff and stylists and assistants, she clung on, like he was the one steady thing in a storm. Leo kept his gaze faraway and distant, looking over everyone's head. His mouth kept tugging down. He forced it into line.

The wind slipped under his collar. Win was whisked into a trailer, no doubt to be put into something far too flimsy for the weather. He remembered joining her for filming two or three Octobers ago, on a bright icy day in New England. In between takes they'd bundled her into a big fluffy dressing gown and she came to huddle under his arm, stealing sips of his coffee because she was on another weird diet and wasn't meant to be having any.

Win returned, a dark, tense slip of a figure on the other side of the field. They'd put her in a high-necked, nearly transparent Edwardian dress. Leo yawned, unimpressed, and she looked in his direction, a trained, loving glance that was for everyone watching. Leo raised his hand and pointed his fingers into a gun, cocked them at her, and Win put her hand playfully over her heart. There was a little murmur of appreciation, quickly stifled.

Riva arrived around lunchtime, rushing into Win's arms. Leo drew closer, hands in his pockets. "Oh my god, honey," Riva was saying. "Your mom? I'm so sorry. Is she going to be okay? Are you okay?"

"We'll both be fine," Win said, and made quick, annoyed eye contact with Leo, jerking her head. He closed the last few feet between them, put an arm around Win's waist, and drew her in against him. "And I'm not on my own."

Riva shook her head, still clutching Win's hand. "I'm so glad you two found each other. I'm going to get made-up, but then I want to hear everything, okay?"

"How about it?" Leo said as she left. "Going to tell her everything?"

Win's smile didn't change.

She was called away again to sprawl against a tree, and after a while Riva joined her, the two of them winding their arms around each other and staring glassy-eyed into the camera. Leo's fingertips were tingling with fury. At least he could stand here scowling and everyone would just label him as protective.

When they moved on to solo shots of Riva, Win dropped into the chair next to him.

"Riva said that you're the dream boyfriend but I should be careful," she said, eyes glittering. "Apparently rich white guys always go bald really young."

Leo was startled into a shout of laughter. "Marie'd ship me off to some retirement home for ex-boyfriends."

"You'll like it," Win said sweetly. "You and Nathan can be poker buddies."

He leaned in toward her, already smirking, but his phone chimed in his pocket. Her face tightened.

"It's just Gum," he said. "Don't worry."

"I'm not worried." Win pulled her hair out of her face. She wrapped her fingers around the arms of her chair. "You can speak to who you want."

"Well, don't lie," Leo said. Win was ready with a comeback, he could tell from the short inhale, the raise of her shoulders—but then there was a flash, and they both stared up into the dark eye of a camera lens.

"Don't mind me!" the girl behind it said. "This is just for the press package, if that's okay?"

Win said, "Sure," and leaned over the arm of Leo's chair, her cheek on his shoulder. Her mouth was almost touching his shirt and she murmured, "Touch me."

"You guys are so great." The camera moved around them, the girl ducking for a new angle so the sea made a murky backdrop. "Just ignore me."

"Okay," Leo said. "We'll just act like normal, then."

He was irritated again. The afternoon had gotten away from him, and he didn't know what Win wanted, so he put two fingers under her chin to angle her face up, and he leaned down and kissed her, light, her mouth just open against his. She shuddered.

Leo knew how it felt when Win liked it. He knew the way tension ran through her like a thread of gold, the way if he pushed a little she'd fold and curl against him. This was not that. It was revulsion.

"Okay," Leo repeated. He didn't let go of her too quickly, because their camera girl was still hovering. "When can we leave?"

Win didn't answer, just shot a smile at the camera. "I better get back to work."

It was hours before they escaped. The clouds were just beginning to open up when Win was released, trailing affectionate goodbyes and fervent promises to see Riva again soon.

"I thought we'd head back ourselves, just the two of us." Win's gaze was clear and attentive, her fingers resting lightly on his forearm. "Does that sound nice? I'll drive."

Leo was in trouble, then. He smiled back at her, gentle and supportive for the cameras and their audience. "Sure."

Her bodyguards took her driver and followed in a car close behind, and Win and Leo pulled down the long, windswept road, not looking at one another.

Leo spoke first. He was miserable and exhausted and he kept thinking of the jerk of disgust in Win's body, like his mouth was just another forced compromise she had to suffer through. "You can tell Marie we won't kiss anymore, if you hate it that much."

"Jesus, Leo," Win said, smacking one hand against the steering wheel, like she'd been waiting for the chance to explode. "Are you serious? It's bad enough that you come out here and force me to parade around with you, now I have to enjoy it?"

"Who's forcing you? I'm helping you."

"You are torturing me," Win said.

Leo could see only half of her face in the streetlights. He wished he could open the door and jump out, but the storm was descending now, rain slamming against their windows in the growing dark. He could feel a headache brewing.

"Win," Leo said. "Why don't we just talk about it?"

"Okay," Win said. "Sure. Tell me about her, then."

Leo stopped. He looked over at Win, white-knuckled on the steering wheel, in the middle of a conversation he hadn't realized he was having. He said carefully, "I meant us."

"There's nothing to talk about with us," she said. "I thought we were friends and you clearly didn't, or else you wouldn't have lied to me—"

"We were friends," Leo said. "We can still be friends. You're the one who won't fucking look at me."

"I'm sorry," Win said, and gave him a sweet, dangerous look. "Tell me about your secret wife, friend."

Leo's mouth tasted sour. "I'm sure you've already compiled a dossier. Likes and dislikes, strengths and weaknesses—"

"Fuck you," Win said, voice shaking, a dull flush clawing up her throat, making her blotchy and horrified. "I haven't. I don't know anything about her, and whose fault is that?"

"I— Fine," Leo said. "Let's play your weird, nasty game. Lila's great. She's a really good musician, and she's always working on a random new project. She built me a bike from scratch while she was writing a song for some *America's Got Talent* star, that Christmas one that was everywhere last year—"

"I fucking hated that song," Win said.

"Good for you," Leo said. "She's allergic to bees, and every time we went hiking we had to carry extra-strength repellent and an EpiPen. She doesn't take shit from anyone and she's not two-faced, she tells the truth. She's always got seven things on the go, but sometimes I think she still hasn't decided what she wants to do. She understands not having a—a vocation, she understands wanting to figure things out, she doesn't have every fucking detail of her life planned out to a fine fucking art and judge anyone who doesn't—"

"I get it," Win snarled. "She sounds perfect. It must be so refreshing for you to be with someone who never has to care about anything—"

"She's kind and she's patient," Leo snapped, "and she's my friend and I love her. That's all."

Win blanched. Leo sat silent, almost breathless, waiting. He wanted a response, some modicum of understanding, but Win's face was tight with anger and she didn't look at him. It was as though there was nothing he could do, no way to win. He could resist or give in, and it didn't matter; he was always left on the outside of Win's fury.

"If you don't want me to tell you anything, you shouldn't ask," he said. "I'm not sorry for having a life outside of *The Whitman Tagore Show*. I should have told you about Lila, and I want to make up for that, but—"

"You can't make up for Lila," Win said. Her voice was very low. "Not ever."

Leo stared at her. "What do you want me to do, then?"

"I keep telling you," Win said. "I want you to leave."

Leo looked out the window. Rain-dark hills, a broiling sea. He didn't know what he was doing here anymore.

"Fine," he said. "I will."

When they got back he slammed out of the car without speaking. Maybe they'd get a photo of him storming into the house, but he didn't care. It couldn't hurt him, couldn't touch him; it wasn't true, unlike the real people in his life, and Leo wanted those people: Gum's nasal pronouncements, Thea's indulgence, Hannah coming home and stealing all his beer. His heart was pounding like he was struggling against a net. He wanted out; he wanted to believe there was something else for him. Win didn't even want him there.

Behind him, he heard the door bang as Win came inside, then Pritha's voice, surprised, cut off by Win's sharp retort. Leo scowled. Maybe he'd go to the gym on his way home, run or box it out. His whole body was sparking and jittery with anger.

Upstairs, he shoved his clothes into his bag, gritting his teeth. He wanted out. He threw the bag over his shoulder and headed back downstairs.

He almost made it, too.

"Shit," someone said, low and annoyed in the living room.

Leo paused. He stuck his head around the door. "I didn't know you swore."

Pritha looked up, eyes narrowed and frustrated. She looked more like Win than he'd noticed at first. "Why, because I'm over sixty, or because this isn't my first language?"

"Oof," Leo said.

"I can't make this stupid machine work," Pritha said. She was kneeling by the enormous TV, in front of a slim white box trailing cords. "I don't know why I have it. I liked the DVD player."

Leo shrugged. "So use the DVD player."

"It was disconnected and packed away. I was told this would be much better."

Leo's grip flexed around his bag. He was *leaving*.

Pritha's nose wrinkled. "Useless," she murmured. It was unclear whether she was talking about Leo or the box.

"Let me have a look," Leo said, and dropped his bag.

Forty-five minutes later, Leo was cursing and Pritha was sitting serenely on the sofa, a pashmina wrapped around her shoulders and her feet folded up underneath her.

"It just doesn't make any sense," Leo said. "It's all connected, the image is working, why isn't there any sound—"

"I told you you should have kept the yellow cord in."

"But that's when we couldn't get the Wi-Fi to connect."

Pritha shrugged. "It is a stupid machine."

"It *is*," Leo said, and dismantled it, started putting it together again.

This time the sound worked, the image worked, and the remote didn't, meaning they couldn't get off the incessantly cheery welcome screen.

"I don't understand the point of all this," Leo said, grimly yanking cords out. "Why can't we just keep using DVDs?"

"That's what I said. You've just unplugged the television."

Leo swore, then looked over his shoulder. "Sorry."

Pritha made a magnanimous gesture.

Leo turned it off, then on again. The image flickered back into life. "No sound."

Leo made a frustrated noise and banged on the box. The sound of a woman sobbing filled the room, and Pritha said, satisfied, "Oh, it's *Yeh Rishta*."

Leo stumbled back and slumped on the opposite end of the sofa to Pritha. "What's that?"

"TV show," Pritha said, already absorbed. "Very silly."

Leo tilted his head to the side. "Are they speaking Bengali?"

"Hindi," Pritha said.

"You speak Hindi, too?"

"I spent some time in Delhi," Pritha said. "I can follow it."

"Right." There were some dramatic close-ups with lots of heartfelt violins in the background. Without letting himself consider it, Leo asked, "Does Win speak Bengali?"

Pritha looked at him. Leo set his jaw, kept his eyes on the television.

"I think she understands some but can't speak very much. We always spoke English to her, we didn't want her to struggle at school. She used to talk to her grandparents on the phone sometimes, but after Jotish died, we lost touch with them. And my parents died before Whitman was born."

"Oh. Sorry," Leo said uselessly. Pritha didn't dignify that with a response. Leo sank back into the couch.

He watched three episodes without thinking. He didn't understand most of what was going on, but when he asked, Pritha would explain in short, uninterested sentences, and every once in a while there was a dance number, which he liked. Pritha looked tired and ill, waxy in the dim light. Leo went into the kitchen and made them cups of tea, shuffling around the cupboards until he could find a packet of biscuits.

When he handed them to Pritha, she said, "This is not on my diet plan."

"You can blame it on me. Win's not my biggest fan at the moment anyway."

"Yes. She said you were a prick, and that you were leaving."

"She's a . . . ," Leo started, and drew in a breath. "Well, I am leaving. I just want to see who Kartik's gonna marry."

"Mm," Pritha said. "It is hard to guess." While he was gone, she had turned the subtitles on for him.

The fizzing energy of his anger started to change shape, shifting into a gray lead that lined his bones. It sank into him and made him gloomy and exhausted. When the biscuits didn't hit the spot, he went back into the spotless kitchen to warm up a pizza. There was no sign of Win. Pritha managed a slice and a half of the pizza before she looked wan and worn out, pushing the plate away. Leo removed it without commenting. He brought her a bottle of soda water and she sipped slowly at it, eyes glazed.

"How were the doctors today?"

Pritha shrugged.

He wondered if she was frightened, if she was thinking about her husband, who had died of the same malignant cells, only an inch or two lower. Mostly she looked annoyed.

"Give me the last biscuit," Pritha said. Leo handed it over. When she switched the channel to an old *MasterChef* rerun, he didn't say anything, didn't make any move to get up. There was plenty of time for leaving.

He woke up to the bleary white light of the television screen saver, a logo bouncing around. His mouth was dry and fuzzy. He wasn't sure what time it was. On the other end of the couch Pritha was asleep, too, head hanging back against the cushion, mouth open.

Win was standing over them, her expression inscrutable. She was in the same clothes from earlier, and she looked perfect and untouchable.

"I asked Gus to give you security clearance," she said.

Leo, thick mouthed, licked his cracked lips and tried to speak, but his first attempt came out grinding and hoarse, and he had to clear his throat and try again. "What?"

"So you can come and go how you like," Whitman said, gaze cool and assessing. "It's late. You should go to bed."

CHAPTER THIRTEEN

They were unfailingly polite to one another for several days after that.

They shared the house like distant roommates. Win wasn't icy when he saw her, just absent, treating him with the same diffident civility as she did journalists.

Most of his time was spent with Pritha, as she was the only real living thing in the house for him to interact with. The cat was no good. Leo didn't mind cats, but this one had decided to hate him since he interrupted its nap, and now it hissed and put its back up whenever he came near it. He got Win's first actual smile when he walked past it sitting on one of the kitchen barstools. As he put his hand out to pet it, the cat turned its head, lightning fast, and nipped at his fingers.

"Ow, Jesus!"

"Ha!" Win said, so unexpected and genuine that he stared at her. She rubbed her nose. "She's shy."

"Is she," Leo said, and Win drifted out of the room again.

Leo's days took on a new routine. He would go out in the morning, taking a car with the windows down and drawing the paparazzi away so that Win and Pritha could slip out an hour later for hospital appointments. Sometimes Win would come with him, and they would sit in a cleared-out restaurant, ignoring each other in favor of their phones.

He went back to the house after lunch, where if she hadn't come with him, Win would be waiting out by the gates as though to welcome him home, nestling in against his side and then breaking apart the moment they were through the door. Sometimes she said, "Thank you," and Leo ran his hand over the back of his neck, and they slipped away into separate rooms. Once she said, "Marie said I should put something online," so Leo pretended to cook, scraping onions into a cold cast-iron pot, and Win posted it with the caption what's cookin good lookin. Comments flooded through, endless heart-eye emojis and #relationshipgoals.

He spent the afternoons crashed on the couch with Pritha watching Indian soap operas or cooking shows or interminable BBC period dramas that Pritha scoffed at to hide her clear devotion. Pritha complained for a few days about the pain in her lower back— she was too weak to exercise and her muscles were aching—until Leo spent an afternoon clicking through online shops and reading reviews out loud. Pritha pursed her lips and seemed unconvinced, but she allowed him to order her an ergonomic pillow. "Not bad," she said when it arrived, and nothing else, but after a few days Leo noticed her carrying it from room to room, propping herself up on the couch or slipping it behind her on the kitchen chairs.

He knew he and Pritha weren't friends—she didn't like him enough for that—but she was entertaining. On the days she was perkier, when there was good news from the doctor and the chemo was showing results, she interrogated him relentlessly about the fact that he'd never had a job, or what he wanted to do with his life. Leo surprised himself by enjoying it; it didn't feel vicious and pointed, like Win's accusations. Instead Pritha was utterly bemused by him, and wondered aloud what unfortunate combination of breeding and indolence and global economic forces ever led to people like Leo, strong and intelligent people who never worked and did not suffer for it.

"Your parents must be so ashamed," she said to him one day. "All that time spent raising and educating you. All those expensive schools."

"Well, sometimes I help my dad. He runs a hotel chain and I pick out art for some of the more upmarket ones."

Pritha looked incredibly unimpressed. "So you buy things for a living."

"It's not really a living," Leo said. "I mean, uh, I don't need to do it. And I've always been into art, it was my best subject in school."

"In school?" Pritha pulled herself up from the sofa, scowling at Leo when he motioned as if to help her. She shuffled over to the cupboard and then returned with a pen and notepad. "Show me something, then. Draw..." She cast about for inspiration. "Draw Whitman."

Her expression was blank, but he could see disapproval lurking. Something caught in Leo's chest; she reminded him of Win in her iciest moods, already sure of her disappointment and just waiting to be proved right. He didn't need Win in front of him to draw her. She was burned into his brain now, as if her dark, furious gaze followed him even when she wasn't there. But without really meaning to, he sketched her like he'd seen her in France, leaning on the balcony of her suite, one hand leafing through her hair, her mouth half caught in a smile as she turned and spotted him.

Pritha took the sketch and looked at it in silence. Leo's face went hot; he could feel himself getting angry again without knowing why.

"Not bad," Pritha said at last. "There are careers that involve art. Maybe you could be a graphic designer."

Leo laughed and relaxed back into the couch. "Maybe," he said, and turned the volume up.

Most of the time she was too exhausted to push him further, and they sat in silence on the couch, taking turns channel surfing. Once they hit on a Western, sweeping panoramic shots of red canyons and grassland, a slight, dark figure limping away on a horse. The camera swung around to the hero's face. Somehow it took Leo almost twenty seconds to realize it was Win.

"Oh," Pritha said, and they sat frozen in front of the screen. Leo's heart was thumping in his chest like he was doing something illegal. It didn't make sense; he'd seen this one. He'd seen all of Win's movies, either as her date to the premiere or just so he could call her afterward. But watching her now, while the real Win was so determined to avoid him, felt strange and invasive for no real reason. He was almost ill with anxiety. The moment when he'd finally realized it was her on-screen kept replaying in his head.

The cowgirl had a low, Texan drawl and a way of holding her mouth like she was ready to spit out teeth. Her laugh was low and wheezing, a chortle that was nothing like Win's own laugh, which was full-bodied and startled and pleased. But even as Leo listed the differences, there was still something else he couldn't touch, like Win's very energy changed when she was playing a role. It was like a stranger was wearing Win's face, or like Win had stepped aside and revealed herself to have been the stranger all along.

"She should have won the Oscar for this," Leo said. His voice sounded strange, like it was coming from far away. He was worried Win was going to walk in on them and catch them, but he didn't move, and Pritha didn't change the channel. "She got the nomination. I can't remember who won instead."

Pritha's mouth was close and tight. She was silent, watching Win. After a moment she said, "Yes. She was always like that. Of course, she has got better. But when Jotish and I went to see her first play, it was this little group of schoolchildren doing their best and...her." She paused. "We didn't know. Jotish thought it would be a good after-school activity, especially because she was a little shy, she had trouble making friends, we thought it would break her out of her shell. We didn't know it would be like this."

Leo turned toward her. "Were you pleased?"

"I don't know," Pritha said. "I can't remember. I know we were very proud. Jotish thought everyone had one thing they were meant to be. He believed in vocations. He always thought he was meant to teach. I enjoy my work but I don't think it defines me. I didn't want Whitman to feel that there was only one choice for her. But it's hard to argue with . . . "

She gestured loosely at the screen, the raw slide of a fiddle, the way Win leaned down over her horse and murmured something in its ear and then shot across the plains.

"And of course," Pritha said, "Whitman did not become famous until after Jotish . . . It was always the thing they did together. I wonder sometimes what he would have thought of all this. I didn't want to interfere in something that had been so important to the two of them."

"That makes sense," Leo said, but if it did it was in a kaleidoscopic way, blurring images he couldn't entirely comprehend yet. He remembered attending one of Win's London premieres and asking why her mother hadn't come. *Oh, she doesn't really get acting*, Win had said, *she thinks I picked a weird career*, and changed the subject. Another premiere, years later: *She doesn't like crowds.* After that he stopped asking.

Pritha looked annoyed with herself. "Anyway," she said, searching for an out.

Leo gave it to her. "I'm actually pretty sure I visited her when she filmed this. She had an afternoon off, we went riding. It was a nice set."

Leo hadn't been riding since school, but he'd settled into it pretty well, and Win laughed at him, called him a rich kid, and raced him across the scrappy ground. Despite her skill on horseback she'd been taught only recently, and when they stopped for lunch, she slung her legs up over his lap and groaned with relief as he dug his fingers into her hamstrings. They stayed up late drinking bourbon on the steps of her trailer. Win had a scene the next day where she lassoed an escaping oil tycoon, and Leo had stood patiently in the moonlight while she practiced tossing the rope over and over, slinging it over his head until it caught around his waist.

"Was it a nice set?" Pritha asked, giving him a strange look. "I thought the director was rude. She got in all that trouble after."

Leo blinked. "What trouble?"

"When they didn't win the Oscar," Pritha said. "There were some other nominations, too, but it didn't win anything. And the director was very angry and said the film was too anachronistic for audiences to accept and he'd been forced to water his story down for..." She waved her hand vaguely. "Political reasons. Representation."

"She didn't tell me any of this," Leo said, shocked. "What an asshole. She shouldn't work with him again."

"Well, she says he wouldn't cast her again after she responded, in any case. Everyone was very cross with her when she said she didn't know why her involvement automatically ruined a film. They said she was deliberately ignoring the point."

"What?" Leo stared. "Why didn't she tell me any of this?"

Pritha gave him a puzzled look. "She said it wasn't a big deal. These things happen all the time. I think she and Marie fixed it."

"Right," Leo said. He had a faint, fleeting memory of being involved in a burst of publicity not long after those Oscars. He vaguely remembered the old bubbling spring of rumors starting up again that Win was too difficult, that she had a victim complex and a problem with men. He'd flown out to LA and they'd gone to a series of industry parties together, Win laughing and happy on his arm, Leo chummy with the other guys there. *Just be your friendly self*, Marie had said wryly.

Asshole, he'd always said when he heard these stories, *what an asshole, what a jerk*, and he wondered suddenly what you did when so many people you met and worked with were assholes: whether it still felt like just a few bad guys, or if instead it felt huge and all-encompassing, impossible to stop.

Echoing through the house, the front door opened. Leo and Pritha both jumped, and Pritha switched the channel to a game show. They exchanged wide-eyed, guilty looks, like small children in trouble.

At night he left Pritha and Win to their weird, uneasy dinners and ate in his room. After he'd been in the house for three weeks, he called Lila.

"My absent husband," she said when she picked up, her voice dry. "Baby, it's like you went to *war*."

"Yeah, I'm sorry," Leo said. "It's kind of intense here, I haven't had a lot of time."

"I know, I saw on Twitter." She sounded sour under the cheer, like she knew he was lying. "Everyone thinks you've saved her life."

"Everyone?"

"Well, the internet."

"Yeah. I know it's weird."

"It's only as weird as when you were flitting around the Mediterranean with her," Lila said. "And at least now you don't look like such a dick. You can have your mopey English holiday, no judgment. Are you at least having fun?"

"It's pretty much the exact opposite of fun," Leo said. He didn't like lying, and he spent all his time pretending with Win. "She's still pissed. We don't really speak."

Lila cackled with laughter. "You dick."

"It's not my fault," Leo said, grinning. It was nice to hear her laughter, to turn this awful month into a sly anecdote. "I've told her about my secret wife. I don't know what she's mad about now."

"She should get over it," Lila agreed. "She kind of comes across like a control freak."

"No, because she doesn't think about it as control. She thinks it's just pragmatic. Like if she just follows all the right steps she won't have to really confront anything. She does it to her mum, too, like you can cure cancer with scheduling."

Lila squawked. "You're *such* a dick," she said. "That is a dick thing to say."

Leo could hear the warm affection in her voice. He and Lila had always understood each other; it had been part of the pleasure of her company, that they worked and thought in the same way, had the same easy, uncomplicated approach to life and fun and relationships. The only thing Lila had never fully understood was Win. For a minute he was back with Lila in LA, forgetting to rub the sleep from his eyes, chilled with a guilt he couldn't name.

He hung up an hour later and wandered around the house, stir-crazy. None of the clocks had been wound back for daylight savings, so he hunted them through the rooms, fixing the wall clock in the entranceway and the digital timer on the fridge. He followed the noise of the television into the lounge room, but it wasn't Pritha watching shitty game shows; it was Win, a glass of wine in her hand and a bottle to her right.

"Oh," Leo said, startled and nervous, like she might have heard everything he was saying, like she knew he'd been talking to Lila. "Sorry, I thought you were—your mum."

Win looked over at him, and Leo had an odd shock: in the blue light of the television, she looked awful, with deep shadows under her eyes that must have been there for days but only properly stood out now. He didn't think she was wearing any makeup. Her hair was scraped back, and she was wearing an old, soft shirt with a neckline that hung low over her collarbone. He stretched out his hands, let them curl in again.

"Sorry to disappoint," she said. "I know you're great pals."

Leo set his jaw. "I just meant—"

"I know," she said, tired, and then repeated, "no, I'm sorry. What-ever. She's gone to bed."

"Okay," Leo said, and had the ghost of an old instinct to cross the floor to her. He wanted to touch her hair. She looked so weightless, like he could scoop her up with one arm and heft her off to bed. He looked at the ceiling instead. "Everything okay?"

"Just fine," Win said. Her eyes went back to the TV, worn. She took another sip of her wine. Leo let her be.

He'd never seen her like this. He wondered how many people ever had. Win had played vulnerable for the cameras once before in her life, and even that had been for him, giving that interview about her father. When Leo had watched it, sick with relief and gratitude, he'd thought that it would be obvious to everyone how much she hated it, her whole body rigid with tension. But everyone just talked about how sad and lovely she was, like a drooping, delicate flower that had to be nurtured back to health.

The show's host had asked her how she'd managed after her father's death. "My mum is a very strong woman," Win said. "I followed her example. I looked ahead."

At the time he'd admired the idea without being able to picture it. Now, looking around the bleak, impersonal house, Leo realized that he'd been looking for loving memorials to Win's father, imprints of his life, traces of grief. He'd thought he couldn't find it, but it was here; it was all around him. Pritha and Win were still swamped in it. They could barely see each other through the fog.

———

Win announced coldly that Leo had not proved himself to be the right kind of distraction at the last Chanel shoot, and she took Emil to the next one instead. Emil flew in on a red-eye and made a brief, bleary appearance at the house to drop off a box of files and scripts and a jar of sea urchin roe from Palermo. Leo and Pritha gamely tried it, dipping in their pinky fingers and bringing them, flinching, up to taste. Emil and Win had a brief, whispered conversation before they left, which made Emil cast disappointed looks at Leo, like Leo was a racehorse who had let him down at the last hurdle. He wished Emil would laugh in the next room, that it would be the familiar dynamic of Win and Emil fondly rolling their eyes at him, but instead Emil was serious and professional, and he and Win left without looking back.

Resigning himself to boredom, Leo startled when he came across Pritha on the back porch, half-hidden in the gray morning, staring out at the high hedge and the waves breaking beyond. She was such a lost, lonely figure that Leo demanded, without thinking, "Where *is* everyone?"

Pritha blinked at him.

"If my mum was sick, we'd need a bouncer on the door," he said, throwing a hand out to encompass the huge, empty house. "We'd have about fifty cousins round and Thea's artist friends would be burning sage in the kitchen and me and Gum and Hannah would probably have to share a camp bed to make room. Where are your *people*?"

"I have a book club," Pritha said mildly, "but we're reading *Infinite Jest*, so we're skipping a month to give everyone time."

Leo pushed a hand over his hair, bristling prickly against his palm. "I'm sorry. That was rude. I know it's different, I know—obviously you're out here, and my family's in London and I have siblings, it's a totally different situation. Sorry."

Pritha didn't say anything, but there was something about the straight line of her eyebrows that made Leo think she was trying not to laugh. He wished she would, but she just kept peering at him, as if waiting for him to continue. Eventually he said, "You're reading *Infinite Jest*?"

"We wanted to see what all the fuss was about," Pritha said, and after a moment Leo dropped onto the wooden bench next to her.

"Well, let me know." He dragged his palm over his face. He imagined Win at the Chanel shoot, in an empty swimming pool, green-lit and red-mouthed. He could see her turning slowly in the vacant space, high vaulted ceilings, one foot curling dangerously over the other.

"My sister lives in Birmingham," Pritha said, perfectly naturally, as though Leo had just been making polite small talk. "She visits when she can, but she has four children, and two of them are still small. Besides, she's ten years younger than me, and we've never really been that close."

"Oh." Leo swallowed. "Me and my siblings were all born within four years of each other," he offered. "We think our parents had kids just for something to talk about."

"Jotish and I had some trouble conceiving," Pritha said. "We discussed having more children, but it took a long time, it was hard, even after Win was born and they thought it might be easier. By the time she was six . . . I thought the age difference would be more trouble than it was worth."

Leo waited. He kept himself still, not wanting to spook her.

"Jotish was one of eight siblings," Pritha said. "He always wanted more room and attention to himself. He wouldn't admit it, but I think he quite liked the idea of having an only child who he could spoil." She paused to reach for the tea at her side. "But most of his family stayed in India. When he died, they wanted me and Win to move to Kolkata, to be closer to them. I thought it would be a bad idea, to lose her father and pull her out of school and away from her best friend and—even acting, I wondered, I wasn't sure whether the transition would be too hard, and she didn't speak the language well enough. So I said no, they kept pushing and . . ." She grimaced. "I was not particularly polite. Occasionally I lose my temper," she added, and Leo thought of Win and almost laughed. Her narrowed eyes and snarl, her tendency to leap straight to shouting when she was angry—clearly a family inheritance. "I lost touch with his family. We never got back in contact."

"Right," Leo said. He paused, thinking. "And your parents died a long time ago, you said."

Pritha nodded.

"So it's just been you and Whitman?" Leo said. "For . . . ten years?"

"Fourteen," Pritha said. "So actually, everyone *is* here. She came back."

Leo stared at her, but Pritha didn't seem lonely or sentimental or regretful, just matter-of-fact. Her and her daughter, and the old cat, and the big house, and Leo: everyone.

Any last vestiges of guilt about talking to Lila again disappeared a week later, when he walked into the kitchen while Win was making a video call. He took a step back, said, "Hey, sorry," and then did a double take.

"Oh, right," Nathan Spencer said, voice tinny over the connection. He was wearing a jaunty polka-dot tie with a thin knot. "I forgot you were there."

Win looked at Leo over her mug of tea. She was perched on one of the kitchen barstools, ankles hooked underneath her, and there was some quirk of amusement in the corner of her mouth.

"Nathan was just telling me about the guests he's got lined up for his show this week," she said. "It's a reality TV special. Maybe you and Ma can watch it together."

"I don't care for reality TV," Leo said. "You guys have fun." He gave the screen finger guns as he left the room.

An hour later, Win drifted across his path in the living room, though Leo doubted it was an accident. He looked up at her. "I didn't know you were still in contact with that asshole."

"He called me when he found out about my mum. We've decided to be friends."

"Oh, great idea. He was an awesome friend to you this summer."

"That was a long time ago."

"Who gives a shit when it was?" Leo said. "He made racist jokes about your mum!"

"You don't have to tell me when people are being racist, Leo," Win said, voice low and thrumming with anger. "I'm actually pretty good at noticing that for myself."

"I—yeah, I know," Leo said. He pushed two knuckles against his eyebrow. "I get that you can't call him out, but do you have to be *nice* to him?"

"I don't like wild cards," Win said. "If he's not angry with me, he's not going to go to the press."

"So that's what it is? Making sure he's still obedient?"

"Yeah, that's exactly it. Thanks for reminding me I'm a psychopath, once again."

"It'd be harder to do if you didn't treat everyone like they're a liability."

"Nathan knows things about me, and I don't want him to hate me. That's common sense." Her voice was still cool and aloof, but her chin was tilted up, and Leo narrowed his eyes. He knew what Win looked like when she was spoiling for a fight. Part of him had been waiting for another break in the tension; he was surprised it had taken this long. He sprawled his legs out across the living room floor.

"Sure," he drawled. "I guess that does make sense. Anyway, it must be tricky to find new people to talk to without Marie here to vet everyone."

"Marie's vetting system isn't perfect," Win said. "It turns out you never know what people are hiding."

"Oh, Whitman," Leo said. "I thought we were friends again."

Win rolled her eyes, turned, and walked away. "Say hi to your wife for me," she said as she ducked out of the room, and Leo lost his temper. He jumped off the couch and swung into the hallway.

"You're allowed to talk to Nathan but I'm not allowed to talk to Lila?"

"Get out of my way, Leo."

"She didn't do anything to you," Leo said. "Nathan, on the other hand—"

"It's none of your business who I talk to," Win said. "And I haven't told you not to—"

"Oh, and a little dig like that doesn't mean anything?"

Win raised her eyebrows. "You had a go at me first."

"That's mature," Leo said.

"I don't have time for this," Win said. For a moment she was all warmth and breath against his side, and then she slipped past him and walked off down the hallway. "I'm going for a run."

"You're always running away from me!"

Win looked over her shoulder. "Don't be dramatic."

"I'm not," Leo said. "I barely see you. I know you're mad, but Christ, Whitman, you can't just keep walking out of rooms when I walk in—"

"We're basically living together. I see you all the time."

"We used to be friends."

"I'm not the one who fucked that up," Win said, low and furious, stepping back toward him. "I'm not the one who lied. I trusted you, and you—"

"I know," Leo said, and felt ruined. "I know. I'm sorry. I've been trying to show you."

"I don't care. It doesn't—it doesn't matter—"

"It does." They were nearly nose to nose, staring at each other. Win was almost breathless with anger, her eyes dark. When Leo reached out, she caught his wrist, so all he could feel was the cool loop of her hand on his skin, the pads of her fingers cupping his wrist bone. She'd done that a lot, in Saint-Tropez, taking quiet, possessive hold of him. He stared at her.

Win blinked, shook her head, and let go of his wrist. "Fine. Go put your running shoes on."

"What?"

"You wanna *hang out*? I'm going for a run. Go get changed. I'll wait five minutes."

Leo glared. "I don't like being told what to do."

"Imagine my surprise," Win said, and checked her watch.

Leo made an awful face and stormed out of the room. When he got to his bedroom, he hesitated, then pulled out his sweatpants.

Win ran every day. If it weren't for the height Leo had on her, he might have had some trouble keeping up. His heart was still hammering from the fight, his breath coming hard.

But he wasn't going to show it, with Win loping along by his side. They ran out the back and through the shady wooded paths that trailed down toward the sea. It was a cold, blue-dark afternoon, the sun already setting, a thin layer of fog around their ankles. Win took the inner path, and Leo kept pace next to her through the sludge of fallen leaves, slipping on the corners.

They ran downhill, which gave Leo enough of a start to bound ahead for a few meters as they came out of the undergrowth. He looked over his shoulder. "Keeping up, Tagore?"

Win's face tightened and Leo laughed, narrowly avoiding running into a tree. Then Win sped up, until she was jostling at his shoulder, and Leo started running harder, too, going all out, heart pounding and chest tight, breath coming ragged. His vision swam. He kept on, with Win furious at his side.

They ran down an empty road and over the bridge. The trees were bare and stark against the gray sky. He could hear the waves. Everything looked bleak and awful, and Leo was still angry. Win slammed her shoulder against his, and he jostled back against her. A couple of meters back, Win's security team's SUV was crawling along, keeping them in sight.

"I go left here," Win panted. Leo ignored her, heading straight for the sea. Win spat a curse and ran after him, overtaking so Leo had a view of her ponytail bouncing and flashes of her long shins. He put his head down and sped up.

They came surging over the bank of the empty beach together, pebbles spilling underfoot, and tumbled down the slope, nearly falling. Leo couldn't pull himself up until he was at the water, and then he stopped, gasping for breath, and Win toppled right into him.

Leo grabbed her forearms hard. They nearly fell, both of them stumbling about, red-faced and panting.

"You're such a *show-off.*"

"What? You said you wanted to go running." Leo swiped his wrist over his sweaty brow and tried to affect nonchalance. It would have been more impressive if he weren't still breathless. "Jesus, it's hot."

"It's not."

She was right: it was dismal, close to winter.

"It's a really warm day," Leo said, and jerked his shirt over his head. He put his hands on his knees, head reeling, and when he looked up, Win was smirking again, and Leo's eyes narrowed. He toed off his sneakers.

"What are you doing," Win said, sounding very unimpressed.

"Cooling off." Leo shoved his sweatpants down, hopping out of them where they tangled around his ankles. Win's mouth was a tight, disapproving line. Leo stretched in his briefs, and turned toward the ocean.

"Don't be stupid. It's November."

"Thanks, most of the time I can remember what month it is," Leo said, and headed into the water. "Anyway, you can do what you like. No shame if you can't handle it."

"Oh, come on," Win said as the first waves lapped around his ankles. Leo froze, hunched his shoulders, then kept going. "*Leo.*"

"*Whitman,*" Leo mocked.

Win cursed and Leo heard a rustle of clothing but didn't dare turn around. He edged farther into the icy water. It left pinpricks of pain everywhere it touched. He gritted his teeth, trudging deeper until it was freezing all around his knees, his feet aching like the sea had taken a hammer to them. "Christ," he mumbled, mostly to himself.

There was a determined splashing sound, and Leo turned around just in time to see Win in—*Christ*—her sports bra and underwear, charging past him and into the waves.

Startled out of his annoyance, he said, "You're so competitive," and Win dove. Her body made a low, close curve against the ocean, and then the waves swallowed her up.

"We've made a bad decision," Leo said to no one, and followed her in.

He came up gasping and shaking his head, his whole body simultaneously on fire and trying to shudder out of its skin. Win was bobbing a little way away from him, her eyes huge, teeth chattering. Every joint in his body was stinging in protest.

"Oh my god," Leo said.

"You're so fucking stupid," Win said.

"I know that now," Leo said, and dove in the vague hope that he might get used to the cold if it submerged him. He didn't, and in the freezing dark he dove too far and scraped his knee against the rocks on the bottom and swallowed a mouthful of seawater in surprise. He came up spluttering and choking.

"You're bad at this," Win said.

"I can still outrun you, though."

"Oh, fuck you," Win said, and launched herself at him, clinging to his back and trying to push his head underwater. Leo fought back with interest. They shoved each other around, ducking under the waves, coming up gasping and fighting to get their hands back on each other.

"You are such a *prick*," Win said.

"It drives me crazy when you won't talk to me," Leo said, and pushed her underwater. Win stayed under, grabbed his ankles, dragged him down. He caught his shin on another sharp rock.

When they came up again, he was cursing, and Win was coughing like the salt water was in her lungs. She spat, a line of spittle connecting her and the ocean.

"You drive me crazy," she said. "You're always *there*. I can't get away from you."

"I barely see you!"

"You've got a very loud presence!"

They stared at each other.

"I don't think that's a thing," Leo said.

"I'm so fucking cold," Win said.

Leo yanked her ponytail, but gently. "Is that you giving in and getting out first?"

Win sank down until the water was up to her chin.

"Fine," Leo said. "But only because I'm a gentleman."

"And a baby," she said, but he'd already turned and was wading back to the shore, his limbs shaking. He folded his arms over his chest.

Win came stumbling out a second later, tripping and catching his arm. She was freezing against him. They held on to each other almost by habit, her hand tight on his forearm, his arm around her waist, and then Leo remembered that they weren't playing for an audience and there were no paparazzi, and he froze. There was nobody to see them on the beach. Win's eyes were wild. Leo's teeth started to chatter.

"We don't have any towels," he said.

"I hate you," Win said, but she didn't look like she meant it.

CHAPTER FOURTEEN

They ran back up to the house together with their T-shirts drenched in seawater clinging to their shoulders. Win's lips were blue, and the cut on Leo's shin was tracking blood behind them, and the cold chased them home through the trees. Leo bent at the door to untie his shoes, and when he looked up, she had paused at the foot of the stairs, considering him.

"Meet me in the kitchen in twenty minutes," she said.

He nodded. "Okay."

After showering he stood undecided in his doorway before he back-tracked and rummaged through his bag. He came downstairs with the bottle held aloft. "I've got whisky."

"Oh." Win looked up at him from where she was holding the kettle. "I'm making hot buttered rum."

"That wins." Leo sat on one of the stools on the opposite side of Win, watching her carefully. She stared right back at him, and he resisted the urge to straighten up. Something had shifted, some new knot lodged out of place, but he wasn't sure exactly what had changed, how he was supposed to be.

Win's hair was still damp and she'd tied it up out of the way, a dark knot that left her neck bare, the line of her shoulder clean. She was wearing a soft, draping black shirt and an old pair of blue jeans. Without trying he could track every patch of bare skin, from the dip of her collarbone to the cautious curl of her fingers out of her sleeves to her long, bare feet.

"Nathan was calling about my mum," Win said. Despite the polite tone there was a dark sheen of warning in her eyes. "She's just finished her chemo course. He was checking in. His mum had breast cancer, a few years ago."

"I didn't know that," Leo said. "That the chemo was finished, I mean. You haven't been telling me much."

"You haven't asked."

"No," Leo agreed. He took a careful sip of his drink. "I didn't think you'd react very well."

"Hmm," Win said, but didn't fight him on it. "Well, it's early days, but the doctors are—optimistic." She rubbed her forehead, looking annoyed. "She already wants to go back to work."

"A workaholic Tagore," Leo mused. "Such a strange concept, let me have a minute to come to grips with it…"

He was worried Win would spark up again, but she was grinning reluctantly.

"Shut up," she said, and touched his wrist, like a counterargument: *No, don't.* It had been easier to touch her earlier, shoving past her as they ran or wrestling with her in the sea, when the adrenaline and the biting cold could distract him. They were being so careful with each other now. It was breaking Leo's heart a little, the way they tried out their gibes as gently as they could, talking like it was a boardroom negotiation. He knew things couldn't go back to normal, but suddenly he wanted Win as she used to be, the daring, laughing way she ran through his life, the fierce determination of her gaze when she came up against him.

After a moment Win said, "My dad would have convinced her to retire. She doesn't listen to me." She was mostly talking to herself, and Leo watched her without responding. She was staring into space, entirely separate from him, like a stranger in a dream. Then she shook her head, and refilled their drinks.

"I wish there were more people around," she said. "For her to talk to when I'm not here. She was never very good at making friends."

"That big falling-out didn't help, either," Leo said.

"What?" Win's gaze jerked up.

"You know," Leo said uneasily, aware he was treading delicate ground, "if she could still call your dad's family, sometimes—"

"What big falling-out?"

Leo stared at her. "You didn't know?"

"*Leo,*" Win began, her voice rising.

"You didn't know," Leo repeated, affirming this time, and recounted the story as concisely as he could. He almost felt a thrill—finally, something useful to tell her—until her face went ashy and shocked as though he'd slapped her. He said, voice thin, "I thought you knew."

"No. She never told me that." Win was still staring at him. "Did she want to go back to India?"

"She just said she thought it was better to stay. Because of your friends, and school." Leo cleared his throat. "And the acting, maybe."

"I don't understand," Win said. "How did you find out? Why did she tell you?"

"Well," Leo said, uncomfortable, "I asked."

Win barked a laugh, harsh and uncompromising. "That's it?"

"Yeah." Leo hesitated, then said, "Did you ever ask?"

When Win's expression didn't budge, jaw clenched and eyes dark with shock and fury, Leo began, despite himself, to laugh. These two stubborn women, and everything was so obvious. "Win, come on, just ask her." Something occurred to him. "Did you ever actually invite her to any of your premieres?"

Win's jaw worked. After a moment she said, "She came to a few but she didn't seem to enjoy them, so I just...I assumed she didn't like them..."

"I am begging you," Leo said, half-laughing and half-sincere, leaning over the counter to catch Win's hand, "I am *begging* you to talk to her. Just ask some, like, some basic questions—"

Win was shaking her head, although she didn't pull away. "We don't understand each other at all, we're different people—"

"How do you expect to understand her if you never talk?" Leo demanded. "Win, I'm on your side, but your mum is not exactly a closed book. She's just a grumpy old lady, it won't kill you to talk to her a little bit about your life."

Win was still scowling at him. "You're on my side, are you?"

Leo swallowed. "I'm always on your side. You just forget sometimes."

"Sometimes you don't particularly act like it," Win said.

Her jaw was tilted up for a challenge, and they glared at each other, the weeks of ugly fighting rising, the afternoon's peacemaking slipping back like a weird blip that could be ignored. It would be easy to fight with Win. It had always been easy.

"Sometimes I fuck up," Leo said. Her hand was still in his, he realized, and then he was hyperaware of it, her long fingers, knuckles still pink from the cold. "But I'm still on your side."

The air felt thick, the way it had on the beach this afternoon, the way it had in Saint-Tropez before everything shuddered apart. Leo didn't leave. Neither did Win.

A few days later Marie sent them to an art gallery. There was hardly any press about, just an in-house photographer for the gallery's website, and an exhibition by Lian Shen, who painted huge watercolors of siblings and was famously averse to showings. Leo had wanted to go to one of her exhibitions for years.

The gallery opened tall windows so clear autumn light trailed through cloister-like rooms, old stone and the sound of waves cresting beyond. "I like these," Win said. "Why doesn't she do more exhibitions?"

Leo shrugged. "I've never met her, but I read an interview where she said the work is what's important. Everything else is vanity, apparently."

They paused in front of a painting of three sisters on a stoop, the palest colors and sweeps of a brush, their heads bent together and glowing in a faint, radiant light. Thea had painted Leo with his siblings once, as a Christmas present for Gabrysia when Leo was fourteen. She had posed them sitting on a red velvet couch, holding whichever object was most important to them. Seventeen-year-old Hannah had her Super 8 camera in her lap, an act of pretension she had long since regretted. Sixteen-year-old Gum brandished a leather-bound copy of *The Complete Works of Cato the Elder*. Leo had spent hours sifting through various sketchbooks, postcards, and prints before he finally scooped up the family cat, and Thea painted it curled up asleep in his lap. Gabrysia had the portrait hung in her study, and it was still Gum's phone screen background.

"I think that's why I never started on the studio," Leo said, trying to make it sound like it was just occurring to him now. "It feels too much like a vanity project."

"I mean, obviously," Win said. "You can do anything you want. Anything you choose is going to be a vanity project."

Leo felt something seize in his throat, a cold hit of embarrassment and indignation.

"Just covering up how empty my life is?" he said. He couldn't look at her. He wondered if she'd forgotten saying it.

"No. But you're going to have to get over people calling you privileged. I think you use that as an excuse to do nothing."

Leo kept his gaze straight ahead. "That's a weird-sounding apology."

"It wasn't an apology," Win said. She paused. "But I am sorry, for what it's worth. For being rude. I was . . . angry."

"Yes," Leo said. "That I'd screwed up your narrative."

"Yes," Win echoed. "Well, you made things a lot harder for me."

They moved into the next room, smaller and suffused with light. The gallery's publicist had been hovering about them for a while, but now she hung back, and they were alone.

"I'm not trying to start a fight," Win said. When he didn't say anything, she shook her head, started again. "Really, I'm not. But you don't see things the way I do, you don't live the way I do. I'm one of the only Indian women to make it in Hollywood, really make it and not just be a bit part, and if I fuck up, that's it. This industry isn't meant to give second chances to people who look like me."

"You don't know that for sure," Leo argued.

"I think *you* don't know that," Win countered. "Because if you did, you wouldn't have kept Lila a secret."

Leo swallowed. "Not telling you about Lila was a mistake. The whole thing was—"

Win's face shut down. "Don't apologize to me about your marriage," she said. "That's the kind of thing that makes me feel like I'm a—a Machiavellian monster."

"Okay," Leo said. "But I didn't mean to make things difficult for you."

Win drew in a breath. "It's not just about me. Look, I know you don't really read my press, but it's significant when I get cast for a role, and it's significant when some director takes a chance on me, because that doesn't happen often. So it's significant when I fuck up as well—it makes them think that maybe it wasn't worth the risk. So maybe they won't do it again."

And if she pointed that out, how heavily the scales were weighed against her, in the same quiet, tired way she was doing for him now, people got angry at her, too. Leo thought about Pritha's story about the director, or he himself urging her to lash out against Nathan. It's bullshit, Leo wanted to say, but Win already knew it was bullshit.

"I should have told you," Leo said. "I wasn't thinking about any of that."

"You don't have to," Win said.

"No," Leo agreed. He hesitated. "I guess I've always thought of it as something you could win one day. If you made the right move, or said the right thing, or . . . made out with me in the right exotic location."

"I thought that for a while, too," Win said.

They looked at each other, quiet and serious. Leo almost wanted to apologize, but that felt like another thing he would be putting on her shoulders, making her solve. He said, "Is there anything I can do to help?"

"You do help." Win sounded surprised. "You're here right now and you . . . you are helping a lot. I'm grateful. I know Marie forced you, but I appreciate that you came anyway."

Something hot and anxious fluttered in his chest.

"Marie didn't force me," he said.

Win blinked. "What?"

"Marie didn't send me." Leo wasn't sure where to look. "I saw all the tabloid stuff and I called her and told her I was going to come out."

Win's face was wiped clean with shock. "But you were angry."

"Yeah, I was furious," Leo said, and laughed awkwardly. "But . . . I don't know, everything looked awful, and I knew how it was with your mum the last time she was sick. I thought maybe I could help and I wanted—I wanted to see you."

"Marie didn't say—"

"I asked her not to tell you," Leo said.

"Well," Win said, still with that odd, unreadable voice, her eyes wide. "I'm . . . surprised."

"Yeah." Leo cleared his throat. "I just wanted you to know."

As they were leaving, a group of fans had amassed outside to greet them. Win paused to say hello to a few of them, and Leo hung back, watching her. The cold sun seemed almost harsh, streaming over her dark hair and her high cheekbones. It was barely autumn anymore, and the orange-red leaves littering the car park were already turning brown.

"You're such a sweetheart," Win was saying, as she stooped down for a photo with a young girl. In the afternoon light Win's face looked softer, dreamier, some of the hard exhaustion and worry of the last few weeks dissipating. It was as though she was backlit, the spotlight never leaving her, even out here in the middle of the day.

In the car on the way home, she dozed off leaning back against her seat, and then drifted to his shoulder. He stayed perfectly still, not daring to touch her, not even to keep her head from slipping off when they hit a bump. She jerked awake and stared at him, dazed, before she said, "Sorry," and Leo shook his head. She scooted to the far side, out of his reach.

He wondered if Win was ever not tired. It tired him out just think-ing about her, the days without end, the exhausting and never-ending professional activity of being Whitman Tagore. While their car wound through country roads, he realized he had been thinking about this— him and her, her and Pritha, all of it—as an essentially personal issue, with some demands from the outside. But Win wasn't allowed to have purely personal issues; everything was outside, everything was on show. It was all high stakes all the time. Win fell asleep again with her face pressed against the window, and Leo thought that there would never be a moment when Win was done, when she didn't have to care about these things anymore. It was never going to stop.

That was when he thought of it, the first quiet solid plan slotting in. He needed to call Lila.

CHAPTER FIFTEEN

Leo woke with a jerk to Win shouting below. He couldn't hear what was being said, but every so often she would pause, and a quieter, harsher voice that belonged to Pritha would respond. Leo stared at the ceiling, scratching his chest. He wondered what his chances were of getting yelled at if he went downstairs.

The need for coffee eclipsed everything else. In the kitchen Win was standing by the sink, gripping the silver rim, back stiff. Pritha sat at the counter sipping tea.

"Morning," Leo said.

Win mumbled something in acknowledgment, but Pritha turned to him, looking him up and down.

"Why aren't you dressed yet?"

He shrugged. "I just woke up."

"It's almost midday."

"I wanted some coffee—"

"Perfect, you can go fetch some. We also need more of the little biscuits."

"You're not supposed to eat those all the time, Ma," Win said, still turned to the window.

"I will eat what I like."

"I'm not trying to upset you," Win said. "This isn't about me, your doctors said—"

"Whitman," Pritha said. "Please let me get rid of Leo before we continue this conversation."

Win glanced over her shoulder finally to look at him. She'd been for her run already, her hair curling and stuck to the sides of her face, dark hollows beneath her eyes. "Fine."

Pritha nodded to Leo pointedly.

"Right," Leo said. "I'll go get—biscuits, then."

He saluted her, which made Pritha squint in suspicion, but she let him leave without further comment. He dressed quickly and carelessly, and flung himself out of the door and into the car without saying goodbye. He could hear them starting up again behind him as he left, Win's voice rising: "How can you call me selfish, after everything that's happened?"

He stayed out all day, driving up and down the coast, eating Pritha's biscuits and killing time. There were only a couple of paparazzi on his trail. Leo thought he saw one of them yawning while they waited for him to leave a coffee shop with his third latte. He'd downloaded an audiobook of *Wolf Hall*, on Pritha's suggestion, and he let it expand through the car and settle around him, the fraught tapestry of British history, feet in the mud, solitary fishing boats moored on the beaches at Dungeness.

Around four his phone buzzed, and he picked up without looking at the screen, expecting Pritha summoning him back with a longer shopping list. Instead Gum's nasal, caffeine-laced voice chirped out, "Please god tell me your self-imposed exile is over soon."

Leo laughed. "Who said it was self-imposed?"

"Come to New York," Gum persisted. "Dad's given me the junior suite of the Kenmare until next week. I'd prefer the penthouse, of course, but beggars can't be choosers."

Leo grinned. He could picture Gum sitting by the window in his huge, empty suite, a crumpled collar, methodically running through his phone's contact list—Leo, Charlie, Hannah—as though he were running a tragic telethon.

Right now Gum was making a crunching noise into the receiver, as if he was snacking on peanuts. "Charlie's arriving on Tuesday, we're going to pick his suit colors and get them fitted. Poor guy's not used to choosing his own clothes, and apparently the selection in Montreal is *dismal*. Did you know he's sold his New York apartment? He says they've decided to live there permanently. What is that going to do for Charlie's career? Did you ever hear of anyone successful living in Montreal?"

He said Montreal as if it were the name of a field hospital or a maximum-security prison. Leo pinched the bridge of his nose. Sometimes Gum reminded him so much of Bernard. While Leo had spent most of his charmed childhood swanning around Europe with his mums, Gum had spent most of his trailing hopefully after their father. Hannah seemed independent of all of them, and fonder of everyone for it.

"I'm sure they have a plan, Gum."

"Well, he's got plenty of plans for the wedding, at least. I've snagged him a tasting session next week, at some couture cake maker the moms know in the Village. I told him they're all booked up and he'd have to settle for donuts, so it's a total surprise. He'll probably cry," Gum added with satisfaction. "I'll send you a video."

"I'll look forward to that," Leo said. Gum could get it right sometimes, and Leo imagined he'd have a great time shepherding Charlie from the bespoke tailor to the artisan florist, offering to pay for all sorts of extravagant extras, one arm thrown jovially around Charlie's shoulders.

"I assume I'll see you both at the wedding, in any case," Gum said. "You and your beloved prima donna." Gum's voice was friendly enough, but he sounded slightly disapproving. Leo wondered what sorts of conversations were churning through the family rumor mill, Hannah and Gum syncing up across time zones to theorize about Leo's motivations.

"I don't know if I'm going with her," Leo said. "We haven't discussed it." His invitation had arrived in the mail a few weeks ago, and he had slipped it into the bottom of his bag. He had been afraid Win would see it and tell him not to come.

"Honestly, Leo," Gum said, in the same exasperated voice he'd used as a child when Leo asked for help tying his shoelaces. "I'm drowning in commitments, but I still have the grace to send an RSVP. You know he's got a *Vogue* profiler coming, plus a photographer? He might make the cover. It's ridiculous, I've been vying for them to profile me for years, but apparently I'm *outside their focus*. He does one Burberry photo shoot and then it's 'Chazzy Chazzy Chaz: The Chaz Story.'"

"Is that what they're calling it?"

"Anyway, you need to be there. It's a big deal and I haven't seen you in forever." Gum sighed. "It's hard not to feel abandoned. Hannah's still filming in Cambodia. The moms seem to think you might bail on the wedding. They said you've been quote-unquote unavailable for the last two months, they think you're avoiding them."

"Why do they always jump to me avoiding them?" Leo demanded. "Can't I just be a good old-fashioned negligent son?"

"The eternal question," Gum said. "They should have given up on you years ago."

"I'll have dinner with them next week," Leo said.

Gum clucked his approval. "Take the movie star with you, they'd love that. Either way, Leonard, you are coming to this wedding. I won't ask you to swear it, but I'm counting on your sense of fraternal duty. All right, I have a meeting with Mimi. I'm going to take her a box of truffles. See if it makes her sweeter. Ciao."

"Hey, wait, Gum—can you ask Miriam to call me?"

There was a pause. "My Mimi?"

"She isn't your Mimi," Leo said. "She's been Dad's lawyer for years."

"But she always tells me I'm the best client she's ever had."

"I bet she can buy a new house every time you pick up the phone."

"Don't you go turning her against me, Leonard," Gum said. "What Mimi and I have is the only functional relationship I've ever had with a woman."

"Because you're paying her?"

Gum sighed wearily. "Yes, I'll tell her to call you, and to expect something scandalous. See you at the wedding. Text me your measurements and I'll order your suit."

"I just want her advice on something," Leo said, but Gum had already hung up.

It had been dark for a while by the time he got back. There was music playing from the kitchen. He kicked his shoes off noisily and jangled his keys a little for good measure. It was a surprise to find Win waiting, rather than disappearing back up the stairs at the sound of his return. Their newfound peace felt fragile.

She was up at the counter in an oversized fisherman's jumper and leggings. There was a glass and a bottle of wine next to her, both empty.

"You're back," she said. Her voice was implacable, her posture very straight. She was in a dangerous mood. Leo paused in the doorway, taking her in.

"I am," he agreed. He tossed his keys onto the counter, and they both watched as they hit marble and then skittered loudly over the other side and onto the floor. Win snorted.

"We're out of wine," she said. "Do you want a drink?"

"Yes," Leo said. Win pulled herself up and went for the closest cupboard, rummaging through it.

"I think there's some old stuff in here—aha," she said, pleased, fishing out a tall green bottle from the back of the shelf. She shook it at him.

Leo stuck his hands in his pockets, looked her up and down. "You're drunk."

"Yeah," Win said. "Do you want some or not?"

"Sure."

She dug out two more glasses and filled them with ice from the machine on the fridge, jumping as the cubes clinked together like it startled her. She poured them both tall glasses topped up with a finger of water. The drink was yellow and sweet, reeking of aniseed. The bottle was labeled in Deco script: *Pastis Henri Bardouin*. A note had been added underneath: *With compliments from La Réserve, Saint-Tropez*.

"It's like we're in France again," Leo said.

Win glanced up at him. "Not really."

Leo couldn't disagree with her, so he changed the subject. "Is your mum okay?"

"Oh, yes," Win said, as though she'd been waiting for him to bring it up. "Thank you for that. *Why don't you just talk to her?*" Win waved her glass around, sending the liquid sloshing up against the sides and putting on a high, gormless voice that Leo hoped sounded nothing like him. "*I'm begging you, Whitman, ask her a question.* Nice one, thanks."

"She didn't react well?" Leo said, a little amused.

"No," Win said, and knocked back a good portion of her drink. "I told her that she shouldn't have kept the family stuff from me—"

"So you started by telling her off."

"Not everyone is a Pritha Tagore whisperer," Win snapped. "It's not as easy for me to talk to her. There's a lot of history there."

"I— Sorry," Leo said. He paused. "My family talk all the time. About everything, even when we're fighting. Especially when we're fighting. I think I . . . don't completely get this."

"No," Win said. "You don't."

"Sorry," Leo repeated. "No more advice."

"Really?" Win said sardonically. "Not about my mother, or about which directors I should blow off, or how to get Nathan Spencer canceled? No brain waves about race relations you want to share with me?"

Leo's face was hot. "No."

Win surveyed him intently, narrow-eyed. The kitchen was close with tension, and then she shrugged sharply, like she was throwing all of that away, and slumped, turning her face down. "I should have asked her to the premieres. God. I really thought she thought they were stupid. That my whole career was just—frivolous."

"But?"

"She thinks I'm embarrassed to be seen with her," Win mumbled. She still wasn't making eye contact. "She thinks I only see her as a burden." She palmed her hand over her face. "It would be easier if my dad was still alive."

Leo went quiet. Win almost never talked about her dad. It was as though she'd given any confidences she might share with him to the talk show host instead, all those years ago, when Leo needed her and Win had saved him. When she began to speak, the words came slow and rough, as though she were excavating them from somewhere deeply buried: hard, heavy work.

"It was always my dad who was interested in film," she said. "When I was little we used to watch classic comedies together—his favorite was *Some Like It Hot*, I think. And then Bollywood, too, stuff he watched when he was a kid that he thought I'd like. I got obsessed with Waheeda Rehman. Every December he took me to all the different Christmas shows in London, and afterward we reenacted them for Ma. And it was his idea for me to audition at this local theater, for *Oliver!* I got stuck in the chorus. Ma said if she heard 'Consider Yourself' one more time, she'd move out. But Dad loved it. He found me an after-school acting troupe."

"So it was just your and his thing?" Leo asked, something slotting into place: the way Win was inclined to think of her mum and dad as opposites, constantly at odds, Pritha the stubborn misanthrope versus Jotish the bright optimist. But Win was shaking her head.

"Maybe a little, but Ma was always— She indulged him. She loved it. She came with us to shows, every so often. She still loves the Globe.

I think she liked how happy it made him when she joined in. She used to sing along off-key when we were blasting musicals in the kitchen, and when we performed stuff for her, she always gave us a standing ovation. I mean, she let him name me after a dead poet—an American, too. Dad dragged her out into the world, he took her to all the family gatherings and evenings out she would have avoided, and then, you know, he'd rub her feet when they got home."

Leo laughed without meaning to, picturing it, and Win smiled absently back at him.

"After he got sick, Ma took over all the driving me around and watching rehearsals, fixing my stage makeup. She didn't quite get it, but she didn't complain." Win went quiet for a moment. She touched her mouth. "It was...a pretty horrible time. Just a lot of hanging around in hospitals. Dad used to make faces at me behind the doctor's back and hold my hand like everything was normal, even though he was getting thinner and thinner and he looked—he looked old. Then, you know. He died."

She reached for the bottle of pastis. Leo watched her without speaking, his mouth thick.

"I stopped going to the theater group," Win said. Her gaze was far away, a little clouded over. Leo wanted to touch her, and didn't dare. "I don't know. I stopped doing everything. But after a few months, Ma was like, *Come on, after-school theater*, and I just got up and followed her. It distracted me. It made me feel like I could control something. And then an agent called us.

"Ma said if I was going to do something, I might as well do it properly," Win said, a little amused twitch at the corner of her mouth. Leo could hear Pritha's businesslike tone. *Maybe you could be a graphic designer.* "Then the agent lined up all these auditions for theater and then some movies and TV shows. You know the rest."

"But you were fifteen," Leo said. "It must've been terrifying."

"Yeah, well," Win said, something lonely and still about the slope of her shoulders. "I spent the year before that with doctors giving us terrible news, so it didn't really compare." She looked up and met Leo's gaze, her mouth a grim, satisfied line. "Plus I kept getting the parts."

"You were a prodigy," Leo agreed.

"Finally, some recognition," Win said, but she was still distracted. She topped up their glasses again. "Anyway. I think if Dad was still alive, he would have come to all the premieres, and he would have dragged Ma out, like he dragged her to everything, and then it wouldn't be so hard, there wouldn't be this . . ."

She swept her hand through the air, like she was mapping out treacherous territory. Leo thought of Pritha and Win, yelling at each other in the kitchen this morning. They looked more alike when they were angry. They'd been standing separately, opposite sides of the room, as though the space between them was too charged to chance.

"Well," Leo said. "Isn't it . . . isn't it easier to know that at least the problem isn't that she thinks you're an idiot? This is the kind of problem you can work on."

"Yeah. If I have time."

Leo's gut twisted. "But the doctors said—"

"God, no," Win said, blanching. "Not—not that. I just mean . . ." She glanced up at him, quick, and Leo suddenly knew what was coming. He picked up his glass so he was drinking when Win said, "I need to leave soon, get back to work."

The pastis was sharp, almost bitter taken in one hit like that. He set the glass down and smiled. "Right, of course."

"Leo—"

"You were about to start working on that Hemingway film, right?"

Win paused, watching him closely. "Right. So when Ma got sick we had to push that back. They've been . . . quite understanding." Leo took the tiny hesitation to mean that they had been talked into under-standing by Patrick and the rest of Win's team. "We're going to start with the winter scenes in France and then move back to Spain in the spring." She rubbed her hand over her face. "But the *All Rivers Run* press tour has to fit in as well, so now I'm going to have to film the first part of *The Sun Also Rises* and then go straight to that. And then somehow get to Montreal for the wedding, as well."

"That's going to be crazy."

"It was always going to be tight. I guess that will probably be the end of this." She flung one hand out between them and made a face. She looked almost regretful, like she was telling a dog when it would be put down.

"Right." Leo nodded. He was aware that he was letting her take the lead, in a way that had caused trouble in the past. He never stopped to read the small print before signing his name beneath hers, but he worried that any hesitation would turn her against him, like she was doubting his commitment. "Makes sense."

"I want to wait until at least a few weeks after she's been given the all clear," Win said. "But Ma thinks I should go back now."

"Oh," Leo said. He wondered for the first time where he would go after Win had left. Maybe Pritha would let him stay.

Win was playing idly with the ice in her glass, swirling it around. "I'm not being selfish. I'm trying to . . . find a compromise with her."

"I know."

Win sighed and looked up at him. "She likes you, you know." He raised his eyebrows, and she added, "Not a compliment."

"Makes me feel special, though," Leo said. He ran a hand back through his shorn hair, ruffling it.

Win didn't smile. "I hate that she likes you."

Leo paused, trying to think of a safer subject. "Emil will be happy you're back at work. He must miss you."

"Oh, he's been keeping busy. Last I heard he was in . . . Milan? I think he's running three different fashion weeks at once. He said to tell you to cut your hair."

"I knew he liked the buzz cut," Leo said. He ran his hand through it again, the first longer tufts of curls soft like lamb's wool. "I could shave it again. Maybe I'll go to London next week."

"You don't need to go all the way to London for a buzz cut," Win said.

"People pay good money to see pictures of my scalp," he said. "I owe it to them to do it right. It's a duty."

"A cross only you could bear," Win agreed. Her expression was unreadable; she was still eyeing his head critically. "I could fix it. I probably have a razor somewhere."

"No, you couldn't."

She glared at him. "Yes. I could do it." She looked up at him properly, setting her glass down. "I could do it right now."

He didn't like where this was going. "Maybe tomorrow."

"I want to do it now," she said. "I think it would make me feel better."

"I really think we should stop and think about this," Leo began, but the idea had seized her, and she was already lurching up out of her chair and darting out of the room. He could track the sounds of her journey through the house, thuds and grunts and the rattle of drawers, and finally an *aha!* that made him wince. She came back toting an electric razor and a smug expression.

"You found it."

"Here," she said, draping a towel around his shoulders. "I'm so excited."

"I'm very happy for you." Leo took a final sip of his drink, wishing they had something stronger. At least Win seemed happier, stirred out of the dreamy, awful recitation of her father's death. He let her tilt his head forward, cool fingers behind his ear and on his brow.

"Gross," Win said as she shaved the first line. "This is going to go everywhere."

"You can't stop now," Leo said. "I don't want half a shaved head." The buzzing was right next to his ear, and he could feel the little metal teeth against his scalp. Win had gone quiet. He held himself very still for her.

It didn't take her long to do the back of his head, and then she ducked around, buzzing in wide, loose lines along his ears all the way down to his jawline. She thumbed over his ear, tucked her knuckles under his jaw, tilting his head to the side and examining him.

"Here," she said, "I need to get the front," and she pulled him down onto the stool so his back was to the counter, and stood between his legs.

"Whitman," Leo murmured.

"Mmm," she said. "Almost there."

"All right," he said.

She spent another five minutes on him, veering dangerously close to his eyebrows at one point so Leo had to duck back and say, "Whoa, hey." Then she switched the razor off and set it down beside her, reaching up to stroke across Leo's temple the way she had in the lobby of La Réserve, months ago.

"Feels nice."

"Win." His voice was low. His thighs were pressing against her hips. He could not stop looking at her mouth.

The cat yowled, twisting around Win's legs and swiping a paw at Leo. Win startled backward, hitting her side against the counter and cursing. Leo's hair was all over the floor, and now the cat was pawing through it.

"I hate that cat," Leo said. Win paused from where she'd been rubbing her side.

"It's my cat," she said. "I've had her for years."

"It hates me and I don't know why," Leo said. He poked it with a toe, and the cat spat at him. "Bad cat. Bad, bad cat."

And for the first time since he'd trapped himself here, since they'd last been together, since that final night in Saint-Tropez, Leo made Win laugh. She had one hand pressed to the side of her face like she wanted to stop, but she was laughing, clear and golden in the cool, dark house.

The next day they had to make an appearance away from the house so that one of Pritha's colleagues could visit in peace. They drove to another art gallery farther down the coast, and Leo took a selfie of his new haircut in the bathroom and posted it online. Back to business, he wrote.

"Nice hair, Leo," one of the photographers called as they were leaving.

"Hey, thanks, man," he said. Win stroked her hand over the top of his skull, pleased.

CHAPTER SIXTEEN

The thought that Win might leave at any minute gave the days a solidity they'd lacked before; they fell past Leo with an urgent sort of weight. The house was shifting, the jagged shadows of autumn giving way to the clear, gray light of winter. Win seemed half-in and half-out of the world, sitting beside her mum with a strained, frightened look about her, like she was fighting hard against the current. He had to resist the urge to grab at her, hold her to him. Sometimes she caught lightly at his shoulder as she drifted past, like she was anchoring herself.

Pritha was getting stronger, and she and Win circled each other like boxers, but the tension didn't flare into anger. Instead they eyed each other up, tried out conversations as though for the first time. He'd always been the peacemaker with his siblings, but this was something new, a not-quite conflict he didn't know how to defuse. Pritha kept him busy with a litany of tasks, helping reorganize the bookshelves in her room and bringing flowerpots from the garden inside for the winter, rehanging some pictures in the hallway that she insisted were off center. He enjoyed it for the most part, but it struck him one evening that maybe she, too, had realized that soon he wouldn't be there anymore, a thought that left him cold and tired.

They'd started eating dinner together, all three of them grouped around the kitchen island or in the lounge with food that Win's people had sent over, or takeout, or—rarely—their own cooking. ("What is this?" Win asked. Leo poked at the dish and said, "Casserole, maybe?" and Win propped her elbows against the counter and laughed help-lessly, her head falling forward, hair tumbling down. They ate it with spoons straight from the dish, poking through for what was edible and fighting over the unscorched vegetables.) They never used the dining room; Pritha said it was too big and Leo thought it was too formal and Win didn't care.

The night Pritha's doctor called to say that the first scans had come back clear, Win gave in and they ate pizza, sprawled on the living room floor with *Yeh Rishta* playing in the background. Even Pritha sat on the floor, her back against the couch and Win lounging by her side. Win could barely take her eyes off her mum.

"I don't get why you two are so obsessed with this," Win said, gesturing at the screen. "It takes, like, two hours for anything to happen—"

"That's why it's great," Leo said. "You can have a conversation halfway through and not miss anything."

"Leo likes Kartik," Pritha said. "He thinks he is also a bad boy."

"That's not true!" Leo said, though it was.

Win rolled her eyes at both of them. "God, this is good," she said, taking another bite of her pepperoni slice. "I haven't had pizza since that night we went swimming in Saint-Tropez."

Leo's head jerked up despite himself and he met her gaze. She was wide-eyed, as though she'd surprised herself, and the memory flashed across Leo's mind like lightning: Win's dark skin and smooth strokes in the pool, the long line of her legs, the dip of her collarbone. At the time he had tried to be gentlemanly and not look too closely. He'd thought cockily that he already knew the easy curves of Win's body, the press of her nipples against her bra, the shadows on the inward dip of her thighs. Now he thought there was a difference between knowing and getting to look again.

"You'll be back soon enough," Pritha said.

"Ma." Win's voice was quiet.

"Back where?" Leo shook his head. "Back in France?"

"It's not like I eat pizza all the time in France," Win said, mostly to herself. "It's just, you know . . ."

"When are you going back?"

Win hesitated. "I'm going over to La Roche-Guyon next week."

"Wow," Leo said. He could feel himself smiling, a weird horrible rictus of a grin, but couldn't get rid of it. "That's so soon."

Win swallowed. "It's only for a few days. Then I'm flying to Montreal for Shift's wedding, and—well, hopefully I'll come back here . . ."

Pritha was already shaking her head. "You said Patrick said that they'd want you back in France after the wedding, and then you have to be in New York until Christmas."

"That's what they want, Ma," Win said, "it doesn't mean I'm going to do it. I need to be here with you. They'll want to do at least one more follow-up scan—"

"I am fine," Pritha said. "I could come out and visit you. There's no need for you to babysit me."

Win flinched like she'd been hit. Leo leapt in, still feeling a little dizzy at the speed with which everything was happening. "Win, it's just that you've already taken so much time off, so if this is important—"

"Yes, thank you, I don't need you to interpret my mother for me," Win snapped, and all three of them went silent. After a moment Win passed her hand over her eyes and handed Leo the soda, like a peace offering. "Sorry. It's not certain, that's all. Everything's up in the air."

"It could land anywhere," Leo said, solemn, trying to make them laugh, but Win and her mother just looked at him as though he was right, and they were worried about it.

Leo slept late more than ever as time took on a momentum he couldn't fight. He went on the occasional date with Win—they were petering out now that Win and Marie were quietly preparing the world for when Win and Leo went their own separate ways again—and he spoke to Lila every so often. Win's phone calls with Marie were switched out more and more often for sessions with Emil: "Always a sign my life is back on track," Win said drily, surrounded by piles of paperwork, printed out calendars and schedule suggestions. One morning Miriam, Gum's lawyer, called to tell Leo that everything was done and she was sending the paperwork, and he panicked and had her redirect it to Hastings Post Office, where he could pick it up himself without worrying about Win or Pritha watching him sign for it.

Win was gone when he got back, and Pritha was having coffee with a woman from her book club, who scrutinized Leo with far too much interest for Leo's liking. He made a hasty retreat upstairs and wondered what he would do, now that it was nearly over. There was the wedding coming up, but that would only be a weekend.

Maybe it was time to actually start on the studio, though the idea of committing to it made Leo anxious, something twisting in the pit of his stomach. Everything felt uncertain. But he didn't have to tell Win he was doing it; he didn't have to tell anyone he was doing it. If he was desperate, he could tell Pritha, who would frown and declare that he should have done something like this years ago, making it seem inevitable, rather than frightening.

And it might be nice to have a real project, the way the last few months had been a project. He'd been here helping, not just jetting around for a series of photo shoots and living a charmed life for both the public and his own selfish enjoyment. It had been different this time. Even when it was awful, it had been satisfying to be useful, a tool rather than an ornament. He could go after the studio in the same way.

Maybe Leo had spent the last few years searching for the wrong thing. All those times he'd told himself he was "location scouting," searching for a space, as if lofts and studios were hard to find in capital cities. The location wasn't the problem—the problem was Leo. Leo as director, Leo running his petty vanity project. But it didn't have to be like that. Leo had friends, he had contacts, he had Lila and Riva and the thousand other people who had offered to put him in touch with artists they knew, real artists with the vision Leo lacked and the requirements Leo could fulfill. Leo felt he understood art, but he didn't understand what fledgling artists needed, or how to bring them together, or what to offer them. What he did have was money to burn and a name that would open a few doors. It was a start.

He was driving into London for dinner with his mums tonight, and he resolved to ask Thea's opinion. She would encourage him no matter what he planned, but she was thoughtful and cleverer than him and would spy out any major flaws in his plan, and explain them to him gently. Dusk was encroaching, and Leo felt restless. He was standing out on the porch smoking in the semi-dark when Win reappeared.

The gravel crunched under Win's feet as she walked over from her car. Frost was already setting in on the grass and the last withered leaves of the trees, and everything looked like it would crumble away if you tried to touch it. Their cohort of photographers had started to dwindle in the falling temperatures, and the ones that remained stayed shut up in their cars until there were signs of movement. Leo had seen one with a paraffin stove set up for hot tea and coffee.

"You shouldn't smoke here," Win said to him as she held her hand out for the cigarette and took a slow, satisfied drag.

"Your mum's asleep already," Leo said.

Win nodded, still mostly preoccupied by the cigarette. Leo rolled himself another, and they stood together in silence.

Win broke it. "I'm leaving on Thursday."

Leo nodded. "For France."

"Yeah," Win said, "but I'm not coming back. Maybe for a day or two over Christmas, that's all."

He'd been expecting it, but something still dropped in Leo's stomach, a stone fallen into a well. "Oh?"

"Ma's fine. The doctors think she's recovering well. They said she can do a few hours at the office next week if she wants to."

"How can they tell?"

Win shrugged her shoulders mutely. She looked younger than usual in the porch light. Leo wasn't sure if the photographers' lenses could see them at this distance, but it was probably best to assume the attention. He put his arm around her shoulders, thumbed at her collarbone.

"How can they tell?" Win echoed, and laughed. "Leo. They're *doctors*."

"Okay, I just meant—"

"They have quite a lot of very impressive scientific technology," Win said, clearly enjoying herself, "and they can run tests, and take blood, and do these special things called X-rays, which is where they look *inside* you—"

"Okay, okay," Leo said. Win laughed again and dropped her cigarette half-smoked on the wood, ground it out with the toe of her boot. Leo took another drag. His chest was tight. His mum was always going on at him to stop smoking. "Well. That's good, then. That your mum's all right, I mean."

"Yeah," Win said.

"It's a relief," Leo said.

"Yes," Win said, quiet in the gloom, warm all along his side. She reached out and took Leo's cigarette again, contemplative like she didn't really know what she was doing. "I don't know. It's not like it's easier when she's sick, of course. It's awful. It's so frightening. But at least there are things I can do to help. It's harder when it's just me and her, to work out what she needs. How to—how to be a good daughter."

"Mums are tricky," Leo said.

Win huffed a laugh. "Like you can talk. You have two mums and they both adore you."

"You don't know that!"

"I can tell," Win said. "You're the most obvious Mummy's Boy I've ever met."

"Fuck you," Leo said, laughing, and nudged at her. "I've got plenty of daddy issues, if that helps."

"That's so original of you," Win said, but he could see the edge of her smile in the shadows. She rubbed her hand over her face. "God. It's—it'll be fine. It's just...I keep thinking about when my dad got sick. They didn't tell me he was dying, even though they knew it was terminal. Him and Ma, I mean. Ma told me that Dad said it was too hard, and unfair, that I was going to have to deal with it anyway, so why not give me a year when it wasn't hanging over me. It was—it was an okay year, even though he was so sick. They acted like he was going to be fine. I think it was better than it would have been if I'd known he wasn't going to get better. We hung out all the time and..." She shook her head. "But when he died it was like the world ended and it turned out everyone knew it was going to happen but me."

"That's shit," Leo murmured, trying to deflect attention, not startle Win into stopping.

"It was so surreal. I still can't decide if it was a good idea or not. Ma told me later that they fought about it tons, that she wanted to tell me really badly."

She paused. They contemplated the dusk, the last of the light. Leo's head was reeling; he couldn't even wrap his head around the idea of one of his parents dying. He tried, "To...give you the chance to say goodbye?"

"I think I did get to say goodbye," Win said. "Not consciously, but we spent so much time together, it was like the Year of Dad. Ma told me that Dad said that him dying was going to make me grow up, that it would be the end of my childhood. And he wanted me to hold on to it for as long as possible."

Leo nodded. Win ran her hand through her hair.

"He was right," she said. "But sometimes I think...he never got the chance to see me grow up. Didn't he—didn't he miss out on something that he could have had, in a way?"

"Win," Leo said. He wanted to touch her very badly.

"Anyway," Win said, mouth quirking self-consciously. "I just keep thinking about it."

"You have plenty of time left," Leo said. "It won't be like that. She won't miss out. Neither will you." He wanted to add, *I promise*, but it wasn't anything he could give her, wasn't a promise he could make, and Win looked at him like she knew it and was pretending she didn't.

"I know," Win said. Her shoulders straightened, a door closed. "And it will be good to get back to work. Even besides filming, I've got a lot of scripts to look through and there's this thriller, we want to sign the contract later this week. And Shift's wedding, obviously. And then it's awards season."

Leo swallowed, trying to get his head back to where she needed it. "I like the Oscars. Excellent champagne."

Win gave him an amused look. "You like the week before the Oscars."

"That's true," Leo said. Hollywood buzzing, everyone excited and a bit fucked up, lots of petty drama, lots of pre-parties. He and Win had gone together, years ago while Win's fame was still only growing. They gave bad advice to fledgling talents and did shots. Leo had dared Win to climb one of the Californian laurel trees in a producer's backyard and was thrilled when she actually did, grinning down at him in her designer gown, framed by green and twigs in her hair.

"It'll be good," Win said, "to be going out for real again, not—" She waved her hand between them noncommittally.

Leo looked down at her, and realized with a start that she was looking up at him. Her breath was warm against his cheek. Leo's stomach knotted.

"I don't know," Win said. "I was so angry, when you came." She swallowed, dry; Leo could hear the tiny click of her throat. "It's probably good you didn't tell me it was your idea. But I'm glad," she said, very low. "I don't know what I would have done without you." She laughed, a little embarrassed. "Even with all the fighting."

"I thought you liked fighting with me," Leo said.

"I guess I'm growing up," she said. He turned closer to her, arm falling from around her shoulders. Win's expression was hidden in the dark. Night had arrived while they were talking, and he hadn't noticed.

"It'll be weird leaving," Leo said. "I'm used to this now. Hanging out here with your mum and your horrible cat."

"She's a nice cat." But Win was nodding. "I'll be glad to get out again. But it's going to be so different. I'm out of practice talking to people," she concluded. "I don't know how to switch back into that world."

Leo hesitated. Then he said, "Well, I have an idea."

CHAPTER SEVENTEEN

Win insisted on getting changed even though Leo said what she was wearing was fine. Then she insisted on him calling ahead to check that it was okay to invite her, even though he told her that absolutely wasn't necessary. Then she sat straight-backed and cold in the car. It wasn't until they got to his mums' street in Chelsea that he realized she was nervous.

"What," Win said, when he accused her of it. "I haven't met them before. It's normal."

"It's not normal," Leo said, laughing. "You don't get nervous. Don't pretend like this is your typical form."

"I do, too," Win said, affronted.

"I don't think I've seen you nervous since..." Leo stopped, trying to think. He scrunched up his face. "Maybe the first time we went to the Golden Globes?"

"No, I was fine that night."

"You were so mean to me," Leo said. "You told me that you thought my face was overrated. Hey, Ben," he added, rolling down the window.

"Hi, Leo," Ben said, bumping his fist against Leo's. "Just you two?"

"Yeah, thanks. Hey, this is Whitman—Whitman, Ben, he does security for the mums—"

"Nice to meet you," Win said.

Ben nodded back at her. "Head on through."

Leo leaned farther out of his car, twisting to wave at the little line of paparazzi. They were shouting and taking photos out of half a dozen car windows. "Sorry, guys, this is where we lose you!"

The barrier had been set up by one of the other resident millionaires, and it suited the mums well as a deterrent for paparazzi, who still took an interest in Gabrysia Milanowski from time to time. It was a river-front street, everything dark and quiet, looming terraced houses with enormous windows, the Thames quivering and cold at their feet.

Win got out before Leo could get around to her door. "Which one's theirs?"

"Oh, man. Come on, I'm sure I've told you this," Leo said, and gestured toward the pier.

"No," Win breathed, delighted, and took his hand.

Leo's heart skipped quick in his chest. He looked down at their linked fingers and kept talking, putting on the same lofty tones Thea had used. "They don't like to feel tethered to the land."

"Right," Win said as they stepped toward the houseboat. "But isn't that . . . exactly what they are?"

Leo laughed. "Please open with that," he said, and watched her, enjoying the way she took it all in. It was a strange square block on the water, several floors in enamel red and black, a deck that spiraled around the hull, and the bronze figurehead that Thea had sculpted her-self when they moved in. Originally it had been the spitting image of a bare-breasted Gabrysia, but after Hannah said it made her uncomfort-able, Thea added a shawl in burnished copper, protecting Gabrysia's modesty. It was ostentatious, too expensive, but his mums' tastes had always tended that way. Hannah still called the boat the ugliest thing she'd ever seen, but Leo had always liked it. Gabrysia and Thea drew the curtains most of the time, but this close he could see all the lit-up warmth of Thea's studio, and his mum's office with its clean white lines high at the top of the boat.

"It's from one of Dad's resorts. He gave it to them as an anniversary present."

"Your parents still celebrate their wedding anniversary?"

"No, the anniversary of Mum divorcing him. She holds a party every year. You ready?"

Win let out an exasperated breath. "Yes. You don't need to enjoy yourself so much."

"But I like to," Leo said, and looked down at their hands again. He squeezed her fingers. "Uh. Not that I mind, but they know most things about us. So we don't have to—"

"Oh!" Win said, and dropped his hand. "Right. Sorry. Force of habit."

"Sure," Leo said, and knocked.

Thea threw the door open immediately, which meant she'd been watching through the peephole. "*Sweetheart*," she said, and flung her arms around him.

Leo hugged her back. "Hey, Mum," he said. "All right?"

"*All right*, honestly, darling, you sound like a complete fool," she said. She was small and round, freckled with wispy white hair pulled haphazardly into a side plait, like a benevolent fairy queen. Leo had always loved her unconditionally. "It's about time you showed your face. Your mother has been worried out of her mind."

"Has she," Leo said, and added, "This is Whitman. Whitman, Thea—"

"*Whitman*," Thea said, and pushed Leo aside to throw her arms around Win instead. Win grinned at Leo over Thea's shoulder. "I can't say how wonderful it is to see you at last. You're even more beautiful than your photos. And *so tall*."

"It's nice to finally meet you," Win said. Thea stepped back to beam at her, catching Win's hands in hers and pulling them up against her heart. "I've heard so much about you, I felt like I was missing out."

"You're a very sweet girl," Thea said. "I don't know what you're doing riding around with our darling brat."

"I think my mum feels the same way about him," Win said.

Leo preened. "I won Pritha over."

"Of course you did," Thea said, brisk. "Right. Come in, both of you, we've had such trouble with those nasty little men lately."

"Paparazzi?" Win said.

Thea nodded. "One of them climbed into a tree trying to get photos of my studio. Probably trying to scoop my next exhibition."

"Awful," Win said, failing to contain another grin, but Thea just smiled back at her.

"Well, it was fine. Gabrysia howled at him and he fell into the river. Can't imagine that did his fancy camera any good. Come on, come on," she added, as though she weren't half blocking the doorway herself. "Gabrysia is just beside herself—can't wait to see the both of you—"

"She's in the—"

"Living room, of course, of course, darling," Thea said. "In you go. Whitman! Would you like a tour? Let me—"

"She should meet Mum first," Leo said.

"Well, stop dawdling in the hall, then," Thea said, and flapped her free hand at Leo, still clutching Win with the other.

The living room was chaos, as usual. Discarded shirts and shawls hung off the back of every chair, and a pile of Edwardian slips was draped lovingly over a green velvet ottoman. There were ferns on the bookshelves trailing down heavy artist portfolios and midcentury detective novels, and sketch paper lay scattered around an empty armchair, Gabrysia's half-drawn profile winking up in charcoal next to teetering piles of fashion magazines weighed down with empty jars of La Mer. The floor-to-ceiling liquor cabinet was jammed full of heavy bottles of imported spirits, but also gilt perfume bottles, a decanter of turpentine, and an ominous unlabeled flask of black liquid sealed with a cork. A twelve-inch shark jaw lay apparently forgotten on the coffee table. Through the bay windows the lights glittered on the river, and the water lapped gently against the hull, like a farmyard dog come to sleep on the stoop.

Deep in the corner's shaded lamplight was the large wicker rocking chair that Gum, age six, had brought home from his first trip to Portobello Market, and in the chair gazing out over the inky water was Leo's mother. She was wearing a black transparent gown over a slip, her gaze absent, her face peaceful, long legs draped over the coffee table and crossed at the ankle.

"Hi, Mum," Leo said, coming over to her.

"Leo," Gabrysia said, and uncurled from her chair, putting her arms around him. They were exactly the same height. Leo thumbed the streak of gray in her hair. She held him back by the shoulders and looked him up and down. "How are you?"

"Good!" Leo said. "Really good."

"Hmm," Gabrysia said.

"No, really." Leo gave her his best smile.

"Well." She reached for her glass of wine, balanced on a stack of old invitations. "It's good to see you. Did you pussy out of bringing the girl?"

"Thea's got hold of her."

"Thea!" Gabrysia called. "Where are you?"

There was a minor exclamation in the next room, and Thea and Win appeared. Thea still had hold of Win's hands, and Win looked around the room and its explosive contents and didn't even blink.

"Darling," Thea said, "Whitman was just telling me about her latest film, it sounds absolutely wonderful—we must go see it—have you met Whitman yet?"

"I am not sure how you would expect me to," Gabrysia said, coming forward, "given you've been with her every moment they've been here." She took Win's hand. They watched each other for a beat. Leo stuck his hands in his pockets and slouched, feeling oddly on show though nobody was looking at him. Gabrysia said, "It's lovely to meet you at last, Whitman."

"You, too," Win said. They kissed each other's cheeks.

"Right," Leo said. "What are we drinking?"

Wine from Thea's ex-girlfriend's vineyard, it turned out, which was very good. They crowded around the dining table, long and worn and brought from Thea's childhood home in France. Thea calmed down once she'd caught her breath, and Win relaxed halfway through her first glass of wine. Leo was feeling pretty pleased with himself.

"Is your mother doing better?" Gabrysia asked. "I was sorry to hear she was unwell."

"Yes. She's finished her chemo and the first scans have been clear. It's just..." Win made a useless gesture.

"It's much more likely to come back again, isn't it," Gabrysia said. "Once you've already had it."

"Yes. Yes." Win let out a breath. "She's had a double mastectomy now, so." Leo startled, because Win hadn't told him that; it must have been before he arrived. "They weren't sure this time if it was a recurrence or a new cancer, and the chemo was for safety. Hopefully it will have . . . Anyway. The doctors are optimistic. I'm holding on to that."

"She sounds like a brave woman," Thea said.

"She's a champ," Leo said.

"Leo just likes her because she frightens him," Win said, and both his mums laughed.

"Hey, we've bonded now," Leo said. "We're roommates. I've spent a month fixing her TV."

"I didn't know you knew how to do that, darling," Thea said.

"Well," Leo said, resisting the urge to flex his bicep. "I figured it out."

"What *have* you two been up to?" Thea said. "The tabloids have been full of it, I suppose, but you know we don't touch those things."

"Not officially," Gabrysia said, sotto voce, and winked.

"We've just been—you know, keeping busy," Win said. She gave Leo an anxious look. She wasn't used to discussing their agreement openly with anyone but him, Shift, and Marie.

Leo said, "Win fixed my hair. And we went for a swim." Neither of his mums looked particularly impressed; Thea swam all year round. Leo glanced at Win and said, as he lifted his glass to his mouth, "You know, the press were giving Win and her mum a hard time, and if I drop round and pretend there's some big love story going on..."

Win let out a breath, relieved. "It's strange, I know," she said, "but—"

"It makes perfect sense to me," Gabrysia said. "I think I was planning to try it at some point, only then..."

"Scuppered it, didn't I," Thea said. "Ah well. You did just fine, I think."

"Hmm," Gabrysia said, but she was smiling into her glass.

"That's—really nice," Win said.

"Don't get them started," Thea said, nodding at Leo and Gabrysia. "They're romantics, the both of them, if you bring it up too much, they'll both launch into the whole grand tale—"

"I haven't done that since I was fifteen," Leo said.

"Went down *very* well at his birthday party," Thea said. "Rich boys love a lesbian love story."

Win started to laugh. Leo said, offended, "I think some of them were very moved. I told it pretty well. I'm a natural storyteller, Nicholle said."

"Which one of your dad's wives was she?" Win said.

"Third one," Leo said, "the one who got done for—"

"Oh, the embezzler," Win said, and laughed again.

Leo grinned at her, propping his chin on his hand. He hadn't heard Win laugh this much in a while. "You like that, do you? My family's pain amuses you?"

"It amused me," Gabrysia said.

"Not me," Thea said. "That woman spent too much time with the children. I still worry it was her who set Geoffrey on the path to—well." She stopped and sighed.

"Gumbo is not on any path," Gabrysia said. She curved her hand over Thea's shoulder. "Unless you call running headfirst into trouble a path. He just wants to be loved. He had a bad week, poor little frog."

Leo frowned. "What happened?"

"*Forbes* passed him over again," Thea said. "He's very disappointed. It was his last chance for the 30 Under 30, he won't be eligible next year."

"Dark times," Leo said, while Win looked torn between sympathy and amusement. "Why haven't I heard about this?"

"Hannah's been handling it," Gabrysia said. "They were on the phone for four hours yesterday."

"Four hours?" Win said.

"That's not so crazy for him," Leo said. "Gum calls her every day for a family gossip update. So Hannah's sorted him out?"

"Well, I think she would have, but there's the time difference, you know," Thea said, looking dour. "So she went to bed and Geoffrey called up Jim Barnes at the *New York Post*—"

"He did what?" Win said.

"Oh, Gum does this all the time," Leo told her. "He met Jim Barnes at a fundraiser years ago and decided they were best friends—"

"Geoffrey's very lonely, you know," Thea added. "He takes to people—"

"Every couple of months he rings this guy up and tells him he's got a huge scoop, and then just rattles on about whatever he's thinking about for a while," Leo said. "Most of the time it's useless, but every now and then he manages to do some real damage. Once he mentioned that Dad was selling a hotel under the table, just as an aside, and Barnes got curious and looked into it and it turned out the guy Dad was selling it to had mob ties—"

"No," Win breathed. "How did I not know about this?"

"Oh, Dad managed to make it blow over," Leo said. "It was nasty for a minute there, though, I half thought I should call you in to pull focus, but you were dating what's-his-face." He snapped his fingers. "The ugly one."

Win sighed. "Dermott."

Leo shook his head, unconcerned. "No, the other ugly one."

"Adam," Win said. The corner of her mouth was twitching. "You were with Kristina around then, anyway."

"It was after we broke up," Leo said. "That's right, it was too soon after the Met thing. I knew Marie wasn't going to let me near you for months."

"Well, you needed to learn some self-control," Win said, something assessing in her gaze. She turned to Thea. "What did Gum say this time, then?"

"He was very tragic about the whole thing," Gabrysia said. Her accent was getting stronger, normally a good indication that she was annoyed. She leaned in confidingly toward Win. "Gumbo is a bit of a drama queen, I'm afraid."

"I have it here," Thea said, squinting hard at her phone and tapping the screen with one pointed index finger. Her reading glasses, Leo noticed, sat jauntily on the head of a taxidermied pelican in the bookcase. "Hem hem. *Well, maybe I am over the hill! But when those bright-eyed babies finally catch up with me, they'll be singing a different tune. Life is decay. Your friends leave you, your achievements fall by the wayside, Old Father Time marches on.*"

"Jesus Christ," Leo said.

Win looked taken aback. "Is he okay?"

"Oh yes, he's quite cheerful about it now," Thea said. "Getting the quote in the *Post* has rather perked him up. I think he's considering a transition to tortured artiste. He asked me where he could buy a beret."

Win cracked up. Gabrysia smiled at her and said, "These moods never last long."

"Just long enough to ruin a night," Leo said. Win was still laughing, rocking forward in her chair; Leo caught the back of her neck, stroked his fingers over the smooth line of her nape as she let her forehead fall against his shoulder. "You know at least some of this is about Charlie's wedding, right? He's obviously freaking out. What if he turns his best man speech into a eulogy for their lost youth?"

"Oh dear," Gabrysia said, which Leo thought was an understatement. She held her hand out for the wine, and Thea diligently emptied the bottle into her glass.

"I didn't realize he was so upset about it," Win said.

"Poor Gumbo. He's actually very fragile," Gabrysia said. "He struggles with change. I think this wedding will be hard for him."

"Leo will look after him," Thea said.

Gabrysia looked at Win. "As long as you don't mind sharing."

"Whatever I can do to help," Win said.

Something startled in Leo's chest. He'd thought this was over; he'd thought they were nearly done, Win about to split ways again. He stayed quiet, watching her, and Win turned to him.

"You were supposed to be my date." She shot Leo that daring look, the same one she always used right before raising a bet. "Unless you've got a better offer."

"No," Leo said, and touched the curve of her chin. He knew that the mums were watching him, but they would know everything whether he touched Win or not. Leo felt comfortably obvious in front of them, and there was no point controlling himself. "I'll stick with you."

He hadn't had his fill of her, not in France or Sussex or all those years ago in New York. He still hadn't had his fill. She was about to leave, and Leo was beginning to recognize the clawing tension in his body every time he looked at her for what it was. He was hungry.

They sat in front of their empty plates talking after dinner was done; to Leo's dismay, his mums had produced several leather-bound photo albums. Win shuffled her chair around to pore over them, laughing at a series of Leo's bad hairstyles and pictures of Leo and his school friends posing aggressively in front of various European landmarks, chests thrown out, chicken-legged in their tan shorts.

"These kids all look like such jerks," Win said.

"That's a Swiss boarding school for you," Gabrysia said. "I wasn't sure, but his father insisted . . . Well. Oh, look, there's Sami."

Leo groaned. Sami meant they were up to the stage in the photos where Leo had worn a lot of button-up pastel shirts and boat shoes. He wished they would skip past.

Thea looked fond. "What a nice kid. Leo had such a crush."

"Uh, excuse you," Leo said. "I was in love."

"It was very sweet," Gabrysia told Win. "They were best friends."

"Yeah," Win said, throwing him a laughing look. "That's Leo's type."

Leo narrowed his eyes.

"Speaking of photographs," Thea said, and Gabrysia stood up, saying, "Oh yes. We meant to show you—Anya sent it to us."

Win and Leo exchanged quick glances.

"Here," Gabrysia said, recovering the fall issue of *Ci Sarà* with unnerving accuracy from under three empty wineglasses, a pashmina, and several newspaper clippings Leo hoped were about Gum, and dumping it in Win's lap. His own face looked back at him from the cover, gaze faraway and heavy-lidded, and Win's photographed mouth curled into something private and knowing. Leo almost didn't want to touch it. It was another uncomfortable thing they didn't talk about, a relic of the summer before everything fell apart.

Win didn't hesitate. She flipped it open to their spread with a quick, practiced turn of her wrist.

MIKAELLA CLEMENTS AND ONJULI DATTA

"Oh," Leo said, realizing something. He touched her shoulder. "You've looked at this before."

"I think I took it out a few times to deface you."

"A *few* times," Leo said.

Win smoothed her hand over the glossy paper. The Win in the photograph was in her lingerie gazing up at him, her expression cool, her eyes dark. He looked at it for a moment, lingering over the sharp lines of Win's hips, the curve of her breasts against lace, the way the underwear cut in along the line of her thigh. When he glanced back at her, she was still watching him, and there was something satisfied about the line of her mouth, like she'd caught him. Leo looked at her lazily, let his gaze track over her the way it had the photo. "Very nice."

"Thank you." Win cleared her throat and closed the magazine. Leo couldn't tell what she was thinking. "Help me clear the table."

"What? Oh, all right," Leo said, and gathered the rest of the dishes. He followed Win into the kitchen.

Win looked around. "I don't know if this place has a sink. Your parents are—"

"Garbage rats, I know," he said, and placed his teetering stack of dishes on another teetering stack of dishes. He leaned on Win's back, an arm slung loose around her shoulders. Win flicked a look back at him.

"You're drunk," she said.

"I'm not even that tipsy. Well, a little bit. I want more wine—"

"Ah-*ha*," Win crowed, pulling him forward and kicking several drooping ferns out of the way. "Look. Is that a dishwasher?"

Leo blinked. "I don't know if that's ever been used." When Win pulled it open, it was empty and gleaming.

"Come on, let's see how many we can fit," she said.

"It's such fun hanging out with you," Leo told her. Win was laughing quietly to herself, a pleased happy buzz in the kitchen.

"Thanks for bringing me here."

"What? Oh, uh, you're welcome," Leo said. "They're having a *great* time."

Win slotted him a sly glance. "You think?"

"You're up for family gossip and clearing the table," he said. "They're probably planning the wedding as we speak."

He turned away then, not sure if he'd overstepped the mark, but all Win said was, "They'd have to beat Marie to it."

"Really?"

"She's definitely thought about it," Win said, gathering up glasses. "In her darkest moments. I think she has a spreadsheet of worst-case scenarios."

"You can talk," Leo said. "Wait. Do you mean she's going to marry us off if you ever rob a bank or something or . . . is she expecting us to run away and elope?" Win was stacking plates in the dishwasher, her back to him. Leo stared at her, the line of her shoulders, her hair falling to the side, the nape of her neck. He wanted to put his hand there, press his thumb against the top of her spine. He knew how she would react.

"Marie doesn't trust you," Win said at last.

"She thinks I'm going to hustle you off and marry you in secret?"

Win shot him a cool look over her shoulder, and Leo's chest went hot and tight with anxiety. "It wouldn't be the first time, huh?"

Leo swallowed. "That wasn't in secret."

"Ah," Win said. "So you were only lying to me."

She wasn't laughing anymore. She wasn't looking at him, either.

"If it helps," Leo said, "I think I was lying to everyone."

"I told you not to apologize to me about your marriage," Win said. "It makes me feel like I'm crazy—"

"I felt like *I* was crazy," Leo said.

His voice was rougher than he meant it to be. He didn't know what to say or do, except that the tension in Win's shoulders made him feel like she was about to leave the room, and he wanted to catch her and make her stay.

"I was trying to be someone else. Being with Lila was easy, and I thought if it was easy it meant it was good, but then it got— I didn't know what I was doing there. I felt like half the time I was just waiting for you to call me back again. I couldn't get away from you, even when you weren't there. And you barely needed me."

She was flushed like she rarely got, hectic in her cheeks. Leo should have stopped but he plowed on, helpless.

"I wanted something to be real," he said. "I wanted it really bad."

"I didn't know," Win said. There was a coffee cup hanging from her hand, listless. "I didn't know that you were so unhappy with what we were doing—"

Leo laughed, startled. "I wasn't unhappy. It's the only thing I'm good at."

"That's not true."

"Well," Leo said, unable to take his eyes off her. He tried to smile. "It's the only time I feel useful."

"I think maybe you just need some time," Win said, pushing breezy practicality into her voice. "Maybe what we've been doing isn't— healthy. If you had a break from my stuff, you and Lila could make it work again."

"What?" Leo said, bewildered.

Win began, "If I wasn't around—"

"Win, come on. Lila and I broke up. I don't want to be with her."

Win stared at him. "But you said. After the Chanel shoot. You said you loved her."

"I said she was my friend," Leo said cautiously.

"You've been so miserable for weeks."

"Yeah," Leo said. "Because you weren't talking to me."

"Leo," Win said. Leo moved forward, not sure if it was a good idea, except Win was pacing forward, too, nervous steps, setting the cup aside on the bench.

"You thought I was sad about Lila?" Leo said. His hand went up restlessly to touch her hair, her shoulder, trailing down the warm line of her arm. "You thought—"

"I thought you were in love with her," Win said, and took quiet, certain hold of his shirt, a fist at his chest and his heart pounding beneath. "I thought you married her because I was this...this terrible obligation you wanted to escape—"

"I married her because I couldn't escape you," Leo said. His voice came out lower than he'd expected, and Win was much closer. This was not how he'd thought the night would end up; not the way he'd really thought anything would end up anymore. He'd figured he'd blown it.

"That's enough cleaning," Gabrysia said, wandering in. She gave them a curious look. "Are you going to drink some more wine with us?"

By ten, Leo was starting to wonder if his mums were engaged in a conspiracy. Thea kept refilling their glasses, and the one time Leo had started to protest, Gabrysia had given him that look that reminded him of Hannah, dismissive and demanding at once.

And Win was so happy, laughing and leaning forward over the table with all her hair tumbling around her shoulders. She and Gabrysia swapped war stories about freezing photo shoots and asshole casting agents and awful diets. She told a delighted Thea about the occasional camping trips she'd made to France with her parents when she was still a kid, ten years old and too shy to talk to any of the other children at the campground. Leo chimed in with details when he was required— no, he told Thea, it was Gum who got the mumps, he and Hannah had a potent combination of chickenpox and head lice; yeah, he affirmed to Win, it was in Mexico City that they slipped in the back of a grand building to shelter in the air-conditioning and ended up at a rehearsal of Haydn's Seventh Symphony—but mostly he stayed quiet. His chest was tight.

Finally, toward midnight, Thea gave in to her yawns. "Goodness, I'm tired." She stood behind Gabrysia in the chair and wound her arms around Gabrysia's shoulders. She peered at them anxiously. "You can't possibly drive, you've already had too many. Gabrysia, have you readied the guest bedroom?"

"Don't worry," Win said. "We can rough it."

"Are there sheets on the beds?" Leo said, because Win didn't know his mums very well.

"Of course," Gabrysia said. "I think they have even been changed in the last few months or so."

"Few months?" Win said.

"It's a scam that you should change your sheets more often," Thea told her. "The buildup of cells is good for you. You don't have to change your *body* every two weeks, do you?"

"Uh, well," Win said. "I clean my body, too."

"Don't get Thea started on the tyranny of showers," Leo said.

Thea looked disapproving. "Gabrysia insists."

Gabrysia made an elegant gesture that could have meant anything.

"Anyhow, there are sheets," Thea said, "but not enough beds. We downsized the second guest bedroom into my meditation suite. Remember, Leo, you helped me pick out the wallpaper?"

"It all just came screaming back," Leo said. He looked at Win, hesitant, and bit his lip. Win was looking right back at him.

"What do you think, Whitman?" he said. "Put up with me for a night?"

"If you'll be good," Win said, smiling like she had a secret.

CHAPTER EIGHTEEN

They're nice," Win said, leaning over the bathroom sink. She pulled her hair back into a bun, splashed her face, and went through the collection of bottles and glass pots of creams in the cupboard with a curious, assessing eye. "Your parents."

"Mm, they're all right," Leo said, elbowing her for room and getting out a spare toothbrush. "They live in their own little world."

"It's a nice world, though." Win pulled a tall tube from the top shelf, and started smoothing foam over her face in long, easy strokes. Leo watched, half-interested. "They love you."

"Well, yeah," Leo said. Win squinted open one eye, made a face at him, rinsed the cleanser off. He handed her a towel when she reached for one. While her face was pressed against the white cloth, he said, "They liked you, too, I think."

"Me, too," Win said, and looked up at him, mouth twitching. "I think so, too, I mean."

Leo shrugged and spat toothpaste into the sink.

"Not that you lot are hard to charm, as a rule," Win added. "You're like a family of Labradors."

"Mum's actually a very frightening supermodel, thanks very much."

"Ex-supermodel," Win said. "Get out, I need to pee."

Leo rinsed and went back into the bedroom. He closed the door behind him and eyed the bed with a steely gaze.

"This is a small bed, Whitman," he called through the door.

"I guess you'll just have to behave yourself," Win shouted back.

"Hmm," Leo said. He pulled off his sweater and rummaged through the drawers until he found a pair of sweatpants.

When Win opened the door again, she'd shucked off her jeans. She was wearing her silk shirt and a hard look in her eyes like a dare. "I didn't bring anything to sleep in."

Leo sat on the bed, leaning back on his hands. "Interesting."

"I mean, you didn't tell me to bring anything," Win said, voice level. "Which I think is your fault, really, given that you should have known your mums would feed us mostly wine and we were going to be too drunk—"

"I'm not drunk! I'm tired, maybe."

"And tired, maybe, to drive back," Win said. "So, in conclusion—I would like your shirt, please."

"Would you," Leo said, and looked at the chest of drawers, which had plenty of spare T-shirts, his and Gum's and Hannah's. Nice T-shirts, designer T-shirts, or ones specifically meant to sleep in, not the ragged Chicago Bulls tee he was in, a shirt he'd picked up six years ago and hadn't got out of the habit of wearing. Six years meant he'd had it in his life almost as long as he'd had Win.

Win followed his gaze, took in the chest of drawers, and held out her hand. "Yes."

Leo stayed where he was, drinking her in. The quiet certainty of her expression, the line of her neck, her black underwear and her long, long legs. After a moment he straightened, pulled his shirt off, and handed it over.

Win said, "Thank you," and turned around. She didn't tell him not to look, so he didn't bother looking away. Her elbows tucked in against her sides as she let her shirt drop to the floor. Her bra was like her underwear, plain black cotton. She reached up for the clasp.

"Do you need a hand with that?" Leo asked.

"You're very kind," Win murmured, but she unhooked it easily, let it fall down, slipped the T-shirt over her head. Leo had a brief flash of skin before she was turning back to him. His T-shirt was blue and it brought out all the shadows under her eyes, the soft curl of her mouth. It was old and worn and it hung close on her, the curve of her breasts and the press of her nipples. Leo flexed his fingers against the covers of the bed and laughed. She was looking at him, too, eyes tracking the bare length of his chest, his shoulders.

"I . . . ," Win said, and then, "does the window open? It's warm in here."

Leo popped the little window and Win joined him, propping herself up against the sill next to him. There wasn't a lot of space; their shoulders pressed close together, and Leo looked down at the long stretch of Win's legs, the line of her thigh where his T-shirt hung over it. The Thames swept out below them, and the bright lights on the far bank seemed worlds away. It was funny to think that there were people out there reading about Win and Leo, right now, wondering what they were doing.

Win looked at him. Her mouth quirked.

"So," she said, "let's discuss."

Leo dropped his head and laughed. They were touching at the ankles, hips, all the way up the arms to their shoulders. He couldn't look her in the face.

"You're done being angry," he said.

"I'm done being angry," Win agreed. "Are you?"

"Yes." He thought about it, then said, "I don't think I've ever been as angry at you before."

"Yes, you have. What about in Miami, when you wanted to start a band and I said you couldn't buy talent? Or the first week in New York? We argued the entire time."

Leo shook his head. "Wasn't the same. We were kids. I was still going through my rebellious phase."

"Come on," Win said. "Our whole thing is that we piss each other off."

"Is that our whole thing?" Leo said. He meant it as a joke but it echoed in the quiet room. Win reached up and traced her fingers along his head.

"I would have thought I'd miss your hair," she said. "I like it, though."

"I know."

"You do?"

"You touch it all the time," Leo said. Win's cheeks were flushed, but she didn't look embarrassed. He drew in a breath. "It might ruin our working relationship."

"I think our working relationship is pretty much ruined," Win said gladly. "Do you remember what you said to me, in New York? You said the curiosity would eat me up inside, and—"

Leo groaned. "I was twenty years old—"

"You were a real prick," Win said, grinning at him.

He gave up and touched her cheek, her hair, cradling her face in one hand and running his eyes over her. Her long eyelashes, her lips slightly parted, all her warm curves leaning into him.

"Leo," Win said, "I'm pining away."

Leo caught her face in his hands. She stayed perfectly still, the way she hadn't in years. Usually Win was aware of cameras, aware of the best shot; she'd lean prettily into his chest or let her foot pop up, but there were no cameras here and no good shots. She just let herself be kissed.

Leo broke away but didn't go far, their noses brushing, their mouths a breath apart. He twisted his hand into her hair and kissed her again. Win made a noise like an electric current had jolted through her, mouth hungry on his, pressing close like she wanted to climb him and claim him. Leo's heart slammed in his chest. He swung sideways, holding her back against the wall. They kissed slow and bruising, panting into each other's mouths, Win's fingers sliding down his bare skin.

"Fuck, Leo," Win said, ragged over a gasp. It was like she couldn't decide where she wanted to touch him, her hands skating up his back, over his shoulders, clasping at his arms, and when he nudged her against the wall again, she rocked her hips up against his. They both made rough, startled noises, and broke away, staring at each other.

"I'm not very good at being angry at you," Leo said. "I don't think that's my whole thing."

Win didn't move, didn't speak. She was breathing hard, her eyes so dark they were almost black.

His mad, mean, expert best friend. Sometimes Leo felt like he'd spent most of the last decade teetering on the edge of falling in love with her. Two months of seeing her madder and meaner than ever shouldn't have helped. But he felt suddenly as though he'd looked up and found the edge, long tripped over, far above him.

"I think you're my whole thing," Leo said, and they lunged for each other.

Win's arms went around his shoulders like she was swooning, her fingers digging into his skin, gripping him hard and sure to leave marks. He caught her hips in his hands, steering her greedily close, and they stumbled into the wall and then the other wall and then the window before they angled it right and got to the bed, kissing before they hit the mattress.

Win made rough, urgent noises against his mouth, and Leo's breath was coming sharp. They grappled, wrestled to trap the other. A flash of Win triumphant and grinning down at him; Leo tangling a hand in her hair and rolling her beneath him. He thought he was saying her name. She wriggled out of his shirt, clumsy enough that it got tangled around her wrists and he had an opportunity to hold her close underneath him and touch, mouth hot against her throat, her sternum, her nipple, while Win squirmed and swore. He got all the way down to her hip, nose brushing her cotton underwear, before she hauled him back up.

"*Off*, off," she demanded, tugging at his sweatpants.

"Quiet," Leo managed, and then Win's hand was on him, sliding warm and sure over his dick, and then she raised her hand and *licked her palm*, Leo's brain was shorting out—

They jerked against each other frantically, like teenagers. She was as desperate as he was, and they both knew how to touch each other. It had been seven years since they last did this. Right then it didn't feel like anything at all: a blink of his eye, a whirlwind of summers, and Win back in his arms like she belonged there. Her hips twitching up, his fingers hooked in her underwear, dragging them down, both of them laughing soft and breathless in each other's faces, laughing into each other's mouths, his fingers against her and Win saying, "Ah, shit, *shit*," and tossing her head restlessly against the mattress. Leo thought maybe they were sideways across the bed; he wasn't sure. Win wrapped her legs around him, and Leo caught her hip in his hand and pushed deep. They both made noises like they'd been shot. His head rocked against her shoulder.

"Okay," Win said, "okay, okay," and when they moved, they moved hard and fast.

CHAPTER NINETEEN

Leo drifted in and out of vague sleep. They'd stayed up most of the night, hands clasped over each other's mouths to keep quiet. He'd realized at one point that Win was panting high and sweet against his palm, wet mouth open and whining, and had to bite into her shoulder to keep down his own shout. She'd touched the marks he left later, running her fingers over the bruises and blinking at him, heavy-eyed.

"Sorry," he said, tracing over them regretfully. His fingers ended up lingering, and Win shivered and pressed into his touch.

"How far away are your mums?"

"Please don't bring up my mums when you're naked."

Win threw a leg over his hip, sliding up onto him, mouth at his neck, hand hot around him. Leo reached for her, and they fucked again with Win in his lap, moving slow and shallow. Afterward he hauled her up, helping her balance with her hand on the headboard and her knee slung over his shoulder, her hips bucking against his wet mouth as she cursed him out.

"Do you need a moment?" Leo said politely, though his voice was wrecked, his breath coming hard.

"I'll kill you," Win said, and they were laughing again as Leo toppled her beneath him, her fingers digging into the small of his back. A sharp inhalation and then moving like they wanted to crawl into each other.

They fell asleep. Leo woke up again to Win staring at him, the radio clock blinking 4:45. He said, groggy with sleep, "You're not going to run out on me, are you?"

"I'm not going anywhere."

She said it even and sure, the way she always did when she wanted something, and Leo ended up kissing her again, hands framing her face. Win was already wriggling against him, demanding and impatient.

"You are going to kill me," he realized.

"That's what I said." Her legs were falling open for him again. This time when he smoothed a hand over her thigh, it started trembling almost immediately, like all her nerves had come to the surface. They pressed against each other, blind and thoughtless, not even sure what they could manage and unwilling to stop trying.

They slept again, sweaty and gross, messy with sex and exertion, sprawled over each other. Win's nose was tucked against his armpit and he had a mouthful of her hair. It wasn't a comfortable sleep. Fractured as it was, it felt more like a dream.

When he woke up next, it was to the gray light of a London morning and two phones buzzing on wood. It was almost six.

"Mrgh," Leo said, and slapped out his hand. He knocked one phone off the bedside table. It buzzed, muffled now, into the carpet. Leo made a disapproving noise and rolled closer to Win.

"Oof," she said.

"Shh." Leo patted clumsily at her. "Sleep."

"You're on my bladder." Win applied an elbow, making him groan. He rolled away but kept hold of her, urging her with him, and smoothed a satisfied hand down the long, bare warmth of her back when she followed. Win sighed, low and sleepy, and tucked herself in, her back against his chest. She ran her hand along his forearm, and he caught it in his. They twisted their fingers together, yawned.

The phone left on the bedside table paused, and then started buzzing again.

"That needs to stop," Leo mumbled.

"I can't get up," Win said, voice slow and satisfied. "I can't move. It's your fault. You get it." Leo started to move, and she grabbed at him. "No."

"No?" Leo said.

Win squinted open an eye, peering back at him. "Don't show off."

Leo kissed her shoulder. He looked at the tired lines of her face. Sometimes she startled him like this, early in the mornings, sleep-deprived and grumpy: she looked ordinary. It was before her team got to her, the makeup and hair and armor Win wore when she faced the world, gleaming and calculated to catch the light. He loved both versions of her. But here she looked sleepy and she had a whitehead coming up in an awkward spot; she looked like someone who might, conceivably, stay here in bed with him, at least for a little while.

Win flexed her fingers in his, squeezed them. He swiped his thumb along hers.

Her phone buzzed itself right off the bedside table and next to Leo's. Leo said, "Good."

"Mm." Win sat up.

Leo meant to stop her, but she kept hold of his hand, and it meant the blankets falling away, Win naked and sitting up in bed. He ended up just staring, the pointy slope of Win's breasts, the sharp line of her collarbone. He reached out, trailing his hand over her, and Win sucked in a breath and looked at him. Her eyes were dark, her mouth swollen; Leo supposed his was, too. It felt frayed from kissing her. He wanted to do it again.

"Don't you have an apartment in London?"

Leo tucked his face against her hip. "You don't need to go home?"

"Ma's doing better," Win said. "Maybe if we go to your flat for a bit it would be a good test. See how she goes on her own for a day or two, and then I'll know if I can go away and film."

"Right," Leo said. "It's for your mother's welfare?"

"It's not—*not* for her welfare," Win said.

"My flat's like, a thirty-minute drive from here."

Win lifted their joined hands to her mouth, touched his thumb to her lip. "That's not far."

"No," Leo agreed. "And once we get there, we don't have to leave for days."

"Days," Win echoed, looking a little stunned.

He nodded. They were bending into each other again, wilting like flowers.

"You have to go to France," Leo murmured, catching her jaw in his hand, tilting her wide eyes up to him. "Tomorrow? Day after?"

"Yes." Win swallowed, the first flicker of anxiety in her gaze. "It's going to be a hectic month."

"However I can help," Leo said. They were kissing again; he'd almost missed the moment it started, soft, hungry presses of her mouth. "Whatever I can do—"

"You fancy France, this time of year?" Win said, and they both laughed, breathless, the kiss deepening. Leo thought he could probably be convinced.

On the floor, one or both of their phones buzzed fiercely enough to send it bumping against the wooden leg of the bed.

"For fuck's sake." Leo threw himself back against the pillows, and Win laughed and slipped her hand free.

"Oh, Christ," she said as she picked up her phone. "Marie's called me, like, ten times."

Something uneasy slipped in Leo's stomach. "About what?"

"I don't know," Win said, frowning over her phone, thumb skidding along the screen. "There's a lot of texts about TMZ—"

"What?" Leo sat up.

"Hang on," Win said, focused now. "God, there's like six links—Okay, I'm just going to call her, hang on—"

"Win," Leo said.

Win leaned back and kissed him. She caught him at a slant, their mouths almost missing. "It's probably some new Paramount drama," she said. "Don't worry. We'll sort it."

"Whitman," Leo said, and on the other end of the line, Marie picked up.

"Hey, Marie," Win said. "Sorry, I just woke up. What's the crisis?"

Leo couldn't hear anything for a moment, just the buzz of static. Then Win's face paled and she lowered the phone. Leo had a mad, panicked thought that something terrible had happened to Pritha, that Marie had somehow got hold of the information first.

Win put the phone on speaker, and Marie's voice filled the room, tinny and brutally professional.

"—someone called Miriam Rosenblatt," Marie was saying.

Leo startled, reaching out instinctively to grab Win's wrist. A hot flush rose through him, prickling at his scalp.

"I haven't spoken to her yet—it's the middle of the night in New York, hopefully I'll have some answers soon, but until then, you need to get out."

"I don't understand," Win said. "How did it leak? I thought you said that you were going to track down the minister."

Leo shot her a sharp look, and Win made a face at him.

"I did," Marie said. "That's the thing. It's not that they've found out about his marriage. They've found out about the divorce."

Win laughed, blank and confused. "There's no divorce. What are you . . . " She looked at Leo, trailing off.

Leo rubbed his hands over his face. "I was going to tell you."

"Is he there?" Marie said. "Leo, what the fuck is going on? You know this Rosenblatt woman?"

"She's my brother's lawyer. I was— Win, I was going to tell you, but we were fighting and then when we weren't, I thought you'd be pleased. I thought you wouldn't want to talk about it. I thought I'd just get it done, sort it out."

"We need to know this shit, Leo," Marie said, clipped over the speakerphone. "You know there are legal procedures involved in a divorce, right? People are always going to find the paper trail."

"There's a paper trail with a wedding, too," Leo said. Win's face was impossible to read, eyes huge with surprise.

"I know, that's why we were all furious with you!" Marie yelled. "The answer to that fuckup wasn't to go out and fuck up again!"

"Win," Leo said, "Win, I thought it would be good. I didn't want to be married to her. I wanted to be—I want to be with—"

"You have no idea how to be careful, do you?" Marie demanded. "You go out and do exactly what you want, when you want, and you don't care about the consequences of your actions or who you're going to hurt along the way!"

"Win," Leo said. "I'm really, really sorry."

Win put her hand up to the back of his neck, touched his earlobe in a gentle, almost automatic gesture.

"You didn't know," she said. "We don't know what it'll do—"

"Whitman," Marie interrupted, "I've been trying to call you for hours." She sounded grim. "We do know what it's going to do."

Win turned back toward the phone, visibly steeling herself. "What, then?"

"The first headlines were already reporting you broke up the marriage," Marie said, clearly trying now to sound kind. She was mostly failing, voice still tight with anger. "That you're a home wrecker, and that Lila has been heartbroken for months, and that Leo tries to return to her but you have—quote—'an irresistible spell on him.'"

"Whitman." Leo touched her knee. "Can we talk?"

She caught his hand and squeezed it but shook her head. She scooted over to the side of the bed to put on her underwear and the discarded Bulls T-shirt from last night. "Go on, Marie."

"The timeline is too blurred, unfortunately," Marie said. "There's even some paparazzi photos of Leo with Lila that night in Saint-Tropez. It looks like the moment he could he went running back to her. The gossip sites have been having a field day, putting it all together. I think everyone on Twitter has been up all night."

"For fuck's sake," Leo said. He went to find his own underwear, suddenly sure he didn't want to be naked for this conversation. He dug out an old rowing sweater of Gum's and wrestled it on.

"Look, we just need to clarify the timeline," Win said. "It's bad, but maybe if we can get Lila to say something..."

She looked at Leo apologetically, but Leo nodded, eager. "She will. I'll call her and ask. She's a good person, I promise, she'll say something—"

"That's the thing," Marie said. "She already has."

Leo paused. "What?"

"I sent it to you, too," Marie said.

Leo scooped up his phone from where it was still lying on the floor. He opened one of the many links Marie had sent him and held it mutely out in front of them.

It was a video, jumping awkwardly every fifteen seconds, ripped from social media and posted on the front page of TMZ. Lila was leaning against a girl Leo didn't know, with Alex slouched behind them. For a moment Leo felt the usual rush of warmth at the sight of her unruly blond hair, her smeared eyeliner, her brash grin. Then what she was saying sank in.

"Man, everyone needs to chiiiiiiill out," she said, drunk but not wasted, clearly aware of what she was saying. Behind her was the buzz of an LA party, a coked-up guy rambling on, a high pitched shrill of laughter over the DJ set. Leo had been to parties like that with her. She liked to set up camp at a table and turn herself into the social hub of the room, making friends with everyone, telling passing drunk girls that they looked beautiful.

"Have you seen Twitter? It's insane, like—Whitman Tagore broke up my marriage? God, as if, she and Leo are barely even friends. They've got their weird celebrity arrangement and then on the off days Leo can do whatever the fuck he likes—"

"Wait," the girl behind the phone camera said, voice thick with glee. "What arrangement?"

"You know!" Lila waved her hands. The camera jumped; when it came back, Lila was halfway through a sentence, someone out of shot laughing hysterically. "—you suck my dick, I'll suck yours, whatever."

Behind her, Alex said, "What the fuck does that even mean?"

"Yeah, I guess it's not applicable," Lila said. "There's definitely no dick sucking going on—come on, you know what I mean, pretending to date for the publicity and then not even being on speaking terms—"

"Lil," Alex said over her shoulder.

"Whoops, whatever," Lila said, and grinned, the cocky one that she used to get out of whatever trouble she found herself in. She held up a hand, nudging the camera aside, and the picture froze on her smile.

Leo and Win sat silent. Even Marie was silent. Leo's heart was pounding; he felt trapped, like a bad dream where everything was spiraling out of control.

Win cleared her throat. "I'll need to talk to Patrick. Is Emil up?"

"Yes," Marie said.

"Great. Could you get him to send a car—"

"Wait," Leo said. "Wait—"

"It's a private street," Win continued, "he'll have to liaise with security," and she rattled off the Mums' address.

"Whitman," Leo said, "listen to me—"

Win put her hand on his arm. She didn't look angry; her face was clear and calm as the morning. "Marie, I'll need to go to my mum's to pack and then..."

Marie made an affirmative noise, crackling through the speakers. "I'll look into flights and give you a call back."

"*What*," Leo said.

"Whitman," Marie said, "you know this means—"

"I know," Win said. "Thank you. Talk soon."

She hung up.

They sat in silence. Leo's gaze dropped to Win's shoulder, where the T-shirt had slipped to bare her skin. The marks he'd left last night were still there, red and purple, even as the morning light grew stronger. When he looked back up at her, she was staring at him. Her face was all screwed up, mouth squinched to the side, and Leo realized with a jolt of horror that for the first time in years, he was about to see Win cry.

He cupped her cheek in his hand. "We'll fix it."

Win let out a burst of rough laughter that edged close to a sob. She turned her face in to his hand, breathing raggedly.

"We'll fix it," Leo repeated, determined. "Win. Look at me. We'll work something out. I'll say something."

"They'll think you're lying, no matter what you say. They know we've been lying the whole time."

"I'm not lying. I won't lie. I'll tell them it's real. Win, it's *real*."

"Please don't," Win said, voice breaking. She evaded his hands and stood up, facing the door. Her shoulders heaved, but when she turned back to him, her face was dry, her chin tilted up. "I have to go."

"You don't have to go."

Win shook her head. "The paparazzi know exactly where I am. They'll already be out there, and the longer I hang around...it looks really bad. It looks like I'm stupid, like I haven't even realized they all know it's fake."

"It's not fake," Leo snarled. He stood up, too, folding his arms. "Who cares what they think!"

"Leo."

"Fine, okay, it matters what they think. So we'll fix it. Why does Marie want to whisk you away? We just need to control the story."

"Whisking me away *is* controlling the story," Win said. She swallowed hard. "I'll put out a statement, and then I'll have to lie low for a while."

"Okay, yes, you go find somewhere safe and I'll issue a statement—"

"No," Win said, voice jerking out like a slap. "No, you can't. Don't say anything. Marie will handle it, she'll get in touch if we need you to say anything."

"Fine." He hated issuing statements. "Fine, I'll just wait here in London then, and when you're ready I'll come and find you."

Win put her jeans on, hands trembling on her belt buckle. She wasn't looking at him. Leo stared at her, feeling as though he'd just missed something very important. Win wasn't the way she normally got when a crisis broke out, and Leo had seen enough of them to know. She wasn't calm and issuing orders, she wasn't strategizing with Marie, she wasn't even particularly angry. Her hands were shaking, and she was trying not to cry.

Leo repeated, very slow, throat sore, "And then I'll come and find you. Right?"

Win took off Leo's T-shirt, put on her bra.

"Whitman?"

"Leo," Win said.

"What the fuck," Leo said. "We just—"

"I know."

"Are you breaking up with me?" Leo said, putting on a funny voice.

Win didn't laugh. She couldn't look at him, her eyes darting about like she was trapped. Her voice cracked when she said, "Really, I'm really sorry."

"Don't," Leo said. He wanted her to stop.

"You and me together is going to be toxic now," Win whispered. "It's going to be a big deal. This is going to be . . . this is the kind of shit people like me lose their careers over. Break up a marriage, all right, I'd suffer for a bit, but I built *my whole career* on an—an epic romance, and now they all know we're lying about it."

"Are you lying?" Leo demanded. "I'm not."

"I'm not lying." Win closed her eyes, then picked up her sweater. "But no matter what happens, it's going to look cheap. It's going to look like we're pandering, and also like we're fucking morons, because everyone knows that it's not real."

"We'll show them it is," Leo said. "Let's go dancing right now. Let's go make out on the London Eye. Let's—"

"You could fuck me on the six o'clock news and they'd just say that I was desperate for press attention *and* a slut," Win said.

Leo shook his head, taken aback. "Marie said that a lot of people guessed it was fake anyway. It was about the narrative."

"The narrative's fallen apart," Win said. "And now it looks like I broke up a marriage just to feed my publicity machine."

"There has to be a way," he said, pulse rabbiting in his throat, his chest. Part of him wanted to grab Win by the hand and run. "We'll give an interview. We'll explain, we can tell the exact truth, the whole story."

"Who's going to believe that?" Win checked her phone. Her hands were still shaking. "It doesn't matter what we say now. This is the story. It's done."

"We have too many mutual friends, we're going to end up being seen together at some point—what about Charlie's wedding?"

Win shrugged, narrow thin shoulders and a blank expression that she was holding together only with a lot of effort. "I won't go," she mumbled. "Shift'll understand."

"Look, I won't go," Leo said. "If you think it's going to be too soon, she's your best friend, of course I won't go. But I don't understand how this is going to work. You're just going to, what, avoid me for the next year?"

Win's face fell.

Leo said, "Ah, fuck."

"Listen—"

"I'm such a fucking idiot," Leo said. "I just got it. You mean we're done forever now, huh?"

Win moved like she was going to come over to him, and then thought better of it. They stood staring at each other over the mess they'd made of the bed.

"No matter what happens," Win said, "no matter what we do, or how we do it, they're going to say it's part of my plan to fake date you for attention. That's the story for as long as we're even near each other. Every time we touch, every time I smile at you, it's me doing it for my career, because I'm a bitch, or ruthless, or a slut, or brainless. Probably all of the above. That's the new story."

"Win," Leo said. He knew his voice was too rough. "This is fucked."

"I know," Win said. She looked cracked open, ruined like he'd never seen her. "I'm sorry."

"You're just writing us off."

"My career is important," Win said, the first light of anger dawning on her face. "Don't you get that? Don't you—"

"I actually know perfectly well how important it is," Leo snapped. "I've been a pretty major part of it for the last seven years, I've taken your career pretty fucking seriously. Why won't you take me seriously? This is important, too!"

"I know it is."

"Pick me," Leo said. He felt sick. He didn't think he'd ever experienced a moment like this in his life before. Everything was slipping through his fingers, and he couldn't do anything except beg. "Fuck. I haven't—I haven't asked you for anything in a long time. Pick me."

"We fight all the time," Win said.

"So what?" Leo said. "So *what?*"

"I'd have to be an idiot," Win said, "to throw everything away on ... We slept together last *night.* I don't know how this is going to turn out—"

"I don't, either," Leo said. "Pick *me.*"

"You can't ask me to choose you over my career."

"Why not?" Leo said. "I know it's important. I'll help you however I can. But this is important, too. You and me."

"I know that." Win's phone buzzed in her hand and she looked down at it, tired, almost absent.

This was what she'd meant, the whole time; this was the way the world worked differently for her. There was no carefully written apology, no cutesy *who, me?* smile that could fix it. For once, Leo couldn't flex his position and have the media fall into line. God, the gibes about arranged marriages alone, Leo thought, and had to bite down a hysterical laugh. Win had been trying to tell him all along, and he, selfishly, only understood it now when it applied to him, now that he was, for the first time, going to suffer from the rules she'd been maneuvering herself around for years.

"Listen." Leo folded his arms so his hands didn't shake. He couldn't let her walk out of the room. He knew, from the resolute set of her exhausted, sad face, that if she left, she wouldn't come back. "I know I've been an asshole. I didn't understand and I didn't listen to you, I've been acting like you live in the same world as me and you don't. I get it now. I'm really sorry. But I can't, I *can't* lose you."

"Leo," Win said, her face shocked, blown open. "I'm not doing this to punish you."

"So stay. It'll be bad, but we'll manage it. It'll be okay. We can move to some shithole in the Midlands and you can act in community theater—" Win laughed, watery, and Leo went on, "—and introduce your mum to my mums and—and have roast dinner at the pub, and we'll be so boring everyone will stop paying attention to us."

"I love my job," Win said, "and you and me have never made it work. Not once."

"We've never tried," Leo said.

"Maybe this will be easier for you," Win said, voice wavering. "You won't have all my shit dragging you down, or me yelling at you about how you don't understand."

Leo wanted to laugh and couldn't. "That sounds awful."

"It's good for you," Win said. "You can do what you want now."

"Fuck you," Leo said. "I only want one thing."

Win looked at him. She looked like someone going into battle for the last of several frays, weary and travel-stained. Her hair was messy from his hands in it. When she took a step toward him, Leo jerked backward. He didn't want her to touch him like this, didn't want to watch her say goodbye. He turned around, shoulders tight, hot misery building in his chest like a howl, and he didn't see her leave, though he heard the door close behind her.

MONTREAL

CHAPTER TWENTY

It was Marie who booked the flight to Montreal, and she came with Win on the plane. Her expression was grim, her voice clipped. They went over the situation in clinical detail: *The Sun Also Rises* had dumped her, of course. The producers at Paramount were skittish as ever. The studio had already wasted months waiting for Win to finish tending to her mother and start filming, and the delay until winter had messed up their schedules. The widespread reports that Win was so desperate for publicity she'd break up a marriage were the last straw.

She was also no longer in consideration for the thriller whose contract she'd been days away from signing, and Chanel had dropped her as their campaign lead. Patrick was trying to smooth things over, but there was a chance they would sue her for breach of contract; one clause had promised *reliable, upstanding behavior as a brand ambassador.* Win listened like a president being briefed on a series of military crises. She nodded at all the right moments.

Then they made their plans. Originally Montreal was only meant to be a quick flyby so that Win could be there for the ceremony before escaping back to work. But suddenly Win's schedule was wide open, like a deeply set valley without a bridge, and she arrived over a week before the wedding. It was only temporary, Patrick had already assured her. He sounded comforting and patient on the phone in a way that reminded Win of Pritha's doctors at her worst stages. They all agreed it would blow over, especially if Win was never so much as even photographed with Leo again. Producers weren't stupid; Win's name on a billboard would still significantly raise a film's profile, and she had proved herself an asset on set. Hardworking, focused. Free from distractions. She had cried only once since the news broke.

Emil called when she was at the airport, waiting to board. His voice was quiet and comforting, and he didn't bother with platitudes that he knew she wouldn't believe, just told her that he was on his way to the East Sussex house to pick up her things. Marie had decided it was best not for Win to go back and get them herself, and she'd had to say goodbye to her mum on the phone.

Pritha's voice had been sleepy and confused, and she'd asked if Win was okay. "Ma," Win said, and felt her voice break. She sobbed for two awful minutes while Pritha said uselessly, "Whitman. Oh, *shona*," until Win said she had to go. Her eyes still stung. She had to stop thinking about it.

"Thank you," she told Emil instead, looking over the airfield, tracking the swoop of departing planes. She tried to inject some humor into her strained voice. "Sorry you've ended up caught in all my Hollywood shit. If you want out, I totally understand."

Emil didn't laugh, as she'd expected. He was quiet, and then he said, "Thank you, Win. I'm glad you said that."

She listened to his resignation in numb silence. He swore it was nothing personal. "It's just—the situation is too unstable for me," he said. "I'm not as tough as you, or Marie—although you can't ever tell her I said that. And I'll serve a notice period, of course, as long as you need." Win wanted to argue with him, but she didn't know what to say. He was right to resign. He was ambitious, and she was a toxic entity with nothing to offer him by way of reassurance except money, which he could get elsewhere. Marie bristled and called him a coward, but Win understood.

After a lot of back-and-forth, Marie decided that Shift's wedding would be a "good tone changer." Win could hole up with Shift and be a dutiful bridesmaid, keeping out of view as much as she could without giving the impression of hiding. Win was relieved. She'd thought she would have to hide out from everyone and everything and worried that Marie would tell her to miss the wedding altogether. But Marie thought Win being a good friend in the background of a family ceremony would help, and the *Vogue* profile on Charlie was just the right amount of attention. It would be a signal that life was still moving, the world still turning, encouraging people to forget this mess. It was clear that Leo wouldn't be there.

After the wedding she would find a new project, something small and independent but with enough clout to remind people of her talent. Win would stay busy, and in a few months, once they'd decided how they wanted to frame the narrative, there would be a scripted confessional interview, a few self-deprecating jokes, a new boyfriend. Win just needed to stay cool, and quiet, and as far away from Leo as possible.

Lila had posted to Twitter only once in the last seventy-two hours, brief and vague: lol...believe what u want to believe. It had been re-tweeted hundreds of thousands of times, her follower count climbing, her name trending alongside Win's and Leo's. Win wondered if she'd even noticed.

"It wouldn't hurt *her* to come out with an apology," Marie said as she scanned through the in-flight menu. Win hadn't been able to eat since their early morning coffees. "You don't think, if I reached out to—"

"No," Win said. "That won't be happening."

"Okay."

"I mean it," Win said. "Don't go behind my back on this one."

Marie looked offended. She leaned back from Win in her seat, plush leather creaking. "You know I'll never contact him without asking you first."

"Unless you decide you know better than me," Win said, filled with a kind of reckless righteousness, still stinging from the call with Emil.

She thought of Leo's admission in the gallery. *I thought maybe I could help*, he'd said, disconsolate and annoyed at having to admit it, and Win had felt it, then, the first real stirrings of danger. Something worse than the way they'd been fighting. Something less manageable. "You let me think that he—"

"I'm your publicist, Whitman," Marie said. "I can't be your relationship guru as well."

"You should have told me," Win said.

"You should have told me you were in love with him," Marie said.

Win shut her mouth on a tiny noise. She felt like she'd been punched in the gut. She had never told Marie why Leo had been there first thing in the morning when Marie called. But she supposed she shouldn't be surprised that Marie had worked it out.

Marie softened. "I would have found another way, if I'd known."

"Well." Win's voice was very small. "I didn't know, either." But dwelling on it wouldn't do any good, even if it was all she could think about, the awful realization that had come too late. "What did he— what did he say when he called you in September?"

She tried to pull the gray memories of two months ago into focus. Her anger had cut her off from everyone, like she was locked away in a tower. Then Marie had texted her, Turn on Radio 1, and everything had gone to shit.

Marie hesitated. "He said it wasn't fair that you were on your own."

Win turned her face to the window. Below the sleek wing of the plane, there were only clouds, harshly white and rolling away as far as she could see.

Win was at Shift's house for two days before they talked about it.

She wondered if Shift was restraining herself from saying *I told you so*. But she just asked Win quietly if she'd already known about the divorce.

"No," Win said. Her mouth twitched. She wasn't sure if she was going to laugh or cry. "I think he thought it was going to be a nice surprise."

Shift's eyebrows went up, almost disappearing under her bangs. She had started wearing her hair in a high messy bun, which made her look like a beloved high school art teacher. "Would it have been a good surprise?"

"Yes," Win said. She paused. "I would have been happy, I think."

"Oh, babe," Shift said.

For a long time Win had wrestled with her thoughts about Lila. She had spent months hating her, and feeling cruel for hating her, since it was Leo's fault, and it wasn't like Win had ever really had a claim on him. Then, at home, with Leo so close and her mother so sick, Lila had been like a phantom, reappearing late at night on Leo's phone or in a skipped heartbeat whenever Marie called, or more and more when Leo looked at her, when he drew closer, when he made her mum laugh, when he ran by her side, and Win thought: *Married, he's married.* On the final night in London, the last thoughts of Lila had burst like lazy fireworks, and Win had allowed herself to forget that Lila existed. Clearly, that had been a mistake.

Once, at her mum's house when Win had still been so furious with Leo she couldn't even speak to him, she'd spent an evening watching videos of Lila. She'd felt absurdly guilty, especially with Leo somewhere in the house, sulking in his room and on the phone to one of his siblings or even to Lila herself. She'd felt paranoid, like she was fifteen again and smoking a secretive cigarette before her mum got home.

In interviews, Lila was rude and quick-witted and untroubled. She hung back more than Win would have expected and let the rest of the band answer questions, smirking in the background and occasionally correcting them when she disagreed. Once an interviewer hinted that being a band with a front woman made it easier to get gigs, because venues had to fill their quotas. "Blow me," Lila replied, and walked off camera without turning back. Win had thought, with a stirring of jealousy that wasn't all about Leo, *She says exactly what she thinks all the time, that girl has no filter at all*, and wondered if that was what Leo wanted. But the next morning she woke to the sounds of Leo and Pritha making breakfast together, getting ready for another endless soap opera marathon, and realized she didn't have any idea what Leo wanted.

Win was forcing herself to call Pritha once a day. Every day she came up with new excuses not to do it, and every day she propped her head in her hand at Shift's crowded kitchen table and called the house in East Sussex. Pritha knew something had gone wrong, even if she didn't completely understand the mechanics. Win tried to tell the truth about how bad things were, though she was wary of stressing Pritha out. It made it worse that Pritha herself was dead center of the scandal this time. Their strategy of an appealingly tragic Win had backfired. It was public knowledge that Win had continued the charade even while her mother was being ferried in and out of hospital rooms, flaunting her mother's illness for sympathy points.

It was a physical effort for Win to loosen her resolve on the phone, the recurring embarrassment of getting to the age of twenty-seven and not knowing how to talk to her mother. But she told Pritha everything: Chanel dropping her, the Hemingway project gone, the producers who had stopped returning Patrick's calls. Leo's face in the blue of the morning. Pritha was still incredulous that anyone really cared about Win's private life, let alone Leo's—but she was patient on the phone. She didn't interrupt. A romantic crisis seemed to baffle her, and she didn't mention Leo, but she talked about other things. She told Win she was recovering well; her sister was coming down to visit in a few days. The cat was back to terrorizing seagulls in the garden. "Try not to worry so much," she said, a few days after Win had left. "I think you're handling things very well." Win hung up almost shivering with relief.

Shift had announced that all wedding planning activities were confined to the garage, and the kitchen and living room were strictly off-limits for flowers, confetti, or tulle. In reality the whole house looked like it had been invaded by an overeager events company. Shift was exasperated by the clutter, and had a habit of knocking things over as she passed them, scattering sugared almonds over the floor or nudging piles of sample menus off the side of the couch. Three times already Win had witnessed Shift drag the seating chart out of the room, cursing, only for Charlie to cheerfully drag it back in a few minutes later.

"I'm sorry I've turned your wedding week into this," Win said. She nodded in the direction of the front door, the blinking shafts of camera flashes through the mottled glass.

"It was always going to be a bit like this," Shift said. "And Charlie loves it, anyway. Last night he asked me if he should take out some tea and coffee for them."

"He's too nice for his own good."

Charlie proved her point when he came bounding into the living room half an hour later and expressed his deep, heartfelt gratitude to Win for helping to make the last few seating cards, something he confessed he had been "really worried about."

It was only when Charlie had pulled Win into a tight hug in Shift's hallway on the night of her arrival that Win realized she barely knew him, had met him just a few times, rarely for longer than an hour. Most of Win's time with Shift was snatched when their schedules collided, which meant while Shift was touring through cities where Win was filming. Win would attend concerts and watch Shift leap around, self-contained and wild at the same time under the strobe lights, or else Shift would meet her for breakfast at dawn, when Win had already been up filming for three hours and was due back on set for another twelve. Win had always been secretly proud of herself for finding the time.

Over the last few days she had barely seen Charlie, who was busy with wedding errands and outings to scenic locations with his *Vogue* profiler. Now he pulled a carefully folded scrap of paper from his wallet and said, "Look, we made *Hello! Canada.*"

Win tensed—Marie had warned her she was on the cover this week—but Charlie only had a clipped article. In the photo Shift was tucked under Charlie's arm while they stood in a parking lot, her face scrunched in a laugh, one hand held up to Charlie's mouth, her thumb resting against his lower lip.

"Oh, come on," Shift said.

"No, this one's good," Charlie said, and began to read the caption. "*Adorable scenes this week from Montreal, where Charlie Washington and his longtime girlfriend, British EDM princess Shift, were seen embracing tenderly outside a local restaurant just days away from their wedding.*"

Shift scoffed. "We have never embraced tenderly."

"Of course we have," Charlie said. "*The pair will say their vows this week at the Rosemont Greenhouse with an intimate gathering of family and friends, including*—well, whatever," Charlie said, glancing up at Win. "It's nice, though. The picture's good, too. I might see if Georgia wants to include it." Georgia was the *Vogue* journalist; Charlie had taken to referring to her as though she were a dear friend.

"It's gross." Shift plucked the clipping from his hands, scrunched it into a ball, and lobbed it into a corner of the room.

Charlie settled back into his seat, untroubled. "I have copies," he said.

Shift gave Win a look out of the corner of her eye that Win thought was meant to convey exasperation. Her mouth was twitching.

"Sorry," she said.

"It's okay," Win said.

"Oh!" Charlie said. "So you told her, then?"

"Told me what?"

"Oh," Charlie said again, this time low and anxious. Shift tilted her head back toward the ceiling, her eyes closed.

"Told me what?" Win repeated.

"Come on." Shift looped her arm under Win's, tugging her toward the kitchen.

Shift whipped up whisky sours, the same in the kitchen as she was in her studio, hands flying about and always at least three things in the mix at once. She managed to look busy enough that Win couldn't probe her further, and Win's gaze wandered around the room instead, Charlie's basil plants in the window and the fridge plastered with save the dates and invitation drafts and Polaroids. She caught sight of it, half-hidden under a caterer's proposed menu: Leo's face, a line of beer bottles, his arm slung around a shoulder that Win knew was her own, though the rest of the photo was out of view. Her stomach twisted, a flood of misery and nausea, and she said quickly, "You might as well just tell me. If it's about Gum coming to the wedding, I already know."

She wasn't looking forward to meeting him, but hopefully he would be too caught up in his own drama to focus much on his little brother's—he seemed the type. "Right, Geoffrey is coming," Shift said. "Only . . . he called Charlie yesterday."

She paused. There were fast, unhappy ripples in Win's stomach.

"He won't come to the wedding unless Leo does, too. Geoffrey says the whole thing is a plot to undermine him."

Win's chest tightened. "Okay." She drew a breath. "Has Leo— Is he going to do it?" It hurt to say his name, like an allergy. A swelling and soreness in the throat.

"Leo's said he won't come unless you say it's okay. But Charlie loves Leo, and he's worried about Geoffrey. He's very protective of him," she added, looking briefly annoyed, "as if he's some kind of sensitive child and not an—anyway. Charlie didn't want me to say it to you, but I think he'll be really crushed if they aren't there."

Keeping her voice deliberately level, Win said, "So are you asking me about this, or telling me?"

Shift winced. "Telling."

"Right."

"Win," Shift started, but Win cut her off with a dismissive wave of her hand.

"Right," she repeated. "So I guess Chilton isn't coming, then?"

Shift blinked. "Chilton?"

"Georgia Chilton. The *Vogue* profiler. And whatever photographer she's bringing." Win was surprised that she had to spell it out. "They can't be there if both me and Leo are. It's too risky."

She didn't like the way Shift was staring at her, not quite taken aback but instead with narrowed eyes, her face slowly setting.

"You know how much that profile means to Charlie," Shift said. "It's not even about you."

"You don't think the fact that I'll be there might make it in?"

Shift took a neat sip of her drink. "So Charlie has you to thank for it, then?"

"That's not what I mean. If anything happens..."

"You'll just have to control yourselves," Shift said, and set her drink down. "I know it's a lot. But I don't ask you for much."

Leo and Shift never thought they were asking her for anything, even when they were demanding everything. Win shook her head. "This is too much. I'm sorry. It's either me and him, or me and the profiler. Not both."

"Is that an ultimatum?"

"I'm not trying to force you," Win said. "I told you, it's just too risky."

"Maybe you just have to take a risk."

"It isn't that simple. You know how hard I work."

"You think Charlie doesn't work hard? You can't use your career as an excuse all the time."

Win leaned back, stunned. "This isn't an excuse."

"No, it is. It always is." Shift stood up, pushing off her stool. Her eyes were bright with anger, her chin tilted up. "You think you're being *professional* and making *smart decisions*, but you just make easy decisions. You always do whatever's easiest for you."

"Nothing about this is easy!"

"No?" Shift folded her arms. "You're sticking with what you know. You're clearly breaking your own heart to do it, but that's never stopped you before. You've always played it safe with Leo—"

Win gaped. "Safe?"

"Doing your stupid platonic publicity thing," Shift said. She was speaking very quickly now. "You've always been obsessed with each other. Why didn't you give him a chance?"

"I did," Win said, standing up herself, her stool screeching across the floor. "It didn't work out—"

"Seven years ago," Shift said. "And you didn't, actually, you slept together a few times and then you decided Leo was too *useful* for your career to risk anything with him. You treated him like a tool, and he loved you—"

"Believe it or not," Win said, voice shaking, "I didn't actually come here for relationship advice."

"Good," Shift said. "You've never listened to any, and I don't— I don't care, anyway, this isn't about you, Win, hard as that might be to believe."

"Oh, god, yeah, because I'm so selfish," Win said, chest tight with fury. She felt worryingly close to bursting into tears. "That's why I'm here, just selfishly wallowing around the place and making you talk about my problems. Shift, you're the one who keeps making things worse. I don't need a reporter from *Vogue* anywhere near me right now. Marie wasn't even sure if I should come to the wedding. I'm here and I'm trying for *you*."

"Marie also said that it would be a good 'change of scenery' for you," Shift said. "I heard you talking to her, the night you arrived. Like my wedding is a set backdrop."

"That's not what she meant—"

"You have a busy life, Win, and a job that's more intense than I can understand. But you forget other people want things, too, and even if we don't end up on magazine covers, we're still important. And I think you use your job as an excuse the moment you're scared of something."

"I'm not scared of Leo."

"I think you are," Shift told her. "And it's not just Leo. You never want to commit yourself to anyone. Me, your mum—"

"Don't talk about my mum!" Win was seething: everyone thought they knew her mother better than her; everyone thought they could explain Pritha and Win to each other. "God, I—I'm here, aren't I?"

"Because it works for you," Shift shouted back. "Do you think for one second you would have come if you'd known Leo was going to be here?"

"My career is on the line—"

"I'm your *best friend*! Win, I love you, but for years, every time we've hung out, it's been on your terms!" Shift's voice cracked, like she, too, was trying not to cry. "Sometimes it's like you're just fitting this friendship into your timetable to prove that you're still down to earth. I know your career is important, but does it have to be the most important? Why can't I count first sometimes?"

Pick me, Leo had said. Win turned away, slamming her hand down hard on the counter, taking ragged breaths. They didn't understand; neither of them understood. They hadn't had to work as hard for recognition as she had. They both looked the part, they had no reason not to be confident in being rewarded, and people loved them without their having to try.

And Win's career had to be important now, it had to be the most important thing, because if that spotlight stayed jeering or worse, tracked away and left her in the dark, then everything would have been for nothing. All of Shift's accusations, torn out of her like she'd been thinking them for a long time; Leo's face wiped clean with shock when he realized what she'd meant that morning in London when she left.

Charlie appeared unsmiling in the doorway. "I heard shouting."

"I'm going." Win pushed past Charlie into the hallway and saw the lights flashing at the front door again. She stopped, swung around on her heel, and bit out, "To bed."

As she stormed up the stairs, she heard Charlie say, "Baby," and Shift saying, voice thick with emotion, "Fuck, it's okay, I just— She's just so fucking cold sometimes—"

Win slammed the door behind her and burst vengefully into tears.

CHAPTER TWENTY-ONE

Win didn't really sleep. She exhausted herself with her crying jag, passing out almost immediately afterward with her face wet and her chest still pulsating with anger, but she woke up at midnight feeling cold, and cruel, and alone. She sent Marie a short message explaining that Leo would be at the wedding. She spent some time composing awful, cutting speeches about all the things Shift did that annoyed her: never being able to remember time zones and calling Win in the middle of the night, going absolutely insane every album cycle and acting as though nobody else had ever gotten a lukewarm review, leaving an unbelievable mess in her wake whenever she visited Win. When they were kids, Win constantly had to shake her out of daydreams, and she still had a tendency to zone out in the middle of conversations.

The hour after that, Win stared at the ceiling thinking numbly that none of those things were as bad as what Shift had thrown at Win. That Win was selfish. That Win was cold.

Leo had edged uncomfortably close to those accusations, too, more than a few times. Win couldn't bring herself to think about their fight that morning before she'd left. It hadn't been enough of a fight. It had felt like a breakup, like she was being torn apart, like Leo was sinking out of her reach.

But she thought about Saint-Tropez, when she'd found out about

Lila. Both at the time and afterward she'd been too angry and hurt about the secret marriage to pay much attention to the content of what he'd said. Now she couldn't stop thinking about the astounded fury dawning on his face. *Not everyone lives their life based on what it's going to look like on the fucking internet!* Shift had accused her of that, too. Like the glittering machinery of Win's life was something she was hiding behind, instead of something she was living inside.

Win had to live her life like that because it did end up on the internet, or in magazines, or in the supercilious mouths of talk show hosts. She wasn't being arrogant or self-obsessed; she was being realistic. Win couldn't just hope that people would see her best side. She had to carefully curate her best side so that they couldn't miss it. If she wanted producers to cast her, it wasn't enough just to read the lines well. Win had to make herself impossible to dismiss. She had to make herself so shiny and smooth that all the old excuses—too demanding, too intense, too brown—couldn't stick.

That's not cold, she thought. *It's clever.* Actually, she supposed, it was both.

She tossed around in Shift's spare bed. Other memories came back without invitation. That night in London felt as though it was burned into her brain, or worse than that, her muscle memory, her skin.

If she closed her eyes, she could feel his hands on her, his mouth, the easy way he shifted her about until her limbs felt hot and malleable, like he could just mold her into the shapes he wanted. She'd been avoiding looking at the marks on her hips, her décolletage. In the dark, she pressed her thumb against the bruised remainder of his kisses and hissed. It was such a sharp, perfect little sting; it made warmth pool in her stomach. It made her want to cry.

She felt strangled with the truth of it. She loved him. She wanted him with all the fierce desperation and possessiveness of a child. She wanted to sit in a corner and yell his name and refuse to do anything until he was brought to her.

Leaving him felt like the hardest thing she'd ever done, but she still felt sure that it was easier than the overwhelming nightmare that her life would turn into if she stayed. Her career would probably be over. If it wasn't, it would have to be clawed back bit by bit, three steps back for every step forward. She would have to explain herself or, worse, have to stay silent in the face of a jeering audience, with no opportunity to manage her image. Prior to this her critics had viewed her as a controlling and high-strung talent, the Indian girl who had to have things her way. Now they could call her the scam artist who had snagged the most susceptible man she could find and tricked or coerced him into a life sentence of a relationship. Pritha would be drawn further in as either another of Win's victims or a potential coconspirator, the mother-in-law slash jailer, trapping Leo for all those months in her hideaway mansion on the coast.

Things were bad now, but she wasn't the first public figure to be wrapped up in a scandal of their own making. She had faith in Marie; she had faith in her image and her work. If she turned her back on everything, if she apologized, she could still recover. There was no precedent for staying with Leo, though. Nobody had ever been caught so definitively in a lie and then just continued as if it hadn't happened. Nobody ever said, *I don't care what you know about us*. And there was no guarantee, after all, that she and Leo would last, that they wouldn't have one of their explosive fights, that they wouldn't find they weren't made for a real relationship after all. Pritha's house was a bubble and Win had been frantic, pacing like a caged animal, pushed into telling Leo things she wouldn't have tried to explain before. Alone with her, he had stopped searching for the perfect thing to say, given up on his crusade to fix her life, and offered something more like sanctuary. But eventually things had to go back to normal. Normal meant scrutiny, pressure, wave after wave of outsiders beating against their door.

Even imagining it made her heart speed up, her breath stuttering, panic crawling over her skin. It would have been the most frightening, most dangerous thing she had ever done. And it didn't matter now; it was gone with that clouded dawn in London when she could have made a different decision. She had chosen her career, not Leo. She'd seen the fury and disbelief on his face, the way he'd turned away from her with a violent shrug of his shoulders, as though he was giving her up for good, as though he'd held out some hope that there was something true left in her and been disappointed. He'd laughed when she left the room. She'd heard it echoing behind her as she set off down the hallway, screwing her face up so she would be calm when she faced the photographers. His laughter had sounded low and rough and unsurprised.

At five in the morning she gave up on the possibility of sleep. She padded out to the kitchen and stopped in the doorway. There was a pool of yellow light, and Shift was sitting in it, a cup of green tea in her palms, her face small and pale like a little girl's, her gaze resting on the dark shapes of trees out the window. It was snowing outside.

Win didn't think she made a noise, but Shift looked over anyway. Her face changed in a way that Win couldn't completely track, some realignment of feeling or resolve.

"Can't sleep?" Shift said, before Win could say anything.

Win shrugged. She felt stupid and embarrassed. She felt as though she'd been fighting with everyone for months. She was exhausted.

"Thought I might have a cup of tea," Win said, and put the kettle on. The kitchen was dim and quiet, but she noticed, with a dull flush of embarrassment, that Shift had taken down the photo of Win and Leo from the fridge.

"Yeah." Shift set aside her cup and stood up. "Look, I—I was really angry and—"

"Shift," Win said, voice small. Shift bolted across the kitchen and they clutched each other, Shift's face shoved up against Win's collarbone.

"You're too fucking tall," Shift said.

Win said, with all the fervor of a night spent staring down her ghosts, "I'm really, really sorry—"

"*I'm* sorry! I completely overstepped the line—"

"I was being such a bad friend but I'm going to do better—"

"Oh my god, you're the best friend in the world, I'm such an idiot I shouldn't be allowed to speak," Shift said.

"This is why we're bad at fighting," Win said. "We go right back to being sixteen."

"I know," Shift said. She smiled, a little watery, and tapped Win on the nose. "It's how I know you're still in there."

Win flinched, and Shift began to apologize again, but Win shook her head.

"Look," she said, "I—I don't keep you around to prove anything—"

"I was angry—"

"No, but I need you to know," Win said, because her throat was still tight with misery, and because the idea that Shift didn't know was terrifying. "You knew me before everything happened. Sometimes it feels like you're the only person who actually *does* know me, who doesn't fall for..." She flapped her hand uselessly at herself. "But you're right. I think...my work takes up everything in my head sometimes."

"It's like it's been rewired," Shift said. "I know why it had to be. I wish— You can be hurtful, Win." Win felt her mouth twist down. Shift reached out and caught her forearm. "But listen, you're right. I know you. If you think I didn't know you could be a massive bitch before all of this, you're kidding yourself."

Win laughed, and sniffled so that she didn't actually start crying again.

"If it was just about you being mean now and then, okay, I can yell at you," Shift said. "But I worry that you're hurting yourself."

"I..." Win shook her head, dazed. Her eyes were blurry from the lack of sleep; the light kept fracturing in them.

"It's okay," Shift said. "I've got you. Everything will be okay."

Win couldn't talk about it, couldn't think about it. She said, "I shouldn't have said that. The ultimatum. That wasn't fair. Of course the profiler should come. And of course—of course he can, too, if that's what Charlie wants. I'll just stay out of his way."

"Win." Shift pulled back so they could see each other's faces.

Win looked at Shift's warm, steady gaze, the kindness written into her, and said, in a rush, "What if I made a mistake?"

Shift paused. "Mistakes can be fixed."

"God, sorry. I was meant to be apologizing, not spiraling."

"But if you want to—"

"No." Win shook her head. Her throat felt like it was closing up; she spoke before it could. "No, really, let's not talk about it."

Shift squeezed Win's hand. "I know it's not easy. I'm sorry. But I'll be there. It's just going to be shit, and we're going to deal with it."

Win smiled. She felt horribly guilty. "You don't have to deal with it. You just have to get married and then get drunk. Those are your two jobs."

Shift held up three fingers, counting off her own list. "Get married, get drunk, keep Leo away from you. It'll be fun."

Win put her hand in a loose fist against her mouth. Something hot was rising in her. She hoped it was vomit; that would be better than the weird howl she kept tamping down on, something lost and desperate like a desert wind trapped in her throat.

"I don't think you'll have to keep him away from me." She saw Leo's face again in that pale dawn, the disgust and exhaustion rising, his sharp jawline as he turned away. "I think he's had enough."

"Well, maybe that's good, too," Shift said. "You couldn't keep this going forever."

"I know," Win agreed, because it was true. "Right, I know, except I think..." She paused, unwilling to say what she was thinking. Shift stayed perfectly still against her. "I think maybe I need him."

"Oh, come on," Shift said, gripping Win's shoulder and shaking her a bit. "I'm pretty sure your career is built on a lot more than one relationship."

"That's not what I meant," Win said.

It wouldn't get light outside for hours. They both watched the snow slowly covering the too-long grass. Shift was quiet for a long time.

CHAPTER TWENTY-TWO

Win was sleeping in the loft bed Shift and Charlie had built last summer. There was a triangular window across from her mattress, and lying awake, she watched the tame drifts of snowfall against the dirty sky. They would need to lay something down on the walkway from the road to the greenhouse, on Saturday. Shift was wearing white satin pumps for the wedding, and Win doubted they would fare well on wet, icy ground.

She dreamed about Leo. They were swimming in the pool in Saint-Tropez, circling each other in the blue-green glow, except this time something else was in the water with them, a slow and hulking shadow that followed them. Without discussion they tried to split up to confuse it and then to band together to scare it, but neither seemed to work, and it only drew closer.

When she came out for breakfast the next morning, she told Shift, who snorted.

"Subtle."

"What do you think it means?" Charlie asked earnestly. Shift snorted again, and palmed her hand through his bed hair. She was still watching Win. Win nodded at her.

"It'll be fine," Win said.

For a while yesterday she had thought she might cry again, half-dazed from a sleepless night, but her brain had already moved on from shock into planning mode. Marie had replied to her message with a flurry of activity, floor plans, escape routes, areas of the venue where Win would be able to avoid any kind of photography. Win wasn't sure how she'd gotten hold of a blueprint of the Rosemont Greenhouse, but she was grateful. Security would keep outsiders away from the approach to the venue, only partly for selfish reasons. Win doubted a baying mob would be exactly the background Shift wanted when she made her entrance.

But the security team wouldn't be able to monitor Charlie's *Vogue* photographer, and there was even less defense against wedding guests or staff who wanted to sell a few grainy photos to the media. She would need to keep her guard up all night so as not to be caught even once in the same frame as Leo. Marie raised the possibility of just whisking Win out straight after the ceremony, but Win was resolute. She would stick it out until the end of the night.

Despite Win's attempt to broach the subject with Charlie, no one really knew what Leo's plans were. All Charlie could show her was a determined missive from Gum: He's coming. She agonized for a while before forcing herself to ask Pritha if she was in touch with Leo.

"No," Pritha said, very stiffly. "I am on your side."

Win wished that other people could keep as silent as Leo. Shift shunned TV and had only slow and spotty Wi-Fi, making it easier to ignore the deluge of commentary, but Marie's daily briefings kept her in the loop. Speculation had moved on to Win's other past relationships, with magazines and pundits now leading all-out investigations in order to determine exactly how much Win had been lying about.

Marie was unsurprised and disdainful. "Like children discovering Santa Claus isn't real. All we ever promised them was a good show."

"They're going to get a good show in a few days," Win said.

"We'll just have to deal with that," Marie said. She looked too polished and out of place among the piles of papers and corsages in Shift's kitchen. She was flying back and forth between LA and Montreal with apparently no exhaustion, joining Patrick in meetings with studio execs and potential directors to talk about Win's newly toxic brand, then meeting up with Win for long, intense strategy meetings every couple of days.

The second time Marie had flown back, Win had told her that it was fine if she needed to stay in LA. She'd tried to make it clear that she knew Marie was one of the more successful publicists in the business, that she'd have hordes of people at her door, and that if she didn't ditch Win completely, she should at least make some time in her schedule for other clients. She worried that Marie thought she'd missed her chance to leave; the best time would have been with Emil, in one fell swoop, and now she was stranded on Win's sinking ship without any backup.

"You know," Marie had said, steely-eyed, "if I'd done for any other actress what I've done for you, there'd be almost nothing anyone could do to knock her down. Even the Lila Gardner mess could have turned into a fun love triangle."

Win had stayed quiet. She wasn't sure if this was a rebuke.

"And now you're on the edge of—well . . ." Marie had said. "You can call it professional pride on my part if you want, but I think it's obscene. Fifty years from now people are going to realize you were the best actor of your generation, and I'm not going to let anyone drive you out."

Win had stared at her.

Marie had looked a little flustered. "Anyway, I want a mention in your first Oscars speech."

"Oh, okay," Win had said, and laughed, voice catching.

"Let's see," Marie continued now. "Adam is being his stubborn self and refusing to speak to anyone. A couple of models we hired to go to public events with you are enjoying the attention, but they aren't great at interviews, and people aren't especially interested in them."

Win nodded, trying and failing to recall the names and faces of handsome dates from long ago. If she were a man, Win thought with a particular surge of bitterness, the fact that she'd arranged arm candy for an awards show would barely raise an eyebrow, let alone warrant an interview. Marie had already forwarded her a couple of think pieces on smaller websites arguing as much, but given that it looked like Win had destroyed a marriage in the process of bolstering her image, sympathy for her was thin and sparsely found.

"And then there's Nathan," Marie said.

"God." Win tipped her cheek into her hand. "Okay, hit me. What's he done now?"

"Mostly just the usual thinly veiled references on his show." Marie turned the phone toward Win to play her a clip of Nathan in the opening monologue of his panel show, vibrating with poorly concealed glee. "This week's theme," he said, tinny through the speakers, "is *karma*," and beamed at the wave of audience laughter and applause.

"Original," Win said.

Marie made a dismissive gesture. "Well, you know what he's like. The only problem is someone from the *Daily Mail* actually called him and managed to get a quote. He said, *It makes a lot of sense. She prefers the kind of fantasy she can control.*"

Win nodded, taking it in. Nathan capitalizing on this opportunity was not that surprising. He was fame hungry in a way that she'd recognized too late, and a few semi-friendly calls over the last few months weren't enough to keep his loyalty. Nathan's first and foremost priority, always, was himself.

It was weird to think that she'd liked Nathan so much once, that they'd slept together, held hands, that he'd taken her on a picnic up high in the Peak District and pulled out containers of deli food and premixed Buck's Fizz. She remembered when his quick, laughing voice had given her butterflies. Now he just annoyed her. She wondered what game he thought he was playing, what victory he was trying to seize out of the ashes of her career.

"That guy," Shift said, wandering into the kitchen in time to hear this last, "is really cruising for a bruising."

Win laughed. "Yeah." She held out her hand for Marie's phone. "Do you have his number?"

"I—yes?"

"I'm going to call him."

"He could record it," Marie warned. "He's quick on his feet like that."

"I don't think he'd do that," Win said. "He doesn't want to look like he's planned anything. He likes feeling reckless."

"He could still spin whatever you say against you."

"Yeah," Win said. That had been in her head all year, since they broke up; it was in her head every time she broke up with someone, a rush of fear over how much they knew about her, how much they could tell the press. In the last few weeks of their relationship, Nathan had complained, *You never let me in.* When they broke up and Nathan was a jerk, Win had thought: *Well, can you blame me?*

She wasn't going to waste time feeling sorry for Nathan, but maybe it had been wrong of her to expect something real when she was censoring every other thing she said. It certainly hadn't helped their relationship, and perhaps sitting quiet and hoping Nathan wouldn't spill anything too bad wasn't going to help, either.

"It's not that late in England," Win said.

Nathan picked up sounding tense, that East London accent sharper than usual. "All right, Marie. You're not my boss, you don't actually get to tell me off—"

"It's me."

Nathan was quiet. He cleared his throat. "Been a while."

"Yeah," Win said.

They'd spoken a few times when she was at her mum's house, after he first called. She had kept speaking with him until he'd seemed like he was warming up, and not at risk of bitching about her on his show again. But Leo had been there all the time, inescapable, driving her mad, infuriating her, obsessing her—so she'd stopped returning Nathan's calls. It occurred to her now, belatedly, that over the course of the last few months, even since August, she'd been cruel to Nathan. Not in the way he'd been cruel to her, malicious and pointed—but still.

"I got caught up in some stuff. I know you saw."

"Yes," Nathan said, and then quickly, almost like he was daring himself to say it, "So none of that stuff with that guy was real?"

Win pressed her lips together. "I didn't call to talk about him."

"You called to tell me off," Nathan said. "So while you're at it, I think I'm owed an explanation. You ran straight from dumping me to larking around Saint-Tropez with him, after all—"

"It was a mutual breakup, Nathan," Win said, trying to stay calm. "And I didn't go to Saint-Tropez until you started running your mouth to the press."

Too late, she realized that had been the wrong thing to say. Marie and Shift both winced, and on the other end of the line there was a staggered silence before Nathan said, "Are you serious? That's why you went off with him? To show that you weren't bothered?"

"Nathan."

"That is messed up, babe. That is some fucked up shit. God, everything they're saying in the papers is absolutely right—"

"So I guess I got what I deserved," Win snapped, losing her temper. "They've found out, and it doesn't matter how complicated everything was or how much I *had* to control things. They've found out and you can gloat as much as you like, but I wish you'd do me a fucking favor and do it somewhere I don't have to hear about it all the time. Why don't you go down to the pub and moan to all your mates about it? Or tell your latest date how hard it was to be with me? Honestly, I couldn't care less, but just give me and Marie a break, I can't tell you how bored I am of hearing your name."

"You mean stop bad-mouthing you to the press," Nathan said. "Phrase it nice as you like, but that's what you mean—"

"Yeah, that's what I mean," Win said. "We dated for nine months. We met each other's families. It didn't work out and that sucks, but I didn't ruin your life. Have some fucking respect."

She hung up, breathing hard. Her fingers twitched; she wanted to call him back, apologize, be as charming and calm as she could and sort it out so that he wouldn't talk about her anymore. Then she set her jaw and looked up.

With feeling, Shift said, "That was brilliant."

"That might have..." Win licked her lips. "That might have been dumb."

She dared to look at Marie, and startled again. Marie's face was gently, serenely smug. "He had it coming. Unless he starts out-and-out lying, there's not much new he can say that people haven't already heard. And if he does, we'll either sue him or start lying right back."

Win started to smile, uncertain.

"Benefit of rock bottom," Marie said. "The only way out is up."

Marie flew back to LA the next day. Win wasn't that surprised when she got an email only seven hours after Marie had left for the airport, a roundup of the latest gossip, including a note that the director of *The Sun Also Rises* had at last made a statement. Better not read it, Whitman, Marie had written, but Win opened it anyway. She sat looking at the short paragraph and felt sick.

Authenticity is important to me, as it is to most of the talented people working in film, he'd said. When we're telling stories, we have to be careful that the heart of them is true. I have to know that the actors are there because they believe in the story and want to share it, not because it's part of a personal narrative or quest for fame.

Win swallowed down bile, and went back to Marie's email. The last link was to an essay in the *New Yorker*. Marie had captioned it ?? quite interesting. The headline was Whitman Tagore's Crumbling Castle.

Here's what we wanted Whitman Tagore to be: beautiful, smart, funny, sexy, cool, a spokesperson for all British Indian people ever, not too Indian, romantic, passionate, talented, humble, kind, it started. For the four shining years that she was the queen of Hollywood, she managed it effortlessly, most obviously in that glorious standard of real-life love stories. Last week, it all came tumbling down. But god, it was beautiful to watch her try.

It was a kind article, thoughtful and smart. It felt like a beam of light falling on her, and just as alarming. After a moment, Win clicked back to the director's statement, and then she closed her laptop.

In the lounge room Shift was bent over a synthesizer, headphones slung over her neck, frowning to herself. Charlie was sprawled in his armchair staring at the wedding seating plan. Win threw herself on the couch and touched the back of Shift's knee.

"Whitman," Charlie said, "do you think it's better to put my friends from school on one table and friends from work on another, or do a singles table and a couples table?"

"First one," Win said. "Singles tables are condescending."

Charlie stared at the chart and made a low, mournful noise. "I think you're right. It just has to be perfect, you know? Imagine if there was a fight and *Vogue* wrote about it."

"That would be bad," Win agreed, and asked where he was going to seat Shift's cousins, a family of four boys who were all enormous, played ice hockey, and had a tendency to pick Charlie and his other willowy friends up and lift them above their heads. Charlie launched into a detailed description of how they would be close enough to the bar to keep them happy but blocked from the models by Shift's roadie friends. Win lay back on the couch and listened.

At one point Charlie got up to make drinks, and Win looked down at Shift, still playing with her hardware.

"I'm really glad I'm here," Win said.

"I was just going to say that." Shift wrapped her fingers around

Win's ankle, giving it a comforting little tug, like she was tethering Win to land.

"By the way," she added, "probably better if you can trick Charlie into seating our parents at different tables. I'm not sure they're going to get on."

"Oh, okay, I'll break that news gently."

Shift laughed and unplugged her headphones. The music she was working on shimmered with stuttering rhythms and slow, arctic melodies shifting underneath. It was quiet and calm in the house. Win sank further into the couch and pretended that the intermittent flashes of cameras outside the windows were just lightning, a storm rolling through and past.

Win had a sneaking suspicion that Shift was more excited for the rehearsal dinner than she was the actual wedding. Shift's favorite Chinese restaurant was out of the way enough to be inconvenient for everyone except Shift's group of eco-friendly friends and musical weirdos, and the odd location and awkward side street entrance made it perfect for losing paparazzi.

There wasn't a huge crowd: Shift's and Charlie's parents; Charlie's cluster of male model colleagues who stood in a circle and looked faintly confused, as if wondering when someone would hand them a Bellini and tell them where to stand and pout; Shift's touring band and a few uni friends; and her sister, the other bridesmaid, who was younger than them and had been giving Win nervous, admiring looks since she arrived a few hours earlier with Shift's parents. Win exchanged hugs with them and updated them on Pritha's health. The last time she'd seen Shift's sister, Danielle was seven years old, obsessed with boa constrictors and sure that Win and Shift were deeply uncool. She was clearly reevaluating.

Charlie had taken to calling Shift's parents Maw and Paw in the days leading up to their arrival ("Let's take Maw and Paw to the observatory when they get here!" and "Do you think Maw and Paw would like my three-bean cassoulet?") but once actually confronted with them, he was quite subdued, and said politely, "Nice to see you again, Mr. and Mrs. Scottsdale."

"Oh, sweetie, call me June," Shift's mum said. Shift's dad managed a faint smile and a nod.

Gum had flown in that afternoon, and Charlie had gone immediately to greet him at a bar. Win wouldn't meet him until they got to the restaurant. She'd had a tight knot in her stomach about it all day. She felt strange about the idea of meeting Leo's brother for the first time like this. At least Charlie had confirmed Gum was alone. Leo was only joining them tomorrow.

Win and Shift were the first people there, getting in the waiters' way and tripping over tables. Shift was wearing a suit, her hair swept up into a drooping coiffe, her lipstick bright red, sporting a pair of wingtip loafers with tassels and a bolo tie. She looked like a disreputable cowboy forced into court, and she laughed with real pleasure when Win told her so.

"You just look beautiful," she told Win.

Win shrugged and looked away. Shift wasn't the type to particularly care about bridesmaid dresses, which had been a relief to Win's team if not Win herself. She'd asked her stylist in LA to send her something simple, the kind of dress that indicated a background presence without seeming like she was hiding. They'd slipped her into midnight-blue Balmain, ankle length with glinting silver chains strapped loosely over her shoulders.

Georgia Chilton, the *Vogue* profiler, had stopped by as well. She was friendly, professional but open, and smart enough not to pay Win much more than the cursory attention a bridesmaid deserved, though her gaze was alert and interested. Shift spent most of the time laughing and dragging Win into the conversation all the same, speaking a little faster, eyes bright with nerves. She was unused to a journalist who didn't want to ask her about her latest sampling techniques and what she thought about the return of dubstep.

"I don't know why you need me, really," Shift said. "The profile's on Charlie, isn't it?"

"Well, I've already had a couple of in-depth interviews with Charlie," Georgia said. "I need to know *something* about you."

"As if Charlie hasn't already recited a few melodramatic odes," Shift said. Win stayed behind Shift with a reassuring hand on her arm. She didn't want to appear overbearing, and she didn't trust how Georgia would portray her, no matter how nice she was in person.

At least the photographer wasn't arriving until tomorrow, the wedding day. It meant there was no one to catch the way Win's head jerked up when she heard Charlie's cheerful laugh and Gum's low, throaty chuckle, a sound she already knew, crackled and secondhand from Leo's phone speaker.

They came in together, brushing snow off the shoulders of their heavy coats and stamping their feet. For a moment, Win felt almost winded with relief. Gum, as she had suspected from photos, didn't look much like Leo at all. Now that she'd met Gabrysia, Win could see for herself that Leo took after his mother. They had the same bone structure, the same dark eyes fringed with lashes long enough to make them look slightly secretive. Gabrysia had masculine features; they sat better on Leo, though his looks weren't quite as striking as his mother's.

But Gum clearly took after their father. His forehead was broader than Leo's, and he was shorter, carrying himself with an authoritative swagger, a build like a boxer's with a pouched, American face. He'd struggled with alcohol for a few years, and the remnants of the fight had lingered on his brow, making him look older than he was.

Charlie had a faint flush in his cheeks, like he'd been drinking, and he seemed younger than usual standing next to Gum; it was hard to remember they'd been school friends. He looked around until he spotted Shift and Win and then made a beeline for his fiancée with Gum trailing behind him like an indulgent uncle. They cut an odd pair together, Gum's slicked hair and heavy face against Charlie's angelic golden curls and pink mouth.

"Shift," Charlie said, and kissed her. Georgia Chilton, hovering behind them, made a note. "There you are!"

"Here I am," she said, and touched his hair with a swift, affectionate curl of her fingers. "Hi, Geoff, nice to see you again."

Gum gave Shift a fussy little handshake, half raising her hand to his mouth like he wanted to kiss it before he thought better, and said, "Feeling's mutual."

"And I don't think you've met my maid of honor, have you?" Shift said, like butter wouldn't melt in her mouth. "Whitman Tagore, Geoffrey Milanowski."

"Hi," Win said. Gum seized her hand in a hearty shake.

"Hullo, hullo, at last," Gum said, squinting at her. Win remembered Leo saying that Gum was farsighted, but refused to wear his glasses, and he didn't trust contacts. "Feel like I have met you, all your movies and the fuss with my little brother—"

"It's been a long time coming," Win said politely. Gum pumped her hand a moment longer.

"Excellent movies," Gum said, and turned to Charlie. "Don't you think?"

"Oh, spectacular!" Charlie said, beaming. Shift was leaning in the curve of his arm, and Charlie looked as though there was nothing bad in the world.

"Thank you," Win said. She felt dull and small, not sure what she wanted to say. Gum's mention of Leo had thrown her, though it would have been odd if he hadn't. She wasn't used to thinking of Leo as a little brother.

"I liked the ladies' heist one best," Gum said, and started clicking his fingers. "What was it, what—"

"*Beg, Borrow, or Bleed*," Win said. It had been one of her early films; she'd been a relative unknown in an ensemble cast, playing an awkward computer scientist, pretty beneath the square-framed glasses. Directly afterward she'd left on her Win Gone Wild tour with Leo to prove she could be nasty, and a lead.

"That's the one," Gum said, and gave his churring laugh again. "Good film. Well, Shift, you all ready to throw yourself away on my boy?"

"I've just about resigned myself," Shift said. Win leaned back, effectively if not actually leaving the conversation.

She felt as though she'd walked through a ring of fire. She was almost proud of herself for the way she'd managed it until Gum, frowning, disagreed with something Charlie said and pushed two knuckles against his eyebrow as he thought. It was so exactly Leo's gesture that it knocked the breath out of her. She had to turn away and pretend she'd heard someone calling her name, touching Shift's arm to excuse herself and hoping that her hands weren't obviously trembling.

She walked as quickly and authoritatively as she could until she got to the bathroom, where she stood with her hands resting over the sink, head bowed. She took several shuddering breaths. Then she walked out smiling.

CHAPTER TWENTY-THREE

Rolling clouds came coursing across the sky, blanketing them with cold, clean light, but there was no snowfall before Shift and Charlie's wedding. The morning stayed still, waiting for the clouds to open, and in the quiet before everyone else woke up, Win watched Shift stand in her garden in her pajamas and Charlie's big coat, arms hugged around herself, face turned up to the sky. She looked small and sure, and when she turned back and saw Win through the window, she laughed and waved.

Charlie had spent the night at a friend's apartment—he was, to Win's utter lack of surprise, quite superstitious about wedding traditions. It left Win, Shift, Shift's sister Danielle, and Shift's mum getting ready together. Jada and Matthew, who had arrived a day earlier, flew about the room fixing everyone's hair and makeup. Shift put on a grime mix. Glasses of champagne were passed around. It was easy to keep laughing, keep smiling, and not say much. Georgia Chilton, to Win's relief, was spending the wedding morning with Charlie.

Every now and then Shift threw a worried look at Win, but she was distracted, mostly by arguing with her sister about whether flower crowns were no longer cool.

"You could have said this months ago," Shift said.

"It's coming back round into fashion again," Jada said.

"Hollywood says so, so there," Shift said, glaring at her younger sister. "You shut your mouth."

"Fine," Danielle sighed, and added, with studied carelessness, "Hey, Win, wanna take a selfie?"

Win paused. "Sure." Shift caught her eye and mouthed, *Thank you.* Win leaned in for the camera.

There were dark shadows under Win's eyes in the photo, but Matthew would take care of them before the wedding. He tilted her jaw up toward him.

"How you doing, sweetie?" he asked, voice low enough that it didn't carry to the rest of the room. "Been a tough week."

"I'm okay," Win said. "I don't think I'm going to be doing many public appearances for a while. Your calendar's going to fill up with other people."

"You know I'm always going to make sure you come first," he said. Win smiled at him, worn out with how good everyone was. She missed Emil, who would have been in his element among all the bustle and fraught tempers. He had sent Shift a bouquet of flowers this morning, with his best wishes, and an email to Win with three likely candidates for his replacement.

"Thank you." She didn't feel like she could talk very much. Her throat was small, her mouth all dried up. She kept looking out the window and waiting for the snow. There was frost against the glass even this late in the morning, tapering, spidery lines of gleaming ice.

But it didn't snow, not all through the morning of preparations and mini-arguments and Danielle and Shift chasing each other around the kitchen with their bouquets, and their mother shouting uselessly for them to slow down and look after their pretty dresses. It didn't snow when the cars beeped outside and they went out to find Shift's dad waiting with his eyebrows drawn together in front of a long line of vintage Skyliners—"Oh my god," Shift said, "I'm just going to kill Charlie."

It didn't snow when they got to the venue and hid in a dressing room while guests arrived. Win stood at the huge windows, looking down the long sweep of lawn and tangle of trees stark and lovely against the horizon, snow on the ground from the preceding week. The clouds sank lower and there were strange, dipping moments of sunlight and shade, beams of light shifting through so the sky looked almost lilac. Voices sounded in the hall beyond as people began arriving. Shift said, "Oh, god, why couldn't we have eloped?" and Win had to bite her lip so she didn't end up agreeing.

Georgia Chilton and *Vogue*'s photographer, a friendly guy called Bill who was wearing a nice shirt out of respect and a trucker's cap out of habit, arrived shortly after and took photos of Shift, Win, and Danielle fixing each other's hair. They were businesslike, friendly but distant. Georgia's focus was clearly on Charlie, which Win respected, and she'd already had most of her conversations with Shift earlier. She said, "Nervous?" in a cheerful, friendly way that meant the answer didn't really matter. Win, despite herself, quite liked her.

Then Georgia said, "Okay, we're going to head into the reception hall, set up a few cameras. Don't want to miss anything!" and Win's blood ran cold.

"I hope they get a couple of shots of Charlie freaking out," Shift said. "I would love that." She groaned. "God, I can hear my aunt. She's already complaining."

Win couldn't pick Leo's voice out among the others. She did hear Gum's unmistakable guffaw. Shift looked around and said, "Oh, good, he and Charlie must be here," and a bit of color came into her pale cheeks.

Win smiled at her. "Not so nervous?"

"Well, it's just Charlie," Shift said.

"And two hundred guests," Danielle chimed in.

"You." Shift's mum pointed a finger at Danielle. "Go make sure all the ushers know what they're doing."

"Mum—"

"Go! There's no bad luck about anyone seeing you."

That left the three of them. Shift's mum said, "Oh, Lisa, you look beautiful," and for a moment Win didn't know whom she was talking to. Shift looked equally surprised.

"Thanks, Mum," Shift said. She did look beautiful. Her hair was falling ragged down her shoulders—she'd refused to allow Jada to trim some of her split ends, waving it away as too much bother—but the flower crown added something elegant, delicate fabric gardenias. Her dress was simple white lace, a low-cut neck that showed off her collarbone and the sparrow tattoos lining her clavicle. She looked fresh and happy in an assured, confident way. She looked like she had no doubts at all.

"You look amazing," Win said.

"You do, too," Shift said. Win was in a rose-gold silk gown that fell gently to her ankles, a square neck like Shift's and three-quarter sleeves in a useless nod to the cold. Her hair was down.

"I'm just keeping up appearances for you," Win said.

Shift turned and held out her arms. "You have to come here. I keep tripping over the damn train."

Win walked into her arms and nestled her face against Shift's warm shoulder. Outside the snow had, at last, begun to fall.

She lifted her head when Shift's father sidled in and cleared his throat. "Bridesmaids, you're up." Danielle appeared behind him with a rustle of skirts and a firm grip on Charlie's cousin's arm.

"I suppose this is it," Shift said.

As if summoned, the door swung open fully and Gum appeared.

"Shift!" he cried. "You're the very *picture* of matrimony. You look a treat!"

"Thank you, Geoffrey," Shift said.

"Chaz is peeing his pants," Gum confided. "Well, ladies and gents. I think we're ready to get this show on the road. Can't leave old

Charles waiting up there on his own too long! All set, sir?" he added to Shift's dad.

"Yes," Shift's dad said, eyeing him with dislike.

Danielle and Charlie's cousin moved forward to wait at the doorway. Gum held out his arm gallantly for Win to take, and she turned to Shift one last time.

"Good luck."

"You, too," Shift said. Win's mouth tightened. She turned to Gum, took his arm, and moved with him into place. Through the conservatory, the organ started up.

Leo would be in the room. Win drew in a breath, trying to prepare herself.

Then Gum leaned in, a close, unexpected presence, and hissed in her ear, "You've got some goddamn nerve, showing your face round here."

Win blinked. It took a moment for the words to filter through. "What?"

"The whole family's in an *uproar*," Gum continued in a low, furious voice, all his good humor dropped away like a discarded pantomime mask. "Dad just about blew his gasket when he heard."

"I'm sorry," Win said, bewildered. Danielle and her groomsman had started to make their way down the aisle, Danielle's cheeks pink with embarrassment and pleasure. "Is this the right time to talk about it?"

"What other time is there? I had to get you on your own, without your damn security detail."

"My..." Win trailed off, shaking her head in disbelief, the first pinpricks of anger rising in her. "I actually don't want to discuss it."

She made a point of shutting her mouth as they moved forward into the doorway. Gum ignored it.

"But Leo's not allowed to say anything." He looked up and winked at Charlie as they began the slow march down the aisle. "So it's up to old Uncle Gerry to tell you what for. Poor boy can't even defend himself! God knows I've never been one to cause a scene—"

"That's not been my experience," Win said coolly.

Gum's scowl darkened. "Oh yes, know all about us, don't you! I bet you've had your people working on me for years. Hollywood types digging their noses in—it's been an awful strain on Leo."

"Really," Win said, through gritted teeth, as they moved forward down the aisle and a crowd of interested faces craned their necks toward her. "Can we talk about this some other time?"

"I hope to God there's never another time," Gum hissed. "I'm not sure Leo could bear it. I certainly couldn't."

"Is..." Win's throat felt like it was closing up. She whispered, "Is Leo—"

"Excuse me, we're in the middle of a wedding," Gum said. "You LA people have no sense of manners."

Win stared at him.

I'm British, she thought, but by then they were at the altar and Gum was kissing her cheek and handing her off to the bride's side. The familiar chords of the Wedding March rose through the conservatory, the greenery shivering and the snow drifting past the windowpanes, giving the light an eerie turquoise glow.

Win turned toward the door, and, without even trying, Leo's face leapt out at her as though he were Technicolor against a black-and-white crowd. He was close to the back, like he'd slipped in at the last minute. She saw him in a blinding flash: his sharp cheekbones, the clean line of his suit, his expression tired and polite as he, too, turned his head toward the door. Heat and misery rushed through her, so overwhelming and sickening she thought she might need to sit down.

Then Shift appeared in the doorway, hugging her dad's arm and beaming, and Win drew in a steadying breath.

The ceremony passed in a blur. Charlie cried prettily through most of it; Shift got the giggles between her vows. There was a warm, generous air of indulgence, unusual in a room with this many famous people. Charlie's vows reduced nearly everyone to happy laughter and tears. Behind him, Gum nodded genially along, a king at the nuptials of his most favored princeling.

Win stared straight ahead, fixing her eyes on Shift and Charlie. She tried to pay attention, but her heart thudded so painfully she felt sure it was audible; she'd forgotten how to breathe steadily. She was so conscious of Leo in the same room as her that it dwarfed everything else. It felt like if she turned and looked out at the crowd, he would be the only one there.

Then it was over, Charlie dipping Shift extravagantly to kiss her, Shift laughing and throwing her arms around his neck. The crowd burst into cheers, and Win remembered they were there, after all. Win stood frozen, her fingers numb around her bouquet, until Shift took hold of her elbow and said, "Come do this weird receiving thing with me."

Win followed her gratefully to the door. Guests were passing through into one of the smaller adjoining rooms, where champagne would be served until the main reception hall was ready; as they did so, they stopped to shake Charlie's hand and tell Shift how lovely the ceremony had been. Win stood behind them, trying not to shiver. She felt stupid. She hadn't thought it would be this physical a reaction.

She kept her gaze pleasant and fixed over Shift's shoulder, smiling at the people who smiled at her. There were a lot of curious looks; there were already people trying to push Shift and Charlie aside and talk to her. Two separate men she'd never met said, "Oh, it's no good what they've been saying about you," with smirking winks, like they knew her real story. She smiled and demurred from conversation, saying, if she had to, "I'm really glad to be here with Shift and Charlie," until they got the hint and told Shift how beautiful she was. Shift, at least, didn't seem to care. She just rolled her eyes at Win and turned smiling to the next guest. Every now and then she ruffled Charlie's hair while he beamed at her.

Even with the bustling crowd as a distraction, Win's attention was fixed on the point, right at the back of the line, where Leo was moving quietly and inevitably closer. She cut her eyes toward him in urgent, guilty glances, sure that someone was going to catch her looking. Probably the *Vogue* people, who would be under instructions to look out for it. The smart thing to do was keep her gaze facing forward, and deal with Leo when he came. But Win couldn't help herself.

He was wearing a two-piece black suit, his shirt white and crisp, his tie loosely knotted. He wasn't quite clean-shaven, but the stubble looked deliberate, and it made his jaw firm and his mouth warm and full. He'd buzzed his hair down again, and when she caught him shaking hands with someone, her mind went momentarily blank. He'd taken all his rings off, every single one of them. His long fingers were bare.

"Loved your latest," a woman told Win, after kissing Shift on both cheeks. "My boyfriend dragged me along, but you really made *Transformers* watchable."

Win hadn't been in the latest *Transformers*. "Thank you," she said.

She wasn't sure she was capable of talking to him, but the doorway was small, and Leo was squeezed between other guests. Even if he wanted to get away and skip the receiving, he wouldn't manage it. She wasn't sure she was going to be able to stand within a meter of him. She wasn't sure whether she most wanted to step into the warm circle of his arms, or turn on her heel and run for the closest taxi. He was coming closer, though, steady and unhalting; soon he would be within reach.

"Whitman," Shift said, in a clear, carrying voice. "I think I've left my phone in the bathroom. Do me a favor and grab it for me?"

Shift caught her gaze, and Win gave her one overwhelmingly grateful look before she fled. Behind her, she heard Leo say, "Hey, Shift. You look nice."

Then confetti, and drinks, and a party. The conservatory led into a wide, wood-paneled reception hall that had been decorated according to Charlie's specifications. He'd taken the plant theme and run with it so the whole room was flush with greenery like a 1930s salon: tall monsteras surrounding the bar, wide banana leafs sheltering the velvet-seated lounge area, sprawling earthenware bowls of winter wildflowers on the tables. To compensate for the excess in plant life, the furniture was relatively understated, with the exception of Shift's and Charlie's chairs, which were wound with pepperberry foliage and cactus dahlias. To Charlie's left, Gum picked one of the leaves and sniffed it. To Shift's right, Win focused on her drink and tried to resist the urge to lift her head, knowing that if she looked out across the room, she would immediately fix on Leo.

Shift told her that Leo was at a table in a far corner from the wedding party, with the rest of Charlie's younger male friends and their dates. That information had induced another guilty pang, and Charlie's assurance, in a comforting voice, that "Leo won't mind, he said whatever's easiest will suit him," didn't help settle Win's stomach at all. She wished he could have left at the end of the ceremony, but Gum's attitude made it clear that this was going to be an endurance test to last all evening. She kept her head down, and ordered another vodka soda.

Georgia Chilton and Bill appeared to take photos of the speeches, pointing and conferring quietly, and Win lifted her head up to smile properly. Shift's parents had made a PowerPoint presentation of Shift's life, running through baby photos to the present day and featuring several photos of teenage Win and Shift, glaring from under terrible haircuts during their emo phase, posing back-to-back with their arms folded in an apparent promo for their short-lived band. Danielle nervously read a Mary Oliver poem. Gum's speech rambled over "the hills and dales of mine and Charlie's youth" before delving into the postcards Charlie had sent him from wherever in the world he was working, the hangovers they'd endured together, the "mystery noodles" that Charlie used to make on a hotplate when they shared a dorm room, the time Gum broke his leg at school and Charlie snuck into the infirmary after hours to read Gum op-eds from the *Financial Times*.

"He has had the opportunity to sit by my side at many hospital beds since then, I'm sorry to say," Gum said, with a jocular little laugh. "On the upside, I claim complete credit for his excellent bedside manner." He raised his glass. His smile was tight. "I am extremely happy for him and his bride."

Once he was done he looked a little lost, collapsing back down into his seat. Charlie patted his back and was immediately distracted by an errant aunt, but Georgia Chilton sidled closer, a calculating look in her eye. Win could understand the appeal: Gum and his big mouth was a golden opportunity for background dirt.

"It's Geoffrey, isn't it?" she said. "You've known Charlie a really long time, then."

Gum stood up to shake her hand, chest puffing out. "There's not a thing I don't know about that boy," he declared. "I was wondering when you'd come to find me—"

"Gum!"

Win fixed her gaze on the table. There was bright confetti scattered over the surface, and she stared at it until her vision blurred. But Leo was careful. He stuck close to the left, as far away from Win as he could manage while still coming up to snag his brother's elbow.

She heard his voice, low and warm. "Nice speech," Leo said. "Come get a drink with me."

"Well..." Gum hesitated, gesturing at Georgia.

"You're very busy," Leo said firmly. "Lots of best man duties. Gum."

"Yes, excuse me," Gum said, seeming to remember himself. "I have to look after my brother, you know. He's having a rough time, poor fella."

Win knew that if she looked up, Gum would be glaring at her. She wasn't sure what Leo would be doing. She stayed perfectly still and watched their feet move away, toward the bar, and then she threw back the rest of her drink.

Danielle, on Win's other side, asked tentatively if Win was having a good time. After a few awkward moments of small talk about her school and her friends, Win asked if she knew anyone else at the reception.

"Well—kind of," Danielle said, glancing around. "Some cousins, and I recognize some of Charlie's friends. That one"—she pointed at a short blond boy who was pretending to eat one of the plants while his friend filmed, expressionless—"has a pretty good YouTube channel. And that other one is maybe dating Isaac Bronstein right now, did you hear about that?"

She looked at Win excitedly as the idea dawned that she might have come across a source of potential insider gossip. But Win didn't really know the guy.

"Right, sure," Danielle said, changing tack. "I don't believe in all that gossip stuff. It's so childish."

Win shrugged. "I think people just like entertainment."

"Right but..." Danielle shifted in her seat, clearly regretting this line of conversation. "I think there's stuff that's there for entertainment, and stuff that's more private, you know?"

"Oh, *I* know," Win said, and grinned when Danielle blushed and giggled.

"Well, I think," Danielle started, but paused. Knowing that she shouldn't, Win followed Danielle's gaze over the tables of shining guests to where Leo was leaning with one elbow on the bar, looking with a determinedly vague expression toward the south windows, the snow still coming down outside. The shelves of bottles behind him were backlit in blue neon, and his outline cut against them in a soft silhouette, his tie already loosened and one hand in his pocket. Win's whole body stung as if she'd fallen into poison ivy. She stretched her hands out on the tablecloth. He was alone.

"He shouldn't have come," Danielle said. Win glanced at her in surprise. Danielle held her chin up, stubborn. "He's just here for the drama."

"He didn't have a choice," Win told her.

"Everybody always has a choice," Danielle said. Win wanted to tell her how wrong she was about that, but she couldn't do it without revealing how helpless she felt. She wanted to be like Danielle, young and hopeful enough to believe it. She wanted it to be true.

After collecting his drink, Leo slipped back into hiding at the corner table and didn't resurface for another hour or more. Win finished dinner in relative peace, doing her best to give Danielle sage advice on college choices and how to apply winged eyeliner. She startled when Danielle asked her what her plans were after the wedding, remembering again with a jolt that there were no new projects on the horizon. Patrick had been sending her scripts, but it was piecemeal, uninspiring stuff. He told her at the end of every phone call that he'd keep working on it.

"I guess I'm taking a break right now," she said.

They all got up and gathered around for the cake cutting—"It's *vegan*," Charlie announced, and it tasted like dust—and then made a haphazard crowd around the dance floor for Shift and Charlie's first dance, to a sweet, playful Fleetwood Mac song. Charlie held Shift's hands with earnest reverence and seemed almost overwhelmed by the moment until Shift started mouthing campily along with the chorus. He cracked into a smile, resting his brow for a second on her bare shoulder. Danielle squeezed Win's hand in the dark. The spotlights were so bright that she couldn't see anyone else in the crowd, and she was grateful for it.

After the dancing really got going, the room began to heat up. Shift commandeered the DJ booth as soon as she could, playing Top 40 hits that swung into stuttering EDM beats, twisting her shoulders back, witch house and something she'd once described to Win as "tropical goth" and then a pop hit that made all the seventeen-year-old cousins throw their hands up and scream. Charlie danced right in front of the turntables, swiveling his hands and surrounded by his cheerful crowd of boys. Every now and then Shift broke out of her reverie to beam at him, her train hooked artlessly over one shoulder. Bill the photographer was ducking in and around the edges of the crowd, his camera a natural extension of his eye, whose gaze Win avoided.

Win turned down several offers to dance, including one from Gum, which was delivered with such a threatening grin that she only very narrowly resisted the urge to slap him. What she wanted was to return to her table and drink until it was time to leave, but the specter of blurry videos surfacing online, depicting her sitting depressed and alone at her best friend's wedding, kept her on her feet. She stuck by Danielle, who had become a welcome ally. They danced goofily together and drank virgin versions of Win's favorite cocktails, and Win helped her curate a tasteful Instagram story of the evening. With Danielle keeping up a constant, delighted stream of conversation, it was easier to forget the eyes that must be on her, the guests nodding knowingly at her as she passed.

Toward the tail end of Shift's set, one of Charlie's younger cousins approached them. He looked hesitant, and across the floor a couple of other suited boys watched his progress with glee. Win tensed, but he fixed his gaze on Danielle.

"Fancy a dance?"

"Oh. I'm a bit busy right now," Danielle started, gesturing to Win.

Win shook her head. "No, you're not. Off you go."

Shift switched the track from a bopping Japanese pop song to a smooth soul number, winked at Win, and flipped a switch to turn the floor lights pink. They both watched Danielle and the pretty boy move together, swaying with only a touch of teenage awkwardness. Win blew Shift a kiss and stifled her desperation to grab Shift's arm and drag her away. Instead she stole Shift's purse where it was hanging over her abandoned chair, and took Charlie's discarded tux jacket as an afterthought.

There was an official smoker's area, a section of the terrarium opened up to the chill night sky, but it had been jam-packed with guests all evening, trampled through with ash and snow and heaving with laughter, and Win wanted more than anything to get away from everyone. It only took a second on her phone to find the emergency routes Marie had sent her. She slipped out through the service exit to the kitchen, smiling apologetically at the gaping waiters, and ducked past endless shelves of dishes and glass, around another corner and out the side door.

She found herself in an external storage space, dirty gray concrete and steel bars and a line of neglected cheese plants. She sat down on a discarded beer crate and picked through Shift's purse for her rolling papers and tobacco. She rolled a clumsy, terrible cigarette—she didn't smoke often enough to do this, and normally Emil rolled them for her—and sat trying to keep it alight with short, sharp puffs while the clatters and calls of the kitchen staff drifted out behind her. It was freezing, even with the jacket.

When the door pushed open again she looked up, expecting a waiter. It was Leo with his phone in hand.

"Fuck," Win said.

Leo blinked down at her, mouth falling open, eyes wide with shock.

"Sorry," he said, and added into the phone as he turned, "hang on—"

"No, I'll go," Win said, standing up and dusting herself off. There was a garbage disposal area on the other side of the kitchen that would probably be just as empty, and maybe it would have a door with a lock.

"You don't have to go," Leo said, with one foot in the doorway.

"*You* don't have to go," Win replied, and gestured for him to get out of her way. She felt suddenly stubborn. Leo had lost his tie and turned his coat collar up against the cold, and he looked so good, and Win was drowning out here, caught in a whirlpool with no way to come up for air. Then the rest of the world raced after her.

"Did anyone see you follow me in here?"

Leo's expression flickered, but only just. "I didn't know you were here. I don't think anyone else does either." He glanced down at the spindle of paper clutched between her fingers, and raised his eyebrows. "Is that supposed to be a cigarette, Whitman?"

"Fuck you," Win said. "I needed a break."

Leo watched her. He put the phone back to his ear. "Listen, Han, I have to call you back."

"You don't need to," Win started, but Leo was already pulling up his own beer crate and holding his hand out for the tobacco. She paused, then handed it over, and Leo pinched out paper.

"I'm sorry this ended up happening," he said. When Win didn't reply, he glanced up, and elaborated. "Us both being here, I mean."

Win sagged. "It wasn't your fault."

"I know, but." Leo shrugged, fingers quick on the cigarette. Win tried not to sulk about the fact that Leo's cigarette was looking much better than hers, which had just sputtered out for the third time. She flicked the lighter at it uselessly.

"I wanted to tell you," he continued, speaking quickly now like he was forcing the words out, "that I'm not going to make it worse. I won't talk about you. I won't call. After tonight I'll be out of your life for good."

He didn't look up from his hands. It was good news. It was what she wanted to hear.

"Okay," Win said. "Thank you." She sucked desperately at her cigarette as the wind swept through and extinguished it again.

Leo nodded and smiled, shaking his head at the ground. It seemed like a weird thing to do, when Win was so close to crying she felt like her heart was about to jerk out of her throat. He held the cigarette up to his mouth to lick the paper and seal it, and grimaced, lips twisting in a way that might have been a laugh.

"What's so funny?"

"Nothing, really."

"It doesn't seem like nothing."

"Yeah," Leo agreed, standing again. Staring up at him made Win seasick. "It's just that I spent all that time pretending I was in love with you, and now I have to pretend that I'm not."

Win's breath caught in her throat. "Leo—"

"I'll leave you to it," Leo said, cutting her off. He plucked her cigarette from her fingers and stamped it out, replacing it with the freshly rolled one. Win stared at him, and raised it slowly to her mouth. She turned her face up, and Leo leaned down, hand close to her face but not touching, shielding the cigarette, lighting it with an easy flick. He turned to the door and nodded once more and left her alone in the cold.

She wasn't sure how long she'd sat outside when Leo left her. The night sky was hazy orange with light pollution, and low-hanging clouds heavy with snow traipsed slowly overhead. It had been quiet and cold enough that she didn't have to think about much, but she couldn't stay there forever. She came back inside for lack of any better ideas, and because people would notice if she didn't: Shift, who mattered, and Georgia Chilton, who mattered in a different way.

Shift was perched on the far corner of the wedding table. Win discarded Shift's bag and Charlie's jacket and went to join her, before she noticed that Shift was chatting to Georgia Chilton. She gave Georgia an absent smile and looped her arms around Shift's shoulders, resting her chin on Shift's head.

She'd thought Leo was angry at her. She thought she'd blown it with him for good, and she'd almost been relieved—there was no way to turn back to what was destroyed.

"Are you flaunting your height again?" Shift asked, laughing up at her.

"Never," Win said. Her voice sounded almost normal. "You finished DJing?"

"I've been ousted." Shift nodded over to where a couple of her musician friends were setting up amps. "Green Lantern are going to do a set."

"Are they the screamo band?"

"No," Shift said, with a tragic sigh that meant she'd lost a fight to Charlie. "Apparently the screamo band is not wedding appropriate."

Georgia Chilton laughed. "Are you having fun, Whitman?"

"Oh yes," Win said, vaguely aware that she sounded too polite, like she was commenting on the weather. "It's a beautiful wedding."

She looked over the crowd, trying to take it in as a spectacle. Danielle had been pulled over to the table of models, looking nervous but defiant. Shift's mum was gesturing violently at Charlie's father, who was beautiful and a staunch conservative. She seemed about two minutes away from punching him; Shift's dad, watching, was smiling for the first time all day. Gum and Charlie had commandeered an abandoned table by the bar, Charlie resting his cheek on his palm and smiling while Gum fixed Charlie's tie.

And Leo was leaning over Gum's chair, a hand on his brother's shoulder, murmuring in his ear. Gum seemed to be disagreeing, but half-heartedly. As Win watched, Leo straightened and passed a hand over his face. He looked exhausted.

Win was staring too obviously. Shift cleared her throat, and after a moment, Georgia said, "I thought I saw Leo come out the same door you did a little while ago."

"What?" Win said, distracted. "I—yeah, we talked a bit..."

Georgia looked stunned, as though she hadn't expected an answer, let alone a truthful one. Shift's face went pinched with concern.

"Well," Georgia said. She was speaking very carefully. "That must have been hard, with everything that's been going on lately."

"Talking to Leo isn't hard," Win said, eyes still on him. He straightened, squeezing Gum's shoulder once more, and Charlie stood, too, face open with happiness, leaning in to hug him. "He's always the best person in the world to talk to. Even when we're fighting."

"Win," Shift said.

"Yeah," Win said. Leo was leaving, making his way across the room. He had said his goodbyes. He didn't look in their direction. He knew where she was, just the same as she knew where he was, both of their focuses attuned to the other. Something in Win was rising, huge and insurmountable.

"Win," Shift repeated. "Are you about to upstage my wedding?"

"What?" Win said. Georgia's eyes were wide. Shift was beginning to smile. "No, Shift, I would never—"

"Hmm," Shift said. "Do you think maybe you *should* upstage my wedding?"

"I . . . " Win looked back across the floor. Leo had slung his jacket over his shoulder. He had a last round of backslapping hugs from the handsome young men at his table. He put his hands in his pockets and turned for the door.

"Whitman," Georgia said, "Bill and I are only here to talk about Charlie and Shift. I want you to know that I won't print anything you don't want me to print."

Win thought of the sea in Sussex that day, the sucker punch of the waves and the freezing cold, and the way they'd grabbed at each other's wrists, trying to drag each other down.

"You can print whatever you like," Win said.

Georgia looked shocked. Shift's eyes were shining. Leo was halfway across the room.

"It doesn't matter," Win said. "I won't read it. Leo!"

She followed after him, pushing past clumps of people and dodging a waiter, Shift's brilliant, shocked laughter ringing out behind her. Music was still blaring, and Leo made his way without looking back, his shoulders slumped.

Win raised her voice. "*Leo!*"

Leo stopped and turned. He wasn't the only one, but he was the only one Win was looking at: his face pale, quiet, like he wasn't sure what she was going to do to him this time. But his eyebrows went up, a silent question. He'd help with whatever she needed. She only needed one thing.

Win stumbled, the direct ray of his attention as disquieting as ever.

She didn't know what to say; people were murmuring around her, and she saw more than one phone's camera pointed in her direction. She wasn't sure what was on her face.

"Leo," she said again, feeling stupid, like there was nothing left in her but his name.

And Leo's expression changed, the exhaustion dropping away, something startled and new and uncertainly triumphant taking its place. His mouth crooked up.

"Come on, then," he said, barely raising his voice. Win slipped out of her heels and flew across the space between them and into his arms.

She almost leapt at him; he caught her tight, an arm around her waist, his hand in her hair, and she kissed him. They clung to each other. Win wound her arms around his neck, pressing as close as she could, and he half bent her over, tearing greedy kisses from her, rough enough to set her mouth buzzing. She fisted her hand in his collar, yanking him in. Something inside her was fitting into place, and everywhere else she was hot all over, like Leo was waking her up again, bringing her in out of the cold.

"I'm sorry," she mumbled, their noses bumping, words interrupted by kisses. "I'm sorry, I fucked it all up, I was stupid—"

"We can— There are going to be pictures," Leo said, voice desperate, "should you call Marie—"

"Jesus, I've fucked you up, too," Win said.

They both laughed, cracked down the middle. Leo kissed the corner of her mouth, the tip of her nose, her cheek, the end of her eyebrow in quick succession, hands trembling on her face. Behind them there was a shimmering twist of chords as the band started up, and Win was grateful—Shift must have hurried them on to distract attention—but didn't turn.

"Marie will deal. Everyone can deal. I'm so in love with you, I can't lose you—"

"You've got me," Leo said, and tilted her up to his mouth.

EPILOGUE

PLAYING TO WIN

Emily Wickham, *New York Times Magazine*

"It's weird to be back in California," Whitman Tagore says, leaning over the pool table to line up her shot. "I forgot how friendly everyone is." She flashes her teeth at me in a grin. "To your face, at least."

The surprise announcement that Whitman is a nominee for Best Actress at this year's Oscars probably helps, I say.

"Well," she says. "It doesn't hurt."

It's a relief to find her in good humor. Whitman Tagore doesn't give many interviews, and I was late to meet her. She sent me an address on Crenshaw Boulevard where I spent ten minutes pacing outside what looked, frankly, like a shitty dive bar: a heavy door thick with grease, neon lights spelling out PABST and MILLER LITE in headache-spurring blues and whites, a SAVE WATER DRINK BEER sticker slapped against the half-closed aluminum shutters. I was peering in through layers of filth on glass and wondering if I'd fallen for an elaborate prank, when the door creaked open and Whitman Tagore leaned out.

"Come on in," she said. "It's Tequila Tuesday."

Accordingly, Whitman is drinking a syrupy margarita served from a slushie machine (she declares herself "addicted"), and it won't take long before the first round of slammers arrives. Considering the occasion, Whitman is remarkably relaxed, scruffy in her street clothes with newly short hair curling around her jawline. She has been rushed back to the States for a new round of pre-Oscars promotion from her home in the South of France where she has lived for the past four years, half runaway and half exile. She must be jet-lagged but she doesn't look it. After our first drinks, she challenges me to a game of pool. Considering we are meeting only days after her shock nomination, I was expecting her to be more—well, shocked.

But her surprise has taken the form of high delight, with a dash of wickedness. "I was expecting to pay for my sins for another decade or so, but I guess they let me out of the doghouse earlier than expected."

"Ah," I say. "We're going to talk about it right away."

Whitman leans over the table, her cue balanced, her face intent and focused. As she sinks the ball, she says, "Everyone's always talking about it."

It would be hard not to. Whitman's personal life has captured the public imagination as much as—and sometimes more than—her filmography, but five years ago it exploded into a drama even she couldn't control. Revelations that her longtime boyfriend Leo Milanowski was secretly married to indie musician Lila Gardner were compounded by Gardner's additional, widely circulated accusations that Whitman and Leo had never been a real couple. Whitman's career—never scandal-free—dive-bombed into the dirt. Directors, producers, critics, and the public turned away in scorn, and *All Rivers Run*, her immediate release after the news, flopped at cinemas. Friends flocked to denounce her; hip-hop star Riva Reed released a platinum single that began, "I say he's a king even though he's a bore/tongue tying while I'm lying like my last name's Tagore."

Whitman's response to the scandal was an erratic mix of silence and shameless PDA. She gave no interviews, made no appearances, went quiet on all social media, and accepted her censure without protest. At the same time, she was regularly photographed with Leo, as though she hadn't noticed her elaborate fiction falling apart. Even now, she has never protested her innocence.

"It was a shit time," Whitman tells me. "It really felt like I had lost everything. And then when I realized I hadn't, that there was more for me than everything my life had centered on for a decade, that was also kind of terrifying. But, you know, it was a weird year. It was awful. It felt endless. And at the same time it was the happiest I'd ever been."

It's been a rocky road back into the public's graces since Whitman's weird year. Cast an eye over her output immediately after the scandal, and there's little of note. A handful of independent films, most of them pretentious flops; a bit part in ensemble comedy *RISK*, which relied too heavily on fourth-wall wink-wink jokes; a gesture of reconciliation about as transparent as plastic wrap via her cameo in a Lila Gardner music video, which featured an artillery assault in pastel tones, Gardner ramming a baby-blue army tank through the gates of Whitman's storybook mansion. She failed to land any meaningful roles, and while her few remaining fans were distraught, the majority of commentators agreed that it served her right.

It was around this time that Whitman first considered a switch to TV. Sick of ramming her head against the closed doors of Hollywood, she started hunting through pilot scripts and, late one night over a bottle of red, found *Inter Alia*. She stayed up until dawn reading and making notes, and at 7 a.m., she put in a call to showrunner Omar Shahbazi.

"It was definitely an unconventional pitch," Shahbazi tells me. "She said, 'Omar, everyone hates me, I'm toxic, and every time I try to fix it, I make it worse. I'm perfect for this role.' I was trying to be professional and tell her, 'Yeah, let's meet, run some lines,' and at the same time I'm waving the team over, like, whisper-screaming, '*Fucking Whitman Tagore is on the phone.*'"

HBO's acclaimed comedy-drama stars Whitman as foul-mouthed, over-sexed Cleveland district attorney Mita Khan (with a spot-on midwestern accent). Early promo for the show leaned into Whitman's position as Hollywood's fallen angel and embraced her infamy. BAD REPUTATION, WORSE LITIGATION, the first teaser screamed, over a picture of Whitman dressed as Lady Justice, a sword in one hand and scales heaped with cocaine in the other.

The show quickly attracted a cult following that exploded into the mainstream with its third season, for which Whitman picked up her first Emmy. It has been praised for its nuanced approach to the US legal system and is certainly more explicitly political than anything Whitman has done before. It was a surprising move from an actress of color who has never seemed particularly interested in talking about race.

"We can talk about race," she says now. "What do you want to talk about?"

I pause, slightly thrown, then ask her if she thinks she's been treated differently, as an Indian woman in a historically white industry.

"Yes," Whitman says, and smiles neatly. "Next question?"

I point out that many people, including other people from the Indian diaspora, have felt that she's ignored her own position as a British Indian celebrity, a major woman of color in the industry. She could have chosen to campaign, to make an impact, to clear the way for other women like her. She could have spoken for her community.

Whitman considers. "The thing is, I was seventeen when I won the BAFTA. I was twenty when I stopped being able to go out in public. I've got a bunch of people telling me the best way to help other Indian actors in this industry is to speak up, and another, louder group of people telling me I'll only be useful if I shut up, and I'm also trying to keep my own head above water and not go crazy. That was why *Inter Alia* was such a revelation for me—working with a really diverse team of writers and actors, issues of race and power are always on the table. And we considered it from numerous angles and perspectives, putting these power structures under the microscope, but trying not to draw easy conclusions. That's something I want to keep doing, aligning my work with my values, and not fighting to justify myself and please everybody by saying, or not saying, the right thing."

If I were more cynical, I might argue that Whitman is still avoiding the point. Is "letting my work speak for itself" essentially a fancier way of saying "no comment"? Whitman is infamous for her layers of defense and disguise, and it was her ceaseless tinkering with her public profile that exiled her from Hollywood in the first place. She has a habit of changing her image to suit her latest project: hiking through Utah and frowning into the distance before her compelling, controversial role as a hell-raising Calamity Jane; summering on the French Riviera and drinking Sancerre at the races when she was aiming for a slot as a Hemingway heroine. In the dive bar, she's wearing a battered black leather jacket, big around her shoulders, and a baseball cap tugged low—a classic Mita Khan look, the sort of outfit she'd wear to threaten a state's witness or seduce a Mafia kingpin on the sly. It's as though the real Whitman Tagore is hidden somewhere deep beneath. Why is she so afraid to be herself?

Whitman's smile is gentle and incredulous.

"Emily," she says. "It's just a jacket."

It's perhaps unsurprising that Whitman is willing to wade into these murkier discussions now, given the film that has catapulted her back into the spotlight. There was general outrage among English literature students and right-wing commentators when she was cast as Dorothea Brooke in Sophie Gammage's lavish new production of *Middlemarch*. (if you're GOING to make WHITMAN TAGORE a character in middlemarch at least know your shit enough to cast her as rosamond, one fan tweeted, referring to *Middlemarch*'s infamously manipulative antiheroine.) Casting an Indian actress as the pious, milk-skinned face of nineteenth-century English Puritanism seemed to move beyond colorblind casting and into straight lunacy.

"I don't want to pretend it's just a human story and I connect to the human individual in the text," Whitman says. "That's not true. It's obviously a white story. But I think if you're adapting a text like *Middlemarch* today, it's worth interrogating why it has to stay so white. One of the things that struck me most about Dorothea is that she's such an alien. Her sister doesn't understand her, her guardian doesn't understand her, her husband definitely doesn't understand her. And even the man she's in love with doesn't understand her for a long time, he misinterprets her, he expects her to break out of circumstances that she can't control. That didn't feel so far away from me."

Much of the public outcry about Whitman's casting melted away when the film premiered at Cannes. Surrounded by an eclectic group of British talent, Whitman is staggering as Dorothea, bringing fresh life to a heroine routinely dismissed as boring. There is a moment, early in the film, when Dorothea goes to Rome and realizes that she has married the wrong man. She is standing in front of Bernini's *Ecstasy of Saint Teresa*, and the camera moves slowly through the cathedral dripping in gold and marble before it stills in a wide shot that frames Whitman Tagore's ravenous face against the agony of the saint. Something very minute changes in Dorothea's expression, a flex of the jaw, a darkening of the eyes, and the effect is devastating. In my screening, the stern silver fox sitting next to me burst abruptly into tears.

It's unsurprising that Whitman has picked up a nomination for Best Actress for this lush, clear-eyed film. She speaks of it with obvious pride and delight. "It kind of got into my blood," she says, and adds, "my house is even in it."

It's true: one outdoor scene is shot in the hills behind Whitman's home, offering a brief glimpse of a sloping gray roof and a window-sill laden with flowers. (It's actually her bathroom, she tells me; they added the extravagant window boxes to hide the modern plumbing system.)

Even before *Middlemarch*, the house found its own place in the official Whitman Tagore mythology. It's protected with a state-of-the-art security system and remote location, but once in a while tidbits or even photographs surface. Whitman idly references running through the hills behind her home; best friend and musician Shift posted a photo of Whitman lounging in the long grass on a golden summer afternoon, buttery sandstone walls covered in vines rising invitingly behind her. Last year the *New York Post* shared an exclusive cache of apparent family photos obtained from Leo's older brother Geoffrey Milanowski, who was quoted saying, "Whitman Tagore is a great gal. Nobody's perfect, but once you get to know her, she's quite the treat." Opening the family albums was meant to prove his point, and the internet had a field day over the photos, which included a Christmas scene with Whitman and Leo mid-hysterics presenting a very burned turkey to the camera and one of Leo sprawled out on a carpet, mid-conversation, with Whitman's mother dozing in a chair behind him. The fan favorite was a cheerful shot of Geoffrey and sister Hannah, arms around each other out in front of the French house. In the background, just visible, Whitman and Leo are kissing, Leo's hand gentle and possessive on her jaw. #WhitowskiLives trended for four days, but the most popular tweet of the week came from a pop culture journalist: can't believe you guys are STILL falling for this shit.

Four days later, Whitman picks me up in a sickly orange Lamborghini that she tells me, a little embarrassed, she has borrowed from her publicist for the week. We're headed for a complex in downtown LA, where she and her team are preparing for the first in a long series of dress fittings before the Oscars. "I'm talking to a few designers, but I like a dress that tells a story," Whitman explains (big surprise). "We want to settle on the overall aesthetic before we make any decisions."

Once we get downtown, Whitman is not the immediate object of attention. Instead, we arrive to find Leo Milanowski in a neat black suit, turning obediently from left to right as people flutter around him adjusting cuffs and taking Polaroids. His focus is absolute, his face almost severe in its blankness. His features conjure up classical sculpture, the same commanding beauty of something timeless and implacable, and he moves like a statue easing its way into life. He doesn't react to us entering the room.

"Oh, he's doing his photo shoot face," Whitman says to me, and then Leo does turn, quick as a snake in the grass, to wink at her before his attention is back on the camera.

Leo will be Whitman's date this year, hence the suit, which is not actually the no-brainer it seems. They don't always attend these events together—Leo presumably has someplace to be, sometimes—and Whitman often replaces him with a member of her tight inner circle. Shift is a childhood friend who survived the crony cull to appear at premieres, and Whitman's mother is becoming a recognizable, if not regular, red carpet fixture.

"It's definitely not her favorite activity," Whitman admits. "I think she still finds the whole thing very frivolous, she hates getting her hair and makeup done. She's never been a *stage mom*." Whitman pronounces this with a disdainful, American twang. "We were talking about the Oscars outfit and she was like, *Why don't you just wear what you wore last year?*"

Leo laughs, back in jeans and a T-shirt after his fitting, and Whitman checks her watch. It's already late morning, and she hasn't even tried on the first dress. There's a whole rack of samples from hopeful designers, and everyone has a different idea of what vibe she should be aiming for—metallic, regal, impenetrable? Pale green satin, sophisticated, relaxed? Severe in black? Leo is not consulted for his opinion but offers it nonetheless; he thinks it would be "cool" for Win to wear a cape.

The truth behind the explosive revelations and accusations leveled against Whitman and Leo five years ago remains unclear: whether Whitman broke up a marriage, whether Whitman and Leo were always or never a real couple, whether they were caught up in some seedy polyamorous drama. Of the many hundreds of think pieces published about the scandal, some suggested that Leo was just as invested in the attention as his faux lover, but most agreed that he had been snagged like a fly in a web.

Their relationship is still a subject of tabloid conjecture and feverish late-night forum posting. For those trawling for clues, all I can offer is that Whitman and Leo seem close. When we arrive, she hands him a slim black case that, he tells me with a grimace, contains his reading glasses—he's not used to them yet, and keeps forgetting or losing them. "I'm on my fourth pair," he says sadly. During the fitting of a very intense, geometric dress that keeps Whitman's hands stiffly down at her sides, an assistant announces that Whitman's mother is on the phone, and Leo answers the call for her. "Hey," he says, moving to the back of the room and lowering his voice. "You were right, no one agrees with me about the cape." At one point, tangled in a sheer web of chiffon, Whitman impatiently waves away her stylists and gets Leo to fish her out of the latest outfit. He is neat and capable, and his fingers trail up the back of her neck before he steps away.

All of this, observed from the outside, gives a very good impression of a genuine relationship. Though, of course, it always has.

While Whitman changes again, I probe a reluctant Leo about his latest venture, bankrolling a pair of art studios in London and Paris. His professed mission is to provide a studio space to those who might not be able to afford or find one for themselves. To what extent the pet project of a wealthy celebrity can truly make a difference in the lives of starving or marginalized artists, especially in such expensive, inaccessible cities, remains questionable. Most of the artists currently involved in the project are relative unknowns, and their output has been sporadic. Still, the studios are becoming established on the local scenes. Eloise Teng ran a series of workshops at the Paris location last month, the first big exhibition is expected this summer, and the parties are apparently off the wall.

Leo himself is unforthcoming. "I just pay the rent," he says, and is saved by the bell, as Whitman announces they're done for the day. The team shares celebratory beers; alcohol is clearly part of Whitman's MO, but not one that I complain about, as I'm invited to join the circle. Whitman and Leo reach out to clink bottles without looking at each other, hands meeting naturally in the air.

It's hard to tell what will happen if Whitman wins Best Actress at the Academy Awards this Sunday; it's equally hard to tell what will happen if she doesn't. Her trajectory once seemed like a golden narrative—the young ingenue, the dazzling Hollywood romance, the empress of the silver screen. When she fell, she fell hard, crashing and burning off her pedestal like a plane trailing smoke in the sky. Now she is something else, something that we don't yet entirely know what to do with. If we're not quick to make up our minds, Whitman will make them up for us, sliding a new character under our noses so gently that we'll convince ourselves this version of her must be the real one.

Love her or hate her, it's easy to project a tragic narrative on Whitman. Her troubled rise, her fall from grace. You can read her as an outsider stigmatized by a cutthroat industry or a control freak who remains Hollywood's most high-strung diva. Over our time together, though, I kept noticing her gentle swagger, the easy way she lined up her pool shots, the sure hand she rested on Leo Milanowski's shoulder. She looked amused, as though she had a private joke no one knew about. She seemed calm, in control, her sharp, handsome face relatively untroubled by the scandals cast upon it. It seemed almost as though she was having fun.

We would like to thank:

Seema Mahanian and Frankie Edwards, our editing superduo, who saw exactly what we were trying to do with this novel and knew how to make it happen.

Andrianna Yeatts, dream agent, who sent a kind email that changed our lives and who has never left our corner since. Lucy Morris, UK-wrangler, for everything and especially the laugh over Jeremy in a London café, as well as Sophie Baker and everybody else at Curtis Brown and ICM for their support and enthusiasm.

Tree Abraham and Albert Tang for a cover better than anything we ever imagined, Angelina Krahn and Mari Okuda for their meticulous copyediting efforts, Andy Dodds, Morgan Swift, and everyone at Grand Central Publishing and Headline.

Ulli and Ruby Clements, our first and loudest cheerleaders, as well as our other early readers who offered much needed advice, encouragement, and cheer: Sara Nunn, Emery Kennedy, Rosalie Bower, and Sophie Atkinson. Monica McInerney for her insight, guidance, wisdom, and humor on everything from editing to industry.

Liz and Pranesh Datta, Shirmilla Datta, Marie McInerney, Daniel Clements, Ulli Clements, Ruby Clements and the little Rafster for love, joy, support, occasional mockery, and for buying us so many books. We love you.

All our excellent friends and in particular Sophie Evans, Hannah Wolfram, and Jack Roberts for very politely listening to us talk a lot about fictional people and bringing us beers while we did.

Wulf and Lokhi, who did not help at all.

Finally, thank you to Shibani Datta, my Thakuma, for countless acts of love and encouragement and for being the center of my family, for which I'm so grateful. We love you, miss you, and think of you often.

The View Was Exhausting is Mikaella Clements and Onjuli Datta's cowritten debut novel. They are married and live in Berlin.